CAN CLASS STILL UNITE?

Can Class Still Unite?

The differentiated work force, class solidarity and trade unions

Edited by
GUY VAN GYES
HANS DE WITTE
PATRICK PASTURE

Routledge
Taylor & Francis Group

LONDON AND NEW YORK

First published 2001 by Ashgate Publishing

Reissued 2018 by Routledge
2 Park Square, Milton Park, Abingdon, Oxon OX14 4RN
711 Third Avenue, New York, NY 10017, USA

Routledge is an imprint of the Taylor & Francis Group, an informa business

A Library of Congress record exists under LC control number: 2001091690

ISBN 13: 978-1-138-73413-5 (hbk)
ISBN 13: 978-1-138-73409-8 (pbk)
ISBN 13: 978-1-315-18741-9 (ebk)

Contents

List of Figures

List of Tables

List of Appendices

List of Contributors

David Adamson is director of the Centre for Community Regeneration at the University of Glamorgan. His research fields are poverty, social exclusion, community development policy and working-class communities.

Maurizio Ambrosini is professor of methodology of social research and sociology of work at the University of Genova, Italy. His research fields are labour market, foreign migration, industrial relations and social policies.

Tim Butler is reader in sociology at the Department of Sociology and Anthropology at the University of East London. His research fields are middle class, gentrification of the city and East London.

Hans De Witte is assistant professor in work psychology at the Department of Psychology of the Catholic University of Leuven (K.U.Leuven). He was head of the Labour Section during the period that this book was reviewed. His topics include: working class cultures, trade union participation, psychological consequences of unemployment, job insecurity and flexible work.

Sjoerd Goslinga is researcher at the Department of Social Psychology and coordinator of the CNV/VU Research Program at the Free University Amsterdam, the Netherlands. His research fields are union participation, collective action, industrial relations and I&O psychology.

Bert Klandermans is professor of applied social psychology at the Department of Social Psychology of the Free University Amsterdam, the Netherlands. His research fields are union participation, mobilisation, persuasive communication and participation in social and political protest.

Sherry Linkon is professor and co-director of the Center for Working-Class Studies at Youngstown State University, USA.

David Ost is an associate professor of political science at Hobart and William Smith Colleges in Geneva, New York and visiting professor at Central European University in Warsaw, Poland. His research fields are labour in post-communist Eastern Europe, and the role of labour in democracy and democratisation.

Patrick Pasture, Ph D in history, is research associate of the Fund for Scientific Research - Flanders (Belgium), affiliated to the Faculty of Arts, and research manager at the Higher Institute of Labour Studies (HIVA) of the Catholic University Leuven, Belgium.

Martin Phillips is a lecturer in human geography at the Department of Geography of the University of Leicester. His research fields are processes of class formation, rural social change and the construction and reception of rural images.

Javier G. Polavieja is researcher at the Centre for Advanced Study in the Social Sciences, Juan March Institute, Madrid, Spain and doctoral candidate at Nuffield College, University of Oxford. His research fields are labour markets, class analysis and attitudinal consequences of unemployment and fixed-term employment in Spain.

Andrew J. Richards is professor of political science at the Centre for Advanced Study in the Social Sciences of the Juan March Institute, Madrid, Spain. His research fields are comparative West European politics, labour movements, industrial relations and social democracy.

Ian Roberts is a lecturer in sociology at the Department of Sociology and Social Policy of the University of Durham. His research fields are sociology of work and employment, sociology of education.

John Russo is the co-director of the Center for Working-Class Studies and coordinator of the Labour Studies Program at Youngstown State University, USA. His research fields are labour unions, popular culture and working-class studies.

Mike Savage is professor of sociology at the University of Manchester. His research fields are study of new middle classes, social mobility and urban sociology.

Tim Strangleman is a research assistant at the International Centre for Labour Studies of the University of Manchester. His research fields are sociology of work and employment, the railway industry and railway labour, coal industry and coal field communities.

Guy Van Gyes is research manager at the Higher Institute of Labour Studies (HIVA) of the Catholic University Leuven, Belgium. His research fields are industrial relations and organisational development.

Michael Vester is professor at the Institute of Political Science of the University of Hannover. His research fields are social structures, movements and mentalities.

Acknowledgements

The Higher Institute of Labour Studies (HIVA) is a research institute based at Leuven, Belgium and is specialised in policy-oriented research. This book is the product of a European conference held by HIVA in 1998, attended by both academics and trade union representatives. The inspiration for holding this conference came from two basic premises: (1) in academic circles, the continuing relevance of the class concept as a analytical tool is frequently called into question and (2) the trade union has always been the social movement which has used this class principle to unite and defend workers. The conference was sponsored by the European Centre for Workers' Questions (EZA) and partly financed by the European Commission. We want to thank Leo Pauwels, president, and Joachim Herudek, general secretary, for the EZA support. The views expressed in this book are of course those of the authors and editors and should not be attributed to any of the persons or organisations acknowledged.

Jeannine Hooge, Sandra Volders, Evy Van Dael, Liesbeth Villa and Rudy De Wit helped with the practical organisation of the conference and/or assisted in preparing the manuscript. Each member of this HIVA team played a unique and valuable role for which we are deeply grateful.

August 2001
Guy Van Gyes
Hans De Witte
Patrick Pasture

Introduction: Modernisation of Trade Unions and Class Analysis

GUY VAN GYES

The Modern Legacy

It was a period during which the national constitutional state came of age, urbanisation began to gain pace and industrialisation took hold. During this period of massive social change, perfectly ordinary people were caught up in initially defensive, but later offensive forms of collective protest and action against the proletarianisation to which they were being subjected. In the modern age, which spread throughout nineteenth and twentieth century Europe, such (national) social movements grew up to preserve old traditions and customs and/or demand new rights. The labour movement (with its political translations such as socialism, communism and Christian democracy) was the most significant representative of these modern 'collective challenges of people with common purposes and solidarity in sustained interaction with elites, opponents and authorities' (Tarrow, 1996, 4). It was mainly Karl Marx who provided the trade unions with its basic ideology: 'Our epoch, the epoch of the bourgeoisie, possesses, however, this distinctive feature: it has simplified the class antagonisms. Society as a whole is more and more splitting up into two great hostile camps, into two great classes directly facing each other: Bourgeoisie and Proletariat' (Marx and Engels, 1977, 417). Workers formed trade unions as a response to the imbalance of power in the industrial society, tried to make links across workplaces, sectors and communities: mobilising fellow workers and others for 'working-class politics'; constructing a political force that is independent of business, opposing the status quo, combining the defence of working people in their daily needs and interests with a longer-term utopian vision; building a trade union movement for social change

1

(Katznelson and Zolberg, 1986; Van der Linden and Rojahn, 1990; Buechler, 2000). It was a slow, difficult and not always successful building process. But in many countries, the trade unions and their demands gained recognition during the twentieth century, together with the growth of welfare state policies and the institutionalisation of neocorporatistic arrangements (Hyman and Ferner, 1998; Berger and Broughton, 1995).

Setting the Challenge: Modernising Means Organising the Changed Work Force

However, in recent decades these trade unions have not always had an easy life in most European countries. As proof of this statement, reference is usually made to the declining membership of trade unions in large areas of Europe. It is, of course, fallacious to infer the strength and power of a social movement solely by the number of persons paying membership fees. There is no denying, however, that trade unions have faced recently new challenges. Literature on the subject of the current future of the European trade unions almost invariably redefines this future issue into a problem of reform for these unions - it is a matter of better adapting these organisations to the present situation (ILO, 1998; Hyman and Ferner, 1998; Leisink et al., 1996).

The economic environment became harsh. Market competition globalised and intensified, putting new pressures on the established national regimes of industrial relations. The industrial core of the trade union membership faced massive job losses and rising job insecurity. As governments tried to adapt to the new demands of the world economy, political elites in many countries - with Thatcherism and Reaganism as the benchmarking politics - became far less favourably inclined towards the trade unions. In some areas, trade unions lost their status as 'social partners'. The trade unions had to deal with phenomena such as the (co-ordinated) decentralisation of collective bargaining, more intensive government intervention, concession bargaining, wage restraints, flexible working hours and labour contracts, individualisation of the labour law, budgetary cuts in the welfare systems. At the workplace, trade union representatives faced new forms of work organisation, HRM policies and direct employee participation. Trade unions were confronted with tax-cutting, saving governments, deregulation, the expansion of multinational companies and the rising volatility of financial capital. Furthermore, ecological 'limits of growth' became visible. This series of events and trends did not occur in the same way and with equal strength everywhere in Europe. However, if a comparative picture is painted of European industrial relations and trade unions, these are phenomena which recurrently surface.

This summary can primarily be read as a series of external challenges with which these European trade unions were confronted when they constantly tried to exercise their influence and power on behalf of those through whom and for whom they developed, to whatever extent, into mass movements in the previous period. It was a threefold influencing function (ILO, 1998):

a) a democratic function: allowing all those who have a job or who want one to have a say about their working life;
b) an economic function: helping to distribute equitably the fruits of economic growth or the burdens of economic decline;
c) a social function: contributing to social stability, realising social security and fighting social exclusion.

In its broad or limited acceptance of these functions, the trade unions were the co-founder of Fordism, which was particularly successful during the 1950s and 1960s (Boyer, 1986). The application of a radical division of labour with strict controls and strict separation between control and execution of tasks in large-scale industrial processes made possible the mass production of standardised goods. Productivity gains could thus be generated and to some extent converted into pay increases for the workers. Mass consumption was the complement to mass production. A social security system was then set up to protect workers against possible exclusion from the labour process (as a result of illness, accident or unemployment).

The aforementioned challenges or trends were a consequence of the fact that this Fordist system was approaching its limits, particularly since the 1970s. To explore the crisis phenomena here would be to digress, mainly because this book is not about these external challenges for the modern trade union movement, but about the so-called internal challenge facing the trade unions in Europe today: 'What may be termed the internal challenge stems from changes in the constituencies which unions seek to recruit and represent' (Hyman, 1999). The central line of approach of the book is thus not the external strength and influence of the trade union, but the internal point of view of trade union participation, or the logic of membership (Streeck, 1987).

The target audience of the trade unions in Europe, the work force, has after all also changed considerably in recent decades. This transformation can be described in socio-demographic terms as increasing feminisation of the labour force and as a limited influx of migrant workers. It is also a matter of fundamental changes in occupational structure and the organisation of work. It is these latter changes which receive special attention in this book. We briefly summarise these changes (Meiksins, 1997; Hyman, 1992; Heery and Abbott, 2000; Leisink, 1997; IILS, 1999).

One of the most significant changes in the economic structure has been the shift away from traditional industries towards the service sectors. Traditional manufacturing jobs are downsized, outsourced, re-engineered, delocalised. The classic 'mass' employment in basic industries and manufacturing has diminished. Manual industrial workers no longer form the majority of the work force in most European countries. 'White-collar' work has taken over as a result of rising employment in private services, retail sales, health care, education, the software industry and other business services. When the large industrial companies were downsizing, new small and medium-sized enterprises were established, with employment opportunities for highly skilled and professional workers, rather than poorly skilled blue-collar workers. This development is linked to a transformation of the 'normal' employment relationship. 'Atypical' employment patterns increased, involving part-time work, temporary work, seasonal jobs, flexible working, homeworking, self-employment (both genuine and as subcontracting), fixed-term contracts, special government job creation schemes. The Fordist 'normal' employment relationship characterised by a full-time job with a stable career trajectory, standardised wages and regulated by law and collective bargaining has been seriously challenged.

These trends have led to a twofold adaptation of the trade unions' traditional grassroots. On the one hand, 'winners' with highly professional and technical skills and with a strong individual position in the labour market. On the other hand, 'losers': less skilled workers with marginal jobs and a vulnerable position on the labour market, threatened by job insecurity and unemployment. Unions must mobilise countervailing power resources; such resources consist of the ability to attract members, to engage these members in action and to win the support (or at least neutrality) of the wider public (Barling et al., 1992). This work force which has to be convinced and attracted is no longer (only) the male manual worker in a stable employment relationship. It is a different work force which now needs organising if the trade unions want to enter the twenty-first century with renewed strength and full membership power.

Looking for an Answer: Reconsidering the Class Theory

Class (or its alternative, 'status') was already a central concept in the thinking of the trade unions: working-class position, working-class consciousness, working-class solidarity, working-class action, working-class politics, etc. However, the power of attraction of this concept reached beyond the trade unions ideology. It was also a central concept of sociology which, like the trade unions, grew up in the modern age. In this discipline too, Marx (together with Weber) was a point of reference used to analyse and denounce social inequality in the nascent modern society. The social stratification of industrial society was interpreted on the basis of economic differences, specifically professional positions grouped into classes. A discipline of stratification research was devoted to describing the structure of these social classes and specifying the processes by which they are generated and maintained. The next questions are typical of this field of research: How many social classes exist? What are the principal economic cleavages that define the class structure? What other social or institutional forces determine the occupational attainment and class allocation of individuals? How are lifestyles, attitudes and the political views of individuals shaped by their class positions? Can 'class cultures' and 'class politics' be identified? (Joyce, 1995; Crompton, 1994; Grusky (ed.), 1994; Breen and Rottman, 1995a; Fantasia, 1995.)

Like the trade unions, this stratification research - built up around the class concept - has not had an easy time in the scientific world in recent decades (Geissler, 1998a; Grusky and Sorensen, 1998; Payne, 1996; Mahieu, 1995; Evans, 1999). This class analysis has also been forced on to the defensive. Doubts have been raised about the usefulness of analysing modern society using a class theory. Reference is now made to the structural trends we have just summarised. Radical critics talk about 'the death of class', heralded by the post-Fordism, post-industrialism and post-modernism used by sociological trend-watchers to describe present society. The following academic positions can be distinguished in this 'death-of-class' debate:

a) new fault lines have replaced the traditional division based on class, profession and status as way of explaining social differences. Sociological characteristics such as gender, race and, more especially, education (cultural capital or knowledge) are cited in this context (Meyer, 1994; Pakulski and Waters, 1996);

b) other authors state that economic contrasts no longer determine political attitudes or cultural lifestyles. An 'uncoupling' of class and culture has taken place (Hradil, 1987; Eyerman and Jamison, 1991). This, to a certain extent, is a revision of the somewhat older embourgeoisement thesis (Gorz, 1982);

c) another group of authors goes a step further and casts doubt on every form of determinism (economic or not): today's individual no longer lets himself be led by collective patterns such as a class. This de-traditionalisation has led to the individual's choosing, or having to choose, for himself (Beck, 1986; Melucci, 1989; Beck et al., 1994);

d) other academics associate this theory of individualisation with the idea that values have thereby gained in importance. In order to invest their life-choices with the required or desired meaning, people fall back on value patterns. The post-materialist value pattern - in contrast to the materialist determinism of a class - seems particularly important in this context (Inglehart, 1990; Ester et al., 1993);

e) finally, a number of analysts do not reject the class model, but chiefly rework it by adding new classes to it. One case in point is the middle class. New middle classes are being discovered (Eder, 1993; Butler and Savage, 1995). If previous approaches thus espoused a disintegrative vision of the class concept, this last group of authors looks rather to a further fragmentation or differentiation of classes (Vester et al., 1993; Wright, 1997).

Like the trade unions, academic class analysis has come up against a number of limits in recent decades. Like the trade union, the academic subject area is having to deal with a 'changed' work force. For a number of authors, these scientific limits are so clear that they flatly draw the line at this sort of class-based analysis. Geissler describes the position as follows: 'The increasing dissatisfaction with the caricature of the old paradigm and the fascination with new phenomena combined to form an antithetical alternative, fixated on the new and ignoring the continuation of the old. This process can also be described metaphorically: paradigm revolutionaries are prone to the 'throwing-out' effect - the baby is thrown out with the bath water' (Geissler, 1998b, 229). It is striking here that, in this dismissal, when the view moves to the political field, the trade unions are saddled with the adjective 'old'. From this point of view, the trade union movement is an 'old' social movement because it represents the conflicts of industrialisation, that is, class conflicts. New social movements, such as the greens, or the women's movement, express the contrasts within the new post-industrial, post-Fordist society.

This book does not adopt the position that class is dead, nor does it dismiss the trade unions as 'old and past its sell-by date'. The changed work force is considered at various levels with reference to class-determined concepts and analytical instruments, with the underlying continuity of such questions as how this changed target audience looks at union membership, how European trade unions deal with this changed rank and file, or how they could anticipate the interests and needs of that changed work force. Discussion in various parts of the book therefore turns to academic viewpoints and visions are developed on the current strength and possibilities of class analysis (see also Devine, 1998; Breen and Rottman, 1995b; Rose, 1998). There is no rigid or orthodox reference to class theory, but the schools of thought we encounter in the 'death of class' debate are repeatedly called into play. Non-parallel definitions of class and various research methods are used to that end. A number of contributions are of a comparative nature, most tell a fairly country-specific tale. The material presented does not always make the direct link with the strategic question of the trade union. On the whole, the book hopes nevertheless to make a contribution to the current issue of the modernisation of European trade unions, viewed from the logic of membership and the changed work force.

Following Chapters

In the opening chapter, Richards paints a broad overall illustration of the various developments frequently facing trade unions today, with their shifting and differentiated grassroots support. These trends give rise to two representation problems, i.e. a question of identity (how should these new groups be represented?) and a solidarity question (how to organise solidarity between these groups?). Richards then points to the fact that this issue of representativeness has always been a problem. The recruiting concept of 'working-class solidarity' has always trodden a fine line between sectarianism and general interest. Today, Richards expects great things from a local micro-construction of new solidarity as a basis for trade union action. For this to happen, trade unions once again have to be more of a movement and less of an institution.

Vester's chapter opens with an additional broad picture, compared to Richards. He gives a summary of the postwar, academic 'death of class' debate. Based on extensive empirical German material, he then adopts an attitude which largely opposes these theories, in particular the vision of Beck and Giddens. This he does through a modernising class analysis of present-day society, borrowing concepts from Bourdieu and Thompson. In this way, Vester develops a multi-dimensional, family tree-like division of our society into ten class milieus. These are milieus which can be distinguished by social position and lifestyle and by economic and cultural capital. Today's trade unions - just like the traditional political parties - face the challenge of building bridges between many of these different 'milieux' so as to retain sufficient effectiveness in the future. He accuses political parties and trade unions of not paying enough attention to the levels of social dissatisfaction and disillusion currently prevailing in some of the mainly new employee milieus.

In his chapter, Savage also reflects on the arguments of Beck and Giddens about the changing relationship between class and individual identities. He argues that class, as a collective identity, may well have gained in importance but that, in determining their own identities, individuals still employ notions of class to identify themselves with respect to others. In such self-identification, we still use a form of anti-elitism. 'Being ordinary' remains another important form of self-definition. Savage's theory is therefore that it may well be correct that class no longer unites, but that it certainly continues to divide and that such divisions, if harboured, effectively continue to provide cultural resources for various forms of anti-elitist movement and action.

Adamson alleges that the economic and social changes of the 1980s caused the traditionally strong working class in the Welsh mining region to split into three fractions: a traditional core, a new working class and a marginalised fraction. He then examines this marginalised working class in more detail and the factors leading to its exclusion. He warns against labelling this group as an 'underclass'. By contrast, he claims that collective action has developed within this group. It is a collective action built on grassroots community development and organisation. This successful development is taking place without the use of the class concept and is supported by government grants and social assistance. The trade unions and the socialist party are conspicuous by their absence in this context and, as a result, are facing difficulties.

Polavieja examines the relationship in Spain between fixed-term labour contracts and trade union participation. Using a series of empirical data, Polavieja first states that an uncertain labour market position in Spain is heavily determined by the high level of contractual flexibility. This form of contract creates a split situation for 'insiders' and 'outsiders' on the Spanish labour market. This phenomenon occurs in every professional class. In this context, he refers to the paradoxical action by the Spanish trade unions: within collective bargaining, they play the hand of the insiders, as a socio-political movement, they stand up for the social rights of all (including the outsiders). Continuing his analysis, Polavieja than demonstrates that people in an insecure job participate less in trade union activities and identify less with the trade union. These outsiders seem to reproach the trade unions for their insider action, just as they also turn more strongly against employers and politicians because of their unstable situation. In particular, those outsiders who have the highest expectations of trade unions demonstrate the deepest disillusion.

Based on survey material about the members of the Christian Trade Union Federation (CNV), Goslinga and Klandermans examine the Dutch situation in terms of the trade union participation of what are referred to as new and growing employee groups on the labour market: women, young people, part-time workers and employees working flexible hours. These employee categories are under-represented within Dutch trade unions, where the problem is primarily an 'exit' problem. A great many of these employees do become members of a trade union but do not remain members for long. Goslinga and Klandermans then ask to what extent this exit behaviour can be explained by a difference in trade union satisfaction and commitment. A close analysis of this issue provides them with 'puzzling' results. On the one hand, they ascertain that union dissatisfaction does influence exit behaviour (the intention to leave) and that a high level of trade union involvement (feeling strongly attached to the trade union and understanding the need for a trade union) plays a moderating role in this context. On the other hand, they note that the 'new' employee groups differ only slightly from traditional employees in terms of intention to leave the trade union, union satisfaction and union commitment. In their conclusion, these Dutch authors therefore point out that these new groups cancel their trade union membership perhaps because they are more likely to have to deal with external events, which means that they slip out of regular work. One other important lesson drawn by Goslinga and Klandermans from their analysis is that the performance of a trade union is important. This refers not so much to the 'new' characteristics of employees, but to the way in which the trade union deals with them. Building up stronger commitment when a person becomes a member is an important duty in this respect. Affective commitment can be strengthened by closer contact between organisation and member. Continuance union commitment can be developed by increasing the individual benefits associated with membership.

In his contribution, Ambrosini concentrates on the growing commercial services sector. In this sector, he finds strong representation by a new type of industrial relations and a different type of employee: more flexibility, atypical contracts, part-timers, freelance workers, women and job insecurity. He therefore alleges that this sector needs a different type of trade union action. He calls this the diffuse trade union model and places it opposite the traditional class-determined industrial model. The core of this new trade union model is formed by higher input levels from pragmatism, individualism, territoriality and service provision.

Based on a longitudinal case study in North London, Butler discerns a subdivision in the middle classes. He talks of a separate group, identified by a specific professional career position and by living in up-market areas of the city. This 'cultural new class' differs from the rest of the middle classes primarily in terms of lifestyle, as well as in terms of aspects such as voting behaviour and opinions about social justice and inequality. Their 'leftwards tendency' does not however translate into support for trade unions. Butler seeks a reason for this in the fact that the economic convergence within this group - unlike relational and normative convergence - is not high. The income differences within the group are high. The main binding factor is not class, but living in a similar urban environment.

Phillips also looks at new types of middle class, using Eder's class theory to typify the countryside population of the United Kingdom. Following on from Eder, he points to the importance of the cultural context as an intervening variable within the relationship between class and collective action. Phillips identifies four rural lifestyles. He then states that these correspond to particular forms of participation in associative life. He does however have to conclude that trade union participation does not form a large part of such types of social commitment. He believes that this has to do with the fact that collective action is also associated with risk perception. People who live in the country are less exposed to socio-economic risks, they do not feel threatened and are therefore less likely to commit themselves. However, this does not mean that they are unaware of existing socio-economic inequalities and injustices, they simply react to them in a different way. They are more likely to regard these inequalities as a universal, unchangeable element of social life.

Roberts and Strangleman observe that, in the past, the British construction industry and its labour market was built on what they call a post-figurative, skill-based workers' culture. These micro-communities of construction workers created an almost automatic 'father to son' influx into the building trade. Today, as a result of deregulation, employers are faced not only with a flexible employee population but, particularly, with under-qualified and poorly motivated construction workers. Formalised training systems seem unable to resolve this problem. The British construction industry therefore needs a new form of industrial 'citizenship' which combines the advantages of the previous culture with the current well-developed training systems. The class concept could be a useful instrument in this respect.

Roberts and Strangleman are the first in a series of three contributions which place strong emphasis on the current value of class thinking. For this purpose, Ost draws from Eastern European evidence, Linkon and Russo contribute arguments from the US situation. Ost defends the view that social discontent which produces a market economy can best be channelled along abstract class lines. If this discontent is organised along the lines of collective identities, such as ethnic origin or religion, it leads to an exclusion ideology which is in conflict with liberal-democratic principles. Ost clarifies this theory using a comparison between the democratic strength of Poland and the Czech Republic in the post-communist era. The action of the Polish Solidarity trade union is a central aspect of this comparison. Using American examples, Linkon and Russo state that class can certainly be a recruiting concept. However, changes have to be made to the way in which this class principle is used. Firstly, we have to accept that economic position is only one of the aspects by which people define their interests. Secondly, we must get out of the habit of placing class opposite or above other social categories, such as race or gender, and vice versa. Increased (international) efforts have to be made to build work-related bridges between these different perspectives.

Klandermans ends the book with some concluding remarks.

Lessons to Learn?

These sometimes highly diverse contributions provide a variety of building blocks for enriching the discussion on the future of the European trade unions and for a more accurately positioning of the class discourse in this discussion.

Looking at the differentiated work force, a number of contributions observe an occurring fragmentation within the working class (traditionally the trade union's grassroots). Fostered by job insecurity and a so-called atypical labour position, a marginalised group of workers emerges which takes a less positive attitude to trade unions. In addition, new groups of professionals are forming which are not immediately convinced of the advantages of a trade union. Moreover, a process of individualisation is threatening the class collectivism of the trade union identity.

Despite the difficulties for trade unions to mobilise or to unify this differentiated work force, a series of contributions states just as clearly that the mission is not impossible. Three main arguments are made why it is not impossible. In the past, the trade union experienced similar problems in defending certain groups of workers and uniting them under the class banner. The final result is not only determined by the contextual structure within which trade unions have to act, but just as much by the way how trade unions organise themselves and take action. It is not yet possible to talk of a 'classless' society, but rather to speak of a differentiated, multi-dimensional class pattern in the late modern society.

But to keep the mission possible, renewal is needed. Trade unions have to work out a more differentiated and decentralised type of industrial relations. They maybe can take advantage of new emerging types of life-style, where there is room for community-based action. In order to cope with individualisation and differentiation the trade unions shall have to develop a new definition of solidarity which takes pluralism and diversity into account. The mission is not only about identity (how to represent new employee groups) but also about solidarity (how to create solidarity between different groups of employees).

However, in the book repeated warnings are sounded not to throw the baby out with the bath water: a renewed multi-dimensional class discourse retains its efficiency for trade union action. Individualisation and differentiation does not mean that people don't distinguish themselves from others anymore on the basis of socio-economic position. If trade unions renew themselves in the right direction, class can still unite.

1 The Crisis of Union Representation

ANDREW J. RICHARDS

Introduction

The relationship between trade unionism and working-class solidarity has always been difficult. While an important part of the discourse of trade unionism has been anchored in a claim to represent the interests of workers as a whole, the historical role of unions as agents of working-class solidarity and unity is ambiguous. In terms of their ability - and willingness - to incorporate workers into their ranks, trade unions have just as often demonstrated exclusive, as inclusive, tendencies. Moreover, to the extent that more inclusive, class-wide strategies on the part of trade unions have emerged, they have been heavily contingent and constructed phenomena, and never structurally-determined givens. It is within this historical context that any assessment of the role of contemporary trade unionism in promoting working-class unity should be undertaken.

Nonetheless, even allowing for its historically contingent nature, it appears that in contemporary terms, the problems of constructing and maintaining trade union and working-class solidarity are greater than ever before. Many severe challenges to trade union and working-class unity have emerged during the 1980s and 1990s. Divisions amongst and between both unionised and non-unionised workers have become deeply entrenched. As such, contemporary trade unionism is beset by an acute crisis of representation, rooted in a division between those whom the unions have, historically, sought and claimed to represent, and those whom they now actually represent. Moreover, traditional appeals to class solidarity alone will not resolve the crisis.

This general argument is sustained as follows. First, I describe those trends in the 1980s and 1990s which have undermined the strength of trade unionism, fragmented the ranks of unionised labour, and generated divisions between unionised and non-unionised workers. Second, I explore the nature of the unions' crisis of representation. Third, I place the contemporary crisis of trade unionism in the context of ongoing debates on working-class fragmentation in late industrial societies. Fourth, in the light of such debates, I examine the possibilities for the renewal and reinvigoration of contemporary trade unionism along more inclusive lines. I emphasise the renewal of trade unionism at the local level - both within and beyond the immediate workplace - as the key to promoting greater working-class solidarity.[1]

Challenges to Trade Union Solidarity

The multiple challenges to trade union solidarity that have emerged over the last two decades are complex and manifold. During the 1980s, economic, structural, industrial and (in some cases) political changes interacted, in different ways and to differing degrees, to undermine the traditional foundations of union activity and organisation (Western, 1995) and reshape the composition of the unionised work force. Economic recession and higher rates of unemployment throughout the advanced capitalist countries sapped the bargaining strength of unions and deprived them of members. Unemployment tended to be concentrated in areas of high union density. For example, the geographical distribution of British trade union workers became much more skewed in the 1980s. Most union workers were still to be found in the traditional industrial heartlands, where rates of unionisation remained high (67 per cent in Northern England, 64 per cent in Wales) but where, of course, the brunt of plant closures and redundancies was being borne. In contrast, unionisation rates in those areas where large numbers of new jobs were being created remained low (41 per cent in

---

[1]   In addressing the issues of solidarity and representation, I set aside the related, but separate, issue of union strength. The latter is, of course, crucial, and the source of continuing vibrant debate - is organised labour, or is it not, 'in decline'? Ebbinghaus and Visser (1997), for example, argue that the general thesis of 'union decline' is undermined by considerable cross-national variation in union density rates. Yet while greater union density may be a measure of greater union power, it may not reflect greater union inclusiveness or solidarity across sections of the national work force. In a context, for example, of deep insider/outsider divisions (for example, Spain), trade unionism may well be exclusionary, with any increases in union affiliation rates tending to come from amongst insiders (Richards and Polavieja, 1997).

the south-east, and only 20 per cent in East Anglia) (Maksymiw et al., 1990, 17).

Structural changes also undermined the traditionally strongly unionised sectors of advanced capitalist economies such as heavy industry and manufacturing. In both absolute and relative terms, the manufacturing sectors of most advanced capitalist economies shrank considerably during the early 1980s and showed few signs of robust recovery thereafter. Employment levels in manufacturing slumped, while the percentage of workers employed in manufacturing declined steadily throughout the 1980s (Richards, 1995, 9, 10, 47). Such a trend ensured that unions based in these sectors suffered steady (and in some cases, staggering) membership losses. In the USA, for example, 10.8 million jobs - consisting primarily of full-time, overwhelmingly male, and heavily unionised jobs in basic industries such as steel, transportation, automobiles and rubber - disappeared through plant closures and cutbacks between 1981 and 1986 (Coggins et al., 1989, 404). Between 1980 and 1988, the United Auto Workers lost over 300,000 members. Between 1980 and 1987, the Machinists lost 32 per cent of their membership, the Carpenters 22 per cent, and the Electrical Workers 23 per cent (Salvatore, 1992, 89).[2] Between 1980 and 1993, the USWA's membership fell from 1,200,000 to 560,000 (Noble, 1993, 115).

Similar trends affected the traditional bastions of trade unionism elsewhere. In Britain, during the recession of 1980-81, nearly half of the TUC membership gained during the 1970s was lost (Maksymiw et al., 1990, 17). Between 1979 and 1987, the number of jobs in manufacturing fell sharply by 1.954 million (or 27 per cent), most of these belonging to full-time, male workers. As in the USA, unions whose respective memberships were heavily concentrated in the blue-collar industrial and manufacturing sectors of the economy fared badly. The country's three largest unions suffered considerably between 1980 and 1987. The TGWU's membership fell 35.4 per cent from 2.07 million to 1.35 million, that of the AEU fell 45.6 per cent from 1.5 million to 0.82 million, and that of the GMB by 16.9 per cent from 0.964 million to 0.8 million. Smaller unions fared little better, with the memberships of the NUR, UCATT and USDAW declining by 34.7 per cent, 26.4 per cent and 17.6 per cent respectively.[3] The steelworkers and especially the mineworkers suffered catastrophic losses.

However, the decline in the manufacturing base of late industrial societies not only undermined the ranks of blue-collar workers, but changed the very structure of employment itself, with further adverse consequences for

---

2   In basic steel, production jobs fell from 500,000 in 1975 to 120,000 in 1990 (Brody, 1992, 33).

3   Calculated from Maksymiw et al. (1990, 6).

unions. In the 1970s, trade unionism had been underpinned by 'well-organised, male full-time workers, employed in large manufacturing plants' (Winchester, 1989, 514). In contrast, the 1980s saw an explosion of part-time, temporary and relatively insecure jobs (especially amongst women and youth) located in smaller, more dispersed, workplaces - all of which have been traditionally weak areas of union organisation.[4] While some 9.16 million new jobs were created in the USA between January 1980 and mid-1986, 30.5 per cent were in the retail trade and 58.9 per cent in 'miscellaneous services' areas of the economy with low rates of unionisation and pay[5] (of these new jobs, 84.3 per cent were taken by women). The number of part-timers in the work force rose by 12 million between 1981 and 1987 (Coggins et al., 1989, 404-5). 'Contingent' workers - those in part-time, temporary, leased, on-call or subcontracted jobs - comprised an estimated 25 per cent of the US work force by 1994 (Cobble, 1994, 474).[6]

---

[4] See, for example, Fulcher (1991), Lane (1989), Troy (1986), Winchester (1989). Francis Green (1992, 44) argues that 'females, part-timers, and those in small establishments and lower age groups tend to have below-average union density and to constitute increasing proportions among employees'.

[5] On the issue of low pay in the USA, Parenti (1995, 25) claims that of the 13 million jobs created in the 1980s, 8.2 million paid less than $7,000 annually. In 1986, the AFL-CIO President noted that the twenty most rapidly expanding occupations paid, on average, $100 a week less than the twenty occupations in most rapid decline (Kirkland, 1986, 396).

In Britain, certain types of privatisation have promoted this general trend. Hyman (1992, 154) argues that the 'growing numbers of workers in private services (particularly women) perform unpleasant, insecure, and low-paid jobs'. Fulcher (1991, 245) notes that where local authorities have been required to put services out to tender and accept the cheapest contract (particularly in catering and cleaning), low-paid public sector workers have either lost their jobs, or been forced 'to accept a worsening of pay and conditions, including re-employment by non-union employers'.

[6] In Britain, too, the 1980s saw a significant expansion of self-employment, homeworking, sub-contractual and part-time working (by 1985, there were nearly 4.7 million part-time workers in Britain - one of the highest rates in the European Union). These jobs - overwhelmingly for women, and increasingly for the young - accounted for most of those created after 1980. Yet unionisation rates of only 14 per cent in these sectors of the economy contrasted with those of 45 per cent for the working population as a whole (Coggins et al., 1989, 387).

With respect to the problems of unionisation amongst the young, Salvatore (1992, 89) reports that in the USA, by 1988, less than 10 per cent of the working class under age 25, and only 15 per cent of those aged between 26 and 34, were unionised. In Germany, Kern and Sabel (1991, 375) describe the growing difficulties faced by the labour movement in recruiting young workers - in 1970, 23.2 per cent of employees in the metal working industries under 25 years of age were trade union members. In 1987, the proportion had fallen to 17.5 per cent. In Britain, the proportion of people under 25 in unions fell from 30 per cent in 1990 to 22 per cent in 1993. Fewer than 25 per cent of young British workers are employed in workplaces where employers recognise unions for collective bargaining (*Financial Times*, 1 March 1995).

Furthermore, in the wake of a changing industrial structure, substantial labour-saving capital investment, growing use of sub-contracted work, the export of labour-intensive activity to 'world-market factories' in the Third World and to 'rural' sites in the First World (Lash and Urry, 1987, 6), work forces in late industrial societies are increasingly dispersed in smaller-scale enterprises. In most European nations,

> non-unionised sectors employing many more part-time workers in small establishments and service occupations now constitute the fastest-growing segments of the economy. Hence, women, part-time employees, and workers in services or small industrial establishments, who were formerly marginal to the organised working class, form a growing portion of the labour force (Hall, 1987, 14).

In Britain, for example, the dramatic decline of large-scale enterprises in the 1980s severely undermined the traditional foundations of trade unionism (Beaumont, 1987; MacInnes, 1987). Between 1978 and 1982, the proportion of workers in establishments of 500 or more employees fell from 54 per cent to 48 per cent, while the proportion of enterprises employing 10,000 or more workers fell from 35 per cent to 30 per cent (Maksymiw et al., 1990, 17). The number of workers in closed shops fell from between 4.7 and 4.9 million in 1980 to between 3.5 and 3.7 million in 1984. The proportion of manual workers in private sector manufacturing covered by collective bargaining arrangements fell from 65 per cent in 1980 to 55 per cent in 1984, reflecting both the closure of large plants and the trend toward the unilateral imposition of pay settlements by employers (Coggins et al., 1989, 387).

In addition to the adverse impact of economic and structural change, employers in the 1980s were decidedly more hostile to organised labour than they had been previously. During the decade, a profound change in the structure of industrial relations took place. In a deteriorating economic and political climate, national-level bargaining was undermined as employers largely succeeded in decentralising union-management relations to the company and/or plant level.[7] In the process, the role of labour movements as national institutions - one of the hallmarks of the postwar consensus - was lost.

Such change was driven partly by the structural factors described above. Industrial change and increasingly fierce global economic competition underpinned the emergence of 'post-Fordist' production methods which

---

[7] For a rigorous overview of the trend in Sweden, Australia, Italy, Britain, the USA and the former West Germany, see Katz (1993). For other general overviews, see Hancké (1993), Lane (1989), Visser (1992), Regini (1992), Thelen (1994), Hall (1987). For case studies of Belgium and Italy, see Hancké (1991) and Locke (1990) respectively.

have, in turn, led employers to eschew macro-level systems of negotiation. Instead, during the 1980s, employers became increasingly convinced that 'they had to search for differentiated, rather than uniform, responses to the variability of conditions in different workplaces' (Regini, 1992, 7). Consequently, there was a near-wholesale shift 'in the 'centre of gravity' of economic and industrial-relations systems from the level of macro-economic management to the micro-level of the firm' (Regini, 1992, 7).[8] However, there can be little doubt, given the economic conditions prevailing in the early 1980s, that employers also sought to regain control and initiative in industrial relations at the expense of the unions (Crouch, 1986, 9). In some cases, they were emboldened and supported in their efforts by the presence of conservative governments determined to undo the influence that organised labour had acquired in national economic policy by the mid-1970s (Sabel, 1987, 26). This was particularly the case in Britain and the USA where, arguably, labour movements suffered the worst series of setbacks.

The Unions' Crisis of Representation

These trends have provoked a crisis of representation for the unions. With the demise or disappearance of traditional union constituencies, a changing labour market structure and a drastically decentralised system of industrial

---

8   In Britain, for example, national-level bargaining outside the public sector was rare by the late 1980s; 90 per cent of all private sector pay, and 65 per cent of working hours, were decided at the company level (Visser, 1992, 36).

Nonetheless, two qualifications are worth emphasising. First, Crouch (1995, 73-4) has distinguished between the collapse of centralised co-ordination of industrial relations, and a process of managed decentralisation. For most of the 1980s, both Britain and Denmark appeared to be engaged in a 'deconstruction of industrial relations structures'. However, in Britain, traditionally feeble employers' associations 'simply collapsed, and cross-firm collective bargaining withered away uncontrollably', while in Denmark, 'the central employers' body managed a decentralisation, retaining authority over its pace and extent', leading to the emergence of 'centralised decentralisation'. Should the future need arise therefore, scope remains in Denmark for centrally co-ordinated collective bargaining, whereas in Britain, no such forum now exists.

Second, the demise of national-level concertation does not necessarily signify the complete decentralisation and/or fragmentation of industrial relations altogether. For example, in Spain, from 1986, the government presided over the demise of national-level agreements with the unions. However, the absence of nationally agreed norms has not, in fact, led to a significant decentralisation of collective bargaining. Instead, continuing union strength in industries such as chemicals, metal and construction has ensured the survival of (sub-national) collective agreements. In 1990, 4 million workers were covered by provincial agreements, and 1.6 million by industry-wide agreements (Rigby and Lawlor, 1994, 259, 265). Moreover, see Pérez (1999) for an analysis of the return to national social bargaining in Spain and Italy in the 1990s.

relations, a gulf has emerged between those whom the unions claim and/or seek to represent, and those whom they actually represent. This crisis comprises, in turn, two components.

A Crisis of Identity

The first crisis is one of identity, as a result of important long-term changes in the internal composition of organised labour. Two trends in particular - both of which were well underway before the 1980s and 1990s - have ensured that the male, industrial, blue-collar worker has lost his prominence as the traditional mainstay of trade unionism. First, as traditional heavy industry declined throughout the advanced capitalist world, trade unionism became increasingly white-collar in character. In Britain, between 1948 and 1970, white-collar union membership increased by 80 per cent, while blue-collar membership rose by a mere 0.8 per cent (Walsh, 1985, 75). In 1911, white-collar membership stood at only 14.58 per cent of blue-collar levels. By 1971, however, this proportion had risen to 51.39 per cent. In absolute terms, white-collar union membership levels rose from 2.175 million in 1951 to 3.57 million in 1971, an increase of 64.1 per cent (Bain and Price, 1980, 41-2).

In the USA, white-collar unionism rose from 13.6 per cent of total union membership in 1956 to 26.9 per cent in 1976, and in Germany, from 15.8 per cent of total union membership in 1957 to 24.9 per cent in 1982. In Sweden, white-collar unionism rose from 2.9 per cent to 72.6 per cent of blue-collar union membership levels between 1950 and 1975. During the same period, while manual trade unionism had increased 45.7 per cent from 1.214 million to 1.769 million, white-collar unionism had more than trebled (221.4 per cent) from 0.4 million to 1.29 million. A similar trend was also evident in Denmark. Between 1950 and 1976, white-collar unionism rose from 34.1 per cent to 75.4 per cent of manual union membership levels. During this period, the ranks of white-collar organised labour increased 217.9 per cent from 197,500 to 627,500 (Bain and Price, 1980, 136, 148, 154; Walsh, 1985, 43).

The second major manifestation of the changing identity of trade unionism has concerned the growing entry of women into the work forces of advanced capitalist countries. In Britain, women accounted for 20.8 per cent of all trade union members in 1945, but 29.5 per cent by 1977. Between 1972 and 1979, the number of women trade unionists increased by 34 per cent, compared to only 13 per cent for men. In Germany, the proportion of women members in the country's largest union confederation (the DGB) increased from 16.5 per cent in 1973 to 21.0 per cent in 1982 (or

22.5 per cent of all German union confederations) (Walsh, 1985, 27, 75; Bain and Price, 1980, 38).[9]

Outside Europe, a similar pattern was apparent. In Australia, the proportion of trade unionists who were women increased from 21.6 per cent in 1945 to 30.1 per cent in 1976. During the same period, the number of women trade unionists rose from 259,100 to 841,300. In Canada, the proportion of trade unionists who were women rose from 8.4 per cent in 1945 to 35.5 per cent in 1984, and in the USA, from 16.6 per cent in 1954 to 24.9 per cent in 1976 (Bain and Price, 1980, 88-9, 115, 123-4; Coggins et al., 1989, 68).

Structural shifts in the advanced capitalist countries from blue- to white-collar sectors of the economy, and the influx of women into the work force, therefore combined to change the face of organised labour in the postwar period. Yet such trends, despite taking place in a context of overall union growth and expansion, were potentially troubling ones. Statistics for most advanced capitalist countries demonstrate that rates of unionisation among white-collar and women workers were markedly and consistently lower than those for traditional blue-collar (and overwhelmingly male) workers (Richards, 1995, 6).

Similarly, while the entry of women into the work force was a dramatic challenge to the deeply masculinist culture of Western labour movements, the overwhelmingly white-collar, part-time or temporary nature of most women's work meant that unionisation rates among women were significantly and consistently lower than those for men. In Britain, for example, while unionisation rates for women rose from 25.0 per cent in 1945 to 38.9 per cent in 1977, rates for men during the same period increased from 45.1 per cent to 62.1 per cent - thus unionisation rates among women in 1977 were still lower than the 1945 level for men. In Australia, a similar pattern was evident. While unionisation rates among men increased from 49.3 per cent in 1945 to 59.7 per cent in 1976, rates among women lagged behind, rising in the same period only from 37.0 per cent to 44.9 per cent (Bain and Price, 1980, 38, 123-4).

Given these internal trends, the notion of the postwar consensus as a golden era of growth and consolidation for organised labour must be treated cautiously. In fact, the structural shift from heavily unionised blue-collar economic sectors to more weakly organised service and white-collar sectors meant that by the late 1970s - despite thirty years of growth - the traditional foundations of trade unionism in most advanced capitalist

---

[9]   In certain cases, women even made inroads into traditionally male-dominated blue-collar unions. In Denmark, the proportion of blue-collar unionists who were women rose from 28.1 per cent in 1972 to 41.5 per cent in 1981 (Walsh, 1985, 27).

countries were beginning to crumble. Moreover, the 1980s saw a considerable acceleration of these changes. The most dramatic manifestation of this was the steep decline of traditional blue-collar unionism.[10] In the USA, by 1985, for the first time in the history of the union movement, blue-collar workers no longer comprised a majority of its membership (Troy, 1986, 86). By 1986, fewer than 40 per cent of AFL-CIO members worked in blue-collar jobs (Kirkland, 1986, 397). In contrast, the fortunes of white-collar unions were boosted.[11] Despite a sharp fall in the aggregate level of union membership, the ranks of the Service Employees International Union, for example, grew by 17 per cent between 1980 and 1987 (Salvatore, 1992, 89). In Britain, too, the 1980s saw a growth in the relative importance of white-collar and service sector unions, with the principal banking union, BIFU, and the local government union, NALGO, actually increasing their memberships between 1979 and 1987 by 25.3 per cent and 0.75 per cent respectively.[12]

Additionally, the structural changes undermining blue-collar unionism boosted the relative importance of women within the labour force in general and, by extension, the ranks of trade unions. Between 1981 and 1994 participation rates in the labour force throughout the late industrialised world fell among men but rose among women; the latter, therefore, increased their share of the employed labour force. In the USA, an increase in union membership among women in the 1970s and 1980s partially compensated for a decline among men. By 1992, women accounted for 37 per cent of all union members, compared to 24 per cent in the mid-1970s (Kessler-Harris and Silverman, 1992, 63). In Britain, between 1983 and 1987, the number of women trade unionists increased by 21 per cent from 2.36 to 2.86 million (while the number of male unionists fell 23 per cent to 5.94 million). By 1987, women accounted for 32.5 per cent of total TUC membership (compared to 23.4 per cent in 1983), and six of Britain's twenty largest unions (BIFU, COHSE, CPSA, NUPE, NUT and USDAW)

---

10 See, for example, Crouch (1992), Fulcher (1991), Hall (1987), Hyman (1992), Lash and Urry (1987). On the demise of traditional trade unionism in the European steel industry, see Rhodes and Wright (1988), Mény and Wright (1986). For the European shipbuilding industry, see Strath (1987), for the British coal industry, see Richards (1996).

11 See, for example, Hall (1987), Hyman (1992), Lash and Urry (1987), MacInnes (1987), Winchester (1989).

12 Calculated from Maksymiw et al. (1990, 6). Visser (1992, 28, 30) notes that the largest unions, or cartels of unions, are now found in the public sector. In contrast, in 1985, metalworkers' unions retained their traditional first place only in Germany, Switzerland and one of the two Belgian federations; 'in Austria, they were outnumbered by a general white-collar union; in Denmark, Ireland, and Britain by large, general unions straddling all industries; in Sweden, Norway, the Netherlands, and France by public employee unions; in Italy by pensioners'.

had a higher proportion of women in their ranks than men. In addition, 49.3 per cent of NALGO's members were women (Maksymiw et al., 1990, 1, 7).[13]

In terms, therefore, of the identity of trade unionism in advanced industrial societies, such compositional changes have ensured that 'blue-collar workers ... will become an ever smaller minority within the labour movements of which they were once the proud founders. Inevitably, their voice will carry less weight in general councils, national confederations, and bargaining fora' (Visser, 1992, 28; see also Crouch, 1986, 6).

A Crisis of Solidarity

The second principal crisis engulfing contemporary trade unionism is one of solidarity. This crisis pertains to both the unionised work force itself, and the relationship between the unionised and non-unionised work forces.

Confronted by rapid economic and structural change, management pressures and, in some cases, government hostility, the unionised work force has been increasingly divided. Such conflict has taken place at all levels of union organisation, and has assumed different forms. National union confederations struggled in the 1980s to maintain the unity of an increasingly disparate set of constituent members. Blue-collar unions based in declining industrial sectors were at odds with white-collar unions attempting to organise in expanding and highly competitive areas of the economy. Economic decline, managerial aggression and rising unemployment tended to promote organisational defence as a key union objective. This generated conflict as unions sought to compensate for membership losses by encroaching on other unions' territory (Winchester, 1989, 503, 505-10; Koelble, 1992, 61 ff.). A politically harsh climate also fuelled disagreements between unions over questions of tactics and strategy. In Britain, for example, the TUC was riven throughout the 1980s by divisions between unions, such as the AEU and EETPU, espousing a 'new realist' strategy of accommodation to government anti-union legislation and moderation (including no-strike agreements) in industrial relations, and those, such as the NUM, promoting a strategy of outright defiance and industrial mili-

---

13 Nevertheless, while union membership gains among women between 1983 and 1987 were both absolute and relative, they took place, unlike previous decades, in a context of general trade union contraction. The impressive gains for women between 1983 and 1987 could not offset the devastating losses of the early 1980s. Overall, the number of women trade unionists in 1987 was still some 685,000 lower than the 1979 total of 3.55 million (Maksymiw et al., 1990, 1). Moreover, union density rates among women remained substantially lower than those for men. In 1985, 31 per cent of women workers were unionised, compared to 53 per cent of male workers (Fulcher, 1991, 249).

tancy. Consequently, the TUC's ability to speak for all unions was severely limited.

In addition, individual unions were increasingly fragmented by the process of structural and economic change. This was true not just of general unions (which have always struggled to unify workers in different economic sectors) but also of those based largely in a single industry. In Germany, one of the primary obstacles faced by IG Metall in developing industry-wide bargaining strategies during the 1980s and 1990s was that it organised all metal workers in both declining and growing sectors of the German industrial economy (Allen, 1990, 267; Markovits and Otto, 1992). In Britain, the attempts of the NUM to unify the miners in defending jobs were severely hampered by material differences within the coalfields and the unevenness of the Thatcher government's pit closure programme (Richards, 1996). Such cases exemplify the general process whereby 'the balance has shifted from national policy co-ordination and the pursuit of general interests towards greater local discretion and the recognition of separate interests in some unions' (Winchester, 1989, 514).

Trade union solidarity in the 1980s was further undermined by a general weakening of the authority of national union leaderships and centralised union confederations (Hyman, 1992, 151), and growing conflict between national and local levels of unionism.[14] This resulted partly from the politically-driven demise of neocorporatist structures of industrial relations, which saw unions excluded from deliberations with governments and employers at the national level. In addition, though, the largely successful efforts of management to shift the locus of industrial relations to the company and/or local level further strained the national unity of labour movements (Visser, 1992, 38). Drives for internal flexibility and company-level mechanisms of employee participation threatened the viability of unions' national strategies (Hyman, 1992, 155; Hall, 1987, 10; Sabel,

---

[14] National-local relations have never been conflict-free (Britain's 1978-79 'winter of discontent' is a vivid example of such tensions). Moreover, the strength of centralised union confederations has, traditionally, varied considerably between countries. Nonetheless, Crouch (1992, 180) argues that the 1980s saw a general 'disarticulation' of labour movements towards the local and/or company level. In Southern Europe, the attempts of the Italian, Spanish (and to a lesser extent) Portuguese and Greek governments to continue with some form of national-level neo-corporatist agreement with the unions were undercut by local level protest. In Italy, attempts in the late 1980s by both employers and unions to effect sector-level agreements were frustrated 'by the radical disarticulation of the Italian labour movement and the growth of rank-and-file activist groups (comitati di base, COBAS) autonomous of the unions' (see also Mershon, 1989). Similarly, Spanish, Portuguese and Greek government attempts to encourage national systems of concertación social also 'suffered from the low levels of articulation of the labour movement' (Crouch, 1992, 180).

1987, 45). This 'disaggregation of industrial relations' has intensified the 'obstacles to solidaristic trade unionism' (Hyman, 1992, 155). In sum, 'change works against (unions), isolating work groups and undermining national strategies to reinforce solidarity and the unions' position as the sword and shield of collective interests' (Sabel, 1987, 45).

Additionally, though, changes in the structure of the labour market and generally higher rates of unemployment during the 1980s and 1990s have led, in many cases, to the emergence of an insider-outsider division within national work forces and have accentuated, by extension, the divide between unionised and non-unionised sections of the advanced industrial work force (Hyman, 1992, 151). Continuing structural and compositional changes have created a 'core' of reasonably secure, relatively skilled, full-time, unionised workers, and a 'periphery' of relatively insecure (temporary and/or part-time), semi-skilled, low-paid, and non-unionised workers (Crouch, 1986, 7; Hall, 1987, 10-1; Pérez-Díaz, 1987, 118; Richards and Polavieja, 1997; Taylor, 1993, 146).[15] General management drives for 'flexibility', moreover, accentuated the division. In essence, managers sought to 'isolate a core of privileged employees' (Boreham and Hall, 1994, 334), involving the 'functional flexibility of multi-skilled 'core' workers in full-time employment, and the numerical flexibility provided by the employment of trainee, part-time, temporary, or subcontracted workers. Such tendencies divide labour and set up barriers to its effective organisation' (Fulcher, 1991, 255). Pressures for greater flexibility and higher productivity, when exerted in a context of high unemployment, therefore reflect a wider problem of solidarity for the trade union movement. Hall (1987, 10) describes the 'cross-cutting pressures that unions already feel between the broad demands of their core constituency, who are employed, and the broader penumbra of the working class that is under- or unemployed'. Similarly, Crouch (1986, 8) argues that 'if unions primarily represent the secure work force, their co-operation in restructuring may be bought precisely by requiring insecure groups to bear the brunt of adjustment'. Pérez-Díaz (1987, 118) also observes that 'in hard times (trade

---

15 Rigby and Lawlor (1994, 262, 266) describe the effects of the 'massive casualisation of the labour force' on Spanish trade unions. Currently, some 32 per cent of the Spanish labour force is employed on temporary contracts of differing types and status. This growth of temporary work, when combined with high unemployment (23 per cent at the end of 1993), the predominance of small firms in the Spanish economy, and the large underground, or 'black', economy, make the problem of organising Spanish workers a formidable one. For an analysis of the relationship in Spain between trade unionism and working-class solidarity in a context of deep labour market segmentation, see Richards and Polavieja (1997).

unions) have closed ranks and established a clear hierarchy of priorities at the expense of those below'.

Trade Union Solidarity and Working-class Fragmentation

Continuing changes in the structure of labour markets and of employment itself have therefore contributed to the fragmentation of unionised labour, and generated growing divisions between unionised and non-unionised workers. Yet to what extent do such trends reflect changes in the class structure per se of advanced industrial societies and, more specifically, in the structure and composition of the working class?

Attempts to answer this question, by placing the contemporary problems of trade unionism in the context of ongoing changes in the class structure of advanced industrial societies, have generated a vibrant debate. Even prior to the 1980s, Hobsbawm (1978) warned in an influential essay that the working class was riven by increasingly serious conflicts of interest. The events of the 1980s merely reinforced his conviction that 'workers are crumbling into groups with diverging and contradictory interests' (Hobsbawm, 1989, 74). The demise of traditional blue-collar heavy industry was particularly damaging for the foundations of trade unionism and a dramatic manifestation of the wider process of class change - the old 'smokestack' industries are 'typically seen as a natural generator of solidaristic collectivism' (Hyman, 1992, 153). With the sharp decline of such traditionally militant and cohesive occupational cultures as those of the miners (Richards, 1996), the 1980s saw the disappearance of what has variously been termed the 'classic labour movement' (Hobsbawm, 1989), the 'core working class' (Lash and Urry, 1987, 5) or the 'quintessential' members of the working class (Hall, 1987, 14). This, moreover, was no mere quantitative change, but represented the demise of a set of powerful traditions and cultures within the labour movement. As such, some authors have pinpointed the 1980s as a decade in which organised labour's historic role as a class-conscious movement was lost for ever. Hobsbawm (1989, 71), for example, argues that while the 'working class' has not disappeared as such, 'class consciousness no longer has this power to unite', while Touraine (1986, 161) explicitly links the decline of a 'class conscious labour movement' to the 'disintegration of the 'classic' working class ... the very basis of class consciousness is disappearing and the labour movement is being replaced by interest group unionism'.

Yet the implications of the demise of traditional blue-collar labour for working-class solidarity as a whole are not clear. On the one hand, some have argued that the decline of blue-collar labour and the concomitant rise of white-collar labour do not signal the demise of the working class per se: 'the problem is not so much objective de-proletarianisation which has been brought about by the decline of old-style industrial labour, but is rather the subjective decline of class solidarity' (Hobsbawm, 1989, 73; see also Edwards, 1979, 163). In addition, those who have argued for the growing 'proletarianisation' of white-collar labour also dispute the disappearance of the working class per se (Aronowitz, 1983; Braverman, 1974; Kelly, 1988).

On the other hand, others claim that the demise of blue-collar labour is synonymous with the disappearance of the working class itself. Gorz, for example, states that developments in late industrial societies have replaced the working class with 'a non-class of non-workers or the 'neoproletariat' (...) the old working class (...) is no more than a privileged minority. Most of the population belong to the post-industrial neoproletariat' (Giddens, 1987, 279; Gorz, 1991). Other authors have also argued, in different contexts, that the former working class is, in fact, being broken down into competing groups with no common objective class interest. Thus Lockwood (1989), and Marshall and Rose (1988), have criticised the notion that white-collar labour is being 'proletarianised', arguing instead that it is informed by a very different set of interests.[16] Meanwhile, as Fulcher (1991, 256) notes, the emerging core/periphery distinction between insiders and outsiders within late industrial work forces has been generalised to the level of the class structure as a whole by the notion of dualism. At a minimum, this implies, critically, that class-based strategies on the part of unions will no longer suffice as a means of bridging the divide between the increasingly beleaguered ranks of organised blue-collar labour and the growing 'disprivileged underclass of employees' (Lane, 1989, 605).

However, great care must be taken in referring to unions' class-based strategies or (recalling Sabel's words (1987, 45)) their alleged position as the 'sword and shield of collective interests'. As Hyman (1992, 166) notes, 'a mythical belief in some previous golden age of proletarian unity and unproblematic trade-union solidarity distorts our perception of current labour-movement dynamics'.[17] Instead, historically, the role of trade unions as agents of working-class unity has been deeply ambiguous and problematic. On the one hand, unions emerged as the defenders and promoters of the immediate concrete interests of those workers whom they organised. On the other hand, trade unionism often involved the articulation of an alternative social order comprising a wider class solidarity. As such, the language of trade unionism in capitalist societies has been

---

[16] See also Bain and Price (1972), Hyman and Price (1983), Smith et al. (1991), Smith and Willmott (1991).

[17] On the 'myth of the golden past' (see Miliband, 1964).

complex and often contradictory. MacInnes (1987, 139), for example, distinguishes between the two faces of trade unionism as those of 'sword of justice' and those of 'vested interest'. Aronowitz (1983, ix) juxtaposes the 'heroic' and 'instrumentalist' views of trade unionism. The former 'consists of the task of transforming society - to abolish exploitation and hierarchy and establish a new social order based upon equality'. In the latter, 'day to day struggle is accorded primacy in all actions of workers (...) far from addressing history, workers address their own immediate needs'.

Labour history also teaches us, however, that the relationship between these two 'faces' of trade unionism is one of complexity rather than of mutual exclusion. In the British context, Marshall (1997, 38, 39) observes that 'on many occasions trades unions have organised themselves along exclusionary lines and secured sectional gains at the expense of the working class as a whole. At other times more inclusionary class objectives have been to the fore'. Yet he adds that this contrast 'forces the history of British labour into an implausible dualistic mould: solidaristic and class versus sectional and privatised. The reality is more complex'. Indeed, viewing 'sectionalism' and 'solidarism' as points on a continuum rather than mutually exclusive alternatives reminds us that, historically, trade union solidarity has been a contingent, constructed and often contradictory phenomenon: 'from historical experience we can learn that there are no short-cuts to the identification and (re)definition of interests in a solidaristic manner; it is always necessary to campaign and struggle for (relative) unity among workers and their organisations' (Hyman, 1992, 166). Trade union solidarity, therefore, has always had to be built - even the pursuit of its most moderate and basic demands often incurred the wrath of employers. The physical construction of unions was very much a contingent phenomenon that took place in an extremely hostile environment. Furthermore, uniting workers in the same industry (let alone different ones), and forging a collective class identity, were processes of painstaking construction, usually from the local level upwards.[18] Even in the case of the miners' union, which organised in a single industry renowned for its tendency to promote a powerful collective identity, both the Miners' Federation of Great Britain and its successor, the National Union of Mineworkers, never represented more than an uneasy coalition of fiercely independent localities (Richards, 1996). And even when established, trade unions have, historically, divided, as well as united, workers. The development of unions tended to perpetuate narrower occupational identities rather than broader class identity: 'in embracing particular categories of workers as

---

[18] See, for example, the account by Coates and Topham (1994) of the formation, between 1870 and 1922, of Britain's erstwhile largest union, the TGWU.

members and excluding others, each union gives institutional reinforce-
ment to certain perceptions of common interest while presenting obstacles
to alternative contours of solidarity' (Hyman, 1985, 105). Even in the best
of times, traditional blue-collar trade unionism, based on the skilled, male,
manual working class, was exclusionary in nature (Heery and Kelly, 1995,
163).

Moreover, the precarious nature of constructing inclusive, class-based
solidarity's has always been further constrained by political and ideological divisions both between and within trade union movements. In terms of
their long-term goals and objectives, neither individual unions nor union
confederations have been monolithic entities. More circumscribed versions
of trade unionism as a vested interest seeking incremental reform 'within
the system' did not sit easily with those which viewed trade unionism in
more radical terms, as a means of promoting profound societal transformation. In all western capitalist societies since the industrial revolution, trade
unions have been riven by such differences. Perhaps the classic example of
trade unionism's 'inner conflict' took place in the USA during the first half
of the twentieth century as the American Federation of Labour's (AFL)
dominance of the American union movement was challenged severely
(though ultimately unsuccessfully) by, first, the much more radical Industrial Workers of the World (IWW) and later the Congress of Industrial
Organisations (CIO) (Galenson, 1986, 46 ff). In Western Europe, too, trade
unionism has been deeply divided along ideological lines.

How such internal ideological divisions have been resolved has had
important organisational consequences. In some cases (for example, the
German DGB, the British TUC and the American AFL-CIO), conflict and
dissent have been largely contained (though by no means extinguished)
within the parameters of a single, dominant union confederation. In other
countries, this has not been the case - in Spain and France, for example,
fierce rivalry between union confederations has both shaped and been
shaped by a longstanding parallel rivalry between powerful Socialist and
Communist parties. As such, the particular organisational configuration of
trade unionism has had enormous implications for its ability to promote
working-class solidarity.

In addition, though, ideological and political divisions have reflected
profoundly differing conceptions within trade unionism of class unity and
class struggle - as the presence in Europe of Socialist, Communist, Catholic, Christian Democratic and avowedly 'non-partisan' trades unions
underscores. We should therefore be wary of assuming uncritically the
willingness and desire of unions to adopt solidaristic discourses and strategies of working-class unity. Indeed, more radical critics sustain that even if
they once were capable of articulating the interests of the exploited in

general (and historically, this is in doubt), trade unions have, during the postwar period, steadily retreated (whether through choice or force of circumstance) from solidaristic class discourses and strategies. This is especially so in the case of American organised labour, where the triumph of 'business unionism', with its hard-nosed, anti-theoretical emphasis on the practicalities of bargaining, and an equally forceful rejection of radical social transformation, was particularly emphatic.[19]

The USA undoubtedly represents the extreme case of a union movement eschewing a solidaristic class-based discourse. Nonetheless, it is also true - albeit to a lesser extent - of Europe, where even the postwar period of union growth and organisational consolidation witnessed a general decline of 'solidarism' on the part of trade unions. Many union movements tended to segregate 'politics' from 'industrial relations' (Hyman, 1990, 144). In the case of the British TUC,

> the use of unions' industrial muscle to sway government was normally viewed as improper (...) even when the language of class struggle entered the vocabulary of trade unionists, their actual practice was typically more mundane and more parochial (Hyman, 1990, 144-5).

In addition, organisational consolidation (often achieved through the political victory of social democracy) did little, in and of itself, to promote - and may even have inhibited - strategies of greater working-class inclusiveness. With respect to the postwar trajectory of British trade unionism, 'the unions reached the high point of their 'Magnificent Journey' (...) in 1945, lost sight of their social purpose and suffered a gradual erosion of membership commitment, only to walk off a cliff in 1979' (Ackers, 1995, 150).

In this context, it is worth emphasising that while in sociological terms, the male, blue-collar, industrial worker has lost his role as the bulwark of trade unionism, the political culture, as it were, of trade union movements has tended to remain decidedly blue-collar in nature. Crouch (1986, 6) notes that the central defining characteristic and sense of direction of most union movements have remained the interests of the manual working class, with an especially important part played in defining that interest by the main traditional industries. Given the immense changes in the structure of labour markets and of employment in the 1980s and 1990s, such limitations have undoubtedly contributed to a growing, and profound, dislocation of trade unions, as institutions, from the needs and interests of an increasingly differentiated work force. This, in turn, has led to a serious crisis of

---

[19] On the evolution of trade unionism in the USA, see Aronowitz (1983), Brody (1980; 1994), Cochran (1977), Davis (1986), Edwards (1979), Gordon et al. (1982), Green (1980), Kazin (1988), Lipset (1986) and Roediger (1988; 1991).

representation, or what Hall (1987, 19) describes as the unions' declining ability to summon up 'moral authority' over work forces as a whole. In Spain, for example, where structural economic change has led to a deeply entrenched insider-outsider division, a huge gulf has opened up between, on the one hand, an immense swathe of outsider workers and, on the other, a trade union movement largely confined to the beleaguered 'core' industrial blue-collar work force (Richards and Polavieja, 1997).

Possibilities for the Renewal of Contemporary Trade Unionism

I have emphasised the contingent nature of the relationship between the role and functioning of trade unionism and the emergence of working-class solidarity. However, in focusing on the essentially constructed nature of solidarity, my intention is not to downplay the role of structural conditions in shaping the role of trade unions as potential agents of working-class unity. Certainly, compared to the present, structural conditions in the past (particularly given the prominence of heavy industry) were more favourable for the underpinning of trade unionism. But even then, the relationship between 'structure' and 'outcome' - understood in terms of working-class unity - was anything but clear:

> when we did have a classic class structure of a kind that would have made every Marxist go to sleep happily at night, we always had a Tory government. We never had socialism in the nineteenth century when there was great oppression (...) or in the 1930s when millions of people were organised in unions in their overalls, we never had socialism (Benn, 1985, 14, cited in Richards, 1996, 6).

As such, the task of labour scholars has always been to analyse under what circumstances unions' strategies and struggles, initially forged in terms of immediate sectional interests, might generate wider working-class solidarity.

All this said, the role of contingency in the shaping of working-class solidarity should not be overestimated. Structural changes in the advanced capitalist countries appear, in the 1980s and 1990s, to be increasingly unfavourable to the forging of common interests (Hyman, 1992, 29) along class lines.[20] As such, the questions of whether wider solidarity's can be constructed, along what lines, under what circumstances, and whether

---

[20] Not all union movements have been undermined in organisational terms over the past twenty years. But the maintenance, in some cases, of rates of unionisation (as a result, for example, of favourable labour institutions) and the role of unions as agents of working-class solidarity are two very separate matters.

appeals to class unity will suffice, can only be answered through careful empirical investigation. But it seems that any a priori assumptions regarding the utility of class analysis with respect to trade union behaviour should be set aside, especially given the fact that, historically, the unions' commitment to (let alone ability to forge) working-class unity cannot be taken for granted. Hyman (1992, 166) has posed the questions of whether trade unions must construct 'a new rationale, a new vocabulary of motives', and whether 'scope remains for strategic initiatives by and within labour movements, allowing new means of transcending divisions and forging common interests'. This would indeed seem to be the priority for unions, but evidence from the 1980s and 1990s indicates that appeals to class solidarity - or, at least, appeals to class solidarity alone - will not suffice.

This does not mean that trade union discourse and strategy has collapsed into Touraine's 'interest group unionism' (1986, 161) cited earlier. Trade union struggles and objectives in the 1980s and 1990s have all contained powerful class elements. However, given the general collapse of concertation (at least at the national level), the decentralisation of industrial relations, the demise of large-scale industrial enterprises, the enormous growth of temporary and insecure work, and the growing division between insiders and outsiders, it is clear that the simple adoption by unions of more forceful and radical appeals to class unity, at the national level, are doomed.

Instead, to the extent that unions, in a context of working-class fragmentation, are developing 'new rationales' and a 'new vocabulary of motives', initiative has come from the local level and has not been cast in purely class terms. Two claims may be made regarding the vitality of the local sphere[21] - first, to the extent that unions have moved beyond their traditional 'terms of reference', and constructed new social alliances and solidarity's, initiative has come largely from below; second, to the extent that unions either scored victories or were able to sustain major struggles in the 1980s, they did so on the basis of activism and initiative at the local level.

There are two dimensions to the relatively greater vitality of local level unionism. First, in their traditional role as defenders of workers' interests in the workplace - that is, as institutions of industrial relations - unions have remained remarkably resilient. The power of local unions is, of course, double-edged. On the one hand, local level autonomy has limited the ability of national unions to devise and implement coherent strategies at the national or sectoral level (Locke, 1990; Mershon, 1989; Richards, 1996). On the other hand, local unionism, especially in a decentralised

---

[21] Locke (1990, 351) contrasts 'microlevel effervescence' with 'macrolevel paralysis'.

environment, is obviously that much closer to the needs and interests of the work force.[22] For this reason, a vibrant local unionism has been critical to maintaining overall union strength.[23] For example, vigorous local leadership can generate levels of participation in, and commitment to, workplace unionism even among allegedly instrumentally-minded white-collar workers (Fosh, 1993). Meanwhile, in Belgium, Britain, France, Germany, Italy, the Netherlands and Sweden, unions with strong locals in the 1960s and 1970s - but especially in the 1980s - lost fewer members or actually gained some, while those without strong local structures of participation saw membership rates decline by between a quarter and one third (Hancké, 1993).[24]

The second dimension to locally-generated renewal can only be termed 'non-traditional'. This has partly involved the internal democratisation of union organisations themselves.[25] In the USA, for example, where unions have rarely been models of democratic procedure, important grass roots initiatives took place in the 1970s within the USWA, UMWA and UAW. Within the latter, black autoworkers succeeded in making the union a more racially representative and sensitive institution by forcing it to tackle race

---

[22] With respect to metalworkers' and textile workers' unions in Italy, the reconstruction of the labour movement along more horizontal lines - that is, as a federation of democratically controlled locals firmly embedded in their regional economies - may be the only viable organisational solution for the labour movement as a whole. Just as the national union was the appropriate organisational solution in a previous era of national markets and large bureaucratic firms, a federation of strong locals could be best placed to represent the interests of workers in a period of market fragmentation and continuous industrial change (Locke, 1990).

[23] Sabia (1988) argues that, historically, the presence or absence of strong local-level bases is critical for the successes and failures of many large-number collective efforts by workers. This is true both for the problems of unionising workers and for the generation of mass strike action.

[24] Institutional arrangements may also play a critical role in protecting trade unionism at the local level. In Germany, works councils have helped underpin the continued resilience of trade unions at the factory level (Turner, 1991), while in Spain, high levels of participation in works committees render trades unions far more influential than union affiliation rates of only 15 per cent would suggest (Hamann, 1998, 438).

Meanwhile, with respect to local trade union responses to industrial restructuring in Italy in the 1970s and 1980s, unions have generally been more active in the Industrial Triangle of traditional Fordist mass production. However, to the extent that local unions have maintained a presence in the Third Italy of 'flexible specialisation', this has been a function of both the local organisational strength of unions and the presence of local political authorities able to involve unions in 'local neocorporatist' bargaining (Contarino, 1995, 62).

[25] For a critique of the 'Leninist' manner in which most unions are organised, and the consequent need for unions to cultivate and incorporate the knowledge and competence (as opposed to just the needs and interests) of individual workplace members as a means of overcoming historically passive forms of participation, see Valkenburg and Zoll (1995).

discrimination in the workplace. In so doing, a previously distant institution was brought that much closer to the needs and interests of a large but previously alienated section of the American labour force.[26]

In addition, however, to the process of internal democratisation, local initiative has played a key role in propelling unionism beyond its traditional concerns and into the construction of new alliances. This is a critical development in an era when companies - especially multinationals - have acquired a phenomenal capacity to hire and fire workers, close or move plants, technology and capital within and beyond national borders and, in so doing, fragment and recompose national work forces. In the face of such awesome power, it is quite clear now that even if struggles originate in the workplace, they can no longer be waged solely within its confines. Kessler-Harris and Silverman (1992, 66) argue that just as companies, therefore, are not simply economic actors but social institutions whose activities loom well beyond the immediate economic domain, so unions must, in response, become once more social institutions themselves. These authors present a case for moving 'beyond industrial unionism', arguing that unionism in the 1990s, if it is to reposition itself as 'the voice of the majority of working people' (Kessler-Harris and Silverman, 1992, 64), has no choice but to address the 'quality of life' issues posed by an increasingly heterogeneous work force. Unions must therefore operate not just within but beyond the workplace, involving themselves in new areas such as social policy (especially that which addresses the needs of women and the family). Moreover, developing a new concept of solidarity in the face of corporate power and work force fragmentation means that unions must turn their attention to the communities in which workers reside - that is, building what Hobsbawm (cited in Kessler-Harris and Silverman, 1992, 64-6) has termed 'social fronts' linking workers and their unions to community groups that address family and community problems.[27] In Britain, the urgent need for unions to play a much more extensive role in campaigns and community activities outside the workplace - in order 'to offer the prospect of collective solutions to the problems of individually vulnerable workers and consumers' - was eloquently articulated in the late 1980s by the leader of the GMB (Winchester, 1989, 516). In this context, it is worth noting that in terms of their everyday activity, trade unions - even in the

---

[26] For an account of locally-initiated reform of the Teamsters during the 1980s, see La Botz (1990).

[27] A more inclusive trade unionism means, therefore, that the 'local' sphere should include both the workplace itself and the surrounding community. Community-based activity may be the best means of reaching out to the non-unionised in a fragmented working environment. At the same time, however, it is doubtful that such activity can be informed solely by appeals to, or in terms of, class solidarity.

traumatic years of the 1980s and 1990s - showed signs of moving towards a more social- or community-based unionism in a bid to make themselves relevant, once again, to both actual and potential members. In some cases, this involved attempting to tackle head-on the immensely difficult problem of the non-unionised working poor (often immigrant labour) and the unemployed - that is, those decidedly third-class citizens used so often as sources of cheap labour and strikebreaking.[28] Current research on Spain, however (though Spain may well be an extreme example) indicates that the unions have a long way to go in directly addressing the needs (let alone gaining the attention) of the millions of temporary workers scattered throughout thousands of small-scale enterprises - that is, precisely those sectors of the economy where unions have traditionally struggled to acquire a presence (Richards and Polavieja, 1997).[29]

Inevitably, though, it is concrete episodes of conflict between workers and employers that highlight, however tentatively, both the basis for, and constraints on, locally-driven processes of renewal. As a range of studies from the USA demonstrates (Bardacke, 1988; Green, 1990; Kwik and Moody, 1988; La Botz, 1990; Mann, 1988; Rosenblum, 1995), to the extent that workers were able to score victories in the 1980s (however limited or partial), or sustain major struggles over time, it was because they developed new alliances, from the bottom up, with the wider community.[30] A similar case may be made for the struggles of the British miners during the 1980s, but particularly their spectacular clash with the Thatcher government in 1984-85. The miners, as quintessential members of the 'traditional' working class, were able to draw on important class resources. In this sense, the assistance they received from sections of the traditional labour movement should not be underestimated. At the same time, however, deep material differences within the British coalfield, while not destroying the miners' powerful collective identity, nonetheless generated divisions within the miners' own ranks - thereby providing a graphic illustration of the tenuous link between class structure and class unity. The extent to which such differences were overcome - or at least compensated for - was largely a product of the remarkable extent to which this most traditional

---

28 For brief accounts of such initiatives in the USA during the 1980s and 1990s involving, amongst others, the International Ladies' Garment Workers Union, the United Mine Workers of America, and the Hotel and Restaurant Employees Union, see Aronowitz (1983, 147-8) and Trumka (1992, 60).

29 Though it is noteworthy that in an era of industrial change and working-class fragmentation, the Comisiones Obreras (CC.OO.) in Spain have attempted to broaden both their vision and strategy away from traditional industrial concerns and towards the arena of social policy, as one possible means of addressing the needs of the immense outsider work force (see Lucio, 1990).

30 For a fuller discussion of these studies, see Richards (1995, 41-4).

group of workers was able to construct, at the local level, a new range of social alliances which went well beyond traditional class-based parameters (Richards, 1996).

The 1980s and 1990s have proved to be a period of great change and challenge for trade unions. The composition of the late industrial work force is being rapidly and profoundly transformed, with the collapse of traditional proletarian communities being the most startling manifestation of this process. The leadership of organised labour has tended to lag behind this transformation, and has been slow in its attempts to resolve labour's twin crises of identity and solidarity. In this context, while unions have been, and will undoubtedly remain, primarily institutions of industrial relations, they must, in addition, renew themselves as movements. My principal contentions, though requiring considerable further empirical research, are, first, that such renewal can no longer be undertaken on the basis of appeals to class unity alone; second, to the extent that such renewal is underway, initiative is coming from, and revitalisation taking place at, the local level.

Such a grass roots perspective is not without its problems. Local level power and resilience do not rest easily with the need to fashion strategy at a more general level. Thus, while spontaneous action at the grass roots level has often succeeded in constructing new solidarity's, it is not clear how, in the subsequent absence of the overt threat or general crisis which initially precipitated the struggle, these may be sustained and cemented. In the course of the 1984-85 miners' strike - an example of massive popular mobilisation - many new social alliances were created, and many hitherto passive sections of the labour movement politicised. In the wake of the struggle, however, it became increasingly difficult to preserve the many impressive new networks that had been created (Richards, 1996). Similarly, Zoll notes how 'collectivity is no longer given by tradition or homogeneity of interests, but it can be created temporarily by conscious discourses on specific themes' (Valkenburg and Zoll, 1995, 124).

Nonetheless, local-level renewal is of the utmost importance for the construction of wider solidarity's. Unions, theoretically, may be able to rely on bureaucratised 'insider' strategies of lobbying for reform at the national level, or to await political salvation, as organisations, through the election of supposedly friendly governments and the passage of favourable labour legislation. This, however, would do little, in and of itself, to resolve (and indeed, could even perpetuate) trade unionism's crises of identity and solidarity. Instead, labour solidarity has always been a constructed and contingent phenomenon built on local foundations. It is now more so than ever in an era of generally decentralised industrial relations, increasingly localised threats, fragmented work forces and growing corporate power. In such an environment, no strategy of national solidarity can be constructed or sustained without a reinvigoration of unionism at the local level. The potential exists for unions to reposition themselves both within and beyond the workplace as the representatives of the majority of working people. Structural changes in advanced capitalist societies have, after all, brought to the fore issues of democracy, control and accountability (especially in the face of resurgent corporate power and mobility), and that of job security in an era of increasingly insecure employment (Hedges, 1994, 48-9) - all of which suggest the need for a strong union presence at both the workplace and community level. But in a fragmented and dispersed working environment, with many 'outside' workers currently beyond the reach of unions, taking struggle beyond the workplace and into the wider community will also involve moving beyond traditional appeals to class solidarity alone.

2 The Transformation of Social Classes: From 'Deproletarianisation' to 'Individualisation'?

MICHAEL VESTER

Since the end 1970s, the old theories of fragmenting social classes have increasingly gained credence under the name of 'individualisation'. This interpretation is also increasingly used by trade union theorists to explain the difficulties of mobilising members especially of the younger generation:

> As a consequence of the process of social differentiation we have to note radical changes in the way of life of the individuals and in the structures and institutions which collectively integrate the individual. At the base of these changes there is the general tendency of individualisation. Its effects are ambiguous. On the one hand, it destroys traditional family ties and social structures such as class, stratum and milieu, effecting isolation and loss of orientation. On the other hand, it offers new opportunities of individual self-determination and co-determination and more autonomy of the individuals.
>
> The tendencies toward individualisation produce the dissolution of the remains of 'working-class culture' in the sense of a collective experience of life which was already partly destroyed by fascism and now is connected with the disappearance of narrow housing conditions, the increasing participation in the educational system, the emanation of autonomous lifestyles and the dissolution of the specific associations of the labour movement. 'Classic' institutions of cultural identity production (Sinnstiftung) such as church or family have lost influence (Mueckenberger et al., 1996, 16f).

In this chapter I intend to test the individualisation hypothesis on the basis of qualitative and survey research guided by the relational class theory which is centred around the Bourdieu concept of 'field'. According to my hypothesis, the differentiation of social classes means their modernisation

37

but not their fragmentation. Doubtlessly, this implies new problems of mobilisation. However, the problems seem to be caused less by individualisation than by a crisis of organisational and political representation.

The Postwar Debates on the Making and Unmaking of the Working Class

The working class has always been a central focus of discussions on social stratification and class. This was not only true in the context of the Marxist philosophy of history which attributed to the working class a central role as agent of fundamental social change. It was also true as long as the most important political parties and movements of the developed countries were counting on the working classes. Conservatives, Christian Democrats, Social Democrats and Communists - but also rightist populists or fascists - could not do without being able to more or less mobilise these central strata of industrial society. Equally, the trade unions of the working classes were an indispensable force on the intermediary level of politics.

At the same time, the role of the working class or classes was, sometimes in a less visible way, largely connected with that of a second actor. The political, administrative or intellectual elites understood their historical task as being to give direction to the seemingly undirected power of the working masses. Thus, behind the question concerning the transformation of social classes, there was almost always a second question which concerned the historical role of the intellectuals and other possible hegemonic elites.

Deproletarianisation: 'Embourgeoisement' or 'Employee Society'

The discussions seemingly took a new turn when, after the Second World War, the identity or existence of the working class itself was put into question. Undoubtedly, in the most developed countries, decades of rising standards of living, the welfare state and mass education signalled an end to what was called proletarianisation. But what did this *deproletarianisation* mean? This was the centre of a long sequence of discussions during the early decades after the Second World War.

In the 1950s, there was an influential revival of the theories of *'embourgeoisement'* of the working classes. It was observed that the working classes now participated in standards of living which had formerly been reserved to the middle classes: more rights and bargaining power at work, a secure and rising income, better health and educational systems, the comfort of durable consumer goods and the facilities of expanding mass communication. Many liberal and, increasingly, also left and neo-Marxist theorists argued therefore that the working-class people would tacitly adapt to middle class or petty bourgeois mentalities (Schelsky, 1965) or would be transformed into thoughtless media manipulated consumers (Marcuse, 1964; Gorz, 1965; Touraine and Ragazzi, 1961).

Up to the early 1970s, these theories were heavily contested by new sociological research. The critics did not deny that the times of the militant industrial working class and its solidarity, forged together by factory discipline, urban squalor and class repression, seemed to be definitely a thing of the past. They insisted, however, that class conflict between employers and trade unions was not obsolete. It had merely been institutionalised. Sociologist like Theodor Geiger (1949) and Ralf Dahrendorf (1957) developed the theory of *institutionalised class struggle*. Equally, new studies (Popitz et al., 1957; Bahrdt, 1962; Goldthorpe et al., 1968; Kern and Schumann, 1970; Schumann, 1971; Mooser, 1984; Berger, 1986; similarly today: Schumann, 1999) confirmed that working-class consciousness was still there, although on a modernised level. Class conditions still persisted: capitalist domination, the opposition of interests at work, work hierarchy, and the necessity to work hard for moderate increases of income. Higher standards of living, by themselves, had not changed the ethos and mentality of workers' everyday life. The 'affluent worker', as John Goldthorpe et al. (1968) called this postwar generation, was still a worker, although no more in the old emotional terms of solidarity and militancy but on the less emotional level of a rational and 'instrumental' attitude towards the trade unions and the labour movement. Goldthorpe et al. (1968) also insisted that the mere use of consumer goods did not, by any miraculous mechanism, turn workers into bourgeois: 'A washing machine is a washing machine is a washing machine'.

In the early 1980s, German researchers noted that even the historical cleavages between white-collar and blue-collar workers ('Angestellte' and 'Arbeiter') had diminished and given way to a new 'employee mentality' ('Arbeitnehmermentalität') and consciousness of common interests (Kern and Schumann, 1982). Several authors were able to explain this convergence of interests in terms of the increasing similarities of work and life situations of the two groups and also in terms of the fact that an increasing part of white-collar workers was composed of former skilled blue-collar workers or their sons and daughters (Bahrdt, 1962; Mooser, 1983, 1984). There also was ample empirical evidence that this situation of the deproletarised workers was not a situation of plenty, but of only relative stability and security (Mooser, 1983, 1984; Berger, 1986).

But, according to the historian, Josef Mooser (1983, 1984), this empirical working class of the late 1970s differed strongly from the classical image of the proletariat. According to the statistical data, since the 1920s, all three classical 'tendencies' of proletarian mass formation - urbanisation (the fragmenting of cohesion in large cities), mass production (collectivity in big factories) and deskilling (monotonous and alienated work) - had not been continuing. In the 1970s, one-third of the blue-collar workers still worked in small enterprises (up to ten employees), another third in medium-sized enterprises (up to 1,000 employees). Half of them still lived in communities with up to 20,000 inhabitants, where four-fifths of them also owned their homes. Only about one-third of them were working in large factories (over 1,000 employees) and living in large cities (over 100,000 inhabitants). In addition, blue-collar work was generally carried out by well-qualified workers although immigrant workers formed a new deskilled substratum below them.

In the light of these findings, Mooser even went one step further. He noted that the classical 'mass' definition of the proletariat only applied to a limited historical period of the decades of *transition* to fully developed industrial capitalism which, in Germany, ended in the 1920s (Mooser, 1983, 1984). This corresponds to the relational class theory of E.P. Thompson who insisted that our notion of class is unduly fixed to the 'special case' of class transition during the industrial revolution, while the 'normal case' was a certain arrangement of classes which conceded to the popular classes not equal but relatively stable conditions of work and living (Thompson, 1980b; see Thompson, 1987).

What we think to be 'natural properties' of the working class - solidarity, militancy and social deprivation - were derived from the observations of the class relations between the ruling and the popular classes in a very specific historical period. The seeming homogeneity of the working class was only a myth - possibly concomitant with the myth of charismatic leadership which has been urged on us as long as labour history was written.

What really changed after the Second World War were the class relations in the fields of everyday life and socio-political representation. The different classes aligned with one another on a relatively higher level of participation of the popular classes, but not on a level of harmony and identity of interests. Furthermore, the institutionalisation of class bargaining became a widening base of a worker consciousness of common interests. The sense of social justice was no longer focused on the charity of the well-to-do, but the employed classes, by explicit and implicit class arrangements, felt *entitled* to make use of their social rights as they could make use of their human and political rights. When, mainly on this basis, the German Social Democrats had their sweeping electoral victory in 1972, Willy Brandt felt legitimated in calling this a victory of a new social concept, that of the 'Arbeitnehmergesellschaft' or 'employee society' (Lepsius, 1973b).

Class Erosion: Post-industrial Society and Individualisation

However, just at this moment the model of social integration and entitlement was already in a situation of new change and transition once again. First we witnessed the apparent paradox that, in a situation of rising social integration, new protest movements developed. At the end of the 1960s, these movements also included waves of spontaneous industrial strikes in many developed countries. In general, however, they were centred around the younger generation in the highly developed societies, especially the students.

Until the early 1970s, these movements formed a coalition with the academic left, defending a neo-Marxist revival of orthodox class theories and competing strongly with the 'revisionist' theories of institutionalised class struggle mentioned above. As the 1970s passed, these neo-Marxist theories found it increasingly difficult to find their 'historical subject'. The structuralist Marxists produced theories in which the large majority of workers was defined as a structural proletariat which should develop the appropriate class consciousness but was kept from doing so because of the cultural hegemony of the bourgeois class which, through the mass media and the educational system, was manipulating their minds (e.g. Marcuse, 1964; Poulantzas, 1980; Althusser, 1977). Because of these manipulative effects, another faction, the cultural neo-Marxists, turned away from the working class completely. Authors like Herbert Marcuse looked for the victims of ethnic or gender repression in the First World and the exploited masses in the Third World (Marcuse, 1964). But these hopes were disappointed as the social groups whose humanity was so much 'negated' did not live up to the messianic expectations.

Soon, both historical subjects - the working class and the extremely excluded - were given up. The academic left turned to a new social actor who was, in a way, an extension of its own social group. These *new social movements* were not defined in terms of economic exploitation or social exclusion but rather in cultural terms, as the vanguard of an alternative culture. This group was composed mainly of a segment of the academic class, which was enlarged and rejuvenated by the strong opening of the educational system. The new movements felt themselves to be somehow linked to the discriminated groups in the non-working class, such as women, the old and disabled and ethnic minorities. Their ideology was 'universalist'. They were representing not class or material interests, but rather the interests of humanity as a whole. The idealistic and selfidealising ideology comprised many aims which (little known in the present) initially were also reclaimed by the allegedly 'materialist' working-class movements (Vester, 1970): ecology and health, peace and multi-ethnic solidarity, personal and gender emancipation, and a participative civil society (Brand et al., 1983; Raschke, 1985).

Former Marxist embourgeoisement theorists joined this 'cultural turn'. André Gorz articulated his 'farewell to the proletariat' and invested his hopes in the new post-industrial class of the non-workers (Gorz, 1980).

These new post-industrial visions were largely constructed against the background of the sinister orthodox Marxist mythology of a homogeneous economic class repression or exclusion from power. The new theories aimed at either class transformation, as Daniel Bell's scenarios did, or at class erosion, as with the scenarios of Ulrich Beck.

Bell's book of the 'post-industrial service society' or 'knowledge society' (Bell, 1973) dwelled less on empirical social history - as Mooser's book did - than on a discussion of Marxist theory critics. Unlike Thompson, these theories did not question Marx's scenario of deskilled work and unregulated repression. Instead they took it for an empirically correct description of industrial capitalism. Moreover, they transported the myths of this Marxist scenario to the present. Against the monolithic background of industrial capitalism, the present diversity looked like an entirely new liberalisation of the individual. This seemed to be accompanied by a secular change of mentalities, as described by Ronald Inglehart's theory of the 'silent revolution', i.e. the transition from the 'materialist' values of the industrial society to the 'post-materialist' values of the knowledge society (Inglehart, 1977; Bell, 1973).

On this basis, the paradigm of class erosion and individualisation was developed by a growing number of authors, especially by Ulrich Beck, and increasingly also by Anthony Giddens. Beck (1983) started with the indisputable fact that, after the Second World War, the agrarian and industrial sectors with their relatively lowskilled occupations had shrunk, while specialised modern occupations and the educational system had expanded enormously. In Beck's view, this caused an extreme mobility and uprooting of people from their occupational and local milieus, which brought them into the patterns of destandardised work and discontinuous life biographies, into recurring educational passages and into new and heterogeneous urban neighbourhoods. In this renewed theory of *fragmentation*, Beck sees himself explicitly - and correctly - following in the footsteps of Marx (Beck, 1983, 47; Marx and Engels, 1848). And he notes that the specific reasons for which, at the times of Marx, the fragmented individuals turned to solidarity no longer exist today. These reasons of class formation, namely the economic repressiveness, the homogeneity of industrial work and the declassment, have now been removed by the increasing standards of living, education and welfare.

This theory of class mentality presupposes that the *freedom from external coercion and from material needs sets the individuals free to choose their own lifestyle and milieu membership*. It was on this presupposition that Ulrich Beck and Anthony Giddens founded their theory of an essentially *new model of politics beyond class lines* (Beck, 1983, 1986; Giddens, 1999). By this, Beck and Giddens refer to the new milieus and movements which adhere so-called universalist values such as personal and gender emancipation, civil, ecological and peace activities, and cultural self-development. They assume that these political themes are going to replace the traditional model of 'materialist' class interests.

At times, especially in feminist theory (see the discussion in Gottschall, 2000), this model goes together with other theories which try to entirely replace 'class' by gender, ethnicity, lifestyle group or age group. In general, these theories tacitly or explicitly dwell on the assumption that different life opportunities are no longer determined by significant vertical differences of occupational position, power, income and education. Instead, society seems to be somehow composed mainly of a huge middle class, bottomed by a thin layer of the very poor and topped by an equally thin layer of the very rich. The possibility that social discrimination by gender, ethnicity, etc. might be *combined* with class inequality is more or less dismissed.

Meanwhile, the debate seems to be taking a new direction. Attention is shifting back to the losers of social modernisation. Against the theories of social 'differentiation', which largely neglect the vertical axis of domination, theories of declassment or 'underclass' have made a certain comeback since the late 1980s. The new dynamics of globalised markets, technological innovation and welfare deregulation have encouraged seemingly new theories that take into account the segregation between the winners and losers of modernisation, the latter moving downwards into precarious welfare or into exclusion, into urban underclass quarters, into incomplete families, and into ethnic and generation conflicts. But here again, social cohesion and joint action are not taken for granted. The impact of the theories of fragmentation and individualisation is also to be felt here. There is a process of declassing - but no reconstruction or reinvention of class cohesion and class identity.

The Relational Theory of Class: The Concepts of Field, Habitus, Milieu and Camp

These new theories have undoubtedly been a source of irritation for the proponents of class theory. It seems, however, that this irritation is due to a theoretical confusion. The term 'cultural turn' suggests that the paradigm changed from a 'materialist' approach, centred on economic assets and interests, to a 'culturalist' approach, centred on the cultural self-definition of social groups. These approaches may seem to be opposites, but in fact they are epistemological complementary to one another. The cultural approach is as one-sided and reductionist as the economic approach.

In historical analyses of class relations, like those of E.P. Thompson, we find a different view. Thompson insists that as far as England is concerned, the traditionalist notion of extremely polarised class relations only applied to the 'special case' of the industrial revolution, which differed from the 'normal case' of comparatively stable class compromises (Thompson, 1963, 1980b; Vester, 1970). According to Thompson's historical analysis, this polarisation of the early nineteenth century was not a purely 'economic' tendency. The increase of machine industry, although it exerted a strong pressure upon the whole economy, did not extinguish all the smaller and medium enterprises and their labour force, which were heterogeneous in their skills and ways of life. Neither did it produce a one-dimensional iron law of deskilling and falling wages. Instead, the classes polarised because the class relations had also changed in two other fields:

a) in the socio-cultural field: it was not only economic misery that opened the cleavages between the bourgeois middle class and the poor working class. It was the whole change of the '*everyday way of life*': factory discipline, other working hours, urbanisation, poor food quality, health problems and child mortality - the loss of old liberties and the disappearance of traditional leisure activities;

b) in the socio-political field: *intermediary structures of mobilisation and representation* were victims of what today may be called 'neo-liberal' deregulation and of political repression. During the early decades of the nineteenth century, the old moral institutions of social regulation were suspended in the name of the free market. Social movements, the free press and civil rights were strongly repressed because of the fear that the French Revolution would recur on a European level.

What united the working class during the industrial revolution was not so much its homogeneity in the field of occupations and wages but rather the *change of class relations* in all fields, and especially the *destabilisation of the class arrangements* between the *upper classes* and the '*respectable*' *popular classes*. The impulse of the working-class movement did not come from those who did already belong to the poorest and most powerless classes, as some theories of immiseration do suggest. These groups had neither the resources nor *the habitus disposition* for active protest. This disposition, instead, was mainly to be found in the large skilled and self-reliant sections of the popular classes whose economic and political status was now in danger. Large factions of the middle parts of the popular classes - artisans, skilled workers, etc. - lost their respected status of skilled work, personal autonomy and decent living. When they wanted to fight for this way of life and work, they found their journals, their unions and their movements for universal suffrage suppressed and their leaders persecuted or deported. It was this common experience of opposition on the economic, cultural and political levels that united the working class as a large and militant - however transitory - coalition of the diverse and heterogeneous groups of the popular classes.

While E.P. Thompson used the relational concepts mainly in an implicit manner, Pierre Bourdieu offers a highly developed theory and methodology which enables an analysis of more complex configurations of classes (Bourdieu, 1982). The 'social world' is understood as a multi-dimensional and multi-level field of action and tension. As a whole, society is differentiated into different fields. These are, mainly,

a) the field of the occupational class positions;
b) the field of the lifestyles;
c) the field of the habitus;
d) the political field.

The fields are interdependent but also relatively autonomous, being shaped by the relations and the practice of their actors. These relations are not to be understood only in the vertical dimension of unequal power and distribution of resources, as is commonly done by theories of class and stratification. They are also to be understood as a horizontal differentiation, expressed in the division of labour and in the splitting of class milieus into factions.

Here, I shall try to resume the theoretical implications of this relational class paradigm in five points, inevitably simplifying the case which can be studied in a more differentiated manner elsewhere (Bourdieu, 1982, 1993; Vester et al., 1993).

Class: Social Cleavages under Different Field Conditions

Class is defined not by single properties, but by practical class relations. This means that we cannot relate an individual to a class merely by measuring his or her properties and then forming groups of homogeneous standards of income, education, consumption, values, etc.[31] Empirically, the working-class movements have always been coalitions of actors bridging a certain internal heterogeneity of higher and lower skills, of artisans, wage earners and intellectuals, of different regions, of ethnicities, of religions, of gender and of age groups, etc. What united them was, generally, *not homogeneity* but rather a *common experience* of social values and of being opposed to or repressed by other social groups. What divided them were their internal differences resulting from their heterogeneous composition.

How the actors deal with these internal and external field differentiations is also relational, i.e. neither solely determined by the habitus and neither solely determined by the field conditions. It depends on the inter-action of the habitus and the field. Thus, as a consequence of the *field* structure, the meaning of a single variable or property varies in accordance with its relative position in the field, as Kurt Lewin put it. For example, we cannot define the working class in terms of 'natural' substance properties such as the identity of bodily work, economic 'declassment', collective solidarity and militancy - as this is done in the theories of embourgeoise-ment, post-materialism and individualisation.

Habitus: A Complex Syndrome of Corporal and Mental Attitudes

In no case can habitus be reduced to single traits or dimensions of a mentality - as this is done by the theories discussed above. While they centre on reductionist value dimensions such as material-immaterial, solidaristic-individualistic, militant-discursive, etc. they reproduce a speci-fic intellectual view dividing the world into an elite and a mass. Habitus is a deeper and more general attitude towards the social world, integrating the dimensions of taste, lifestyles, the corporal and emotional attitudes, the patterns of social actions and relations and also the mentalities and ideolo-gical views of the world. Thus, habitus can only be described as a compre-

---

[31] In fact, these standards do often form an uninterrupted continuum rarely showing us where the cleavages between social groups are in fact situated. While these standards are important as indicators, resources or means of a specific way of life, class relations are something we do not see and that we cannot measure in a quantitative way.

hensive combination or *syndrome* of attitudes, classifications and value patterns.

Being so comprehensive, the patterns of a certain habitus type cannot be explained only by certain occupational experiences, economic interests or educational and ideological indoctrination. Biographical habitus formation begins much earlier, in the pre-discursive phases of early childhood, when the principal orientations of taste, bodily attitudes, emotional energy, moral rules etc. begin to develop. For this, the occupation and habitus of the parent family is important, but often in a more unconscious, pre-discursive way. Here, we already see the first typological differences between distinctive and vulgar styles, between active or passive action strategies, between dominative or partnership orientations, between asceticism and hedonism and also between different ways to deal with gender, ethnicity and age differences.

Habitus continues to develop in later life passages, in the peer groups, in the educational and occupational system and in the territorial neighbourhoods. But, as the field of habitus is relatively autonomous, social groups and individuals mainly combine and divide on the grounds of 'moral' sentiments. The lines of reasoning do not centre on naked economic interests but rather on how people and groups should and should not behave. Habitus, as well that part of it which we call mentality, is essentially formed through group or 'milieu' relations.

Milieu: The Everyday Level of Class Practice

To identify these social groups or actors we use the concept of milieu which was the central concept of sociological analysis in Émile Durkheim's study on the division of labour (Durkheim, 1893/1902). Durkheim used the concept milieu to refer to a group which has developed a common 'corpus of moral rules' (related also to a certain 'moral habitus' in the individual) in order to distinguish itself from other social groups. He defined milieu primarily as an *occupational* group in the division of labour which, however, in a differentiated society, also exists as a *territorial* and a *familial* milieu and, possibly, also is represented in an organisation when it participates in the field of power or politics.

Camp: The Politico-ideological Level of Class Practice

Durkheim clearly treats the *political* representation of the milieus as a problem of a different field of social practice. Bourdieu sees a similar institutional and epistemological rupture between the everyday milieus and the ideological factions and discourses of the political field (Bourdieu,

1982, Chapter 8). While *milieus* may be defined by the attitudes regulating the practices of everyday life, the political and ideological *camps* follow a different logic. Class milieus and their subdivisions can be seen as formations on the same vertical level, while camps cross the *vertical levels*. They can be understood as 'vertical coalitions' between specific factions from the lower classes up to the higher classes.

The Axes of the Fields: Domination, Differentiation and Change

A field cannot be understood without a spatial presentation of more than one dimension. Bourdieu's paradigm implies an important innovation in this regard. It enables us to understand social change as a conflict between the dynamics on two different axes of social space. Most theories of class and stratification only take into account the *vertical* axis. This verticalism would only be adequate for a monolithic hierarchical order, in which *all* valued resources of society - economic, cultural and political capital - could be located. Instead, Bourdieu adds a second *horizontal* axis. This axis is more than a technical device for designing maps. It is the methodological expression of a crucial theoretical concept.

The horizontal axis signifies the *division of labour* concomitant with functional specialisation, as described by Durkheim (1893/1902). In Bourdieu's terms, this is expressed by a movement from the material or economic pole on the right margin of social space to the intellectual or cultural pole on the left margin. Émile Durkheim, as well as Adam Smith, made clear, that this development should not be confused with vertical domination. They insist that the increase of cultural and intellectual capacities of the productive forces does occur *at each hierarchical rank level*, not only at the top (Smith, 1776, 3-11; Durkheim, 1893/1902, 444f).

In the socio-cultural field, this horizontal *differentiation* is related to what Bourdieu calls 'class factions'. Thus, horizontally we distinguish:

a) at the top: the elite milieus of property and of education;
b) in the middle: the popular milieus of the smaller owners (or petty bourgeois milieus) and of the skilled employee classes and;
c) at the bottom: the respective milieus of the underprivileged classes.

The vertical axis signifies the traditional dimension of *domination* and power, i.e. the organisational hierarchy of decision-making and of the unequal distribution of other resources and assets. It is the axis of exploitation (as described in Marx' general law of capitalist accumulation) and the axis of the countervailing powers of labour and other social movements, coming from the lower pole. These counter-powers are analysed by social democrat theorists like Myrdal (1974), Galbraith (1952, 1958) and Geiger (1949).

The third axis signifies the dimension of *historical change* in which the constellations of actors and their generations in the various fields do change and latent qualities become manifest and vice versa.

To sum it up, in the economic and occupational field, we still have what Marx described as the *contradiction between the production forces* (developing on the horizontal axis) and the *production relations* (concerning the vertical axis of power hierarchies).[32] This theorem can still be used as one of the central concepts of analysing the change of class relations. However, this largely depends on the corresponding contradictions in the other fields of social action. We therefore have to look at the dynamics especially in the field of everyday class relations (represented by the milieus), in the field of corporate conflict (represented by trade unions and occupational associations) and in the field of political and ideological conflict (represented by the hegemonic elites). Each of these fields, has its own conflicts on the three axes which, although not determined by mere *economic* contradictions, could be expected to have similar structures.

This argument does not dismiss the importance of other factors like gender, ethnicity, age and cultural identity (Bourdieu, 1982). In this argument, these factors aren't seen as an alternative for class differences, but rather operate in combination with them.

Research Hypothesis: The Long Duration of Class Mentalities

The results presented in this chapter are mainly based on a research project structured by the multi-dimensional field approach of Bourdieu and Thompson.[33] The project's initial aim was to test the hypothesis of the new model of classless politics promoted by Beck and Giddens. In the later stages of the work, when we tried to extend the scope of our study to the whole of society, the multi-dimensional paradigm was further developed in

---

[32] We do not discuss here the fact that Marx could not elaborate this theory in full because he did not distinguish the axes consequently. His theory of deskilling was a generalisation of Andrew Ure's book on deskilled and monotonous machine labour in the British textile industry (Blauner, 1964). For the whole economy, this tendency has been counterbalanced at least since the 1880s by rising workers' qualifications (Geiger, 1949). For these workers, proletarianisation did not consist in deskilling but in declassment.

[33] The project 'The change of social structure and the development of new socio-political milieus in the Federal Republic of Germany', supported by the Volkswagen Foundation from 1988 to 1991, is described in Vester et al., 1993/2000.

order to specify the dynamics of the fields more completely. We developed a counter-hypothesis of the long duration of class milieus and mentalities.

If classes are coalitions acting in multi-level and multi-dimensional fields, they principally do have more than one option of combining and mobilising forces. However, the range of possible scenarios is limited.

Firstly, we often have *combined tendencies* where we assume *alternative tendencies* of development. That is, we do not have *either* individualisation or tendencies of class division. We also do not have unilinear tendencies of *either* growing cultural capital (Bell) *or* dequalification of work (orthodox Marxism). Rather we have a combination of the two. In all highly developed countries, there is an immense increase of intellectual and cultural competence almost down to the bottom of the social hierarchy, and - since neo-liberal deregulation has been in effect - an immense depreciation of these same production forces.

Secondly, more cultural capital helps the self-activity of the people. But self-activity is not an automatism, however. Rather, it is a disposition. Its realisation depends on what is going on in the other fields, outside the economic field. As these fields are relatively autonomous, they may follow *different historical* and also *national paths*.[34] But the extent to which these paths differ is also limited.

Our hypothesis of the *change of habitus and mentality types* could not follow the assumptions of the objectivist or the subjectivist theories because these are mostly limited to only one field. Liberal economists and Marxists often assume that material exploitation or declassment triggers off militancy motivated by physical needs (Marx and Engels, 1848; Rostow, 1948; criticised by Thompson (1980c)). Inglehart's and Maslow's assumption that the saturation of material or physical needs will make room to post-materialist values is just another application of the same theory. Similarly, Beck's assumption of the free choice of lifestyles in a welfare society presupposes the autonomy of the socio-cultural field.

Against these 'objectivist' and 'subjectivist' theories, Maurice Merleau-Ponty, in the dynamic social situation of 1945, developed his theory of the *opening of social space* (Merleau-Ponty, 1965). He argued that, as a rule, movements for radical social change are not encouraged by situations of utter repression and exploitation but, on the contrary, by historic situations of opening social space, e.g. rising standards of living and civic liberties. Thus, there is no 'economic necessity' that dictates the precise direction that mental change should take. It is rather the opening of social space that

---

[34] The institutional aspects are taken account of in the institutional theory of stratification developed by Esping-Andersen (1993).

motivates the milieus to unfold and further develop their already existing repertoires of possibilities.

This hypothesis is supported by the Birmingham studies of Stuart Hall and others on youth class cultures (Clarke et al., 1979). They found that the postwar generations in particular did not develop a uniformly classless culture. Instead, the 'bricolage' of their identity was a means of symbolic coping with postwar society by not giving up their class identity but developing new variants of their parent cultures.

On this basis we developed our *hypothesis of habitus metamorphosis*. According to this hypothesis, the lifestyles and habitus of the younger generations were not developed through free and reflective choices but rather relationally, through a process of conflict against and with the habitus patterns of their parent cultures. The new habitus diversities of the younger milieus may be understood as new branches on the family trees of those parent cultures. We might, as we will see later, distinguish more or less five such 'family trees' in our maps of class milieus.

Outlines of the Project: Research Questions, Methodology and Principal Results

Although our basic research project,[35] in its qualitative parts, concentrated on the new social movements and milieus, it had to widen its scope in order to interpret the results within the multi-dimensional context of West German social structure as a whole (especially Vester et al., 1994; Geiling, 1996; Gardemin, 1998; Vögele and Vester, 1999). The research project was designed in accordance with the multi-level field concept by first analysing three main fields (mentality change, occupational change, and the change of social cohesion) separately and then integrating these fields. In the following paragraphs I shall give for each phase of the project a brief outline of the research questions, the methodologies and concepts followed and the principal results (for more details see Vester et al., 1993).

Research Part 1: Mentality Change

The first part involved asking questions about the intergenerational habitus and mentality change: *Was it true that the alternative milieus and the new social movements represented a new 'universalist' mentality and practice*

---

[35] The project 'Social Structural Change and the New Socio-political Milieus', carried out at the University of Hannover from 1988 to 1992, was especially supported by the Volkswagen Foundation. See especially Vester et al., 1993/2000.

which was no longer linked to particular class milieus? This question was studied by a sample of 250 open biographical two-generation-interviews in three selected regions[36] which then were interpreted in order to detect the *mentality types* of female members of the new milieus as compared to their mothers and of the male members as compared to their fathers.[37] Our main result was that the habitus types of the younger generation were not completely different from the parent generation but variations of the same basic patterns. This supported our hypothesis of generational habitus metamorphosis. This hypothesis was constructed with the habitus theory of Bourdieu and followed the ideas of Stuart Hall et al. on class mentality change.

Research Part 2: Dynamics of the Occupational Field

The second part asked for the dynamics of the occupational field: *How was this mentality change linked to changes in the occupational and economic position of the sample? And was this occupational change to be located in the total occupational change of West Germany?* This question was studied

---

[36] These were, for the members of the alternative milieus, urban and suburban regions of the de-industrialising type (Oberhausen), of the re-industrialising type (Reutlingen) and of the tertiarising type (Hannover). The parents we interviewed came from a wide range of regions.

[37] Our way of constructing the types of habitus differed somewhat from Bourdieu. Bourdieu analysed class habitus in many ways, including the attributes and practices of lifestyle. Our work was centred on qualitative interviews, especially narrative and semi-directive biographical interviews. (We also used an enlarged concept of group discussions as a basis for the analysis of the schemes of classification and valuation of the habitus.) On this basis, we made hermeneutic interpretations to detect the *habitus syndromes*, i.e. combinations of attitude traits (or patterns of classification and valuation) that may be circumscribed as 'ethos' or 'ethics of everyday life'.

To understand these better, we also referred to *historical mentality types* and to Bourdieu's *habitus types* (Bourdieu, 1982). Bourdieu's types were not used as typological models into which our cases had to fit but only for purposes of comparison. We constructed each case individually by analysing the interviews and other manifestations of the habitus. We especially concentrated on the balance of value and classification patterns such as: asceticism vs. hedonism (or work vs. leisure orientation), domination vs. co-operation (or hierarchy vs. partnership), individualisation vs. cohesion, patriarchalism vs. gender partnership, popular vs. distinctive culture, etc. For each case, the entire configuration formed by these patterns was outlined. After this, the individual case syndromes were grouped to *types not according to single traits or dimensions, i.e. according to the relational structure of all elements of the habitus or mentality syndromes.* Finally, the types were located in the field of habitus along the vertical axis of distinction (ranking from 'vulgar' and 'popular' patterns to 'distinctive' and 'elitist' patterns) and along the horizontal axis (ranking from 'conventional' and 'authoritarian' patterns to 'rational' 'individualistic' and 'vanguard' patterns).

in particular by means of an analysis of the changes in the occupational field since 1950, in three selected regions as well as on the base of general West German census data. The data were processed according to Geiger's ascending method and Bourdieu's concept of social space.[38] The hypothesis was that mentality changes might at least be partly related to a secular increase of educational and cultural capital on the horizontal axis of social space. In our results, we were able to map a selection of important occupational fields, especially in the sectors of the educational, health, technical and agricultural occupations, which were also divided by gender cleavages. By mapping the changes since 1950, we were able to describe a significant movement from the right to the left pole of social space. This supported the hypothesis of a historical drift towards more cultural capital at all the vertical levels of society. At the same time, we found sufficient evidence of the dynamics of vertical opening as well as closure.[39]

These findings had important consequences for the influential theories of the coming of a tertiary knowledge society. On the one hand, these tendencies were strongly represented in our data. From 1950 to 1990, the tertiary occupations rose from about 20 per cent to almost 60 per cent of the employed population. On the other hand, this growth remained principally a horizontal movement in social space. It did not basically change the vertical relations of domination between social classes, gender, age and ethnic groups.

Research Part 3: Change in Social and Political Cohesion

The third part of our study asked for the change of everyday culture and political camps: *How had the milieus of the new social movements develop their cohesion and identity since the end of the 1960s?* This question was studied on the basis of so-called milieu biographies, i.e. case histories in the three selected regions showing how the new social movements and

---

[38] *Constructing the field of occupational positions*: To detect the dynamics in the field of occupational positions, we defined and positioned 102 selected occupations following the ascending method of Geiger (1932) and the theory of economic, cultural and social capital of Bourdieu (1982). The vertical axial positioning corresponded to the total amount of capital, especially the income. The horizontal positioning corresponded to the relation of cultural and economic capital, i.e. of all the occupational groups occupying the same position on the vertical ladder, those with least cultural capital were positioned to the right, and those with relatively more cultural capital were positioned towards the left pole of the field.

[39] The openings have allowed a certain exchange of elites and academic cadres since the late 1960s. The closures explained the counter-tendencies of continuing discrimination by gender, ethnicity and other ascriptive denominations and of continuing declassment of class milieus possessing little economic, cultural and social capital.

milieus emerged in the regional field of socio-political camps. The hypothesis was that the new identities were not only linked to occupational change but also to a general 'opening of social space' (according to the theory of Merleau-Ponty) and to the intergenerational camp conflicts (according to the theory of Lepsius) since the sixties. The results supported our hypothesis.

Research Part 4: Synthesis

The last part aimed at a synthesis, i.e. the changes of the class configuration as a whole: *How did the dynamics of the different fields studied separately in the first three parts of the project correlate? How representative were the selected milieus for West German social structure as a whole? What was their size and location in relation to the other social milieus?* These questions were studied by a representative survey of the 1991 West German population,[40] including all axes and all levels of social space, in accordance with the theory and methodology of Bourdieu. Thus, each interviewed person could be located on all field levels simultaneously. For each level we constructed independent maps and then we investigated which types of a field were related to which types of another field. In order to avoid economic determinism, our starting point was not the person's occupation, from which, then, we would continue to ask which mentality typically 'belonged' to it, etc. Rather, the analytic procedure took the opposite direction, starting from the mentality type and then asking which occupation, social relations, etc. were 'typical' or 'not typical' for it.

---

[40] The interviews were done in 1991 by the Marplan Institute, with a random sample of 2,699 German-speaking inhabitants of 14 years and older, who were representative according to the demographic structure of the 1988 micro-census.

The mentality types were identified by a 44-statement milieu-indicator developed and validated by the Sinus Institute.[41] Additional dimensions of mentality were explored by three other item batteries[42] and with questions concerning political and trade union participation as well as trade union participation of the parent generation.

From the mentality types we proceeded to the second level, the *occupational field*. Thus, we identified the typical occupational profile of each milieu. It is important to note that none of these profiles followed the distinctions of the official statistics, i.e. between production and services, secondary and tertiary sectors, blue- and white-collar, etc. Instead, according to the data, the occupational profiles of the milieus rather followed (in a loose but clearly significant relation) the capital dimensions of Bourdieu (see Figure 2.2, in the annexe for the detailed profiles).

On the *vertical axis*, we find three layers of milieus which are separated by two cleavage lines. The *line of distinction* separates the upper 20 or 25 per cent from the popular classes. It corresponds to the line of higher education or 'legitimate culture'. The *line of respectability divides* the popular classes in two. Below this line, we see the underprivileged milieus (around 10 per cent), which are stigmatised by poor education and lack of

---

[41] *Basically, mentality types can only be found by qualitative research.* To draw up a valid description of the mentality dimensions of only one type between twenty and thirty interviews are necessary. However, it is possible to reproduce types of habitus in standardised interviews, when, from the qualitative material, extensive batteries of statements are extracted and tested which represent the main traits (or syndrome dimensions) of each type. To represent all dimensions, an indicator needs more than forty statements which may be accepted or rejected by the interviewed persons on a scale of varying intensity. If the dimensions cover a relatively broad spectrum of traits that are possible in a society, it may be possible to detect new types. Technically, these types can be detected in the sample by the multivariate statistical procedure of *cluster analysis*. (Subsequently, the types found have to undergo qualitative and theoretical validation procedures securing that the types are not statistical artefacts but empirically and theoretically possible.) To a certain degree, it is also possible to reproduce the traits of a type by another multivariate procedure, the factor analysis. This, too, is no automatic procedure but needs qualitative and theoretical validation procedures.

The Sinus Institute (SPD, 1984; Becker et al., 1992; Flaig et al., 1993) did important pioneer work to develop the first statement batteries of the milieu indicator in the early 1980s. In principle, their lifestyle milieus can be translated into habitus types, especially those of the three large family trees of the popular classes. For the rest of the social space, the statements of the indicator only reveal the general lines. Here, additional research and additional statement batteries are necessary.

[42] The types of cohesion preferences and the types of politico-ideological camp affiliation were explored by indicators of 39 and 44 statements which we constructed from our qualitative material. In addition, we applied a statement battery of cohesion and leisure practices with 22 items.

skills. Above this line, we find the 'respectable' popular classes, with good skills and education.

On the *horizontal axis*, there are also three groups separated by two cleavage lines. The *line of authoritarian status orientation* delimits the petty bourgeois and conservative groups at the right margin. In the horizontal middle, we find the milieus for whom work is the base of self-reliance and self-consciousness. At the left margin, the *line of the vanguard* delineates the hedonistic or cultural vanguard with its idealistic orientations, and makes it distinct from the balancing realism of the middle.

On the *axis of time*, we can detect the *traditional lines* of class culture which are modified by *historical* slow processes of modernisation. Each tradition line resembles a family tree, the younger branches mainly distinguishing themselves from the older by modernised cultural capital and habitus.

The structures can be better understood with the help of our diagram. Our *synoptic table* (Table 2.1) shows the main lines as well as their internal differentiation. In the case of the 'respectable popular classes', the data enable us to show the family tree differentiation. The category of skilled work (n° 2.1. - the classical working class) consists of three generational groups: the vanishing old generation of the 'Traditional Working Class', the large but stagnant middle generation of the 'Meritocratic Employee Milieu' and the growing younger generation of the 'Modern Employee Milieu'.

When we compare the milieu map of 1995 and 1982, we can also see how change over time happens. What changes in size is not mainly the general lines, but rather new internal differentiations that arise in the passage from one generation to the next. (As the younger branches are distinguished by modernised cultural capital and habitus, they are located a little higher and a little more to the left, symbolised by a diagonal distinction line.)

Table 2.1   Traditional lines of class cultures (milieus) in West Germany

Vertical class pyramid and its horizontal differentiation by tradition lines	Differentiation of the tradition lines by sub-groups (-) resp. generations (*) in West Germany (1982-1995)
1. *Hegemonic milieus*	
1.1. Tradition line of power and property: milieus of the economic and state functional elites (c. 10%)	1.1 Conservative Technocratic Milieu (c. 9%-c. 10%)
1.2 Tradition line of Higher Education: milieus of the humanist and service class functional elites (c. 10%)	1.2 Liberal Intellectual Milieu (c. 9%-c. 10%), with two sub-groups: - Progressive Elite of Higher Learning (c. 5%) - Modern Service Class Elite (c. 4%)
1.3 Tradition line of the cultural vanguard (c. 5%)	1.3 Alternative Milieu (c. 5%-0%) Post-modern Milieu (0%-c. 5%)
2. *Milieus of the 'respectable' popular (or employee) classes*	
2.1 Tradition line of skilled work (c. 30%)	2.1 - Traditional Working Class (c. 10%-c. 5%) - Meritocratic Employee Milieu (c. 20%-c. 18%) - Modern Employee Milieu (0%-c. 7%)
2.2 Tradition line of the petty bourgeois popular classes (between 28% und 23%)	2.2 - Petty Bourgeois Employee Milieu (c. 28%-c. 15%) - Modern Petty Bourgeois Employee Milieu (0%-c. 8%)
2.3 Vanguard of youth culture (c. 10%)	2.3 Hedonist Milieu (c. 10%-c. 11%)
3. Underprivileged popular classes (between 8% and 13%)	3. Underprivileged Employee Milieu, with three sub-groups: - The Status Oriented (c. 3%) - The Fatalists (c. 6%) - The Hedonist Rebels (c. 2%)

This diagram presents the social map in a stylised - and therefore simplified - manner. The empirical complexity of the class differentiation is better shown by the two diagrams in the annexe of this chapter. In the first diagram, we projected the West German milieus into Bourdieu's diagram of social space in France - in order to show the dynamic field of occupations each milieu covers. The second diagram shows the internal differentiation of the largest milieu, the 'Meritocratic Employee Milieu', by occupational and gender groups.[43]

Class Mentalities and Milieu Family Trees in West Germany

In our maps, class milieus are forming certain configurations expressing their relations with each other. However, these are only in part influenced by interests connected with positions in the occupational field. Seeking economic or positional advantage, for most milieus, is not a value in itself but part of a larger value system in which the proverbial happiness lies in the *pursuit* of a specific *way of life* and not in the utilitarian definition of maximum gain or upward mobility.

All milieus have a sense of their interests. But this 'sense of one's place' (Goffman) is embedded in a specific 'philosophy' of how the world should be seen and coped with. Of such 'philosophies', we distinguish seven different traditional types which, however, may be subdivided into a larger and more colourful universe of milieus.

Despite this diversity, there are also common views concerning social justice. As we will see, in most milieus a vast majority of more than eighty per cent supports the model of the Employee Society. On the other hand,

---

[43] If we take more of the illustrating variables of the questionnaire into the analysis, we see that the interior of each milieu is structured by additional *cleavages*, especially those of the *gender segregation of occupations*. On first sight, there is no gender difference by milieu. Each milieu (defined by mentality type) contains as many women as men. However, if we look at the occupational field, the structures both of segregation and discrimination are very obvious.

In our case of the 'Meritocratic Employee Milieu' (Gardemin, 1998), which contains almost one fifth of the population, men are mainly concentrated in skilled blue-collar occupations and women in skilled white-collar occupations. In the central part of the field, this seems to represent a division of labour with a certain partnership equality because many men and women earn similar wages by equally skilled work. Other parts of the field, however, show inequality. Despite similar cultural capital, many women are positioned below that central part by lower income. Equally, the upper parts of the field are overwhelmingly populated by well-earning men and almost no women. However, there is evidence that the milieu members, especially the women, are not content with this discrimination. Moreover, mothers as well as fathers strongly support educational investment also for their daughters (see also Rupp, 1995, 1997).

trade union affiliation differs widely. Even in the popular classes the quota ranges from 20 to 44 per cent.

Work Orientation: The Self-reliant Labouring Classes

We first turn to the traditional milieu of skilled work which formerly was identified with the classical labour movement. Numerically, this historical milieu have not eroded. It still represents one-third of the population,[44] although it changed his appearance. Despite the structural change towards more tertiary and white-collar occupations, this milieu still shares the basic dispositions of mutual help, ascetic work ethics and personal autonomy, though increasingly balanced by a moderate hedonism in the younger generations.

The values of personal autonomy, mutual help and work ethics still point to the classic milieu of skilled labour which formed the core of the labour movements and their historical predecessors. Today, its core groups are the self-reliant and skilled blue-collar and white-collar workers in modern occupations and a smaller section of the small-owners. The value system seems to be rather consistent. While in the petty bourgeois popular classes the central value is social status derived from hierarchical relations, here autonomy is the central value, a value that is primarily based on what a person can create autonomous by his or her work and practice. The other values are more or less derived from this idea.

Thus, solidarity is not a value in itself but a necessary condition of personal autonomy which cannot be successful without mutual help and co-operation. Similarly, education and culture are seen as an important means of developing personal competencies in terms of work, autonomy and orientation.

Accordingly, different personal achievements of work and learning may legitimate *a certain hierarchy in the social order.* However, this hierarchy of skills does *not* legitimate any *class domination.* The sense of personal autonomy does not accept 'natural' or 'power' inequalities and it detests disrespect for other persons as well as deference towards social, religious or political authorities. Instead, work orientation lies at the basis of a meritocratic sense of equality. The value of a person must depend on his or her practical work achievements, independent from gender, ethnic or class affiliations. Just as in the village community of independent neighbours, the residential community of these milieus still rests on the mutual obligation of neighbourly help and emergency ethics (Weber, 1964) which,

---

[44] Bismarck (1957) named the same percentage for the 1950s, and there are indications for a long historical duration of this quota.

however, is only latent in the day-to-day recreational activities of the community and manifestly mobilised only for special cases. If somebody is in distress without being personally responsible for it, help is the neighbours' duty. This principle is also transferred to the political field. The welfare state should not support any featherbedding. But it should help everybody who is in need, provided they are not responsible for their own situation.

Work and lifestyle are largely structured by a special variant of the Weberian 'protestant ethic', a rational and realistic method of conducting life. In this variant, work and self-discipline are for the most part not values in themselves, that lead to a kind of puritan morosity, but are rather combined with the conviction that one is entitled to enjoy the fruits of the own and common efforts and to receive social justice.

As already mentioned, this general value pattern can be articulated in many different ways, depending on the field situation.[45] In addition, the mentality pattern itself may shift the balance of the different traits as each new generation with new formative experiences develops the pattern in its own way. Our data enable us to distinguish three different milieus, each of which is mainly centred around a different age cohort.

a) The *Traditional Working-Class Milieu*, a sort of 'grandparent genera-tion', is still identified with the necessities of physical work and scarcity. In West Germany, this milieu has reduced to little more than 5 per cent of the population. Here, the distance to the powerful is felt most while the relations with friends, work mates and neighbours are still highly valued in the sense of the old working-class culture. The old 'proletarian experience' of insecure and limited incomes and of more traditional work skills is still important. At work, the milieu members follow the disciplined ethos of good skilled work. At home, they are modestly adapted to the necessary. With a realistic scepticism, future perspectives are voiced cautiously.

b) The 'parent generation' grew up during the economic growth decades of the 1950s and 1960s and with the experience of increasing social rights and standards. They developed into a new milieu of about 20 per cent which Goldthorpe et al. called the *'Affluent Workers'*[46] and we call the *'Meritocratic' Employee Milieu* - as they strongly believe in hard

---

45 In situations of declassment and humiliation it may motivate militant or persevering collective action. In a situation of occupational change it may motivate reconversions for new occupational fields by strong educational efforts on a family level. In a situation of prosperity, personal acquisition may become important.

46 Strictly speaking, Goldthorpe et al. (1968) studied a specific group of 'affluent workers', i.e. those in deskilled work and urban living conditions, which is only in part identical with the milieu described here. For a detailed discussion see Vester (1998).

skilled work which, then, legitimates participating in the standards of consumption, leisure and social security of the welfare society. Their skills, education and social standards are better than those of the traditional working-class generation but in no way extravagant. Their occupations are those of modern employees, the men mainly in skilled blue-collar work, the women mainly in skilled white-collar work.

c) The generation of the '(grand) children' has grown up mainly since the end 1960s, in the context of educational reforms, new work and communication technologies, new social movements and a wider variety of both conventional and nonconformist lifestyles. This *Modern Employee Milieu* first described in 1990[47] is growing rapidly, though it still than 7 per cent. These working people are 'individualised' but, in our qualitative interview sample (Vester et al., 1993; see also Vögele and Vester, 1999), in no way socially fragmented. Instead, they represent a specific new ethic of everyday life, structured by the balance of personal autonomy and competence on the one hand, and social cohesiveness and responsibility on the other.

In a way, this is the rebirth of the old cosmopolitan culture of the curious and creative artisan, with his passion for learning and wandering. These people are employed in the most modern branches of technical, social, and organisational work and in academically specialised practical occupations. They are ready to learn new arts and languages, and are convinced of the necessity of good skilled work - and of empowerment both at work and in politics. This work ethic does not operate as an incentive for endless careers and acquisition, however. It is, in their time schedule, balanced by a caring for their friends, neighbours and parents. These people's horizontal solidarity has not at all disappeared, but their autonomous mentality makes them difficult members of trade unions and other hierarchical organisations. However, their openness for non-conventional lifestyles differs from that of the Hedonistic Milieu described below, because they share the sceptical realism of the older milieus in their family tree. Hedonism and personal emancipation are adapted to the mental framework of the possible.

When the social consciousness of the two younger generations in this family tree is described in the literature as 'instrumental' and 'individualised', this description is not inadequate. But it does concern only one trait of their mentality which, in practice, is only part of the common habitus syndrome of the family tree. Their union affiliation is still substantial,

---

[47] This type was first explored by mentality researchers in Hannover (Mueller, 1990; Vester, 1992), Heidelberg (Flaig et al., 1991) and Goettingen (Baethge, 1991).

though gradually weakening. The percentage of union membership is around 32 in the grandparent milieu, around 28 in the parent milieu and 24 in the youngest milieu. On the other hand, all three milieus are highly disappointed by the present situation in which, as they see it, the elites are not keeping their promise of fair chances for the working classes. We will come back to this standpoint at the end of this chapter.

Hierarchic Orientation: The Petty Bourgeois Working Classes

The second family tree goes back to old traditions of the deferential popular classes living in hierarchical agrarian, urban or administrative conditions. Today, it comprises self-employed persons and small business-men in more hierarchical and traditional occupations, mostly not too well paid. This corresponds with a very conventional and often authoritarian mentality. Complying with the conventionalism, hierarchies and duties of work, politics and the family gives the milieu members a feeling of security. Solidarity does not have the same neighbourly connotation as in the first family tree. It is rather limited to the nuclear family - and combined with a hierarchical loyalty of patronage.

However, in this family tree, which traditionally has been the strong-hold of authoritarian politics there have occurred important changes. The hard-core authoritarianism has been modified by individualisation and modernisation. The classical *Petty Bourgeois Employee Milieu,* which had 28 per cent in 1982, lost 13 per cent, and these 13 per cent are now mainly to be found in the *Modern Petty Bourgeois Employee Milieu* of 8 per cent. Here, the striving for security is better satisfied than in the parent milieu as the milieu members have better occupational qualifications and incomes. They belong mainly to the middle echelons of white-collar workers and civil servant employees. Joining the winners of modernisation, they are balancing their authoritarianism in the liberal aura of more modern lifestyles. Their compliance with occupational and familial hierarchies is still dominant, but the petty bourgeois lifestyle has been modernised by elements of individual hedonism and modern comfort.

Politically, the two milieus belong partly to the conservative political camp (which has been eroding for a while) and the authoritarian camp of right-wing populism (which is growing), as we will show later. However, four fifths of them up to now have been for the big conservative or social-democratic parties, still viewing them as a more effective representation of their interests than the rightist parties. In addition, parts of the two milieus are still very important for the labour movement. They are the milieus of the so-called 'authoritarian workers', a membership group trade unions have to take into account. The union membership in the first milieu is around 20 per cent, in the second it is even higher (around 26 per cent), possibly due to a more modern employee orientation.

To understand this union orientation, we have to remember that the conservative pattern of patronage does not mean unconditional obedience. It also implies that the patron has duties which he can be reminded of when he does not comply with them. Of course, this disposition will be articulated differently, depending on the field conditions. When there is strong fear of 'declassment' and disenchantment concerning the Employee Society, significant minorities of the milieu might turn to reactionary or racist resentments - especially rightist populism at the current time.

Orientations of Powerlessness: The Underprivileged Popular Classes

The third main group differs from the first two family trees which, in 'normal times', are integrated into the economic and moral context of giving and taking in society. They enjoy a 'respected' position in the social division of labour and a certain honour of status. The third group, instead, is not stably integrated into this nexus of giving and taking. It is positioned below the invisible borderline of respectability. It especially differs from the traditions of internalised social control of the first two family trees.

The underclass of the *Underprivileged Working-Class Milieus,* which comprise about 12 per cent of the population, are not different in all respects, however. Especially in the self-reliant labouring classes the milieu members share the value of giving high priority to their family and offspring (which gave the 'proletariat' it's name) and also to the friends and peers in their milieu. But they differ in the means. For them, work is not 'fulfilment' (as it is for the self-reliant labouring classes) nor a 'duty' (as it is for the petty bourgeois labouring classes). Instead, it is a necessary burden, especially as they mostly occupy the less skilled, less secure and less paid jobs. For them, the world is deeply divided into the powerful and the underdogs.

This *polarised power image of society* is often misunderstood as the source of clear proletarian class-consciousness and militancy. In fact, their confidence in helping themselves is realistically limited. With little resources of their own in terms of economic and cultural capital, the future of their employment and well-being is insecure. As they are very conscious of their own limits and the risks of being destabilised and stigmatised, they develop strategies of *keeping up* with the standards of the middle classes and of *depending on* stronger actors - the unions, the boss, a good marriage or just lucky occasions. In this respect, they are following the old tradition of the pre-industrial underclasses (see Conze, 1966), which did not belong to the respected artisan and peasant milieus. With them, they share the general belief that *investment in personal relations* (horizontally as well a vertically) is most important for social recognition, while educational achievements or legal equality cannot be trusted.

These strategical viewpoints differ according to the submilieus people belong to. The *Fatalist* submilieu (about 6 per cent) sticks to the underdog philosophy that all personal efforts are futile. Nevertheless, they see the unions as their voice and almost one-third of them are union members. The same is true for the *Status-Oriented* submilieu (about 3 per cent), although it is not so 'progressive' in other respects. Its members pursue an active strategy of adapting to petty-bourgeois conformity, for the purpose of gaining stability and being respected by the other classes. In particular, they conform to patriarchic family structures, discipline and reliability on the job, as well as conventional lifestyles. By contrast, the *Hedonist Rebels* (about 2 per cent) follow the more liberal philosophy of the Hedonistic Milieu and display an explicit distance towards the authorities of state, church, higher education, patriarchalism, etc. Although this is the most 'individualised' of the three submilieus, its union affiliation is the strongest: over 44 per cent (61 for the men and 22 for the women).

Our data show that the 'dependence' strategies of most of the underprivileged workers have been rather successful. Certainly, for the most part they have not participated in the educational revolution since the 1960s (Geißler, 1994). Their school achievements are still low although more stable. Nevertheless, the postwar Fordist model of social integration allowed them rather secure lowskilled jobs in the pits, on the railway, or on the assembly lines and also rather stable incomes. But this model is now eroding, as the less skilled jobs are exported to cheap labour countries and the social guarantees of the welfare state are increasingly being reduced.

Taking all above together, the habitus dispositions may motivate different action, depending on the field conditions. When social change is smooth, the mentioned 'dependence' strategies of keeping up a respectable lifestyle, of union power or of personal protection may well work. In the present crisis, the underprivileged workers are dividing into several parts. Many are now among the main losers of modernisation and globalisation. Laid off, they constitute the largest group of the so-called long-term unemployed. While part of them may enter into precarious living conditions and vicious circles of anomy, others return to the old milieu strategies of combining small job opportunities and of activating their networks in the informal economy. Politically, parts of these milieus may also enter into actions against ethnic minorities or into right-wing populist protest.

Lifestyle Orientation: The Hedonist Popular Classes

On the left margin of social space we see, on each of the three vertical levels of society, a formation which defines itself as a sort of vanguard lifestyle or, in some cases, moral distinction. Our data do not support the interpretation of the theories of individualisation which see this as a proof of the dissolution of social classes. Instead, on every level, the habitus and practice of these groups mainly represents a younger faction or variation of known class habitus types.

In this context, the hedonist faction of the popular classes, the so-called *Hedonist Milieu* (11 per cent), seems to constitute a special case. On first sight, our data show a heterogeneous picture as this milieu unites a younger generation, whose parents and grand parents belong to occupational groups which may as well be located in the petty bourgeois as in the work oriented popular classes. Their lifestyles cannot be defined by common class faction roots. Instead, they are defined *negatively*. What unites them is a strong *rejection* of the sense of *necessity* which (in different combinations) is a common property of the two main family trees of the popular classes. This very strong negative identification disguises the internal differences of the milieu to a certain extent.

The members of the hedonist milieu profess conspicuous anti-conformism, individual autonomy and spontaneous enjoyment of the exciting new possibilities of lifestyle and consumption. They seem to represent a prolonged adolescent rejection of the habitus of their parents, be it the petty bourgeois habitus of duty and order or be it the skilled workers' balancing of self-discipline and quality of life. This indicates that the milieu is a transitory formation constituted by the prolonged adolescent rebellion against the narrow perspectives of necessity, harmony, security and frugality.

However, our data show that about four-fifths of the milieu comply with the usual everyday routines of school, work and other social obligations, and about one fifth also goes to church on Sunday mornings. Thus, for most of these milieu members hedonism means little more than a leisure time compensation.

Moreover, as the Golden Years are over, hedonism gets into difficulties. As the milieu members are concentrated in the age groups up to the early thirties, many of them have not yet left the phases of education and transitional jobs behind them. Others are in the situation of simple blue-collar and white-collar work or are unemployed. Thus, medium and small incomes are the rule, and hedonism touches its material limits, so that the group is segregated into winners and losers.

Especially, the thesis of eroding trade union affiliations is not supported by our data. The percentage of trade union membership is about 26 in the whole milieu, 30 for men and 22 for women. This is around the average for the popular classes.

Hegemony: The Elites of Property and Education

The popular classes and the underclasses are not the only ones for which trade unions are important. The three formations at the top of the social space, uniting more or less one-quarter of the population, are to a large extent milieus of employees - especially of their academic segments. The major part of the social space at the top is occupied by two large groups - property and education - which can be subdivided into a number of important submilieus. What unites them is their open or implicit distinction from the culture of those who do not have academic education and are less propertied.

a) The family tree of the *Conservative-Technocratic Milieus* of about 10 per cent is united by a habitus of a very explicit sense of success, hierarchy and power and manifestly exclusive social networks. They are the milieus of property and of institutional domination. However, they legitimate themselves in a modernised way as a meritocratic elite with academic and technocratic education and republican discourses blunting the edges of authority. To them belong the best-established employers, managers, professionals and civil servants.

   Although they are very conscious of authority, their action vary in accordance to the field conditions. In the decades of economic growth, the sense of authority was mediated by a tolerant and modernised paternalistic style conceding a certain social participation. Since the late 1970s, the neo-liberal rhetoric of innovation has come to the forefront, legitimating the disadvantage of the losers on the grounds of their inferior efficiency.

   Even in this family tree, one-third (half of the men and one-quarter of the women) are employees. 16 per cent of these employees (19 of the men and 11 of the women) are union members.

b) In a sense, the second family tree of elite milieus legitimates itself by distancing precisely from this power consciousness. *The Liberal-Intellectual Milieu* of about 10 per cent feels dominated by the milieus of property and power. Their members reject the materialism and exclusivity of the conservative elite factions by defining themselves as the *critical and universalistic part of the hegemonical milieus*, feeling themselves in a certain way responsible for peace and democracy and for the social and ecological consequences of economic progress. Being the advocates of spiritual progress, however, they do not go so far as to doubt their mission for cultural hegemony over society. Their distinctive lifestyles, which often take the form of charity and volunteer work, express that they should not be confused with the masses they serve.

Their members are the enlightened and well-situated elements of the academic elite working at the higher professional levels of administration, education and the cultural sector. 56 per cent of them are employees, a figure that is higher than the total population (52 per cent). The percentage of male employees equals the average for the total population (64 per cent), the difference being due to the percentage of the female employees which, in our sample, is 46 per cent, as compared to the population average of 42 per cent. This certainly corresponds with the efforts for women's rights in this milieu. The percentage of union affiliation is 28 for the men and 19 for the women in the milieu. This is near the average of the whole employee population (24 and 16 per cent).

The milieu consists of two subgroups. The *Progressive Elite of Higher Education* (5 per cent) is following older family traditions of humanist orientation. The *Modern Service Class Elite* (4 per cent) mainly have occupations in the higher social, medical and administrative services, many of its members being newcomers from the skilled working class.

Both subgroups understand themselves as cultural vanguards of a knowledge society which should be governed by competence and not by power. Their elitist ethos of high professional performance comes to expression in a variety of ways, according to the field conditions. Mainly in the first group, the post-materialist distinction of taste, of self-emancipation and of ecological, pacifist and social responsibility has developed since the 1970s. Since the turn to realism of the 1980s, humanist and innovative lines of reasoning have been increasingly utilised for the purposes of power management. This also explains why, in the 1990s, the old 'Alternative Milieu' merged with the mainstream Technocratic Milieu which, in turn, acquired a more progressive image. At the same time the aesthetic (instead of social) legitimisation of lifestyle as well as the celebration of expensive lifestyles became more important.

c) In this context, we could see the emergence of the so-called *Post-Modern Milieu* (now about 5 per cent). Its growth points to a different recruitment. Its style of distinctive grandiosity, of being not obliged and of apparent self-confidence can be compared with the performances of high wire walkers who know there is a safety net underneath them. The group may, in part be identical with what Pierre Bourdieu called the New Petty Bourgeoisie, who have been recruited from among the declassed parts of the upper classes and ascending parts of the proper petty bourgeoisie (Bourdieu, 1982, chapter 6; Hartmann, 1998; Bürklin et al., 1997). Many of its members are younger than 35, with a higher education and living as singles. They are students or young academics working on a medium employee, professional or managerial level, by preference in the fields of culture, media, new technologies, arts and architecture.

Here, we do not have trade union data, as this milieu appeared some years after our inquiry. The percentages may be as low as for the defunct 'Alternative Milieu' which had an average employee percentage of 52 but few union members (17 per cent). This seems to be linked less to individualisation as the other individualised milieus have a markedly higher unionisation. It may be explained in terms of the identification with upward mobility and the part the milieu plays in exerting cultural hegemony.

As there is not much research on the hegemonic class milieus, their precise internal field structure is not well known. Research on the elite in Germany covers at most small segments, such as the higher managers in business and the power elite, which does not include more than two per cent of the total population. By the criterion of way of life, the hegemonic milieus include at least 20 per cent of the population, differentiated into numerous occupational and mentality groups which, as they are not systematically studied up to now, cannot clearly be identified in the logic of family trees.

A large part of these milieus involve those strata which are commonly called the *middle classes* or the *proper petty bourgeoisie* - to distinguish them from the petty bourgeois or middle-class segment of the popular classes which, in the social space, are clearly separated from them. On first sight, it seems curious to distinguish several milieus with almost identical names. However, this can be explained by the *homology* of their positions: although of different historical descent, they occupy similar structural positions as clients in hierarchies, between the capitalist owner groups above them and the less esteemed groups below them.

The Socio-political Camps and the Crisis of Representation

The relation between the higher and the popular milieus has undergone important changes since the beginning of the international economic crisis in the 1970s and especially since the German unification of 1989. From

1980 to 1997, net wages rose by 20 per cent while net gains of the enterprises rose by 119 per cent. Due to the consequent decrease of effective demand, unemployment rose to more than four million, poverty and precarious social standards (Huebinger, 1996) to about 10 per cent each. This affected not only the underprivileged milieus. Large parts of the skilled employee middle had to cope with precarity as well as with discontinuous work biographies implying decreasing social standards. Since the seventies, more than half of the labour force experienced recurring periods of transitional unemployment. What was experienced were not only economic deprivations but crucial changes of the culturally accepted ways of life, with the result of a deep crisis of social consensus and political confidence.

Soon after the German unification of 1990, public opinion was increasingly confronted with a seemingly new phenomenon called 'politische Verdrossenheit', which may be well translated by 'political alienation'. Ten years before, the distrust in the political representatives had reached little more than 10 per cent in the opinion polls. Now, it scored almost 60 per cent. During the early 1990s, it found a wide variety of different expressions. Public opinion and the media focussed directly on the political patronage system, incited by an increasing number of cases where politicians were taken personal advantage of their power positions. The public was shocked by long months of violent acts directed against immigrants and their homes in Germany. These waves of violence were followed by an equally huge wave of strictly non-violent mass demonstrations against ethnocentrism. In the same period there were also strong pacifist manifestations against the Gulf War and spontaneous relief actions for the people in the new Balkan wars. At first sight, these movements seemed to act according to the 'new political model' of action across the boundaries of vertical class layers which, in the opinion of Giddens and Beck, had replaced the old left-right scheme by the issues of human and civil rights, peace and ecology. However, the waves of xenophobic violence had their social background. This was the rising anxiety of the less well-to-do Germans who were afraid that, after the opening of so many borders, they had to share their precarious incomes, jobs and housing with unlimited groups of new immigrants.

But the decrease of the xenophobic incidents and the confinement of the voting for the ultra-right parties (together with a new policy of more strict immigration control) encouraged the opinion that, in principle, material welfare and social standards of the vast majority were sufficiently secure. Thus, the way was free for an increasing neo-liberal public campaign for social deregulation and cutting costs in the social security system, in order to improve the national business chances in the globalising economy. However, despite the rising export booms, the unemployment rate remained around 10 per cent, and there were numerous small conflicts between the unions and the employers over deregulating working conditions. Nonetheless, the liberal-conservative government of Kohl continued its piecemeal reductions of social guarantees. In 1996, it started to deregulate the salary guarantees for employees in case of illness. This lead to an unexpected wave of forceful protest organised by the three million member Metal Workers' Union. This, and also the consequent actions of other unions, helped to slow down the pace of deregulation policies.

Thus it was no surprise when, in 1998, the Kohl government, just as most other conservative governments in Europe before it, was voted out of office. Now, trade unions hoped that the new coalition of Social Democrats and the Green Party would reverse the tendency of deregulation. However, there was no resolution of the conflicts between different elite factions over the question as to whether Willy Brandt's social model of the Employee Society should be either continued or changed. A liberal-conservative media campaign succeeded in politically isolating the protagonist of that model, Social Democratic Party leader Oskar Lafontaine. His rival, Chancellor Gerhard Schroeder, took over, with policies following the blueprint of the Blairist 'third way'.

But now it was Schroeder who was caught by surprise. In the European elections of 1999, his party lost eight out of twenty million voters. These losses were mainly due to an unexpected mass abstention of the party voters. In the German mass media, Blair's strategists, Giddens and Mandelson, explained that the SPD had only lost the old vanishing working class which did not comprehend the necessities of austerity policies. The SPD would gain much more if it turned to the growing post-modern service classes. This was, in the light of our milieu data, a fatal misunderstanding. As the old proletariat was already down to five per cent, this could not explain the losses. Instead, those who abstained were the very groups the Blairists had in mind: the modern employee milieus. It was exactly these groups which saw social justice in danger.

After the election, Schroeder changed his policy strategy, combining symbolic worship with social justice and an even more forceful budgetary policy. However, in the four subsequent regional elections, the SPD suffered losses of up to 15 per cent. At the end of 1999, fortune returned. What helped Schroeder was the discovery of huge financial irregularities in the Christian Democrat Party.

However, this doesn't mean that the political confidence of the German public is on the rise. The confidence of the social milieus has not been regained. Instead, it seems that the leading political elites (and the ideological camps they are combined with) have lost touch with the large popular milieus they intend to mobilise and to represent. At the same time, the popular classes are in a situation of political disorientation, in each of their camps. This includes the danger of right-wing populism because one of the camps has a strong authoritarian populist potential. Up to now its majority has been bound by the big Christian and Social Democratic parties. If these parties continue to disintegrate, a populist leader like Haider in Austria, could mobilise that potential with the consequence of a fundamental change in the German party system.

The Three Camps of Popular Discontent

What is the anatomy of this discontent? Is it only that the people do not comprehend the necessity of austerity in an economic situation of global competition, as supposed by the politicians? Or is it the return of class cleavages? How can social discontent among the majority of the population like this be explained when the classical parameters of declassing, poverty and unemployment, are limited to about 10 per cent each?

Our survey of 1991 enables us to identify a configuration of six ideological camps by which we are able analytically to explain the distrust between the represented and their representatives (see Vester et al., 1993, Chapter 11). On the basis of more recent data we have been able to verify that this configuration forms part of a long-term structural trend. The six camps are detected by the application of a 44-item indicator of socio-political attitudes; and by using clustering techniques. Only one of these camps, the 'Radical Democrats' of about 11 per cent, has certain characteristics of the post-modern attitudinal model of Beck and Giddens. In a second step, we related the six camps to the class milieu types described in the last chapter. Although all camps spread over all milieus, there is a significant concentration in specific milieus so that each camp has a specific location in the field of class milieus. Each location represents a certain social position and experience of the process of socio-economic modernisation, which has been changing - and destabilising - Postwar societies since the 1970s.

In our analysis (Vester et al., 1993), the journalistic term of 'political distrust' turns out to be an adequate, though undifferentiated description of the situation. It describes the cleavage between two poles. In general, there is an extremely high acceptance of the social solidarity model of the

Employee Society including the role of the trade unions.[48] It obviously is a generally consented value, accepted by 78 up to 95 per cent in most milieus except for the Conservative Technocratic milieu (60 per cent). But in three of the camps large parts of the people (58 per cent of the population) are firmly convinced that the politicians do not act responsibly in terms of the values of social justice.[49] In detail, however, these three clusters differ highly as to their motives and value patterns - which again shows that the Employee Society does function as an integrational ideology capable of defining a common formula for different ethics and interests. For these three camps, this common formula is defined politically negatively. These camps form together a spectrum of popular discontent.

a) The largest group are the *Authoritarian Disappointed* (about 27 per cent). They are concentrated among the *'definite losers'* of modernisation with their low-skill and income standards and their limited social cohesion, being located in the traditional employee milieus at the *right and lower margins* of the social space.[50] They are most brutally confronted with unemployment, decreasing social standards and moral exclusion. Having grown up in authoritarian traditions, they transform their humiliation into resentment, especially against foreigners, modern young people and politicians. Up to now, four-fifths of them vote Christian and Social Democrat. But the sympathy for populist right-wing politics may rise if they are further disappointed by precarious social conditions and by the mainstream parties.

b) Another large group is the camp of those who maintain a *Sceptic Distance* from party politics (about 18 per cent). They are concentrated among the more modern employees who are the *'relative losers'* of modernisation. With their good skills, social cohesion and work discipline, they form the backbone of the labour force. However, they are losing faith in the value of the Employee Society (that their hard work will be rewarded by social justice) since their way of life is being made

---

48 The factor 'Classical Employee Orientation' was mainly described by five statements: (1) the demand for more employee participation rights at work; (2) that the employers' profit thinking inhibited the solution of the unemployment problem; (3) that trade unions demands did not impede economic recovery; (4) that employees may protest when laid off in larger numbers in a firm; (5) that the state has the unconditional duty to stabilise the socially disadvantaged.

49 This was expressed by the factor 'Political Disappointment', which was described mainly by five statements: (1) disbelief in politicians' promises; (2) absence of moral principles in politics; (3) no matter what party you vote for, there will be no change; (4) in politics, it is rare that anything happens in favour of the common man; (5) fear of being unable to keep the present standard of living in the coming years.

50 The Petty Bourgeois and Underprivileged Milieus and smaller parts of the Traditional Working Class and the Meritocratic Employee Milieus.

discontinuous and insecure by decreasing work standards and recurring short periods of unemployment. They are concentrated around the *middle of the middle* in the social space.[51] Having grown up in traditions of democracy and tolerance, they transform their disappointment into distance and scepticism towards all politicians and ideologies, including Social Democracy and Conservatism. Up to now, their votes for the Social Democrats have been above average, and their votes for the Christian Democrats and the Liberals have been around the average. But non-voter turnout abstention may be on the rise in their ranks.

c) The third group of strong discontented is the *Social Integration Camp* (about 13 per cent). It is concentrated among the most modern segments of the employee milieus. With their high standards of education, specialist qualifications and cohesive modern lifestyles, the members are clearly *not* among the *economic losers* of modernisation. They are disappointed, however, by the *authoritarianism and arrogance of institutional power* which is discouraging solidarity and participation from below. They are concentrated in the *left upper middle* of social space, which may be called 'new centre'.[52] Having grown up with high standards of individual and social responsibility, they transform their disappointment into strong participation in grassroots politics and universalistic solidarity, while they refuse participation in institutional politics. Up to now, they have mostly voted for the Social Democrats and Greens, but non-voting may increase.

The three camps of discontent cannot be explained by the vulgar materialist mainstream theory, which only accepts economic deprivation as a motive of discontent. For all three groups, the main motive is the change that has taken place in their 'whole way of life' (Thompson), be it (1) by moral exclusion from modernisation; (2) by destabilisation of the continuity of life or (3) by a general acquisitive and authoritarian 'culture of contentment' (Galbraith, 1992). The economic conditions are important, but only as one part of the their everyday way of life which cannot be reduced to material standards of distribution alone. This becomes especially apparent in the seeming paradox that, of the three camps, the group with the least resources is precisely *not* the group with the clearest class mentality, while the group with the best economic and cultural standards is not only the most critical but also consists of a working-class

---

51 The Modern, Underprivileged and Hedonist Employee Milieus and smaller parts of the neighbouring Petty Bourgeois and Modern Employee Milieus.

52 The Hedonist, Meritocratic and Modern Employee Milieus and smaller parts of the neighbouring Liberal Intellectual, Petty Bourgeois and Underprivileged Employee Milieus.

intelligentsia whose members, in the employee milieus, play a widely accepted role as 'opinion leaders' or 'multipliers'. It is a special weakness of the leading political organisations and camps that, up to now, they have failed to offer this intelligentsia an acceptable basis for co-operation.

The Three Camps of Contentment

The hegemonic political camps and elites do not on the whole think that there is anything wrong with their concepts of the social order and their explanations of rising popular discontent. Due to their position in social space, their mainstream ideology explains the 'political alienation' of the general public mainly as a question of political and economic misunderstanding. However, the crisis of representation could also be understood as what Klaus von Bismarck called 'the narrowing of milieus' to their immediate followers (Bismarck, 1966).

a) The *Traditional Conservative Camp* still does exist in impressive consistency and numbers (about 14 per cent). However, it suffers a strong modernisation lag, clinging to rather rigid conceptions of conservative hierarchy in the family, at work and in politics. Being rooted in the older and best-established parts of the leading employers, managers, professionals and civil servants and their followers in petty bourgeois milieus, the camp is concentrated in the *upper right* of the social space.[53] Having grown up with the understanding that they themselves are uncontested executors of economic and state power, they have long practised a patronage system which, in the current wave of scandals, is openly rescaling itself to be in crisis, a crisis which is damaging the preferred political formations of this camp, the Christian Democrat and the Liberal Parties.

b) The *Conservative Employee Camp* has traditionally combined the *client milieus* which were socially and politically represented and led by the Traditional Conservative Camp. This camp consisted of conservative employees in rather secure social positions that were guaranteed by stable hierarchies led by paternalistic employers, provincial politicians, regional media and church representatives. The camp is concentrated in the *right part of the middle*.[54] Since the 1980s, however, this large camp (about 18 per cent) has been slowly eroding. Part of the younger blue-collar and white-collar employees (up to 1991: about 7 per cent)

---

[53] The Conservative Technocratic and the two Petty Bourgeois Milieus and smaller factions of the neighbouring Liberal Intellectual and Meritocratic Employee Milieus.

[54] The two Petty Bourgeois Milieus, the Status Oriented subgroup of the Underprivileged Employee Milieu and part of the Meritocratic Employee Milieu.

are adopting more modern lifestyles and work qualifications which, in turn, are encouraging the sense of personal independence and gender equality as well as of ecological and civic responsibility. Thus, the hegemony of the Christian and Liberal Parties has also in this camp been challenged. In the 1990s, part of the younger groups started voting Social Democrat. The recent new financial irregularities could also lead to an increase in non-voter turnout.

The crisis of conservative patronage system is only part of the problem because the conservative parties also need substantial support from the camps of the discontented described earlier. The same is true for the Social-Democrat and Green leaderships.

c) The camp of the *Radical Democrats,* which has gained hegemony in the new government, does indeed represent the Blairist new model of politics beyond class. However, with more or less 11 per cent, it depends on support of larger popular camps. It consists mainly of the middle generation of children of academic upper class milieus who have become radicalised since 1968 and now work in the higher modern occupations. In terms of social space, this camp is concentrated in the *upper middle and right.*[55] While this camp professes all the idealistic values of civic, gender and ethnic rights, of peace and ecology, it has a blind spot concerning vertical social inequality. Since 1998, many Green politicians are advocating austerity and asceticism because, in their opinion, most people are made lazy by consumerism and the welfare state. This view caused great losses of voters in the milieus of the modern employees, who had great sympathy with green goals. Similarly, the Blairist new politics in the Social Democratic party lies at the roots of rising non-voting and of protest voters switching over to the Democratic Socialist Party (PDS).

In this situation, none of the hegemonic milieus really respond to the social destabilisation experienced by large parts of the employee majority milieus. Thus, the three forms of 'political alienation' are likely to develop further. On the one hand, the *populist* potential could one day be the basis of a 20 per cent right-wing party after the Austrian model. On the other hand, the disenchanted *democratic* employee milieus are turning away from politics, and focussing higher expectations on the trade unions, in the hope that they will resume their role of countervailing powers.

---

[55] The Liberal Intellectual and the Conservative Technocratic Milieus and smaller factions of its neighbours in the upper middle of the Hedonist, the Modern and the Meritocratic as well as the Petty Bourgeois Employee Milieus.

However, even though trade union strength in Germany is above the European average, it is weakened by two tendencies, the modernisation of the labour force and the problem of union power. From 1982 to 1998, the membership of the DGB (which unites the majority of union members) decreased from 7.9 to 6.5 million in West Germany, in East Germany the loss is 1.8 million. In this total number, the portion of blue-collar workers decreased slowly (to about 5 million), but the growth of white-collar members (to about 3 million) did not compensate for the losses. Union membership is strongest in the more traditional and less skilled employee milieus where trade union membership covers between 32 and 44 per cent of the employed (compared to an average of about 25 per cent in the more modern occupations). The weakness is especially felt among the young, the highly qualified and the female employees in the modern tertiary sectors. At present, these sectors are experiencing an enormous growth, but - contrary to the general consensus - not so much in the electronic and media sectors, but rather in the health, personal and cultural services, which are gaining from the demographic changes and the respective demands (Krueger, 2000).

These deficits relate not only to the problem of the trade union cultural lag (the paternalistic and bureaucratic culture which does not appeal to the modern employees and their participative in values), but also to the problem of organisational power. As we can see from the high acceptance of the Employee society (around 80 per cent), union membership could be considerably higher in Germany. The German unions lost nevertheless many members who entered unemployment or precarious conditions. The highest rates of new membership entrances, in recent years have occurred when the unions showed their competence in conflicts at the enterprise level, when they actively struggled for employment. On the whole, the crisis of class representation - which could be overcome if the younger and female employees would play a more active role - is not only a problem of the political parties, but also of the trade unions.

Appendix 2.1 The position of social milieus in Bourdieu's social space

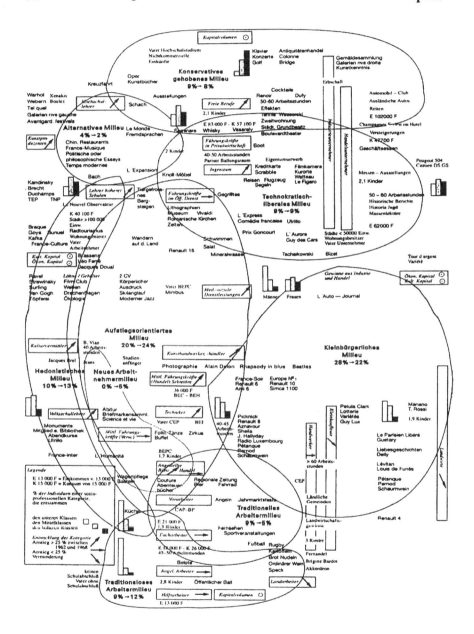

Appendix 2.2   Class differentiation of the 'merocratic employee milieu' by occupation and gender

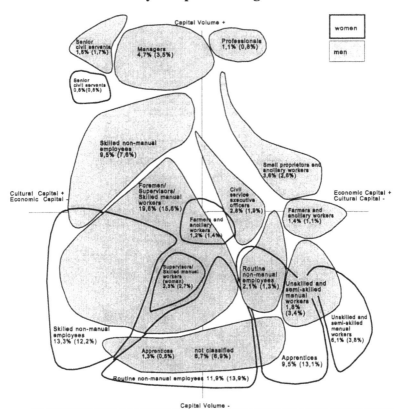

Capital Volume +

women

men

Senior
civil servants
1,6% (1,7%)

Managers
4,7% (3,5%)

Professionals
1,1% (0,8%)

Senior
civil servants
0,6%(0,6%)

Skilled non-manual
employees
9,5% (7,6%)

Small proprietors and
ancillary workers
3,6% (2,6%)

Cultural Capital +
Economic Capital −

Foremen/
Supervisors/
Skilled manual
workers
19,6% (15,6%)

Civil
service
executive
officers
2,8% (1,9%)

Economic Capital +
Cultural Capital −

Farmers and
ancillary workers
1,4% (1,1%)

Farmers and
ancillary
workers
1,2% (1,4%)

Supervisors/
Skilled manual
workers
(women)
2,3% (2,7%)

Routine
non-manual
employees
2,1% (1,3%)

Unskilled and
semi-skilled
manual
workers
1,8%
(3,4%)

Unskilled and
semi-skilled
manual
workers
6,1% (3,6%)

Skilled non-manual
employees
13,3% (12,2%)

Apprentices
1,3% (0,5%)

not classified
6,7% (6,9%)

Apprentices
9,5% (13,1%)

Routine non-manual employees 11,9% (13,9%)

Capital Volume −

*The relative position of occupational groups in social space; representative sample 1991, agis, University of Hannover
(see Vester et al. 1993, pp. 251-256, pp. 286- 294), placed in Bourdieus space of social positions
(see Bourdieu 1984[1979] pp. 126-129).
Percentages of the: Meritocratic Employee Milieu (in parenthesis: percentage of total population)
Example: foremen/supervisors/skilled manual workers, 19,6% (15,6%) = 19,6% of the sample of the Meritocratic Employee
Milieu are foremen/supervisors/skilled manual workers; 15,6% of men in the sample of the whole population are
foremen/supervisors/skilled manual workers.

Arbeitsgruppe interdiszipilnre Sozialstrukturforschung (agis), University of Hannover

3 Class Identity in Contemporary Britain: The Demise of Collectivism?[56]

MIKE SAVAGE

In the past decade influential social theorists as well as politicians have proclaimed 'the end of class'.[57] The rise of new social identities based around consumerism, 'post-materialist' concerns, and lifestyle now command particular attention (see e.g. Melucci, 1996). The idea of 'individualisation', found prominently in the work of Ulrich Beck and (in somewhat different vein) Anthony Giddens' recent writings, is especially important in suggesting that the old collective identities of class have been displaced by newer modes of self-identity. Both these writers see class not as a modern identity - as Marx and Weber did - but as traditional, ascriptive ones, which have no place in a dynamic modern and globalised world in which individuals have to construct their own biographies and identities. In the context of the issues discussed in this book concerning the potential of class to be a continued political force, they raise fundamental concerns which emphasise

---

[56] I would like to thank the conference organisers, as well as Rosemary Crompton and Alan Warde for comments on an earlier draft of this chapter. An earlier draft which includes more empirical discussion of survey evidence and contemporary potential for class solidarity has been published as Savage (1998). The themes developed in this chapter are developed in Savage (2000).

[57] In the UK, both John Major and Tony Blair have made statements along these lines. Academics arguing for the demise of class include Clark and Lipset (1991), Giddens (1990), Beck (1992), Pakulski and Waters (1996) and Lockwood (1992).

how contemporary social change has fundamentally disrupted older repertoires of collective action and class based politics.[58]

In this chapter I critically reflect on arguments about the nature of contemporary social change and the changing relationship between class and
individual identities. My intention is to show that whilst old models of
collective class cultures are indeed dead and buried, we should not leap to
the other extreme of positing thoroughly individualised beings whose cultural framework does not draw in some ways on notions of class. I will
emphasise that the kinds of analytical oppositions between traditional class
cultures and new individualised ones, which itself draws on other well
rehearsed oppositions (between modernity and post-modernity, organised
and disorganised capitalism, and so on) fails to capture the complex interweaving of class and individual identity.

I begin by examining the arguments of Beck and Giddens in some detail
in order to draw out some of the theoretical ambiguities in their formulations, and in order to show that the underpinnings for their ideas are in
many ways deeply conventional and rather 'dated'. I will argue that for all
their sophistication they ultimately posit an a-social account of the individual. What worries me about their arguments is that they draw on the long
standing and now thoroughly discredited notion of a golden age of class, in
which it is assumed that there was an historical period in which class
identities were bound up with collective sentiment. I draw upon the arguments of Bourdieu to emphasise the need for a more developed 'relational'
recognition of the intermeshing of individual and collective identities.

In the second part of the chapter I draw upon diverse recent research
undertaken in the UK to examine the nature of contemporary class awareness. Here I show that class as a *collective* identity is rather weak and
appeals for class unity are therefore likely to have little impact. However,
people still tend to define themselves in opposition to other groups, and
social divisions continue to have some pertinence in shaping diverse
aspects of individual identities. I emphasise that the way explicit class identities map on to these relational attitudes is in many respects arbitrary, but
that it is possible to show that individual identities and relational identities
are more closely inter-related than theorists of individualisation suppose.
The final section of the paper explores some of the broader issues concerning the changing nature of class identities and argues and examines how

---

58 Giddens and Beck are only the most celebrated of a number of social and cultural
theorists who elaborate similar themes concerning the decline of collective class based
cultures and the rise of new forms of fragmentation (for other examples see Harvey,
1989; Lash and Urry, 1994; Castells, 1996) but their work is especially important in
emphasising the erosion of class identity.

we might think about the meshing of individualistic and class identities. I draw some conclusions regarding the relevance of these findings for the role of trade unions.

Class and Individualisation

Both Beck and Giddens insist that contemporary individualised cultures break from the ascribed culture of class. This is a major theme of Beck's book on *The Risk Society*,

> it is no longer social classes that take the place of status groups, or the family as a stable frame of reference that takes the place of social class commitments. *The individual himself or herself becomes the reproduction unit for the social in the lifeworld* (Beck, 1992, 130).

> class loses its sub-cultural basis and is no longer experienced (Beck, 1992, 98).

This theme is echoed by Giddens, who in the 1970s and early 1980s adopted a class-centred interpretation of modern societies from which he has now distanced himself. An important indication of this shift is his work on *The Consequences of Modernity* (1990). Here he argued that modernity produced four types of social movements (labour movements, free speech/democratic movements, peace movements and ecological movements), oriented to each of the basic institutional dimensions of modernity (capitalism, surveillance, military power and industrialism) which he identifies. Although Giddens recognises a role for 'class politics' through the significance of labour movements (it is not clear how the industrial/political movements of employers, professionals, bureaucrats or peasants fit into Giddens' scheme), it becomes clear in his later work that he sees a shift in the political agenda from one where 'emancipatory politics' held centre stage to one where 'life politics' jostles with it and possibly shifts it from its central position. For Giddens, as for Beck, 'life politics' indicates a new role for the individual in politics:

> while emancipatory politics is a politics of life chances, life politics is a politics of lifestyle. Life politics ... is a politics of self-actualisation in a reflexively ordered environment, where that reflexivity links self and body to systems of global scope (Giddens, 1991, 214).

Even in his recent work Giddens does continue to acknowledge the continuation of old style 'emancipatory' concerns (e.g. Giddens 1994), but it is clear from his brief statements that he has no ready theoretical handle on their relationship to life politics, and hence seems to see them simply as a 'throwback' to times past.[59]

Beck and Giddens are aware that their arguments pose important issues in reflecting on theorising 'individualisation' in a sociologically convincing way. The 'individual' and 'society' is one of the classic, much discussed tensions in social theory and both Beck and Giddens are keen to search for a way of avoiding positing a dualistic relationship between these two terms (for instance by claiming that individual freedom entails breaking from social forces).[60] The way they do this is to argue that a culture of 'individualisation' does not entail the weakening of the power of social relations but is premised on the specific, contemporary character of such relations so that the two can only be understood alongside each other.

In fact, this does not stop either of them from adopting, from time to time, formulations which appear to be consistent with the conventional Enlightenment humanist idea that individualisation depends on 'freeing' people from social constraint.[61] Thus Beck makes reference to 'Enlightenment' notions of individualism whereby people free themselves from social constraints, and at times sees late modernity as simply a democratisation and extension of this long-term development (e.g. Beck and Beck-Gernsheim, 1996, 34; 38). Giddens also incautiously refers to lifestyle in terms of 'forms of self-actualisation and empowerment' (e.g. Giddens, 1991, 6). However, in general both authors are clear in their intent to distance themselves from this 'humanistic' reading of individualisation. 'Individualisation' Beck argues, is a triple process involving,

> disembedding, *removal* from historically prescribed social forms and commitments ..., the *loss of traditional security* with respect to practical knowledge, faith and guiding norms ...; and ... re-embedding, a *new type of social commitment* (Beck, 1992, 128).

The first two of these echo the classic sociological dualism in which individuals are freed from social constraints, and from social norms and values. However Beck's final point insists that they are re-embedded,

---

59 See notably Giddens' uncertain statements about class and lifestyle in Giddens (1991, 5-6).
    'One might imagine that 'lifestyle' refers only to the pursuits of the more affluent groups and classes ... In some substantial part this is true ... yet it would be a major error to suppose that the phenomena analysed in this book are confined in their impact to those in more privileged material circumstances ...'.

60 See especially Beck and Beck-Gernsheim's (1996) criticisms of the German writers Ostner and Roy and Mayer.

61 See for instance Lash's commentary on this work which refers to its 'core assumption' as the 'progressive freeing of agency from structure' (Lash, 1994, 119).

finally, back into society. Beck adopts arguments from Habermas and Luhmann to argue that individualisation is not to be understood as a process which allows the 'free individual' to emerge, but rather, 'how one lives becomes the *biographical solution of systemic contradictions*' (Beck, 1992, 137). What Beck appears to mean is that individuals are able to reflect on the implications of various structural processes, and can thereby choose which of them to become involved with. Individuals cannot escape structural forces in general, but they can decide which ones to act on, which to ignore, which to oppose and so on. Reflexive modernisation does not create the 'free' individual but the individual who is in a sense, able to choose what kind of social relations to act on.

Beck's arguments about individualisation therefore attempt to avoid the excesses of methodological individualism and sees the individual as embedded in social relations. Here his arguments are linked to his claims about the 'universalisation of risk'. In contemporary societies, he claims, risks cannot be attributed or apportioned to specific social groups, but are universalised, so that anyone can, potentially, be affected by any risk. Since risks are not the attribute of social groups, so they cannot be shrugged off by individuals (in the way that individuals who thought that a risk was integrally related to a specific social group could shrug off their own responsibility onto that group - even if he or she was a member of that group). Thereby Beck feels he has evaded the classic sociological dualism: individualisation depends on a particular configuration of social relations, not the collapse or erosion of society in general. Now of course the 'universalisation of risk' idea is a controversial, and probably overstated, argument,[62] but the important theoretical point I want to concentrate on here is the way that it leads him to see the reflexive rational individual as the product of specific global and system wide social conditions, rather than linked to more proximate social relations around the firm, family, neighbourhood, and social network.

Before discussing this, I want to say a few words about Giddens' related arguments. He links individualism to the growing problems in sustaining ontological security in a globalised world. Giddens is less cautious than Beck in adopting teleological language to describe individualisation, i.e. a language which imparts certain inherent self developing processes to individuals which will be realised once the individual is freed from societal 'checks'.

---

[62] I don't know of many men who are concerned about contracting breast cancer, for instance. Other examples whereby risks can be integrally and not just probabilistically linked to specific social groups can also be readily found.

> The more tradition loses its hold ... the more individuals are forced to nego-
> tiate lifestyle choices among a diversity of options (Giddens, 1991, 5).

Nonetheless Giddens is keen also to locate the contemporary 'dynamism of
modernity' in terms of the separation of time and space, the disembedding
of social life from face to face contact, and institutional reflexivity (and
hence the decline of tradition) as fundamental to the development of a 'life
politics' where we search to create a coherent biography in a fractured
world. Once again we see the 'externalisation' of the self from social
relations so that the former can reflect and plan on its future actions.

The individuals which Beck and Giddens discuss are lonely. Their individualism is constructed not with respect to other people or social groups,
but in relation to the de-traditionalised, globalised world system as a whole.
To be sure they search out others, for instance as they seek the kinds of
'pure relationships' that Giddens (1991) emphasises as a key feature of late
modern identity, but such relationships remain contingent.

Despite their caveats, we can still doubt whether all this provides a satisfactory theoretical account of individualism, for it ultimately presupposes
an a-social concept of the individual. It is partly this point which explains
why both authors situate their ideas in opposition to the idea of collective
class cultures, for by doing so, they can attempt to sociologically ground
their arguments against some kind of an alternative. However, in this process they rely on the rather old and venerable tradition of counterpoising
individual against collective class cultures, and seeing the rise of the former
as detracting from the significance of the latter. In the British case the roots
for this theoretical move go back at least to the 1950s and the work of
writers such as Raymond Williams and Richard Hoggart. Here working-
class collectivism was invoked as a foil in order to provide a cultural critique of the competitive and individualistic character of capitalist, middle-
class Britain. The work of Hoggart (1957) had a key role here, in his
attempt to see his own working class upbringing in Leeds as a counter to
the commercialising and Americanising influences found elsewhere in
British society. For Hoggart,

> in any discussions of working-class attitudes much is said of the group
> sense, the feeling of being not so much an individual with a 'way to make'
> as one of a group whose members are all roughly level and likely to remain
> so ... (this feeling) arises from a knowledge, born of close living together,
> that one is inescapably part of a group (Hoggart, 1957, 68, 70).

The idea is perhaps found more clearly and directly in the writings of
Williams. For him, working-class culture

is not proletarian art, or council houses, or a particular use of languages; it is rather, the basic collective idea, and the institutions, manners, habits of thought and intentions which proceed from this. Bourgeois culture, similarly is the basic individualist idea ... the culture which it (the working class) has produced ... is the collective democratic institution, whether in trade unions, the co-operative movement or political party (Williams, 1958, 327).

Like Hoggart, Williams articulates a vision of the essential collectivism of working-class culture in opposition to the individualism of orthodox middle-class cultures as providing a lever for cultural critique.[63] But, in this process, the road is paved for subsequent critiques of the role of class which points to the absence of working-class collectivism. The 'classical' dichotomy between collective class cultures and individual cultures is firmly put in place, and this allows Beck's and Giddens' arguments to follow in their wake. Thought about in this way, individualisation is seen almost in definitional terms as bound to bring about the decline of class. Rather than class identity and individual identity as being intermeshed, the two are seen as inherently in contradiction.

It is worth noting at this point that most current defenders of class analysis do not in fact defend the idea of that collective class identities are strong in contemporary social life. Indeed, the work of Mann (1970, 1973), Goldthorpe (1988), Marshall (1988) and Scase (1991) has all emphasised the complexity and contingency of the relationship between class and cultural values (see also for a further discussion Savage, 1998). Leaving this point aside, however, we might draw theoretical sustenance from Bourdieu's (e.g. 1984) arguments about the relationship between class and identity. For Bourdieu, the struggle to define oneself as an autonomous individual cannot be distinguished from classification struggles in which other people are simultaneously de-individualised (i.e. that their claims to individuality are denigrated). Bourdieu thus emphasises that the 'taste of reflection' - which might be seen as the precursor to the kind of reflexivity emphasised by Beck and Giddens - is associated with what he terms a Kantian aesthetic. This is not a socially neutral 'habitus' which arises from the abstract position of the individual in the global social system, but is rather one which rests upon social struggles, as it comes to define itself against 'popular', 'natural' aesthetics (see Fowler, 1996, for a recent account, and Savage et al., 1992, for an application to the analysis of the British middle class). For Bourdieu, the kinds of reflexive practices heralded by Giddens

---

63 This theme also plays a key role in Williams's novels which examine the relationship between communal ties and individual liberties, in ways which often conflate these issues with those of class.

and Beck involve people not simply responding defensively to a globalising world, but actively distanciating themselves from the world of the immediate and the sensuous. They therefore involve modes of exclusion. Within this perspective the reflexive individual is less a product of global restructuring and more the product of a particular class habitus, associated with the academic and intellectual middle class. Their ability to stand outside social relations and reflect on them is a fundamental part of their specific class based exclusionary culture.

Bourdieu provides important insights about why the social distinctions he discusses might not always be apparent to people themselves. For the culturally advantaged to recognise their taste explicitly as a class taste would be to devalue it, to contaminate it with a pragmatic and instrumental meaning which is utterly at odds with its claims to be universal which lie at the heart of the entire Kantian aesthetic. It is hence the very salience of class struggles over distinction which explains why it is so difficult for them to be explicitly named and identified by their protagonists.

Bourdieu's argument therefore gives an importantly different gloss on the relationship between the individual and social class. Individualism should not be conceptualised as breaking from class relations but as interweaving with them, so that individual identities are seen as socially grounded. Bourdieu shows how claims to individuality are social claims which are only meaningful as relational claims. Defining what individuality is entails defining what it is not. Put in these terms, this is a rather familiar idea, which has surfaced in writings on identity and difference. Feminists have shown how the development of the idea of individual democratic freedoms were premised on gendered models in which male individuality was contrasted with female dependency (Pateman, 1990), whilst Said (1978) has examined how Western freedom was defined in relation to the Orient.

What Bourdieu's arguments point towards is the need to consider again the nature of contemporary class identities in ways which are not premised on simplistic notions of class collectivism but which can explore more fully the intermeshing between class and individual identities. In the next section I draw upon recent research to show that whilst it is indeed manifestly apparent that the idea of the collective class actor has no empirical warrant, nonetheless it would be quite wrong to assume that notions of class are not evident in other ways, which suggest the intersection of individual and class identities. I briefly discuss some of this material as a means of providing some material to return to some general issues in the last part of the chapter.

Individuality and Contemporary Class Identities

If we firstly consider evidence from social surveys, the messages concerning the contemporary salience of class are mixed.[64] It continues to be true that most people can place themselves in class categories when they are asked to by sociologists[65] and it is also clear that people recognise that societies are unequal and that inequality is structurally produced (see for instance Kluegel et al., 1995). However, what remains unclear is whether lay perceptions of inequality draw directly on class terms, or whether such categories tend to be ones which sociological researchers use to gloss their findings. In British research this issue has surfaced with particular acuity in the context of Marshall et al. (1988) claim that class remains of major cultural significance to the British population. However, as Saunders (1990) points out, the survey itself asked a battery of questions about class which might have 'encouraged' respondents to think in these terms. It is also interesting to note that this survey is something of an anomaly in showing that as many as 40 per cent of British people in 1984 did not think of themselves as belonging to a social class. It is also noteworthy that Evans (1992) has also used the same data as Marshall et al. (1988) to suggest that there is little clear indication of consistent class attitudes.

Recent surveys indicate how difficult it can be to demonstrate that there are deeply held views about social class. Table 3.1, drawn from the British Social Attitudes Survey, asks respondents about the kinds of factors which they think affects people's chances of getting ahead. The first three rows offer responses which can all be seen as indications of class based forces, and there is a significant minority agreement about the role of such factors. Interestingly these are mentioned more frequently than are the ascriptive factors or gender, race and region, which are offered in rows 4-6. This would appear to be in general line with the comparative research of Kluegel, Cspeli et al. (1995) concerning the general endorsement of social explanations of poverty and wealth as well as individualistic ones. But it is the responses given to rows 7-9 which are really striking. People give almost universal assent to individualised and meritocratic factors. The responses given do not suggest that people themselves see the world as one where class determines all: rather it is 'performative' factors which are emphasised.

---

64 This is of course a well established point, first emphasised by Michael Mann (1970) in his emphasis on the 'split consciousness' models of class consciousness.

65 Young (1992) shows that the proportion of British people identifying as working class and middle class has changed relatively little.

Table 3.1   What factors influence people's chances of getting ahead?

Factor	Essential/very important	Fairly important	Not very or not at all important
Coming from wealthy family	20.5	33.3	43.9
Knowing the right people	39.4	40.7	19.5
Having well educated parents	26.5	45.1	26.8
Being born a man or a woman	11.3	21.5	62.5
A person's race	16.2	30.8	49.5
The part of the country a person comes from	7.3	20.6	70.8
Having a good education yourself	71.8	23.8	3.5
Ambition	79.4	16.7	2.8
Natural ability	57.0	37.3	4.7
Hard work	83.5	13.7	2.1

Source: British Social Attitudes Survey (1987).

Table 3.1 indicates that whilst people are aware of class inequalities, they simultaneously are drawn overwhelmingly to a focus on individual properties as determinants of life chances. And indeed, this point is well known even by those who defend the relevance of class in general. Few leading sociologists who rely on survey evidence make any claims about the existence of collective class identities. Goldthorpe (1988) and Evans (1992), both of whom are committed to the importance of class and to the use of survey methods, doubt that class is of major cultural significance. Evans's (1992) critique of Marshall et al. (1988) is perhaps of particular importance here, in showing that there are few consistent class values. Goldthorpe's (1996) recent work on class differences in educational attainment indicate clearly his attachment to showing how class is structurally significant in ways that do not depend on a theory of class culture or identity.[66]

It is of course entirely consistent to point out that the lack of direct recognition of the relevance of class is in fact an indication of its real power. Skeggs (1997), develops this argument. She reports interviews with young working-class women in the Northwest of England, which show that these women were generally unwilling to talk openly about class, precisely because its scars were so deep, and so personal. Repeated interviews showed Skeggs that it was the deep and pervasive effect of class which explains the very difficulty of explicitly recognising it. This research has clear affinities with the American research reported by Sennett and Cobb (1971), in which the power of class was registered individually, in terms of the senses of failures it instilled in working-class people.

> This fear of being summoned before some hidden bar of judgement and being found inadequate infect the lives of people who are coping perfectly well from day to day: it is a matter of hidden weight, a hidden anxiety, in the *quality* of experience, a mater of feeling inadequately in control where an observer making calculations would conclude the workingman had adequate control (Sennett and Cobb, 1993, 33-4).

These studies all suggest, in line with Bourdieu's thinking, that the lack of a clear recognition of class actually demonstrates the hegemonic power of the middle classes to stigmatise, and thereby undermine working-class identities (Skeggs, 1997; Reay, 1998). Discussions of class do not 'unite' people into a proud collectivity, but because they refer to various processes of division and inequality they raise fraught recognition of the extent to which promises of equality are not kept.

There are, however, problems in using qualitative research to show the 'hidden' aspects of class, since there are dangers, rather akin to those found in survey research, of reading class into people's own accounts. A good example of these problems can be found in Reay's (1998) study of the class awareness of working-class mothers in London. She emphasises the ways in which class affects the lives and outlooks of these women, but does not actually indicate their own perception of class.[67] It seems vital not to 'smuggle' class into such account but to make a serious effort to register what people themselves actually say about class. This attention to the 'languages of class' has attracted considerable interest amongst social

---

[66] Goldthorpe's chosen framework here is rational action theory. See Savage (2000) for a fuller discussion.

[67] The only exception (Reay, 1998, 269), is a case where the respondent explicitly denies the existence of class.

historians in recent years, but we still lack any detailed knowledge of contemporary 'narratives of class' (see, for instance Somers, 1992). As a preliminary step to this end, I want to present some provisional, early results from a research project I have been conducting with Brian Long-hurst and Gaynor Bagnall.[68] This research project is primarily concerned with studying social networks and leisure interests, and has carried out 200 in-depth, qualitative interviews with men and women living in or around the Manchester area to explore these themes.[69] Towards the end of the interviews respondents were asked firstly whether Britain was becoming a classless society, and secondly whether they saw themselves as members of social classes. These questions provoked some interesting reflections which can develop our analysis of the complex nature of contemporary class iden-tities. The discussion below is based on only a few of the early responses taken at random and should be seen as suggestive only.[70] I am not in this paper interested in generalising about the frequency of responses which we received, for instance about whether people tended to identify as middle or working class. Rather I want to present a few illustrations about the 'style' and the narrative structures in which class was discussed. I pursue this objective by using relatively lengthy quotations which report the full dialo-gue between respondents and interviewer on those issues bearing on class.

One of the important points is that most people could give some sort of 'account' of class, but that there were often differences in the kinds of accounts given to explore general social and political issues and more personal ones. The words of a 38 year old male computer programmer indicate this point particularly clearly.

---

[68] This research has been funded by the Economic and Social Research Council, 'Life-styles and social Integration: a study of middle class culture in Manchester' project num-ber R000236929.

[69] The project does not attempt to interview a representative sample of the population, but instead has chosen four samples from areas chosen for theoretical reasons to represent different types of middle class lifestyles. These four areas are Wilmslow (taken to repre-sent the high status, affluent suburban middle class), Cheadle (representative of the lower middle/upper working class living in semi-detached inner suburbs), Chorlton (typical of the young, gentrifying middle class living in inner Manchester) and Ramsbot-tom (taken as typical of mixed groups living in rural villages within commuting distan-ces of Manchester). Here I say nothing about these local differences and concentrate only on the narratives of class used.

[70] The five cases I discuss are drawn from the first ten interviews to be transcribed and do not represent a 'selection' of typical cases.

Do you think Britain's becoming a classless society?

That's a tough one. In many ways yes. In the sense that I think many of the old boundaries of class, the old distinctions and mechanisms that held the class system in place are being eroded by education, by change in the way we live, by other factors, but I think these things change very slowly. I think a lot of change might be superficial, and people might ... my perception is that people who are middle class or above would seem to like to hold onto something ... in conversation when you scratch beneath the surface sometimes you pick out people wanting to have this sense of 'well, we've moved on', or 'we're not like that ...', you know and I like to pursue that often in conversation just to see what people mean.

How do they react when you pursue it?

Sometimes by ... when they realise that you're on the hunt for something, by denial - 'oh no, that's not what I meant' kind of thing and sometimes by being quite ... by being defensive about it.

Do you think of yourself as belonging to any particular social class?

No. I was going to say ... I didn't ... I wouldn't put myself as ... I'm working class ... by background and upbringing and I'm still working so in that sense I'm working class. I find it a difficult area to make distinctions in. Again, it's a scale or criteria that I prefer not to use so I don't find it helpful or meaningful.

There are a number of interesting points about this extract. This man begins by providing an articulate account both of issues around 'classlessness', and of the nuances of class as a general cultural issue, and the kinds of denials which are linked to claims about class. In his early statements he shows he has thought about class, indeed that he is interested in pursuing the issue in his interactions with others. In the later parts of the extract, however, this man exhibits the same defensiveness about class that he claims to find in others. He finds it easier to talk about class as a general social process than as an individually relevant one. However, this can be taken as evidence, in Bourdieu's terms of the importance of class, rather than its reverse. Here we see a striking bifurcation between people's awareness of class as a social and political issue, and as one which relates to their own individual identity.

Two other subsidiary points can be gleaned from these quotes. Firstly, although the respondent states that he is working class ('by background and upbringing') it seems that this class label is not something which is salient to him. Secondly, we see also how this claim to 'working classness', though rather diluted, follows a rather halting attempt to define himself as 'not' something else, and seems linked to a claim to be 'ordinary', 'un-snobbish', in a sense outside the class system. The claim to be working class in this case is also acceptable because it is outside the individual's control (in that it was due to the fortune of upbringing) and thereby does not 'contaminate' his own sense of self.

Let me turn to a second example. These are the responses of a 43 year old female self employed cleaner. The answers are less articulate but indicate a not dissimilar narrative structure.

> *There is some discussion going on about whether Britain is becoming a classless society, what do you think of that?*
>
> No.
>
> *And why do you think that?*
>
> I don't know really, I don't think it will ever be classless, I think there will always be filthy rich Conservatives.
>
> *And do you think of yourselves as belonging to any particular social class?*
>
> No, not really.
>
> *You don't think in those sort of terms? How would you describe yourself?*
>
> I would describe myself as a very normal lower middle-class person. (Daughter interjects: I would say upper lower class, no working class, upper working class').[71]
> I get on with most people - I have friends that I mean are very nice people but obviously have come from nice backgrounds, and I know people that are in the poverty trap, but I would not say that I treat them any differently.

Here the response to the question concerning class evokes a less articulate response, but nonetheless, does appear to tap felt beliefs about class inequality. In her later responses to questions about self-identity it is clear that although she gives a class label to herself - in this case lower middle class - it is one which is relatively arbitrary. What it said with more feeling is the last sentence, which is that she can 'get on with most people'. Here we see a concern not to use class as a basis for personal taste, with the subsequent concern to be 'outside class'. Class is something which this individual strives to leave behind.

This same point can be found in a third case, of a 55 year old unemployed woman (formerly a typist and housewife), living in relatively

---

[71] Although we attempted to conduct interviews with individuals alone, in some cases other household members were present and we made no attempt to exclude them.

modest conditions in Cheadle, Manchester. Here we see some differences from the first two cases, in that this respondent finds it initially difficult to get any grasp of the concept of class. Interestingly, however, when coaxed, she does show that terms such as middle and working class are meaningful. At the end, it is clearly the idea of 'ordinariness' which is attractive.

> *You might know that there's been some discussion going on these days about whether Britain is becoming a classless society or not. What do you think about that? D'you think it is?*
>
> [pause] Er I don't know. This is where you get me, when you get technical. [laughs]
>
> *Well you know, d'you think there are things like you know an upper class and middle class and working class, all that sort of thing?*
>
> Oh I think yeah. I think there's still the upper class there isn't there? You know but er you know *[pause]* perhaps the working class has gone up into the middle class haven't they really. And then I don't know, er but I think there've always been 'haves' and 'have nots' really.
>
> *D'you think of yourself as belonging to any particular class?*
>
> Well it's not the upper class. *[laughs]* I'll tell you that. I, well I don't know whether you'd put us working class really or I should imagine, I don't think we're middle class but we, I don't know, I don't know where we come in that really. *[laughs]*
>
> *No. D'you, would you think of yourself in those terms, you know terms of class? You know when you're describing yourself?*
>
> No, I don't think I would really but er you know. No.
>
> *No. What ways would you describe yourself, you know if you were thinking of ...*
>
> I'd just say ordinary. *[laughs]*
>
> *There's no other, there's nothing you'd use to describe yourself?*
>
> No, not really.

These three examples all indicate a particular style of talking about class. Clearly the idea of class means something to people, even in the last case where the replies are hesitant. Crucially, rather than evoking a sense of *belonging* to a collective group, it invokes the sense of *differentiation* from others. In all three cases people's sense of self identity is linked with a claim of 'ordinariness', or 'normality', which is seen as at odds with claims to pretensions towards exclusion and distinction.[72] We see here the desire for claims to 'naturalism' which Strathern (1991) sees as lying at the heart of modern Western identities (see also Anthias, 1998). In some respects, this profoundly undermines the salience of class. The way in which this desire for 'ordinariness' maps onto class identities is arbitrary. For some people it is linked to a definition of being working class, since this is regarded as the least 'snobbish' case, but in others, 'middle class' self-definitions are preferred. This suggests that Reay's (1997) and Skeggs's (1997) emphasis that 'working classness' is a stigmatised identity may overstate the case. Rather, these limited cases chimes in better with Devine's (1992) study which shows that even amongst manual car workers, the most common identity was that of the 'ordinary working people', which continues to offer some positive evaluations of working-class identification. However, this is not an important point, since there is little evidence that the respondents place much store on defining themselves in class terms: what matters to them is their emphasis on being 'ordinary'. In other ways, class continues to profoundly affect these self identities, since people seem to see class as threatening to 'pollute' ordinariness. 'Ordinariness' is also seen as a relational construct in which people draw contrasts with others who place themselves above them.

Whilst at one level, individuals seek to 'escape' class in ways which have superficial resonance with the arguments of Giddens and Beck, it seems also to be the case that class reappears as a reference category which makes people aware of the possibilities of not being ordinary. However, at this point I should note that not all respondents are so shy as these previous three in adopting a more personally involved sense of class, and I want to consider some of these cases in a little more detail. The first is of a male, 38 year old printing worker, perhaps the most class conscious of any person we interviewed. When asked whether relations between the shop-floor and managers were harmonious he responded,

> It is harmonious to the degree that we all agree that they're a set of wankers ... You're frightened of people. I don't know if it's indicative of like what's happening all over the country, but we're frightened of our management ...

---

[72] Skeggs (1997) emphasises the importance of discourses of 'respectability', which from the limited cases analysed so far do not appear to be so prominent in our research. However, as explained in footnote 11 above, different sampling strategies were adopted.

Is Britain becoming a classless society?

The middle class have been educated, yeah, they know which knife and fork to use ... yeah, that's what it is, it's natural to them. Do you use your soup spoon like this or like that? I'd have to remember and they would just do it automatically ...

Do you consider yourself working class or middle class?

Well, if I had a five-figure income and you had, you know, the car of your desire and shopped at Sainsbury's and Kendal's in Manchester, then I might consider myself middle class ...

This man had no difficulty in articulating a strong sense of class injustice and inequality, and in thinking in terms of class, both generally and personally. Interestingly, he was the only respondent reported here whose sense of class was related to employment based relationships. Strikingly, all his references to class are relational. Rather than emphasising that he is working class, he stresses that he is not middle class. Furthermore, the language of the 'natural' is directly used to compare the table manners of working and middle-class people. In this case, it would appear the respondent is aware that what is 'natural' to him, is not 'natural' to the educated middle classes, and it is this sense of the way in which he is thereby forced not to act naturally which is a major part of his indignation about class. The 'natural' is a battleground in which class identities are forged.

The same kind of issue is apparent from another case, this time someone who sees himself on the other side of the class divide. This respondent was a 45 year old self-employed landscape gardener who made great efforts to distinguish himself from the working class.

Do you think Britain is becoming a classless society?

No, I don't.

Why?

Classless. Because I think there's a lot of people like me that enjoy a certain class. You'll always have the poor, you'll always have the lower working class, middle class and upper class; I think I'm ... I like to think ... I *never* class myself as working class. That's awful isn't it! But I have high values, I have high goals - I set my goals high. I don't want to be in this situation in another year's time - I want to be wealthy for many different reasons. Whether I will be, I don't know, but I always used to say ... people used to say 'you set your sights too high Dave' and I'd say 'yeah, but there's one little philosophy that I live by; if I set my sights very, very high and only reach half way and you only set your sights there and you only reach half way - I'm an awful lot higher than you are'. So, you know, I'm always looking I suppose - I'm a dreamer. I'm definitely a dreamer.

Do you think of yourself as being ... you mentioned you don't think of yourself as working class; would you think of yourself as middle class or ...

I'd like to think of myself as middle class. I don't always think I have the money to be middle class; I certainly have the ideals and the dreams and I have a lot of class. I don't like common people, I don't like drunkenness, I don't like ... I don't like a lot of things ... oh, this is awful, it sounds terrible, that you see around you on a Saturday night when they're kicking people out of the pub; I can't stand bad language, can't stand women using bad language, can't stand swearing in the street, boozing - I just can't stand that kind of thing. Now whether that makes me middle ... I like nice things, I like buying antiques, I like buying ... I like a nice car, I like to eat well, I like nice things around me and my son says it's really strange when he goes into people's houses he says 'it's amazing what they don't have dad', I said 'yeah, I know what you mean' and I can only deduce ... 'cos there are some of these guys are on decent money and that their life is spent, football, in the pub and that's where the money goes because they don't have things around them that would sort of denote that they enjoy the home, you know. My home is important.

For this man, there was no difficulty in thinking about class in personal terms, and clearly his strivings about class were important to him. Clearly, they were also bound up with a sense of who you were not, a means of distinction from others. In this case, the idea of 'ordinariness' was not the key to self-identity. Instead the idea of 'niceness' is articulated, and although not used by name it is possible to see this in terms of the desire to be 'respectable' (Skeggs, 1997).

The evidence from our qualitative interviews is limited and it would be unwise to easily generalise from it. However, it gives us insights on class identification which helps explain the patterns found in surveys. Our evidence suggests that people are ambivalent about class, but for consistent reasons. They wish to pursue ordinary lives in which people are treated fairly and equally, as individuals who are treated on their own terms. The idea of class threatens this, and is therefore regarded with some suspicion as a means of explicit self-identification. However, since ideas of 'ordinariness' (or, less commonly, 'niceness', or 'respectability') can only be given substance by being contrasted with something else, discourses and idioms of class are smuggled back into people's thinking. It is, after all, members of 'other' classes who are not ordinary. As Marshall et al. (1988) suggest, this points in some respects to considerable consistency in people's outlooks. The survey evidence is entirely consistent with this basic structure, because it shows that people are aware of class whilst they also seek to deny it. I will develop these points more generally in the last section and think also about the extent to which we can talk about new forms of self identity emerging in recent times.

Individualisation, Class Identity and Social Change: Critical Issues

In this section I return to the broader theoretical issues with which I began this chapter. Firstly, let me briefly repeat a point which unites virtually all the writers I have discussed in this chapter. Class is clearly *not* an important sense of collective identity in contemporary Britain. In this respect class identities seem rather different from those of gender, race and ethnicity which appear to permit a greater sense of mutual identification (see the general discussion in Anthias, 1998). There is in fact very little dispute on this point. Defenders of class analysis such as Goldthorpe and Marshall (1992) are - perhaps despite appearances - in broad agreement over this point with those such as Beck and Giddens who proclaim the idea of individualisation. However, the point should be pressed a little further by emphasising that it is unhelpful to continue to counterpoise the idea of collective class cultures with those of individualised cultures as if these were antinomies. Part of the intuitive appeal of claims for individualisation comes from the way these claims are defined in terms of the alternative of the collective class actors. Once one dispenses with this assumption, however, notions of individualisation themselves begin to lose their coherence.

It is clear that we need to have a more fully developed theory of identity, which is able to examine the complex interplay between the 'social' and the 'individual'. The evidence I have discussed in the previous section indicates how identities can be seen as relational constructs, in which individuals develop a sense of their own selves by comparing themselves with 'meaningful' others. Bourdieu offers one valuable source for this argument,[73] but the evidence in the second section suggests the need to modify Bourdieu's emphasis on the social legitimacy of cultural capital. One of the most frequent criticisms of Bourdieu's work is that he finds it difficult to come to terms with working class or popular culture (e.g. Jenkins, 1991). At times Bourdieu patronisingly seems to see working class and popular culture as close to 'nature'. This is the way it may look from within the

---

[73] Though there are numerous others which might be drawn upon to similar effect, for instance symbolic interactionism or network theory (see White, 1992).

Kantian aesthetic that Bourdieu aims to critique, but it is also possible to invert such meanings, and to criticise the deployment of cultural capital as 'unnatural' and elitist. As I showed in Section 2, a common theme in people's perspectives on class is their desire to be 'ordinary' and not to appear to be 'above' others. This marks something of a different emphasis from Bourdieu's emphasis on the struggles for cultural distinction. Of course this is largely a difference in focus. Although it is true that Bourdieu's emphasis has been on the dominant cultures and their denigration of popular aesthetics, there are no reasons in general why his approach cannot be reversed to explore how 'working-class' symbols of individualisation are related also to their relationships to the middle class.

I now want to say a few words about how the relevance of my argument for considering the role of trade unions in contemporary conditions. It may appear that if my arguments are correct, this has gloomy implications for trade unions, but in fact this need not be the case. The starting point, however, should be to emphasise the weak appeal of collective class identities (see also Marshall et al., 1988). Insofar as these have ever been the bedrock for union support (and the historical evidence suggests that this has by no means been the case), they no longer perform such a role today (Savage, 1999). Attempts to appeal to class unity or class loyalty are likely to have little resonance except amongst a few groups of atypical workers (for instance those still living in 'occupational communities').

However, if we start from a different premise, that individualistic cultures need not be inimical to class cultures, then it is possible that the implications for trade unionism are somewhat different. Notions of 'ordinariness' do encode certain types of class awareness. It is possible to see how the need to 'perform' individual identity can be related to class aware frameworks which celebrates the advantages in being free from power networks and hierarchical structures (see Savage, 1998). Indeed, the whole idea of working-class instrumentalism, which entered the British sociological canon in the 1960s following Goldthorpe and Lockwood's (1968, 1969) affluent worker studies might be seen in these terms. Goldthorpe and Lockwood's 'discovery' of the instrumental affluent worker in the 1960s showed how the workers often saw themselves as having more freedom and autonomy than did managers. Research I carried out in the early 1990s as part of a project examining the career paths of men and women in banking, nursing and local government (Halford et al., 1997) indicated also how individualised and class-aware sentiments might interrelate. One privatised, individualised, bank clerk explained to me why he identified with the staff rather than with management:

Q: Do you identify with staff or management?

I would personally identify with the staff, I mean I have never wanted to go beyond where I am now.

Q: Why is that?

It has never appealed to me, because of the way I look at work it is only a means to an end to me. It has always seemed, for many years, it has always seemed to me that if you aspire to the management side of it you have to devote more of your time and personality to the bank, which I am not prepared to do.

In this example, this man's individualistic and instrumental orientation was simultaneously class-aware. The logic of his view was that as a clerk he could be an 'individual', unlike the manager who had to sell his soul to the bank. This kind of interpretative step, in which clerical workers critically react against management might even be seen as being more important historically as a source sustaining labour politics as the much vaunted notions of collective manual cultures. For instance, it can be traced through in Huw Beynon's (1975) classic study of shop stewards in Ford's Halewood plant in the 1960s. Beynon shows how the militant, class conscious shop stewards were not some kind of throwback to the kind of primordial collective working-class communities of the 1950s celebrated by Hoggart and Williams but were archetypally modern men, keen on fashion, music and pleasure. Their celebration of individuality was again highly class conscious:

The shop stewards weren't interested in promotion, in becoming 'dedicated Ford men'. For them to take the white coat at Halewood would be to join the other side: 'I couldn't do that. Leave the lads? Not in this firm anyway. They're a crowd of gangsters here' (Beynon, 1975).

The celebration of individual identity can, in some cases, be seen as simultaneously drawing upon class identities, not as marking a break from it. This insight can allow us to rethink the dynamics of working-class collective action in ways which depend neither on ideas of cultural collectivism or of disembodied individualism (as in resource mobilisation perspectives, for instance). We can instead draw on a more nuanced perspective on historical shifts in class awareness and identity than that offered by the rather simplistic claims about the shift from collective to individual cultures (see the critical discussion in Marshall et al., 1988). It is by no means clear that the somewhat halting and ambivalent attitudes to class revealed both by survey evidence and by qualitative research mark a major break from older patterns of class awareness (this is an issue discussed further by Savage,

2000). Possibly there is evidence of a slight tendency for the salience of class to decline (see Young, 1992), but this is not particularly marked.

The union movement can take heart, then, from historically having been an important vehicle for the defence and advancement of individualised notions, such as dignity, self-respect, individual autonomy, and so forth. The task facing unions today is to find a way of appealing to these individualised notions in rather different conditions. Today, managerial cultures have taken up individualised idioms (by devices such as performance related pay, etc.), with the result that it is more difficult for unions to define themselves as bastions of individual values. However, it is clear that the labour movement has retained its power more effectively in countries such as Germany where it has been able to emphasise that individual health and prosperity is related to the employees need to keep distance from their employing organisation - in the form of ensuring working hours are limited. If unions see their role as defending the ordinary worker, and the individuals need for autonomy, then it may have the potential to advance a popular and attractive sentiment against the 'greedy' organisation always concerned to take up more of an employees time and effort. I have shown how individualised cultures do not create 'individualised' actors, but rather appear to be consistent with the existence of a 'plebeian' culture, which still takes its cues by distinguishing itself from elites. In this way, unions may be able to play on some of the individualised cultures delineated by Beck and Giddens and may be able to inflect them with modes of class identity (as discussed in this chapter) that could prove to be a critical resource in future years. It is possible to conclude this chapter by suggesting that while class does not unite, it certainly continues to divide, and that such divisions, if harboured effectively, continue to give cultural resources for diverse forms of anti-elitist social movements.

4 Social Segregation in a Working-class Community: Economic and Social Change in the South Wales Coalfield

DAVID ADAMSON

Introduction

The South Wales coalfield, situated in the British Celtic fringe, is the most populous region of the principality of Wales. The region was the seat of the industrial revolution in Wales and contributed significantly to the nineteenth century development of Britain as an industrial power (Williams, 1985). The coalfield is divided by steep-sided valleys[74] running from north to south which provided the physical conditions for the emergence of highly cohesive and solidaristic working-class communities by the end of the nineteenth century. The periodic struggles between labour and capital played out in the coalfield have entered popular culture through film and literature and the image of the coal-smudged, cloth-capped Welsh miner has become a universal icon of working-class radicalism. As with all such representations there is a strong foundation for this imagery and historically this region contributed significantly to the development of the British socialist tradition and to the general labour politics of the United Kingdom. From the early nineteenth century onwards a radical tradition presented itself as the most powerful force in the politics of the region. Labour historians trace the emergence of that political tradition in the rural economy

---

[74] The political and cultural configuration which emerged in these valleys has dominated the Anglo-Welsh culture of the region to the extent that the whole coalfield is referred to as 'the valleys'. This term has become a shorthand for the distinctive social and political praxis of the region as well as denoting physical location.

and follow its emigration, with rural labourers, to the new centres of iron and coal production which developed as the century progressed.[75]

Trade unionism was an early and central feature of this political tradition, with embryonic organisations emerging from the 1830s onwards. Followers of Robert Owen had considerable success in the region and by the 1880s the increasing radicalism of the work force had prepared a fertile ground for the emergence of the Miners Federation, a trade union of great political significance throughout much of the current century. 'The Fed', as it was known by its members, became a militant force for change in the region, articulating by 1910 the radical syndicalist philosophy of the Miners Next Step (Jones, 1973). This radicalism eventually coalesced in the form of support for the British Labour Party which has remained consistently the political party of the region, even throughout the period of New Right hegemony in British politics. The South Wales region has continued to fuel a radical working-class politics expressed in trade unionism throughout the twentieth century culminating in the fierce resistance to the pit closure programme which triggered the year long Miners' Strike of 1984-85. However, the closure programme which followed that strike marked the final chapter in the long decline of the industrial base which had given rise to the organised industrial work force of the region. The last two decades have seen the virtual elimination of trades unions as agents in the politics and culture of the region.

Leaving aside the political reforms of the successive Conservative governments, the membership of trades unions has fallen directly as a consequence of the closure and downsizing of key industries. Britain has experienced a dramatic decline in its manufacturing industrial base which has seen trades union membership fall consistently since the early 1980s from a peak of 53 per cent of the work force in 1980 to 32 per cent in 1994 (Office for National Statistics, 1997). Disaggregation from UK statistics for trade union membership in Wales presents some difficulty as even the Wales Trades Union Council has no historical records. Current Welsh membership suggests that the fall has not been as dramatic, with 41 per cent membership in 1996, the highest of the UK regions. However, the trend continues to be downwards and recent trades union strategy in the region has centred on acceptance of single union, plant based recognition,

---

[75] From the beginning of the nineteenth century nascent working-class organisations were emerging. Amongst the earliest rural groups was the Rebecca movement which protested against toll gates. This radical protest tradition re-emerged in the growing industrial centres in the form of the Scotch Cattle nascent unionism, the Merthyr Rising of 1832, and the Chartist movement of the late 1830s. The South Wales region was at the forefront of the emerging organisation and political culture of the British working class (Morgan, 1995; Smith, 1980; Williams, 1985).

which have been negotiated with some of the key inward investors into the region in recent years. This has been seen by the major unions as preferable to non-unionised plants which are also now not uncommon in the region. Additionally, the developing retail and service sectors which are dominating the economic recovery of the region are predominantly non-unionised.

This chapter traces some of the underlying social and economic processes which characterise the postwar period generally and the last twenty years particularly. The chapter also considers the implications for the survival of a radical, collectivist politics, of the effective demise of its primary vehicle of expression in trades unions. The chapter suggests that the very structure of the working class itself has changed dramatically and that innovative and adaptive social organisations are emerging to replace and to an extent replicate the functions of trades unions in the communities of the South Wales coalfield. The conclusion drawn is that social class remains a key component of the self-identity of the region and that it contributes significantly to new strategies of collectivism and mutuality which are emerging in community based organisations. Whilst trade unions are not organisationally important in the emerging strategies of the working class today, the culture, traditions and values of traditional unionism are an important influence.

The South Wales Coalfield: Patterns of Socio-economic Change

The economic structure of the South Wales region has historically demonstrated the features of what Lash and Urry (1987) have characterised as an 'organised' capitalism. With industrial production centred on coal-mining and steel manufacture, both highly unionised and state managed, the region manifested clear patterns of a highly structured and directed economy. The range of social experience in communities intricately connected to a single place of employment was necessarily relatively homogeneous and the communities of the region have often been presented as a political monoculture, wedded to an almost automatic support of the Labour Party. However, the last twenty years have seen a change to a more 'disorganised' process of capital accumulation with the effective demise of coal production, the rationalisation of the steel industry and the drastic reduction in associated heavy manufacturing which has accompanied these changes. For Lash and Urry and other writers who identify similar process (Gorz, 1983; Offe, 1985) the disorganisation of capitalism entails a reduction in the significance and political role of trades unions and the demise of class based political action. The experience of South Wales in the last two decades appears to support such claims. Central to this process has been the changing nature of economic activity in the region which has created a more differentiated work force with clear implications for traditional patterns of class identity and political solidarity.

The economic changes which underlie this process have been well documented through these decades (Cooke and Rees, 1981; Edwards, 1985; Rutherford, 1991; Williams and Boyns, 1977). Consensus exists in identifying the primary features of the changes which have occurred. There has been a significant decline in the heavy manufacturing and extractive sector, a diversification into light manufacturing and electronics and a major growth of the financial and service sectors. Central to the first of these changes has been the demise of the coal industry. Employing 100,000 miners at nationalisation in 1947 the figure fell to 24,000 by the early 1980s (Rutherford, 1991). The 1984-85 Miners' Strike provided the political climate for a further programme of closures and the eventual privatisation of mining in Great Britain. In the wake of the strike 14 of 26 pits closed within two years and the remaining pits followed by 1992. The attempts at economic diversification, whilst having notable success in attracting inward investment to the region, are not credited with providing sufficient alternative employment (Lovering, 1997). Additionally, much of the new industrial development has focused on the coastal belt south of the coalfield which is outside of reasonable travel to work distances of the northern reaches of the mining valley's communities. There has also been a significant skills mismatch between personnel shed by the old industries and the skills required in the manufacturing and electronics sector which has emerged. Finally, the recruitment strategies and gender identification of the labour processes involved have created an increasingly female work force with little employment opportunity for men redundant from the old industrial base industries.

Of equal impact has been the rise of a significant retail and service sector in the region with major infrastructural investment in the coastal cities by both the state and private sector. Government has transferred key administrative offices to the region and there has been a significant private sector development of financial and retail services. As a consequence the coastal plain has seen an emerging affluence and a false climate of economic progress and development has been fostered by successive administrations in the Welsh Office. The claims for the success of the economic strategy for the region hide an increased polarisation (Morris and Wilkinson, 1995). Significant economic recovery in cities such as Cardiff and Newport is in contrast to continued economic decline in the valleys towns of the South Wales coalfield only twenty miles to the north. The consequence is that the ex-mining communities of the South Wales valleys have become characterised by sustained and excessive levels of unemployment which have remained stubbornly at about twice the British average rate throughout the 1980s and 1990s (Adamson, 1996).

Inevitably, these changes in the economic activity of the region have had consequences for its social, political and cultural character. Economic polarisation has had a disruptive effect on the traditionally homogenous lifestyles of valleys residents. In the early 1980s patterns of outward migration emerged, as those with qualifications and appropriate skills moved socially and physically to take advantage of the new employment opportunities (Rees and Rees, 1983). The unskilled and unqualified have remained in communities increasingly characterised by poverty, marginalisation and social exclusion. The consequences have been an increased differentiation in working-class communities between those who remain locked in traditional patterns of work and its culture, those who have transferred successfully to the new industries and those who have been effectively excluded for the contemporary labour market by their lack of skill and qualifications. I will examine this process in more detail in the next section of the chapter.

Difference and Social Segregation in Working-class Communities

Before addressing the implications of economic change for the class structure in Wales, it is first necessary to address briefly two issues that underpin the analysis offered. Firstly, it is impossible in the scope of this chapter to address the current debates about the saliency of class analysis within sociology generally (Goldthorpe and Marshall, 1992; Pahl, 1993). Whilst many sociologists continue to work comfortably with the concept of class there is a justifiable debate about the continuing relevance of both Marxist and Weberian class analysis and a growing conviction that gender, ethnicity and sexuality constitute more important determinants of both identity and social action. For post-modernist writers social structure is transitory and fluid with social restructuring evident as a constant process determined by a broad range of social and cultural phenomena (Holmwood, 1997). In this 'retreat from class' (Meiksins-Wood, 1986), class is seen neither as a useful means of understanding the social structure or of analysing the political processes of advanced societies.

The research underpinning this chapter points to a rather different conclusion as clear structures of disadvantage and social difference can be seen to relate directly to the labour market in the South Wales region, as elsewhere in the UK (Jones, 1997). Additionally, analysis of changes in the nature of that labour market have offered effective understanding, over a prolonged period of time, of social change in the region.[76] The saliency of class in structuring social identity in the region is also evident, although in complex interaction with both national and highly localised identities (Thompson et al., 1996).

For the purposes of this chapter I have assumed a 'strongly relational' class model (Gubbay, 1997). In this model Gubbay suggests that there are clear and strong patterns of influence by the economic structure on the constitution and structuration of social groups. Gubbay's model suggests that specific forms of industrial organisation and economic relationships lead to the formation and persistence of social classes with strongly allied social and political interests. The model seeks to recognise the strong causal link between economic and social organisation whilst avoiding the implicit economic reductionism of orthodox Marxism. It achieves this by recognising the mediation of that link by social and political processes located in the state and civil society. In this sense he echoes Wright's (1989) distinction between *class structure* as a macro-level outcome of the economic mode of production and *class formation* as the specific historical manifestation of class relations. These relations, whilst significantly structured by the underlying capitalist mode of production, are additionally mediated and conditioned by the cultural, social and political environment of the specific social formation. The Welsh social formation has moved over the last century from a direct and unmediated set of capitalist relations of production to a more mediated and differentiated formation resulting in an ideological and cultural fracturing of the working class. However, the primary influence of economic relations of capitalism remain powerful and Gubbay's 'strongly relational' model is apposite. The primary boundaries of the class structure remain unchanged whilst the specific cultural, social and political characteristics of the social formation have become more complex. The Welsh social formation remains characterised by a significant working-class presence which occupies a specific relationship to the 'overall flow of value within the generation, appropriation and allocation of surplus value' (Gubbay, 1997). However, a fracturing of that class along cultural, social and political fault lines is occurring.

Secondly, it is necessary to qualify the extent to which working-class communities can be presented as entirely culturally, politically and socially homogenous. Whilst we can sometimes usefully employ a working characterisation of such communities as having a virtual monocultural environ-

---

[76] There has been a self-conscious 'sociology of Wales' since the early 1970s in which sociologists working in the region have identified Wales as a social formation in its own right and worthy of discrete sociological investigation. Analysis of economic change has been a central feature of much of the work undertaken to date. The annually published journal *Contemporary Wales.* University of Wales Press reports much of that research.

ment, we also have to recognise the internal differentiation in working-class communities which has always existed. This is a prerequisite for the analysis of contemporary differentiation. Such communities have always been marked by social divisions deriving from gender, religion and political beliefs. Even the archetypal working-class communities of the Welsh coalfield produced support for the British Liberal and Conservative political parties. Furthermore, even the radicalism of the region was sectarian with clear antagonisms between communists, syndicalist and reform socialists. Additionally, important social divisions emerged around the various schisms in non-conformist religious denominations which were highly influential in the last century. Most fundamentally, social and status division emerged from the structure of the workplace itself with fine gradations of skill and authority in the place of work which were reflected in social hierarchies in the community.

However, relative to the wider society this differentiation was limited and the wage structures, patterns of housing, leisure activities, levels of education, marriage patterns and the experiences drawn from employment in a single industry represented a compressed range of social experience. The lifestyle and cultural activities of residents of the Welsh coalfield valleys were comparatively uniform and the cultural patterns associated with mining communities are remarkably similar (Gilbert, 1992) across all the British coalfields. Certainly, within the mining valleys of South-east Wales there emerged by the 1930s a distinct cultural practice and class identity.

In summary, the economic restructuring described above has had major consequences for the survival of that working-class identity in the region. Increased differentiation in working-class lifestyles has derived from diversified experience in the labour market. The changes impact on a wide range of cultural, and especially, consumption practices which are too detailed and varied to examine fully here. These issues have been examined in greater depth in other publications (Adamson, 1988; Adamson, 1991b; Adamson and Jones, 1996). Here I will be concerned to map the broad divisions that have emerged in the Welsh working class.

Toward a Tripartite Working Class

At the start of the twentieth century in Wales we could identify a working class which, despite the internal differentiation discussed earlier, was nevertheless characterised by a relatively uniform cultural and political experience. Today we recognise a more highly differentiated working class which is manifesting social disintegration and internal fracturing. This section will delineate those fractures and describe the key characteristics of the social fractions which are identified. These groupings are presented as ideal types in the Weberian sense in that they are described here in their pure theoretical form. In the social reality of the South-east Wales region the class structure is in a complex process of change and the three primary categories presented here do not have rigid or clear boundaries. Individuals move in and out of employment, they become reskilled and move between industrial sectors. Additionally, these fractions are largely determined in the social, cultural and political fields and do not relate directly to occupational structures, although heavily determined by them. For example, as the new working class has grown numerically its cultural influence has increased and many of its social consumption patterns are aspired to and mimicked by both the traditional and the marginalised working class. Empirical verification is consequently difficult and the argument is presented here as a theoretical explanation of changes which have some empirical basis in the changing sectoral structure of the Welsh economy, some observational basis in changing consumption patterns and some experiential basis from community based action research in the region. The class structure of the region is currently dynamic and fluid. The classification presented here attempts to recognise and categorise the differentiation in the Welsh working class which has been developing since the early 1980s.

The model presented is of three distinctive class fractions which collectively constitute the working class. It is not suggested here that any fraction itself constitutes a separate or new class. No change in the underlying mode of production has occurred and the class structure in the sense portrayed by Wright (1989) remains constant. Each fraction remains characteristically working class but experiences and manifests the culture, politics and consumption practices of that class position differently. That experience is determined by a complex mix of economic status, cultural values and political practice (Adamson, 1991b). However, the three fractions discussed continue to share an objectively identical relationship to capital and the creation of surplus value and continue to constitute a working class within the overall class structure. The differentiation is internal and the economic restructuring of the region has not created new social classes, rather it has created fracture lines in the solidarity and relative homogeneity of the Welsh working class.

The Traditional Working Class

The resilience of the cultural and social practices of mining communities is remarkable. Despite the virtual disappearance of mining and related activities in the region, the political practice and cultural activities associated with the mining industry survive relatively unscathed in ex-mining communities. In the Mid-Glamorgan county area,[77] 20,200 jobs (83.3 per cent) in the energy and water supply industries were lost between 1977 and 1989 (Welsh Office, 1990). This loss was almost entirely in the mining industry. Those men retired and redundant from coal production and related industries have retained the political culture of their past occupations. There still exists a fierce loyalty to the British Labour Party. Until 1999 the Labour Party maintained a hegemonic status in the region, both in the form of unchallenged support for election of members of Parliament, and majority control of all local authorities. Successive campaigns by Plaid Cymru, the Welsh Nationalist Party consistently failed to gain ground in this region until the surprise victory on nationalists in the 1999 elections to the key local authorities and the newly established Welsh Assembly. Whilst key cultural institutions of the heyday of coal production (the miner's institutes and welfare halls) have all suffered closure, working men's clubs remain a central feature of the social life of the community. However, many are now financially precarious and dependent on an increasingly ageing clientele. In the Regional Research Programme survey, over a third of respondents reported regular attendance at a working men's' club or equivalent organisation, but were largely older males (Adamson and Jones, 1996).

As well as this vestigial mining culture those redundant from the traditional manufacturing sector also contribute to the maintenance of the traditional working-class identity of the region. In this sector, Mid-Glamorgan job losses in the traditional heavy industries have been masked in part by some limited growth in light manufacturing which created 10,000 new jobs between 1984 and 1989. However, even with this growth the sector declined by 30 per cent (21,400 jobs) between 1977 and 1989. Labour losses in this sector have contributed significantly to the high long-term unemployment rates of the region which in Mid-Glamorgan have remained at nearly twice the UK level throughout the period 1980 to the present. The job losses in these two major industrial sectors in the Mid-Glamorgan region create a potential 27.3 per cent of the total 1989 work force which has left traditional working-class occupations. No study has tracked their destination but the continuing high unemployment rate, the significant rise of permanent sickness and disability rates and the high female participation rates in the new jobs which have emerged, show that a high proportion

---

[77] This local authority was abolished by the creation of Unitary Local Authorities in Wales in 1996. The location is retained here as it forms the basis for a 1993 empirical study which is not possible to replicate until the Census of 2001. The locality also contains the two Rhondda Valleys and the Cynon and Rhymney Valleys which exemplify the experience of the wider region.

have become permanently economically inactive. It is this section of the population that constitutes the most significant component of the traditional working class.

Central to the culture of this region is a highly developed sense of community and community association. In the 1995 survey, issues of community were central in the responses of the survey population to questions about identity and social change (Adamson and Jones, 1996). Residents reported very high levels of contact with neighbours and family members and relied on both for social and economic support. This level of communalism is a clear legacy of the collectivist politics of the area but also derives from the clear connection between the workplace and the place of residence. The traditional practice of a community growing around a pit led to a highly developed sense of local identity and pride in the community. Workmates were also neighbours and shared their leisure time with men from the same mining shifts. Local identity meshed with the workplace identity and in turn with the particular union lodge. Traditionally, the union also played a central role in social life through its welfare function and its social and recreational roles. This was never more clearly demonstrated than during times of industrial action when community defences were brought to bear in the resistance to the privations of a lengthy period on strike. In 1984-85 this manifested in a host of community strategies and a clear and active involvement of women from mining communities in the whole fabric of the industrial dispute.

In terms of the spatial organisation of working-class communities in the coalfield the traditional working class can be most clearly identified with the terraced housing of the mining villages, established from the 1850s onwards. Often built by co-operative organisations such as building societies and clubs (Fiske, 1996), costs were kept low by shared, continuous roof design, creating the familiar 'valleyscape' of long terraces following the steep contours of the ground. The history of self-building by the community has created a high level of owner-occupation and a fierce pride in the upkeep of external appearance, aided in recent years by state financed housing improvement programmes. However, this housing stock is now aged and the basic fabric of many homes is increasingly poor by modern standards.

In summary, the traditional working class consists of those workers and their families made redundant from the mining and heavy industrial sector of the economy in the past twenty years. They are located in the traditional terraced communities of the area and maintain political and cultural consumption practices which demonstrate a continuity with the past and the central role played by the workplace, its trade union and associated leisure and political practices.

The New Working Class

In earlier work (Adamson, 1988; Adamson, 1991b), I have described a process whereby new patterns of employment in the light manufacturing, service and retail sectors of the Welsh economy have created a section of the Welsh work force with a very different experience of the relations of production from those traditionally identified with the region. Historically, the mining industry has represented a very direct and unmediated relationship between labour and capital which sponsored a radical trade union culture. That culture remained largely unaffected by the nationalisation of the industry. In contrast, employees in the new industries and the service sector in South Wales have significantly different experience of the workplace in that many of the new employment opportunities fall on the mental side of a mental/manual division of labour. This division has long been seen as central to the structuration of classes in capitalist society (Lockwood, 1958; Poulantzas, 1975) both in Weberian/neo-Weberian models of occupational class (Goldthorpe et al., 1980) and in Marxist concerns with the determination of classes by the relations of production (Wright, 1985).

In the South Wales context, the rapid expansion of non-manual employment has created a more differentiated occupational structure with a significant increase in white-collar, supervisory and lower managerial employment. In Mid-Glamorgan the period 1977-89 saw an increase of 20 per cent (15,200 jobs) in the service sector. The nature of this employment is in sharp contrast to the traditional work which dominated the region. In working-class culture the difference between mental and manual labour is highly significant and is represented in numerous dichotomies which resonate in workplace culture. The difference creates social divisions based on work distinctions which include 'dirty/clean, quiet/noisy, dangerous/safe, salary/wages, or workers/staff' (Adamson, 1988). In British working-class culture anyone in white-collar or supervisory positions is perceived as 'management'. Crompton effectively encapsulates this cultural tendency in her quotation of the parody of the socialist Red Flag which employs the words 'The working class can kiss my arse; I've got the foreman's job at last' (Crompton, 1993, 61). Implicit in this quotation is the self-perception of employees in even low-paid, routinised clerical and supervisory work who regard themselves as following middle-class occupations. This leads to an experience of the social relations of production in the workplace which militates against traditional working-class values of trade union activism and which predisposes members of this 'new working class' to managerial ideologies. It is contended here that the experience of the workplace by the new working class develops a distance from traditional working-class values, even when the individuals concerned have a working-class background. However, the new working class does not constitute a new class category, nor do they join the ranks of the middle classes. The majority of such new jobs are in routine clerical and low-grade office work. Much of the increase is accounted for by the transfer of key government departments to the region and the increasing range of services offered by the financial sector of banks, building societies and insurance companies, several of which have relocated their national headquarters in the region. Many of these jobs remain relatively low paid and are lacking in professional structures of advancement and promotion. Entry qualifications are low and the field is not professionalised in ways associated with middle-class categories of employment. Additionally, these new jobs do not create a new location in the division of labour in relation to the accumulation and control of capital. The economic interests of the new working class are inseparable from those of the traditional working class.

Therefore, whilst I do not believe that the new working class constitutes a new class, its workplace experience mediates its relation to capital differently, and creates an ideological context in which the relationship is obscured in ways which militate against its participation in the political action and trade union activity of the traditional working class. Rather than constituting a new class it does form the basis for a significant fracturing of the working class in terms of its ideology, class practices and class identity.

Furthermore, this class fraction develops new consumption practices to distinguish itself from the traditional working class (Bourdieu, 1984). Such practices focus especially on housing and leisure consumption (Adamson, 1991b) as the new working class develops a distinct social identity and cultural practice. In reality, this cultural practice remains a complex hybrid of the traditional working-class base from which the individual members of the class fraction have emerged and the relative affluence of their new social standing. The consumption practices of the new working class are fuelled by the opening up of credit opportunities and the retail revolution that has simultaneously occurred. Because of its stable employment, the new working class is better placed to secure financial credit even though wages are similar to traditional working-class occupational categories in the region. In terms of the spatial location of this class fraction it is increasingly found in new housing estates created by the national commercial building companies. Built in non-traditional materials and non-regional designs, the housing emulates the affluence of the South-east of England and offers a ready opportunity for the new working class to mark itself from its traditional counterpart, resident in the terraced valley floor.

In its workplace experience and cultural practice the new working class becomes a distinct and separate class fraction. Its political values are also changed in the process. Attitudes to trade union membership and trade union activism become complex. Many members of the new working class have been socialised in a strong culture of trade unionism and retain trade union membership as a consequence. However, the membership is habitual rather than politically motivated and levels of activism and militancy are low. In many ways the politics of this social class are contradictory and vacillate between the ideologies which pull them towards their origins in the working class on the one hand, and their contemporary location in the new working class on the other (Adamson, 1988). This has manifested in electoral politics in support of the Nationalist Party, Plaid Cymru and in a temporary occupation of the coastal constituencies by conservative members of Parliament in the 1980s. The 1997 Labour landslide has reversed that situation but it has demonstrated the potential fluidity of political support in constituencies with a clear presence of the new working class.

The Marginalised Working Class

The chapter has until now reported work completed in the early 1990s which investigated the political and social impact of the development of a more diversified economy. The publication of 1991 Census data offered an opportunity to provide some empirical verification of these largely theoretical arguments and in 1993 the Regional Research Programme, based at the University of Glamorgan, began an exercise to map some of the social changes which had occurred. Very early in that project the central feature of change that emerged was the significant growth of a section of the population characterised by poverty rather than the relative affluence of the new working class. All the key poverty indicators demonstrated significant clustering in the ex-mining valleys and the first publications employing 1991 data revealed a clear polarisation between communities in the South Wales valleys and those on the coastal belt (Morris and Wilkinson, 1995). The Regional Research Programme project also noted clear polarisation within valleys communities, with local authority (social) housing estates in themselves accounting for much of the apparent poverty at ward level. Close analysis of Enumeration District data revealed pockets of exceptionally high levels of unemployment and benefit dependency with associated high levels of single parenthood.

Visits to the locations revealed in this analysis also pointed to physical and environmental decline, exacerbated by the collapse in public services which was being experienced as a result of central government underfunding of local government. Housing estates were deteriorating physically and public facilities such as schools and hospitals were in acute decline and showing signs of physical disrepair. At the same time as high unemployment became the norm for such communities, the social welfare system was subject to reform and there was a decline in the real value of benefits along with withdrawal of support for key sections of the population. Crucially, 16-18 year olds were being denied benefits unless in attendance on government training schemes. For many there were no places on such schemes or the quality of training and level of remuneration offered were too low to attract participation. The consequence has been the emergence of a population of 'status zero' youth (Istance et al., 1994) with effectively no income.[78]

The complex and multidimensional nature of poverty in such communities led to an analysis in terms of social exclusion, in an attempt to capture the subjective experience of poverty in addition to its objective measurement by traditional indicators. This approach moves the analysis away from empirical measurement of poverty to the consideration of social relationships between sections of the community. Consequently, quantification of the socially excluded is difficult. Standardised poverty indicators applied in South-east Wales, including the Department of the Environment Index, Breadline Britain and the European Threshold of Decency show that between 20 and 25 per cent of the population of the region can be defined as poor.

The term social exclusion is enjoying greater currency in European debates on poverty and British sociologists are gradually overcoming objections to the term (Chamberlayne, 1997). With its origins in French social policy debates it has become the dominant framework in which the European Union both analyses poverty and seeks to structure its anti-poverty strategies. The concept shifts the focus away from analyses of an absence of resources associated with a conventional poverty based approach and begins to address instead the relations that the poor have with society as a whole.

> The notion of poverty is primarily focused on *distribution* issues: the lack of resources at the disposal of the individual or household. In contrast, notions such as social exclusion focus primarily on *relational* issues: in other words inadequate social participation, lack of social integration and lack of power (Room, 1995, 105; my emphasis in italics).

Room's analysis suggests that the contemporary nature of poverty is significantly a feature of practices of social exclusion which overlay the material disadvantage experienced by the poor. Silver (1994) identifies a pattern of exclusion from 'permanent employment; earnings; property,

---

[78] The term 'status zero' was coined to describe those young people who were not in school, in receipt of benefits or participating in government training programmes.

credit, or land; housing; the minimal consumption level; education, skills and cultural capital; the benefits provided by the welfare state; citizenship and equality before the law, ...' (p. 541). These and the other factors she identifies correspond closely to the pattern of social exclusion evident in the marginalised communities of South Wales.

The research by the Regional Research Programme suggests four fields of exclusion exist.

Material

This refers to an individual's or family's economic status and includes factors such as housing tenure, work status, benefit dependency, educational qualification, car ownership and ownership of consumer durables. Here unemployment or benefit dependency are the primary indicators of exclusion. This field closely coincides with conventional analyses of poverty and the use of standardised poverty indicators provide well-tried methods of initial identification of social exclusion.

Environmental

This field refers to the quality of the physical environment and includes housing quality, housing density, housing cost as proportion of income, transport links, location and its proximity to key services including education and health facilities. Many estates in the valleys demonstrate acute environmental decline as poorly conceived housing and estate design become exacerbated by the collapse of repair and maintenance programmes in the 1980s.

Social

This field refers to an individual's overall status set, including marital and parental status, age, disability and incapacity. It also includes analysis of family and neighbourhood relationships such as the extent of contact with siblings and parents, neighbours and communal informal support networks. Such factors determine considerably the individual and, ultimately, the communal ability to resist and adapt to negative socio-economic change and the resulting patterns of social exclusion. Where high levels of community support exist social exclusion does not necessarily follow from poverty.

Relational

This refers to the standing of the individual, family and community in relations with external agents. Those defined as 'problem' in some way will experience relations characterised by 'labelling' and 'self-fulfilling' prophecy. Key indicators will include referral to police, education and health authorities and registration on 'at risk' or special need registers. At the communal level localities with high prosecution/victimisation rates, social work caseloads and health problems will be defined by professionals as risk areas for all residents.

Communities which feature these four fields of social exclusion are also often physically separated from the wider community by their location on hilltop plateaux between the valleys. The shortage of land space in the 1960s and 1970s forced new house building on to this high ground, legitimised by a 'Garden Village' ideology which saw this as new, quality housing away from the grime and industrial environment of the valley floor. The intervening years have instead demonstrated rapid decay of the housing stock in the face of severe climatic conditions, coupled with extensive problems with damp walls and expensive-to-fuel heating systems. Few estates were provided with social or retail facilities and the lack of adequate public transport has rendered such locations socially isolated. Consequently, by the late 1970s, housing on these estates became difficult to let and the locations were characterised by transitory populations 'serving time' on waiting lists for better accommodation elsewhere. The resulting social decline of the estates and high incidence of crime and drug related activities has led to these estates becoming local 'folk demons', perceived as 'dangerous places' (Campbell, 1995). Reinforced by negative media coverage, key estates in the South Wales valleys have become permanently associated with high levels of family breakdown, youth disaffection, and car and drug related crime.

The popular culture of these communities in many ways echoes a commonsensical expression of the 'underclass' model of the new poor (Murray, 1989). The populations of the estates are seen as unemployed from choice, with residents preferring a lifestyle fuelled by criminal activity and drug abuse. Attitudes to single parenthood and the negative perceptions of single mothers are fuelled by wider national discourses which have placed many of the problems of working-class communities at the door of 'families without fathers' (Dennis and Erdos, 1992). Unsurprisingly, communities characterised by high levels of male unemployment and single parenthood have become stigmatised by the traditional working-class community which derives its social identity primarily from highly gendered roles associated with working men supported by women locked in a highly traditional role of mother/housewife. The stigma and prejudice which results operates both informally in the way such estates are blamed for many of the problems of the valleys and more formally in a kind of 'postcode prejudice' operated by utility companies, telephone companies and, most importantly, prospective employers. It is the perception of many residents of such estates that their dealings with the wider world are almost entirely conditioned by the notoriety of their place of residence.

Survey evidence from 1995 (Adamson and Jones, 1996) provides a useful counterargument to the recognition of an 'underclass' in the region. Residents of highly excluded estates demonstrated similar propensities to move or retrain to find work. In more general terms of contacts with neighbourhood and kinship networks, there was no discernible evidence of difference. However, residents were aware of the stigma they suffered in the eyes of the wider community and generally expressed the view that a tiny minority of the population of the estate earned an undeserved reputation for the majority of residents. The existence of an active informal economy and a constant high response rate for the limited employment opportunities which emerge, also suggest a continuing commitment to the work ethic. Rather than discovering an underclass the survey identified a population, which in times of full employment, would have moved seamlessly from school to work. In this sense, populations of even the most marginalised estates constitute 'imminent labour' which would rapidly enter the labour market should significant opportunity present itself.[79]

The Regional Research Programme study concluded that an underclass did not exist in terms of either the 'conservative' or 'radical' usage of the term (Robinson and Gregson, 1992). Rather it concluded that a 'marginalised working class' had been brought into existence by significant labour market restructuring (Adamson, 1995; 1996). In that sense the marginalised poor of the region remain a fraction of the working class. They have not abandoned traditional commitment to the work ethic, nor deliberately chosen a deviant lifestyle. Rather, their values still predominantly reflect the values of the working class. However, realism in the face of acute economic and social decline has created a climate where low self-esteem, collapsed aspirations and social stigma have created a major social division between the poor and the remainder of the working class in the region. Rather than identify an underclass, the Regional Research Programme has identified practices of social exclusion by the wider

---

[79] Evidence from Scotland suggests that young people in particular enter the labour market rapidly when opportunity occurs (Payne and Payne, 1994). Similar conclusions are drawn by Gallie in his analysis of ESRC Social Change and Economic Life data (Gallie, 1994) when he fails to identify changing or different social values in the long-term unemployed.

society. The trigger for marginalisation of communities was the exclusion of poorly qualified and unskilled populations from a redefined and physically relocated economic activity, not the adoption of those populations of deviant and 'underclass lifestyles'. Members of the 'marginalised working class' are capable of rapid re-integration into the labour market should economic activity revive in the locality.

Fragmentation in Working-class Communities

The clear consequence of the process of social and economic change identified above is the movement, in a relatively short time scale, from a highly solidaristic and politically organised working class to a fractured and fragmented working class. The three class fractions identified in the analysis presented here; the traditional, new and marginalised working class, remain a single economic class defined by relations of production and their particular relation to the 'overall flow of value within the generation, appropriation and allocation of surplus value' (Gubbay, 1997) original emphasis). However, if they share an objective, common class interest, their social and cultural practice does not recognise it. Distinctive consumption practices and associated lifestyle and values render the three fractions of the working-class distinct. Most marked is the separation of the marginalised working class from both the traditional and new working class. The stigma and isolation it experiences prevents any sense of solidarity or community between this fraction of the working class and the other two, which retain a respectability and legitimacy both with each other and the wider society.

This fault line is of key significance in that it opens sections of the working class to neoliberal and right-wing explanations of poverty and promotes the adoption of punitive and discriminatory beliefs about welfare dependency and the poor generally. In these explanations the poor are blamed for their condition of poverty. Poverty is seen as an individual failing, promoted by a dependency culture which looks to the state first for economic security. The unemployed are caricatured as lazy and unwilling to work. They are portrayed as enjoying a parasitic relationship with the employed, creating a tax burden that punishes the hard-working majority. Such explanations of poverty achieved an official orthodoxy during the years of Conservative government in Britain and the traditional working class and new working-class sectors readily accepted such explanations of the rise of the new poverty. This constituted a significant weakening of working-class culture and traditional political practice in regions such as

South-east Wales as the marginal working class were effectively shut out of the politics of the region.

In many ways the marginal working class has been completely forsaken to its own fate by all the traditional working-class political agents and institutions, including the trade unions. Ironically it is within the marginalised communities of the socially excluded that we are beginning to see some challenge to this situation with the emergence of innovative, collectivist strategies, centred on a community based culture of economic and cultural survivalism.

Community Development, Mutuality and Solidarity in Marginalised Communities

In the 1995 survey described above it was concluded that 'a sense of community is an embedded aspect of valleys culture and identity' (Adamson and Jones, 1996, 9). It is therefore unsurprising that the clearest response to the deprivation and exclusion of the marginalised working class is originating from the marginal communities themselves. The political parties, local government and the Welsh Office were virtually silent on the issues of poverty and exclusion (Adamson, 1996) until the election of a Labour government in 1997. In that policy vacuum there emerged a growing number of community based initiatives which seek to address directly the problems of life in deprived areas. This growth of community development strategies has also been dependent on changes in the funding environment, which have made available significant funding opportunities. This has partly resulted from growing international evidence of success for community development schemes, especially in rural communities (Cinnéide and Grimes, 1992; Twelvetrees, 1996). Furthermore, the European Union appears to have shifted significantly towards an acceptance of the viability of community development strategies and such approaches figure significantly in EU funding strategies (Commission, 1996). Finally, increased availability of funding for community groups from sources as diverse as the Welsh Office and the National Lottery has created a solid financial base for the growth in numbers of community development groups.

The pattern of this growth is in itself interesting in that it demonstrates considerable diversity in the origins of groups. Often arising from single-issue campaigns which upon resolution take on additional community defined tasks, the approaches reflect a considerable diversity in the form of the communities themselves and the specific problems they encounter. For some it has been a spate of drug related deaths which has spurred action, whilst for others it is coming together to write a social and oral history of the community. Regardless of the original motivation there is a common pattern in which, following initial success, confidence and capacity builds towards grant application, receipt of funding and subsequent employment of 'professional' community development workers. Despite the diversity, I have made a preliminary attempt to categorise the strategies which are emerging (Adamson, 1997). Three broad approaches can be identified.

Resource Development Approach

This approach seeks to revive community processes by providing the facilities for social and leisure activities. The decline of community is seen as the consequence of the decline of dense community relations and community association. By providing the physical space for such activities to occur, the community can be recreated. Such programmes frequently centre on the creation of a key resource such as a community or leisure centre. One of the key features of the marginal social housing estates has been a lack of social and leisure facilities. Frequently devoid of any form of public space, meeting facilities, public houses, religious premises, shops or surgeries, there is literally no physical location for public and communal interaction. High density housing with no private gardens exacerbates an individual isolation which corresponds with the ways in which the community is itself isolated form the wider society. Provision of a specific social facility is frequently the starting point for broader strategies of community development.

Community Enterprise Approach

The community enterprise model seeks regeneration of community through the creation of employment opportunities. Less emphasis is placed on socio-cultural factors and the primary strategy is one of economic development through infrastructural strategies, small business development and associated attempts to train and reskill the unemployed work force. The approach rests on ideas associated with the full employment of the 1960s when these communities were high income communities with a relative degree of affluence and associated consumer based lifestyles. The objective is to create employment opportunities by raising individual and collective capacity to recreate economic opportunity. The model is based on ideas of social entrepreneurship and identifies risk-taking as the primary source of increased wealth creation in communities which have lost the capacity to be self-organising and self-directing. This is potentially more of an individualistic philosophy and seeks to regenerate communities through the efforts of key individuals operating in conditions made more favourable by the process of community development. The approach advocates not-for-profit activities that support community based objectives, but tends to be weighted more towards a 'business' model of organisation.

Holistic Community Development Approach

Projects working from this ethos generally have a strong emphasis on partnership and multi-agency approaches. This approach to community regeneration attempts to establish a process of empowerment at the individual and community level. Concerned with social, economic, environmental and cultural impact such projects stress the need for sustainability and independence from short-term funding initiatives. The holistic community development strategy also identifies a long-term process where unemployment will be a key feature of community life for the foreseeable future and seeks to build activities which enhance individual and community experience despite this inevitability. At the same time it seeks to build employment opportunities through community enterprise and small business development. Major emphasis is placed on the building of social capital and support networks. The strategies adopted are difficult to evaluate in conventional terms which have tended to emphasise job creation as the major tangible outcome from past models of urban regeneration funding. Inevitably the number of jobs created at current levels of funding are small and judged by orthodox criteria such schemes compare badly to conventional economic development strategies. In the South Wales context those advocating this approach point to the success of Tower Colliery which has recently completed in profit its first year of trading as a worker co-operative. The colliery defines itself clearly as a 'community enterprise' and plays an active economic, social and cultural role in the community of the Cynon Valley, last year spending £50,000 on supporting community based organisations.

This latter approach has become represented in a growing ideology of 'transformation from within' which informs the activities of community groups in the area. They have pessimistically, but perhaps realistically, concluded that no direct help with their problems will come from outside, but that responsibility for change rests with those who live there. This 'grassroots' organising is emerging in communities marked in the early 1980s by a deep political apathy and a moribund and conservative organisation of labour. The Labour Party itself has become the party of a localised municipal establishment with little vision and even less policy for the alleviation of poverty. The community development movement has grown outside of that and other conventional political structures, bringing into political and community activity groups not previously politically organised. Women have played a key part in these developments and their significant participation in the 1984-85 Miners' Strike provided clear role models and practical experience for the initiatives which have emerged in the communities of the region.

Drawing funding from diverse sources which include the European Union and the National Lottery Fund community development groups are providing an increasing range of training, social care, leisure and recreational service, entirely outside of the structures and control of both the local and central state. The Welsh Office and Local Government have only an indirect involvement as gatekeepers to some funding sources, whilst some groups have established considerable funding portfolios, frequently in excess of £1m and drawn almost entirely from European, charity and Lottery Fund Sources. The voluntary sector has played a key role in community development initiatives with basic skills training, capacity raising initiatives and support services. As yet the political significance of these major developments is not clear but crucially, a key arena of social policy provision is emerging outside of the formal state structures which have dominated for most of this century. Early indications are that local authorities find the situation highly challenging and are beginning to target funding to their own community based initiatives. Local authority members also see community activists as challenging their local hegemony and friction between community development teams and local councillors is not uncommon. More commonly the attitude of local Labour Party councillors is one of indifference.

Discussion

The chapter has described a process of fragmentation of a traditionally solidary working-class region, characterised historically by a collectivist and highly organised labour movement. Three distinct class fractions have emerged in the form of the traditional, the new and the marginalised working class. Relations between these fractions of the working class are at best limited and at their worst reflect a growing stigmatisation and social exclusion of the marginalised working class. Traditional working-class organisations have little relevance to, or resonance with the lived experience of any of the three social classes identified, other than a residual attachment of members of the traditional working class to the values of trade unionism and labourism. The majority of ward Labour Party groups are populated by a dwindling and ageing population of active members and trade unionism is increasingly irrelevant in communities of high unemployment. The Labour Party enjoys significant electoral support, but no longer directly as a result of a grounded workplace culture. It derives largely from the place of Labour Party loyalty at the centre of the Anglo-Welsh political culture of the region. That support is in effect a cultural legacy and no longer owes its existence to an informed and politically committed working class deriving its political praxis from the lived experience of the workplace.

Social innovation in the form of community development initiatives is emerging from within the economically and socially distressed communities of the marginalised working class. Completely outside of the traditional social and political organisations of the region, community development groups are demonstrating a 'grass roots' activity that attempts to promote social and economic regeneration. The objectives of community development organisations are not overtly political in orientation but their consequences have a deep political significance. The breadth and scale of the movement is considerable (Community Enterprise Wales, 1995) and few communities in the region can be found without some level of community activism.[80] This situation is reminiscent of the level of mutuality and self-organisation evident towards the end of the last century. Then building clubs and societies, miners' welfare halls and institutes and health insurance schemes were forming across the coalfield of South Wales to provide for the needs of the working-class community. As the twentieth century progressed, more and more of those functions were taken from the realm of community provision and became the domain of the welfare state. In the late twentieth century those same communities have witnessed the partial withdrawal of the welfare state and have rediscovered mutuality and community provision. In this the community development initiatives link with the political culture of the past.

The central question arising from the circumstances described in this chapter is whether class remains a source of political unity and cultural identity in the working-class communities of the South Wales coalfield. In many ways the answer is not yet clear, in that the social and cultural changes arising from the economic restructuring of the region have not yet fully matured. The processes identified here are very much in their infancy and the reworking of the political culture of the region is by no means complete. However, it is clear that the community activism which is growing in the region retains a direct and transparent connection to the class derived, traditional political culture of the region. The response to severe economic decline has been framed entirely in a collectivist ethos. Community development initiatives based on the 'holistic' model descri-

---

[80] A baseline study by Community Enterprise Wales (1995) claimed that 500 groups existed in 1995. This is likely to have increased considerably in the intervening period.

bed earlier are the clearest example of an approach to economic renewal founded on an inclusive and solidarity definition of the community. Even the more individualistic 'community enterprise' approach is founded on the objective of improving the collective good in communities characterised by distress and economic hardship.

Furthermore, the emphasis on community shares many features with the syndicalism of the region in the opening years of the century, which opposed the nationalisation route for the coal industry and favoured 'localism' in which the place of work was the heart of the community. Community development initiatives are attempting to combine economic renewal with 'welfare' provision in ways reminiscent of the relationship between union lodge and wider community. The flagship of the current community initiatives is Tower Colliery at Hirwaun on the northern edge of the coalfield. Tower survived the closure programme by a worker buy-out, supported and funded by the whole South Wales community. Employing over 300 miners with conditions and wages better than found in the privatised mining industry, Tower is being seen as an inspiration for the many community initiatives which are trying to build employment opportunities in the heart of the South Wales valleys communities. It is little surprise that the Tower team cite the influence of the National Union of Mineworkers' education programme and their consequent familiarity with the writings of leading syndicalists as one of their primary inspirations in the buy out process.[81] The buy-out is seen as a return to localism after the failure of coal nationalisation.

Patterns of participation within community development groups are also similar to those of conventional labour organisations. Just as activists lead the labour and union movement, community activists play a central role in community development initiatives. Drawing implicit, and at times active support from the community, it is nevertheless the activists who identify need, marshal resources and provide the labour power for the programmes. The situation is not unlike that of a trade union where the majority of members remain passive until called on at times of dispute, while the day-to-day affairs of the organisation are administered by a dedicated minority. Prime movers can be identified in most community programmes, providing inspiration and energy for a wider body of volunteers. Interestingly, the current terminology of the Welsh Office and more orthodox development agencies labels them 'community entrepreneurs'. However, they are in

---

[81] The link with the philosophy of the Tower buy-out team and the writings of the Miners' Next Step are clearly evident in the transcript of an interview with Mr Philip White, member of the team and now Personnel Manager of Tower Colliery. The interview took place at Tower Colliery on May 15th, 1997. The interviewers were the author and professor M. Majumdar of the University of Glamorgan.

many ways the 'organic intellectuals' of an innovative political praxis emerging in depressed communities.

Class, Trades Unions and Contemporary Collectivism

Whilst the above points indicate a very direct connection between the community development sector and traditional models of working-class practice, the emergence of 'community' as the key organising principle presents the possibility of organisations and practices emerging which are not necessarily classed based. The role of the conventional organisations and structures of the working-class movement are not currently evident in the community regeneration strategies of the area. Labour Party dominated local authorities have been slow to respond to the community development movement and many Labour Party councillors and officials regard such groups as a challenge to their traditional power base. Consequently, many community based initiatives have received a hostile reception from the local Labour Party, despite a growing community rhetoric at the national level.

The trade unions are also noticeable only by their absence. In this situation trade unions have become almost obsolete, demonstrating no linkage to the lives of the marginalised working class. The Wales TUC has been consistently blind to the deprivation of marginalised communities in Wales as indeed has the Labour Party until very recently (Adamson, 1996). Anti-poverty strategies have been slow to emerge from those agencies with statutory obligations and it is the voluntary and community sectors which have been attempting to alleviate the consequences of social exclusion in South-east Wales. No significant attempt has been made to organise the unemployed by any of the trade unions in the region and membership of a union effectively lapses once employment in the relevant industry is lost. Unemployed Workers Centres have been funded by the trade union movement in several valleys towns but they have settled for a role as job clubs, where ex-members are assisted in their search for employment. They have not become engaged with recovery strategies within the community. The key barrier to their participation in the community regeneration process is the historical concern of British trade unions with a limited protectionism in the place of work. In the postwar period, the connection between trades unions and the social and cultural activities of their members has been minimal and with the advent of high unemployment in the region of South-east Wales there was no surviving mechanism which allowed the trades unions to develop a more social role of this kind.

This effective demise of the active role of traditional working-class organisations in South-east Wales opens the way for new modes of political organisation based on non-class identities. The centrality of the concept of community presents a significant potential for mobilising political action. Currently, the traditionally close connection between class and community in South-east Wales makes it exceptionally difficult to separately identify an emerging political and cultural praxis which is entirely located in community identities. However, the centrality of notions of community to Welsh political culture has recently been the focus of increasing attention (Borland et al., 1992; Day and Murdoch, 1993; Thompson et al., 1996). This literature convincingly demonstrates the key role of the concept of community in the formation of personal and collective identity in rural and urban Wales. These community identities have traditionally existed in complex relationship with class identities and have been primarily constituted by class relations (Adamson, 1991a). However, the fragmentation of the working class raises the potential for community based identities to fill the vacuum which class fractions may experience following the demise of the traditional, solidary class identity of the region.

For members of the new working class, community identity may have more direct relevance, allowing a nostalgic identification with the mining community which is not contingent on adhering to its traditional class practice. For the socially excluded and marginalised populations of the deprived social housing estates of the region, a community identity and political praxis may be the only alternative in the context of effective exclusion from the orthodox political institutions of the region. In the face of indifference to deprivation the deprived are finding that community development initiatives provide a means of giving them voice in a world which has largely ignored them. High profile successes have ensured that this message is being widely disseminated and the example quickly followed by other communities. In this lies the potential for developing broader campaigns for change which can potentially unite the broad community of the coalfield.

There is already a growing self-perception of the region as a 'community of communities' suggesting a disarticulation of the direct link between community and class. There is some growing evidence for institutional recognition of this trend. A Federation of Enterprising Communities exists which is attempting to disseminate good community development practice. The Community University of the Valleys has emerged as a partnership between the University of Glamorgan, University of Wales (Swansea) and the Open University to develop higher education strategies which meet the needs of the local population through community rather than campus based delivery. Amalgamation of FE colleges in the region is creating a distinct regional pattern of provision centred on coalfield communities. Politically, the region is looking increasingly to Europe and not London, with a growing perception of Wales as a region in a Europe of regions. The 'Yes' vote in the 1998 Referendum for a Devolved National Assembly and the success of Plaid Cymru, the Nationalist Party in elections to that Assembly signifies a key change in the politics of the region. The loss of Labour Party support in its traditional heartland clearly adds immense impetus to a politics associated with regional identity rather than the traditional class identity conventionally associated with the political culture of the region. Within such emerging frameworks a traditional politics of class becomes increasingly divorced from the social environment.

This discussion is necessarily speculative given the recent emergence of a fragmented working class in the coalfield of South-east Wales. The discussion suggests a continued saliency for the concept of class in the analysis of social and economic change in the region. Complex connections between class and community identities are a legacy of the close connection between individual collieries and the communities which grew around them. This complexity remains evident as class and community are fused within local culture. However, the emergence of a highly organised community development sector questions the long-term survival of this complex articulation of class and community. With the disappearance of the collieries as workplaces, the articulation is no longer evident to anyone other than the older generation, largely associated with membership of the traditional working class. The ability of that class to maintain an identity based on a reality that no longer exists diminishes rapidly with time. Relations between the class fractions identified above are complex and divisive and the evident social divisions have created opportunity for innovative responses to social exclusion. The resulting emphasis on 'community' as an organising principle contains serious implications for the internal integrity of the Welsh working class.

5 Labour Market Dualisation and Trade Union Involvement in Spain

JAVIER G. POLAVIEJA

Introduction

In 1984, after eight years of an employment crisis in which 1.9 million jobs were lost, and at a time when unemployment rose to over 20 per cent for the first time, fixed-term contracts were introduced in Spain through the *Reforma del Estatuto de los Trabajadores* (Reform of the Workers' Statute).

The flexibilisation strategy implemented in the 1984 labour market reform - which was reinforced through further legal changes in 1992 and 1994 - set in motion a process of dualisation of employment. Flexibilisation only affected new entrants into the labour market, while workers on permanent contracts continued to enjoy the privileges of a rigid employment security legislation inherited from the Franco regime, which makes their dismissal comparatively costly for employers. The consequence has been the increasing differentiation of the Spanish work force along the lines of an insider-outsider divide. Employment adjustments have mainly involved fixed-term workers, while the employment security of permanently employed insiders has remained largely untouched. Spain not only has the highest proportion of temporary workers of all OECD countries (33 per cent) but also the highest rate of unemployment of all OECD member

129

states (around 15 per cent in 1999)[82] (OECD, 1988, 1991, 1993, 1997; Esping-Andersen, 1995; Argentaria, 1995).

This chapter analyses the process of labour market dualisation and its consequences for the relation between workers and trade unions in Spain. In particular, it examines the effects of the progressive fragmentation of the Spanish work force - i.e. the growing differentiation of a core of workers with stable jobs and a periphery without - on workers' patterns of collective action, as well as on their attitudes to, and perceptions and evaluation of, trade unions.

The chapter is structured as follows. In part one, the process of labour market dualisation will be analysed by looking at the relationship between fixed-term contracts and employment precarity. This analysis will be based on an original treatment of data from the Spanish Labour Force Surveys (LFS) for the 1987-97 period. Special attention will be paid to the interplay of class and type of contract in the distribution of unemployment risks. Following Goldthorpe's latest contribution to the development of class theory (Goldthorpe, 1997), an explanation will be offered as to why a clear correlation should be expected between class and labour precarity. This class hypothesis will be tested by analysing the effects of class and type of contract on the chances of being unemployed in Spain. Our main finding in this respect is that the institutionally driven process of contract flexibilisation in Spain has given rise to high levels of labour precarity *in all classes,* and that having a fixed-term contract in Spain constitutes in itself a stronger predictor of unemployment than class. In fact, it is because the type of contract determines the individual chances of being unemployed to a higher extent than occupational class, we can speak of an acute process of labour market dualisation in Spain. Part one will conclude with a discussion of the effects of labour market dualisation on collective bargaining in Spain. I will argue that the differentiation of unemployment risks by type of contract has produced a two-tier system of employment relations, in which the interests of fixed-term and unemployed workers are largely disregarded. Evidence on the insider character of the bargaining process, which is the main determinant of wages in Spain, will be provided.

In part two, I will argue that labour market dualisation has an impact on *union involvement* - i.e. the degree of workers' participation in the different forms of collective action and the intensity of subjective identification with unions. Given their precarious market situation, outsider workers - i.e. the unemployed or those with fixed-term contracts - will show less levels of

---

[82] *Spanish Labour Force Survey, 1999.* Undoubtedly, this national aggregate figure conceals significant regional variations in the rate of unemployment. In the third quarter of 1999, unemployment varied from 26.8 per cent in Andalucía and 22.9 per cent in Extremadura to 7.5 per cent in Navarra and 6.1 per cent in the Balearic Islands.

union involvement than their securely employed counterparts. In order to test this hypothesis, I will study, on the one hand, the extent to which the labour precarity attached to fixed-term employment reduces the levels of participation in different forms of union action - i.e. union membership, union voting, and participation in strikes. On the other hand, I will test the extent to which labour precarity reduces the degree of subjective identification with unions. This analysis regarding the effects of labour market dualisation on union involvement is based on original usage of the Spanish Survey on Class Structure, Class Consciousness and Class Biography (SCSCCCB), carried out in 1991 (Carabaña et al., 1993), and of the Centro de Investigaciones Sociológicas the Survey on Trade Union Activity (CSRSTUA), which dates from 1994 (CIS, 1994, 2,088). Multivariate modelling of data from these surveys will provide empirical support for the hypothesis that labour market dualisation does have an impact on union involvement.

Part One: Labour Market Dualisation in Spain

Defining Labour Precarity

It is important to approach the study of labour market dualisation from a dynamic perspective that stresses the longitudinal character of the phenomena of employment stability and instability. Labour precarity should be conceptualised as a particular type of unstable labour market trajectory which can manifest itself either as long-term unemployment or as a rotation between unemployment and short-term work.

From this perspective, labour market dualisation is understood as that phenomenon whereby a particular labour market is divided up between those who, by virtue of their employment security, enjoy stable labour market trajectories and those who, having the same labour market capacities, are nevertheless incapable of abandoning labour precarity. In this section, I will provide evidence of how the introduction of fixed-term contracts in 1984 produced labour market dualisation in Spain.

Hypothesis: Two-tier Flexibilisation Produces Dualisation

The flexibilisation strategy implemented in the 1984 labour market reform - which was reinforced through further legal changes in 1992 and 1994 - constitutes a prototypical case of what Esping-Andersen (1998a, 1998b) has recently labelled as *two-tier selective labour market policy*. Two-tier selective policies deregulate conditions only for some workers but not for others. In the Spanish case, flexibilisation through fixed-term employment was exclusively applied to new entrants in the labour market, while workers on permanent contracts continued to enjoy the privileges of a rigid employment security legislation inherited from the Franco regime, which makes their dismissal comparatively very costly for employers (Polavieja, 1998a).

Fixed-term contracts may be used for any activity (temporary or otherwise), may be signed for short periods (six months until 1992, one year since then) and renewed for up to three years (four years since 1993). When the period of the last possible renewal expires, the firm must either offer the worker a permanent contract or dismiss her. Non-renewal of fixed-term contracts entails very low firing costs and cannot be challenged in court. While the redundancy compensation for permanent contracts varies from 20 to 45-days wages per year of employment, the compensation for fixed-term contracts (depending on their type) various from nothing to maximum 12 days wages (Bentolila and Dolado, 1994, 67).

The differentiation of employment-termination costs by type of contract, together with the *expiration* date incorporated into fixed-term contracts, gives incentives to employers to manage labour adjustments exclusively through fixed-term work. Fixed-term contracts, therefore, become both the principal channel of entry into employment and the principal channel of exit from employment to unemployment. The outcome of this process is dualisation. The labour market increasingly divides up into, on the one hand, a core of permanent workers and, on the other, an enlarging periphery of insecurely employed ones who bear the brunt of employment adjustments. While the former group continues to enjoy stable employment trajectories, the labour market histories of those in the latter group are likely to consist of a combination of recurrent unemployment and short-term work.

This process can be studied by looking at: entries into employment; exits from employment to unemployment; and indirect indicators of labour turnover.

Entries into Employment

From an employment perspective, *two-tier flexibilisation* implies that fixed-term contracts, given their low costs, become the main channel of entry into employment. In fact original analysis of data from the Spanish Labour Force surveys for the period 1987-97 shows that the proportion of fixed-term contracts amongst the newly employed - i.e. those employees who were unemployed a year before the survey was carried out - rose from 59 per cent in 1987 to 84 per cent in 1991 and further to 88 per cent in

1997 (second quarters). This meant a dramatic increase in the total proportion of the Spanish work force on fixed-term contracts. Between 1987 and 1991, the rate of fixed-term work in Spain doubled from 16 per cent to 33 per cent (Bentolila et al., 1991, 237-8; Jimeno and Toharia, 1994, chapters 1 and 4). Thereafter, the rate of fixed-term work further increased to surpass the 34 per cent level by 1995 (Polavieja, 1998a). The sheer scale of fixed-term work in Spain is unparalleled anywhere else in Western Europe[83] (Jimeno and Toharia, 1994, 96).

There can be no doubt, therefore, that the flexibilisation policy has meant that temporary work has become the principal channel of entry into employment in Spain. Yet the rate at which fixed-term contracts have been converted into permanent ones is very low. For example, between the second quarter of 1987 and the second quarter of 1988, when employment was rising, only two out of ten temporary workers were given permanent contracts (Jimeno and Toharia, 1994, 111). Later data show that this rate declined significantly thereafter, remaining at around 10 per cent per year in the 1990-1995 period (Güell-Rotllan and Petrongolo, 1998; Alba, 1997, 1991; Segura et al., 1991; Bentolila et al., 1991; Polavieja, 1998a).

The introduction of fixed-term contracts increased the sensitivity of employment to the economic cycle and facilitated the creation of employment in the growth years. The world-wide economic recovery and Spain's entry into the European Community in 1986 provided the Spanish economy with a very favourable context for employment growth. Between 1985 and 1991, 1.7 million jobs were created at a rate unknown even in the years of the economic boom in the 1960s (Toharia, 1994, 112). Yet, by the same token, higher employment sensitivity implied that when the effects of the world-wide economic recession of the early 1990s hit the Spanish economy in 1992, levels of employment fell dramatically (more than one million job losses between 1992 and 1993) and unemployment reached 24 per cent of the active population at the beginning of 1994 (Antolin, 1995).

Fixed-term Contracts have become the Principal Means of Exit from Employment to Unemployment

Temporary work has become the principal means of exit from employment at least since 1987, which is the first date for which we have reliable data on fixed-term work (Encuesta Sociodemográfica in Argentaria, 1995, 57-9; Jimeno and Toharia, 1994; Polavieja, 1998a). Original analysis of the LFS

---

[83] In 1992, the proportion of the working population in Spain on temporary contracts (32 per cent) was nearly four times the EC average of 9 per cent (Martinez Lucio and Blyton 1995, 351).

data shows that as early as the second quarter of 1987, 56 per cent of the unemployed had become so following the termination of their fixed-term contracts. This proportion rose to 73 per cent in 1991 and since then has never fallen below 72 per cent. Meanwhile, the proportion of unemployed coming from permanent employment has dropped consistently. In 1987, 28 per cent of the unemployed with job experience had agreed to early or health-related retirement, forms of termination of employment contracts exclusively applied to permanent workers. Yet, by 1991, the figure had fallen to 12.3 per cent. Moreover, despite the massive destruction of employment in the period 1992 and 1994, the proportion of unemployed people coming from permanent contracts only increased to 12 per cent in 1993 and 14 per cent in 1995. In 1997, 73 per cent of the unemployed came from fixed-term employment, whereas only 13 per cent of the unemployed had become so following the termination of their permanent contracts (calculated by the author using LFS data for the period 1987-97). Downsizing has, therefore, essentially meant the destruction of fixed-term jobs (Polavieja, 1998a).

Two-tier Flexibility and the Increase in Job Turnover

With the extension of two-tier flexibilisation, growing numbers of workers on fixed-term contracts move back and forth between unemployment and temporary work. This has led to the emergence of precarious labour market trajectories characterised by recurrent periods of unemployment and temporary work. Evidence for the existence of such unstable trajectories comes from a variety of indirect indicators obtained from the LFSs.

One such indicator is the duration of fixed-term contracts. Original analysis of the LFS data shows that the average duration of temporary contracts in the period 1987-97 was around 12 months. Despite the fact that, from 1984 until 1993, the maximum legal duration of fixed-term contracts was three years, and that thereafter the legal limit was extended to four years, the average duration of fixed-term contracts has consistently been less than half the legal maximum. This is a clear indicator of labour precarity[84] (Bentolila et al., 1991, 237-8; Polavieja, 1998a). In sharp contrast, the average duration of permanent contracts is 10 years (calculated by the author using LFS data for the period 1987-97).

Another particularly interesting indicator of the spread of precarious labour trajectories is the evolution of the proportion of fixed-term workers who were employed in a different job 12 months before the LFS was carried out. An increase in labour turnover should be reflected in an increase in this proportion, since it is reasonable to believe that a short spell in unemployment might have been experienced between the previous job and the job held at the time of the LFS. In fact, data obtained from the LFS confirm this hypothesis. In 1987, 20 per cent of temporary workers had been employed in a different job 12 months earlier. This proportion shows an increasing trend in the period 1987-97, reaching 50 per cent by 1995. Meanwhile, in the case of permanent workers this figure remained more or less constant at around 3 per cent (Polavieja, 1998a).

Conversely, the proportion of fixed-term workers who had been employed in the same job one year before the survey took place, after increasing from 30 per cent to 36 per cent between 1987 and 1991 (the years of economic expansion), dropped to 25 per cent in 1993, and still further to a mere 12 per cent in 1997. This is a clear indicator of labour precarity. Yet for permanent workers, the proportion of those who had been employed in the same job 12 months earlier rose from 89 per cent in 1987 to 94 per cent in 1991, and remained above the 90 per cent level thereafter. The contrast between both figures is striking and gives a clear sense of the unequal distribution of employment security between the two types of workers.

Thus, all the indicators presented in this section suggest a steady increase in labour turnover among fixed-term workers over the period.

---

[84] Other secondary data reinforce our findings regarding the brevity of the fixed-term contract duration. For instance, Martinez Lucio and Blyton (1995) calculated that in 1991, nearly 90 per cent of *job creation contracts* (*contratos temporales de fomento al empleo*) - which accounted for around 20 per cent of all employment contracts registered with the INEM (*Instituto Nacional de Empleo*) - were for a period of no more than six months. Furthermore, contracts for specific services *(contratos para obra o servicio)* and casual contracts (*contratos eventuales*) - neither of which were subject to any specific legal minimum period - accounted for 60 per cent of all new registered employment contracts (see Martinez Lucio and Blyton, 1995, 351). Equally, the European Industrial Relations Review (1997) has estimated that by 1996, 70 per cent of the temporary contracts signed for a specified fixed-term had a duration of less than three months, and only 0.4 per cent for a duration of more than one year. Of the 14 types of contracts available, 80 per cent of new contracts signed in 1996 belonged to the three categories of casual work (*contratos eventuales*), contracts for work or services (*contratos por obra o servicio*) and part-time contracts (*contratos a tiempo parcial*) (EIRR, 1997, 25).

Two-tier flexibilisation has led to the emergence of a new pattern of unstable labour market trajectories with recurring periods of unemployment and temporary work. The rapid spread of this type of precarious trajectory has become one of the main features of the Spanish labour market.

Class, Type of Contract and Unemployment Chances

The process of dualisation in Spain has been so intense that type of contract has become a better predictor of unemployment chances than class itself. Certainly, class has an effect on an individual's chances of being unemployed, but the main component of this effect relates to the different distribution of fixed-term employment within each of the occupational classes. In other words, in Spain unemployment is heavily concentrated among manual workers *mainly because* the proportion of fixed-term contracts is significantly higher in manual occupations. When we control for type of contract, however, the effect of class diminishes significantly.

The Class Hypothesis

Why, however, should class have an effect on unemployment chances in the first place? To answer this question I will now turn to John Goldthorpe's latest contribution to the theory of class differentiation, which will be taken here as the class hypothesis to be tested.

In a recent seminar paper, Goldthorpe (1997) has elaborated on the theoretical principles that guide the EGP class schema (Erikson et al., 1979) by drawing on some aspects of organisational and personnel economics (for example Milgrom and Roberts, 1992; Lazear, 1995; Goldthorpe, 1997) as well as on the new institutional transaction cost economics (e.g. Williamson, 1985, 1996; Goldthorpe, 1997). In this approach, the main axiom of Goldthorpe's class theory, namely that class positions can be understood as positions defined by employment relations (Erikson and Goldthorpe, 1992, 35-47), is explained within a new rational action framework.

In this new framework, the causal mechanism which accounts for the class differentiation of employees - divided into a service class, working class, and 'mixed' forms of employment relations - is related to: (1) the costs involved in monitoring and measuring the respective types of work performed by the different classes of employees; and (2) the extent to which productive value would be lost if each class of employee left the firm - which is a function of the level of specificity of the human assets or human capital required to perform each type of work. Depending on these costs, workers will enter a different employment relation with employers.

The 'labour' relation - which applies to the working classes - is that which may be expected to generate the lowest costs for employers. The absence of serious work monitoring problems implies that workers can be paid in direct relation to their productivity, while the absence of serious problems of asset specificity means that no specific productive value is lost if the employee 'leaves' the firm. In labour occupations, the characteristics of the work and the assets required to perform it make the employee easily replaceable. Thus, labour contracts can take the form of discrete and short-term exchanges of money for effort and come '*as close as is possible to a simple spot contract - albeit perhaps of a recurrent kind - for the purchase of a quantity of a commodity*' (Goldthorpe, 1997, 12). Hence, there should be a clear correlation between labour precarity and working-class occupations.

Conversely, the 'service' (or 'professional') relationship implies the highest monitoring and human asset specificity costs. Service work-tasks are diverse and multifaceted, making them very difficult to monitor. In fact, monitoring these tasks would require as much expertise, specialised knowledge, and delegated authority as the expertise, knowledge and authority being monitored. Service tasks also require a highly qualified work force. With this type of work force, it is very likely that there will be an advantage to the employer in ensuring that service workers' skills are developed and become further specialised in the organisational context in which these skills are to be applied. Therefore, in order to ensure the organisational commitment of their professional, administrative, and managerial employees, and to ensure further skill specialisation, it is rational for the employer to offer a form of contract which establishes a long-term employment relation. 'Service' contracts create the possibility for employees to earn a steadily rising level of compensation throughout the course of their working lives - including salary increases according to a defined 'scale' and promotion opportunities through a relatively defined career structure. Service contracts also give incentives for employers to engage in training and for employees to engage in learning. Thus, the rationale of the service relationship favours continuing employment.

Therefore, one should expect to find a correlation between class and the distribution of labour precarity. In other words, fixed-term contracts and unemployment should be concentrated in working-class occupations, whereas service class professionals should show the lowest levels of unemployment and temporality.

Testing the Class Hypothesis

How does the process of dualisation discussed above affect the class differentiation mechanisms theorised by Goldthorpe? Does this theory hold for the Spanish case? In order to test Goldthorpe's class hypothesis, I will first examine the distribution of unemployment by class. Table 5.1 shows the total distribution of employment and unemployment by occupational class in Spain in 1997.

Table 5.1   Unemployment by class

Occupational classes	Unemployed	
	Count	% class
Service (I/II)	2,793	7.0
Intermediate (III)	9,277	19.8
Self-employed (IV)	428	2.7
Skilled manual (V/VI)	5,752	17.2
Unskilled manual (VII)	5,610	37.3
Total	23,860	15.8

* Counts are given in hundreds.

Source: LFS, 1997 (2nd Quarter) (Calculated by the author). Weighted.

Table 5.1 shows that unemployment in Spain has followed a class distribution, which is consistent with the class theory discussed above. Only 2.7 per cent of the self-employed (class IV) and 7.0 per cent of professionals in the service classes (Goldthorpe's classes I and II) were unemployed in 1997, whereas the unemployment rate among non-manual routine workers (class III) and skilled manual workers and supervisors of manual work (classes VI and V respectively) was close to the 20 per cent level. As predicted by the class hypothesis, unskilled manual workers constitute the class most heavily affected by unemployment, with a staggering unemployment rate of around 37 per cent.

In accordance with Goldthorpe's argument, one should also expect to find a clear correlation between fixed-term work and class. And this is indeed the case. As shown in Table 5.2, where we have cross-tabulated type of contract by occupational class, the proportion of fixed-term workers increases as we move from the service to the labour employment relation. Again, the service class is the least affected by fixed-term employment ('only' 19.7 per cent of the service class has a fixed-term contract), and the unskilled manual working class the most affected (63.2 per cent of the members of this class have a temporary contract).

The data presented so far is consistent with the class hypothesis as developed by Goldthorpe. However, further research on the structure of unemployment in Spain shows that the differentiation between insider and outsider work forces occurs within the ranks of all occupational classes. That is, we can identify both very insecurely employed fixed-term workers in highly qualified service class occupations, and very securely employed permanent workers in working-class manual occupations. Surprisingly, the employment security of the latter group is higher than the employment security of the former. In other words, type of contract in itself is a stronger predictor of unemployment than class. In Spain, workers on permanent contracts in working-class occupations seem to enjoy levels of employment security typical of a 'service' employment relation; conversely, service-class workers on fixed-term contracts show levels of vulnerability to unemployment which one would expect to find in 'labour' rather than in 'service' employment relations. And this phenomenon, which is a direct result of the implementation of a reform policy in a particular institutional setting, does not fit Goldthorpe's class hypothesis.

Table 5.2   Type of contract by class

Occupational classes	Type of contract			
	Permanent		Fixed-term	
	Count	% class	Count	% class
Service (I/II)	19,581	80.3	4,806	19.7
Intermediate (III)	24,260	68.4	11,188	31.6
Skilled manual (V/VI)	16,624	61.2	10,545	38.8
Unskilled manual (VII)	3,411	36.8	5,846	63.2
Total	63,876	66.4	32,385	33.6

* Counts are given in hundreds.

Source: LFS, 1997 (2nd Quarter) (Calculated by the author). Weighted.

In order to sustain this claim, I have applied multivariate logistic regression techniques to a random sub-sample of the 1997 Labour Force Survey (2nd quarter). The sub-sample includes 5,989 economically active respondents, 1,198 of whom were unemployed at the time the survey was carried out. The results of our statistical analysis are given in Table 5.3.

Table 5.3 shows three nested logistic regressions on the probability that a salaried employee is unemployed. The dependent variable modelled in this analysis has a value 0 if the respondent was a salaried employee at the time the LFS survey was carried out, and a value 1 if she or he was an unemployed (ex)salaried employee (employers and self-employed are not included in the analysis). Therefore, the universe of reference in this analysis is the Spanish economically active population of employees. The first regression, Model A, includes age, sex, class, sector of activity of the firm, industry and autonomous community of residence of the respondent as independent variables. Model B, is the result of adding type of contract as an independent variable to the previous equation. The type of contract variable refers to the current job, in the case of employed respondents, and to the last job held, in the case of the unemployed. It has a value of 0 if the respondent is employed with a permanent contract or unemployed coming from permanent employment, and a value of 1 if she is employed on a fixed-term contract or unemployed coming from fixed-term work. Finally, Model C tests an interaction effect between class and type of contract on the probability of being unemployed.

Model A, in which type of contract is not included, suggests that class is a strong predictor of unemployment, even when controlling for age, sex, sector of activity, industry and autonomous community (*comunidad autónoma*) of residence. Compared to the service class, which is the reference category in this model, being a member of the intermediate class increases the unemployment odds ratio by 93 percentage points; being a member of the manual working class increases the ratio by 96 percentage points; and being a member of the unskilled working class increases the ratio by more than 300 percentage points. Therefore, the distinction between service, mixed, and labour employment relations seems to have an important impact on the unemployment chances of Spanish employees, when controlling for other relevant variables, but not yet for type of contract.

Table 5.3 Logistic regressions on the probability of being unemployed

Explanatory variables	Odds R.	Sig.	Model's characteristics
Model A			*Logit estimates*
Age → (Reference 44 and older)			Number of obs. = 4,395
16-19 year	2.28	****	Log Likelihood = -1,852.689
20-24 year	2.28	****	Pseudo R^2 = 0.1128
25-29 year	1.79	****	Hosmer-Lemeshow Goodness-of-fit
30-34 year	1.38	**	Test
35-39 year	1.78	****	P > chi² = 0.9500
40-44 year	0.92	n.s.	
Female	1.17	****	
Class → (Reference service)			Model sensitivity 60.97%
Intermediate	1.93	****	Model specificity 72.08%
Skilled manual	1.96	****	Classification (Cut off point = 0.2)
Unskilled manual	4.77	****	
Model B			*Logit estimates*
Age → (Reference 44 and older)			Number of obs. = 4,316
16-19 year	0.78	n.s.	Log Likelihood = -1,507.6864
20-24 year	0.84	n.s.	Pseudo R^2 = 0.2289
25-29 year	0.87	n.s.	Hosmer-Lemeshow Goodness-of-fit
30-34 year	0.85	n.s.	Test
35-39 year	1.23	n.s.	P > chi² = 0.2289
40-44 year	0.74	n.s.	

Table 5.3   Logistic regressions on the probability of being unemployed. Continued

Explanatory variables	Odds R.	Sig.	Model's characteristics
Female	1.11	****	Model sensitivity 81.27%
Class → (Reference service)			
Intermediate	1.70	****	Model sensitivity 71.78%
Skilled manual	1.54	**	Classification (Cut off point = 0.2)
Unskilled manual	3.26	****	
Type of contract → (Ref. permanent)			
Fixed-term	10.34	****	
Model C			*Logit estimates*
Age → (Reference 44 and older)			
16-19 year	0.79	n.s.	Number of obs. = 4,316
20-24 year	0.84	n.s.	Log Likelihood = -1,498.7016
25-29 year	0.86	n.s.	Pseudo R^2 = 0.2335
30-34 year	0.85	n.s.	Hosmer-Lemeshow Goodness-of-fit
35-39 year	1.24	n.s.	Test
40-44 year	0.75	n.s.	P > chi^2 = 0.5749
Female	1.11	****	Model sensitivity 80.72%
Interaction Type of Contract * Class	1.62	n.s.	Classification (Cut off point = 0.2)
1. Class Main Effect Term → (Ref. service)			
Intermediate	3.41	****	
Skilled manual	6.00	****	Likelihood-Ratio Test

			Comparing Model C to Model B
Unskilled manual	15.31	****	
2. Type of Contract Main Effect Term → (Ref. PC)			Chi^2 (3) = 17.97 Prob > chi^2 = 0.0004
Fixed-term	1.04	n.s.	
3. Class Interaction Term → (Ref. service)			
Intermediate	0.35	***	
Skilled manual	0.46	* (0.78)	
Unskilled manual			

1. Class effect for employees on permanent contracts (compared to service-class).
2. Contract effect for service-class employees (i.e. impact of having a FT for service-class employees).
3. Effect of having a fixed-term contract in non-service classes compared to the effect of having a fixed-term contract in the service class.

**** Significance ≤ 0.001; *** Significance ≤ 0.01; ** Significance ≤ 0.05; * Approx. 0.10 (Significance level in parenthesis).

* Controlling for firms' ownership, industry, and autonomous community of residence.

Source: Subsample of LFS, 1997 (Calculated by the author).

However, when we introduce type of contract in the equation (Model B), the effect of class diminishes significantly. Clearly, type of contract is the variable that has the strongest effect on unemployment chances. In each and all of the occupational classes, and controlling for all other independent variables, having a fixed-term contract rather than a permanent one, produces in and by itself an increase in the unemployment odds ratio of 934 percentage points. As the logit estimates on Table 5.3 show, Model B is a significantly better description of the data structure than the previous model. The introduction of the type of contract variable yields an impressive increase in the pseudo R-square, which doubles, and a very significant improvement of the models' sensitivity, which increases in 20 percentage points. In sum, Model B suggests the existence of a very strong causal relationship between fixed-term work and unemployment risks in all occupational classes.[85]

Notice, however, that Model B assumes that the effect of the type of contract on unemployment risks is homogeneous in all classes. That is, that the relative employment insecurity of temporary workers vis-à-vis permanent ones does not differ by class. Yet, one could argue that the impact of type of contract on unemployment chances might vary by occupational class or, in other words, that there is an interaction effect between class and type of contract. Model C on the third row of Table 5.3 tests this interaction effect hypothesis and finds indeed empirical evidence which suggests that the impact of having a fixed-term contract on unemployment risks is significantly stronger within the non-manual categories of employees. There is strong empirical evidence that Model C provides a better description of the data structure than Model B, as confirmed by the results of the likelihood ratio test shown in Table 5.3.

An alternative way of looking at the interaction effect tested by Model C is to note that class has a stronger impact on unemployment risks in the case of employees on permanent contracts, whereas it is significantly less important for fixed-term employees, who suffer very high levels of insecurity in all occupational classes. In order to better understand the interplay of class and type of contract described by Model C, we have calculated different unemployment probabilities (in percentages) by class, and type of contract for 30-34 year old male and female respondents employed in the

---

[85] Model B also shows, that the inverse relation between age and unemployment, which appeared in Model A, in fact hides a type of contract relation. Once we control for type of contract, age becomes insignificant in statistical terms. The introduction of the type of contract variable in the model also reduces the effect of gender, although it does not eliminate it entirely. As the model shows, women are more likely than men to be unemployed (being a woman increases the unemployment odds ratio by 11 per cent), even when controlling for all the independent variables including type of contract.

private sector using the logistic equation of Model C. Predicted probabilities give us a clear sense of the intensity of type-of-contract segmentation in Spain. The results are given in Table 5.4.

Table 5.4 **Average predicted probabilities (in %) of unemployment by class, gender, and type of contract. Values for private sector employees as predicted by model C (Table 5.3)**

Classes	Men 30 to 34 years old		Women 30 to 34 years old	
	Permanent contract	Fixed-term contract	Permanent contract	Fixed-term contract
Service (I/II)	1.3	21.6	2.3	26.9
Intermediate (III)	2.2	28.4	4.0	38.8
Manual (VI/VII)	5.2	30.6	9.0	42.9

Source: LFS Subsamples (Calculated by the author from Model C on Table 5.3).

According to the logistic equation of Model C, the predicted chances of unemployment for a private-sector male professional in his thirties are 1.3 per cent, if he has a permanent contract, and 21.6 per cent, if he has a fixed-term contract. Model C also shows that the predicted unemployment chances of a male manual worker of the same age and sector of activity are 5.2 per cent, if he has a permanent contract, and 30.6 per cent if he has a fixed-term contract. That is, Model C shows that in Spain private-sector male manual workers in his thirties who are employed on permanent contracts have four times less chances of being unemployed than male professionals of the same age and sector of activity employed on fixed-term contracts. The unemployment chances of the latter category are almost twenty times higher than the unemployment chances of their class, sector, and age counterparts employed on permanent contracts. The effect of type of contract, therefore, cuts across all class categories and is clearly stronger than the class effect (see Table 5.4 for other predicted probabilities). There can be no doubt as to the decisive impact that the contractual distinction introduced by the labour market flexibility strategy adopted in Spain has had on the unemployment chances of Spanish workers of all occupational classes.

To sum up, in this section I have provided empirical evidence showing the highly dualised nature of the Spanish labour market. Labour market precarity in Spain is disproportionally concentrated among workers on fixed-term contracts who have bore the brunt of employment adjustments. Although labour precarity follows a class pattern, since both fixed-term employment and unemployment are disproportionally concentrated in working-class occupations, it has been shown that the type of contract that an individual has determines her unemployment chances, regardless of the occupational class to which she belongs. Furthermore, multivariate logistic regression analysis confirms that type of contract is a stronger predictor of unemployment than class. In Spain, type of contract constitutes a new and important source of socio-economic differentiation that cuts across classes.

Insiders, Outsiders and Industrial Relations

The process of labour market dualisation by type of contract may well be affected by - and depend on - the policies of representation adopted by trade unions. In theoretical terms at least, a union can develop an inclusive strategy whereby it attempts to represent the interests of all workers, both insiders and outsiders. Alternatively, unions can adopt policies that tend to privilege insiders (who are within or near their sphere of influence)[86] to the detriment of outsiders, who in this way are abandoned to the ongoing process of labour market dualisation.[87]

Judging by the results, we have to conclude that Spanish trade unions have not effectively performed an inclusive representation of interests. Collective bargaining, which is the main determinant of wages in Spain, has consistently benefited the interests of insiders. The empirical evidence supports this statement.

First, there is strong evidence of wage discrimination against fixed-term workers. An analysis by Jimeno and Toharia (1992) using survey data (Instituto Nacional de Estadística, 1991) (n = 1,209), which added information on wages to the usual structure of the LFS, has found that, *ceteris paribus*, workers on fixed-term contracts earned approximately 10 per cent less than permanent workers, despite the fact that wage discrimination is forbidden under Spanish law (Fernandez et al., 1991, 74; Toharia and Muro, 1988; Albarracin, 1990; Recio, 1991, 109; Polavieja, 1999a).

Secondly, there is also evidence suggesting that permanent workers have increased their bargaining power with the spread of fixed-term work.

---

[86] See, for instance: Bilbao (1993), Taboadela (1993), Rojo Torrecilla (1990).

[87] For an examination of these issues through a detailed study of four large enterprises in the metalworking sector in the Autonomous Community of Madrid, see Iriso (1993).

Using data from 1,167 manufacturing, non-energy, private firms over the period 1985-88, Bentolila and Dolado (1994) found that the larger the proportion of fixed-term workers in any given firm, the higher the wages that permanent workers obtained from firm-level collective bargaining. For their part, using a combination of data from the LFS and from the Ministry of Employment Statistical Office for the period 1987-91, which included both firm and sectoral level agreements for 44 industrial sectors, Jimeno and Toharia (1992) found that a 10 per cent increase in the rate of temporary contracts produced wage inflation of 0.22 points. Given the existence of wage discrimination against fixed-term workers - confirmed by Jinemo and Toharia in the same study - this figure can only indicate that wage inflation was concentrated among permanent workers (Jimeno and Toharia, 1992).

Finally, evidence also shows that fixed-term workers experience harsher working conditions in terms of hours, rhythm of work, supervision and productivity demands (Argentaria, 1995, 115-6; Recio, 1991; Rojo Torrecilla, 1990), and that their accident rate is significantly higher than the accident rate among permanent workers, even after controlling for occupational class (Polavieja, 1999a; Recio, 1991).[88]

These findings have been interpreted as confirming the insider-outsider theory of wage determination (for example Bentolila and Dolado, 1994).[89] Standard bargaining models based on this theory claim that the outcomes of the wage-determination process depend on the trade-off between wages and the workers' 'survival probability' at each wage level (Layard et al., 1991, chapter 2). The introduction and spread of fixed-term contracts in Spain increased the employment security of permanent workers - i.e. their 'survival probability' - because, given the distinctive layoff costs of each type of contract, it is fixed-term workers who bear the brunt of employment adjustments. Thus, the larger the number of temporary workers in any given firm, the greater the 'buffer' effect will be for insiders - i.e. their protection from the risk of unemployment. If fixed-term (and unemployed)

---

[88] Moreover, fixed-term workers are not entitled to as many welfare benefits as their securely employed counterparts, especially with respect to unemployment insurance (Toharia, 1994, 115-6; Rojo Torrecilla, 1990, 33), and, compared to insiders, they are much less likely to have opportunities for promotion and for the acquisition of skills (Rojo Torrecilla, 1990).

[89] According to this theory, both workers' representatives and firms have some degree of monopoly power and, consequently, some scope to set wages and prices, respectively (Layard and Nickell, 1987; Layard et al., 1991, chapter 8; Lindbeck and Snower, 1988; Nickell and Wadhwani, 1990; Jimeno and Toharia, 1994). Wages are, therefore, the outcome of a bargaining process in which firms and workers' representatives share the economic profit obtained by the firm on goods markets (Bentolila and Dolado, 1994, 72).

workers are ignored in the collective bargaining process, this 'buffer effect' will bolster the monopoly power of insiders (that is, their bargaining position) and insiders will be able to push for higher wages, the negative employment consequences of which will be paid for by fixed-term workers. Thus, the confirmation of the existence of an insider mark-up in the wage determination process constitutes quite convincing evidence of the insider character of collective bargaining in Spain. The differentiation of unemployment risks by type of contract has produced a two-tier system of industrial relations. Under this system, the interests of fixed-term and unemployed workers are largely disregarded. Spanish unions have *de facto* acted as insider organisations in collective bargaining (Polavieja, 1999a).

However, Spanish unions have also been insisting throughout the last ten years on the need to broaden collective bargaining agendas, reduce fixed-term contracts, establish a national employment programme, and secure a general shift in social policy, particularly with regard to welfare spending (Propuesta Sindical Prioritaria, 1989; Iniciativa Sindical de Progreso, 1991; Base para un Acuerdo sobre el Empleo, 1993; Alternativas de los Sindicatos sobre la Reforma Laboral, 1994; van der Meer, 1997). Spanish unionism has, therefore, displayed two rather distinctive representational faces: on the one hand, unions have acted as insider organisations in collective bargaining but, on the other, they have condemned the employment effects of labour market dualisation. This, apparently paradoxical, behaviour by the unions might be explained by the fact that the unions' role in collective bargaining may not respond to their own representation strategy, but rather to their inability to implement inclusive policies, which is, in turn, a function of their organisational power. Weak and competing unions, acting in a decentralised and uncoördinated institutional context which favours inflationary tendencies and hinders inclusive bargaining, are not in the best position to defend the interests of fixed-term and unemployed workers (Polavieja, 1999a).

In any event, this chapter does not seek to explain trade unions' behaviour towards insider and outsider workers, but rather insider and outsider workers' behaviour and attitudes towards trade unions. So the important question here is which of the two faces of Spanish unionism do workers believe: the inclusive and solidaristic face expressed in the above-mentioned union proposals and in the discourses which accompanied the successful one-day general strikes of 1988, 1992 and 1994, or the insider-non-solidaristic face which unions show in their less public collective-bargaining practices? It is our hypothesis that the answer to this question will largely depend on the labour market situation of the workers in question.

Part Two: Labour Market Dualisation and Workers' Involvement with the Unions in Contemporary Spain

The effects of labour market dualisation on trade union support have tended to be studied solely in terms of union affiliation rates. From this perspective, it has been argued that the principal effect of dualisation, within the realm of trade unionism, has been to provoke a growing division of labour in advanced capitalist societies between a core of stable workers (insiders), with generally high levels of affiliation, and a periphery of unstable workers (outsiders), with low or non-existent levels of union affiliation (e.g. Green, 1992; Hyman, 1992; Fulcher, 1991; Coggins et al., 1989; Salvatore, 1992; Kern and Sabel, 1991; Richards, 1995; Richards and Polavieja, 1997). However, this perspective poses serious problems in the case of Spain where, given that Spanish trade unionism is characterised as being more of 'voters' than of 'membership' (Martin Valverde, 1991, 24-5; Martinez Lucio, 1993, 500-1), the level of union affiliation is not a completely reliable measure of union support. Thus, while it appears clear that the great majority of outsiders are not union members, and that the great majority of union members workers are insiders, in Spain - with a level of affiliation of approximately 12 to 15 per cent - the great majority of insiders are, in fact, not affiliated to unions (see below). In consequence, I believe it is more appropriate to extend the scope of the dependent variable, and to analyse the effects of labour market dualisation on union support as effects on a broader measure such as the workers' level of *union involvement* (*implicacion sindical*).[90]

---

[90] By this, I do not wish to underestimate the importance of levels of union membership per se. Indeed, in terms of total union membership and net union density rate (including the unemployed), Spanish unions have staged something of a recovery in the 1990s. Total union membership (that is, the number of workers belonging to the UGT, CC.OO., USO, CNT/CGT and all other confederations) rose from 1.697 million in 1990 to 2.166 million in 1993 (before slipping back to 2.127 million in 1994). The net union density rate in Spain rose from 13.3 per cent in 1990 to 16.4 per cent in 1993 (before falling to 15.8 per cent in 1994). Such data have been used, quite reasonably, by Jordana to challenge the overall thesis of 'union decline' in the Spanish context. However, this trend does not contradict - and may even reinforce - the central thesis of this chapter that trade unionism in Spain is increasingly based on, and identified with, the core permanent work force. Indeed, Jordana himself notes that the recovery in union membership in the early 1990s is based partly on the phenomenon of permanent workers who were previously non-members sympathetic to the unions actually joining. In contrast, union affiliation rates among temporary workers have remained low - in 1992, for example, when 34 per cent of Spanish workers were temporary, only 18 per cent of CC.OO.'s membership were temporary workers (Jordana, 1996, 215-20). As such, fluctuations in union membership levels do not disguise an enduring insider-outsider

Union involvement, as used here, refers to that set of attitudes, evaluations and activities which indicate that a worker feels identified with the union (that is, feels represented by it) and is therefore personally interested in union activity. The ideal-typical *involved* worker, therefore, will not just display pro-union sentiments and attitudes, but will act accordingly. The involved worker will vote in union elections when they are convoked in the workplace, will be personally interested in the activities and functioning of the works' councils in the workplace, and will attend, if they take place, union meetings on collective action. In some cases, the involved Spanish worker will affiliate to the union. This conception of union involvement, therefore, includes both an attitudinal/evaluative component, and a dimension based on concrete behaviour.

It is obvious that pro-union behaviour requires pro-union attitudes. Moreover, however, pro-union behaviour requires an appropriate environment. The involved worker, for example, cannot vote in union elections if no such elections take place in her workplace. Nor can an interest be taken in the affairs of the union committees if the company in which someone works employs fewer than 49 people (the legal minimum for the establishment of works' councils in Spain). Nor can the involved worker participate in strikes if none are called. Involved, or pro-union, behaviour, therefore, requires the institutional and organisational conditions which make possible the direct presence - and thereby mobilisational capacity - of the unions.

Many of these contextual conditions are directly related to the size of the company. The more employees there are in the workplace, the greater the legal and strategic possibilities for effective union organisation. Within the European Union, Spain has the lowest proportion of employees in firms employing more than 500 workers (only 19 per cent of salaried workers in 1989), and the highest proportion of employees in firms employing less

---

division in the *composition* of union membership (see below) (Richards and Polavieja, 1997).

than 50 workers[91] (53 per cent of salaried workers in 1989) (Martinez Lucio, 1993, 494-5). Hence, it is hardly surprising that, according to the Survey on Trade Union Activity, only 39.7 per cent of Spanish workers claimed to have union committees in their firms, that just 38.4 per cent were covered by firm-specific collective agreements, and that only 38.9 per cent had had union elections in their workplaces. Thus, given the institutional framework of industrial relations in Spain, the average size of the firms is of fundamental importance in explaining the weak and unequal distribution of trade union presence in Spain.

But even in large companies with a strong union presence, the likelihood of a worker participating in union organised collective action may depend on other objective factors. Here I argue that having a fixed-term contract, and therefore occupying a precarious position in the labour market, has a decisive effect on pro-union behaviour.

On the basis of his study of four large metalworking companies in the region of Madrid, Iriso (1993, 427) has argued that the fixed-term workers given their weak position within the company, may consider participation in union action to be an excessive risk with regards to the employer. It is the fixed-term worker's weak position in the internal labour market that limits enormously her possibilities of taking part in collective action, regardless of her personal attitudes towards, and evaluations of, the trade unions. As such, it is argued that labour market precarity has a direct effect on pro-union behaviour which is independent of evaluative questions. A precarious position in the labour market makes it unlikely that even workers who are subjectively involved with the unions will turn this involvement into concrete action.

---

[91] Martinez Lucio (1993, 494-5) writes: 'The predominance of smaller firms has been increasing: in 1961, 38 per cent of employees worked in firms of fewer than 50 workers; in 1989, the figure was 53 per cent, while only 19 per cent worked in firms of over 500 employees. Using a different basis of calculation (percentages of total work force rather than of wage earners), Sisson et al. (1991, 97) show that Spain had the highest proportion of any EC country of workers (41 per cent) working in firms with under ten workers, and the lowest proportion by far (8 per cent) in companies with over 500 workers (...) (I)t would appear that conservatism and paternalistic employment relations remain the dominant characteristics of small-scale capital in Spain. The rise in the proportion of small firms probably reflects the elimination of large production units in the course of restructuring of traditional industries. Union membership and organization tend to be much weaker in small firms. Work forces are generally dependent of union bodies external to the workplace, even where elected union representatives exist, and the extensive network of local union officers of the 1970s has been substantially reduced, in great part as a result of financial difficulties and low membership'.

Moreover, I also hypothesise that an unstable working situation will also affect attitudes towards the unions - producing feelings of detachment, estrangement, lack of confidence and disaffection. Trajectories in working life that include temporary work, (long) periods of unemployment, or alternating temporary work and unemployment, can undermine the feeling that the unions represent and defend the common interest of all workers. In a precarious working situation, identification with the unions may be replaced by the feeling that the worker is alone in the face of the employer, or alone in the face of unemployment, and that no-one is defending her interests. Therefore a precarious working situation also diminishes subjective involvement with the unions.

In short, my general hypothesis is that the labour market precarity derived from type of contract reduces union involvement because: (1) it seriously impedes collective action (sub-hypothesis 1); and (2) it produces subjective de-identification with the unions (sub-hypothesis 2).

Sub-hypothesis 1: Labour Market Precarity Diminishes Pro-union Activity

In order to test the hypothesis that the labour precarity attached to type of contract hinders pro-union activity, I have analysed the effects of type of contract on union membership, union voting, and participation in strikes or stoppages in the firm. The statistical source used for this analysis is a sub-sample of the employed work force from the *Spanish Survey on Trade Union Activity* (CSRSTUA), conducted in 1994 (n = 5,900), to which we have applied logistic regression techniques.

(1) Fixed-term Employment and Trade Union Membership

Probably because collective agreements in Spain apply by law to unionised and non-unionised workers alike, and because unions have weak presence and, therefore, rather limited recruitment capacity in most of the Spanish firms (which are small), the union membership rate is very low. According to the CSRSTUA, the affiliation rate in Spain is 15 per cent. If we distinguish by type of contract, though, we see that the membership rate for workers on permanent contracts is 19 per cent and that 80 per cent of all union members have a permanent contract, whilst the rate for fixed-term workers is only 8 per cent and only 20 per cent of all members are fixed-term workers. However, is this highly significant difference in fact attributable to type of contract or is it the consequence of other possible explanatory variables hidden in the bivariate comparison? In order to answer this question, I have undertaken a logistic regression on the probability of being a union member in Spain, the results of which are presented in the first column of Table 5.5 (see below).

In the regression model, I have introduced as explanatory variables of union membership firm-level factors, individual-level subjective factors, and individual-level 'objective' factors. With respect to firm-level factors, the model shows that both the size of the company (measured as number of workers) and the type of ownership (public or private) have an impact on the chances of being a union member. Being in the public sector and in large firms increase the chances of affiliation. The model also controls for industry, yet this variable seems not to be significant (it is not shown in the table). Membership also depends on ideological factors. The more left-wing an individual is and the better her evaluation of trade unions, the more likely it is that she will be a union member. In all the models of this section, ideology has been measured using a ten-point-left-right-self-placement scale. Union evaluation has been measured using a computed scale that combines different opinions regarding the extent to which unions defend different categories of workers[92] with different opinions regarding the characteristics of trade unions as organisations and of their leaders.[93] The general evaluation of unions' scale is a 160-interval scale ranging from -10 to +10. It shows a Cronbach's Alpha of 0.85.

---

[92] There are 8 likert-type questions in the CSRSTUA in which respondents are asked to express the extent to which unions defend different categories of workers (women, young workers, unemployed, permanent workers, fixed-term workers, pensioners, highly paid workers and poorly paid workers). All these 8 questions were added up in a -16 to +16 index. This index was then divided by 8 resulting in a -2 to +2 scale, which was later used as the basis for our union evaluation scale (see footnote below).

[93] These are 3 likert-type questions on the degree of agreement with the following: 'If unions disappeared, nothing would really happen'; 'Most unions are run by leaders who are detached from society'; 'Unions are absolutely necessary to protect the interests of workers'. Finally, the scale includes a question in which respondents are asked to choose between the following: 'Generally speaking, Spanish unions are modern organisations which are adapted to today's society'; 'Generally speaking, Spanish unions are old organisations and they should change to adapt to today's society'.
Pro-union responses to these questions were coded either +2 or +1 (depending on the intensity of the response); whilst anti-union responses were coded -2 or -1. Those who did not answer or answered that they did not know were given a 0. These answers were then added up to the -2 to +2 scale previously obtained from the 8 likert-type questions on the extent to which unions defend different categories of workers (see footnote above). The resulting scale (of approximately 160 intervals) goes from -10 (most negative evaluation of unions) to +10 (most positive evaluation of unions). It has a Cronbach's Alpha of 0.85.

Finally, the model shows that union membership also depends on individual-level 'objective' factors. In a previous model - not presented here - in which type of contract was not introduced, two of these factors were age and gender. The average age of union members in Spain is 41 years, and the proportion of women is 24.3 per cent. However, when controlling for type of contract, both the effect of age and the effect of gender disappear (see Table 5.5). Type of contract, together with class, are the individual-level 'objective' factors that really matter. Indeed, being a manual worker, compared to a service class professional, increases the chances of becoming a union member significantly. Crucially for the validation of our hypothesis, having a fixed-term contract also significantly reduces the chances of becoming a trade union member. Thus, even after controlling for firm-level, ideological, and individual subjective and objective factors, having a fixed-term contract hinders union affiliation in Spain (see Table 5.5 below).

(2) Fixed-term Work and Union Vote

However, in a context in which 85 per cent of the work force is not unionised, the relevance of the analysis of the effects of labour market dualisation on affiliation can be rightly questioned. In voter unionism of the type existing in Spain, it is voting behaviour rather than affiliation which matters (Martin Valverde, 1991, 24-5; Martinez Lucio, 1993, 500-1). According to the CSRSTUA, the percentage of workers who voted in the last union elections convoked at their workplaces was 76.8 per cent. This figure rises to 79.6 per cent in the case of workers on permanent contracts and drops to 61.3 per cent for fixed-term workers. In other words, almost 40 per cent of fixed-term workers did not vote in the last union elections held at their firms. Again, logistic regression techniques have been applied to further investigate this figure.

In the second column of Table 5.5, the results of a logistic regression model on the probability of voting in union elections are presented. Notice that this time firm-level factors are not significant. Although firm-level factors are of a fundamental importance in determining whether elections are convoked or not, once elections take place, they do not seem to affect voting behaviour. Therefore, only individual factors play a role in explaining the decision to vote or abstain in union elections.

Age, class, ideology and type of contract are such factors. The older an individual is, the more left wing he or she is, if he or she is a white-collar or a manual worker and, critically, if he or she has a permanent contract, the more likely it is that s/he will vote in a union election when such election takes place. The model also shows a strong, although not totally significant, correlation between favourable evaluations of unions and vote (0.09 level of significance). In any case, what is clear from our model is that, after controlling for other explanatory variables, having a fixed-term contract also reduces the chances of voting in trade union elections.

(3) Fixed-term Employment and Participation in Strikes and Stoppages in the Workplace

We have hypothesised that the labour precarity of the fixed-term worker places her in a rather weak position vis-à-vis the employer. Since fixed-term workers are easily - i.e. cheaply - replaceable, personal involvement in any form of collective action can be easily sanctioned via the termination of the contract. This could also explain why workers who do evaluate unions in a positive manner nevertheless show significantly lower rates of union vote and union membership. To further explore this hypothesis, I have examined the effects of type of contract on the chances of taking part in strikes or workplace stoppages.

The CSRSTUA includes a question on whether respondents have ever taken part in organised strikes or stoppages in their workplaces. Some 45.5 per cent of all active respondents report that they have participated in such forms of collective action. This rate increases to 53.3 per cent in the case of workers on permanent contracts, and decreases to 35.4 in the case of fixed-term workers. Again, logistic regression techniques have been applied to further investigate this difference. The results of this logistic regression model are presented in the final column of Table 5.5.

Table 5.5   Logistic regressions on different forms of trade union participation

Models	Probability of being a trade union member		Probability of voting in union elections (if convoked)		Probability of taking part in an organised strike of stoppage	
Explanatory variables	Odds ratio	Sig.	Odds ratio	Sig.	Odds ratio	Sig.
Age	1.00	n.s.	1.04	**	1.00	n.s.
Female	0.89	n.s.	1.50	n.s.	0.56	***
Class ⟹ (Service)						
Intermediate	1.45	n.s.	3.60	**	0.82	n.s.
Skilled manual	2.54	***	3.95	**	0.79	n.s.
Unskilled	2.31	**	2.47	**	0.45	**
Public sector	2.25	***	0.86	n.s.	1.59	***
Size of firm ⟹ (less 50)						
From 50 to 500 workers	1.90	**	1.03	n.s.	1.14	n.s.
More than 500 workers	2.45	***	1.27	n.s.	1.79	***
Ideology (L-R scale)	0.84	***	0.83	**	0.79	***
Evaluation of unions	1.07	***	1.05	(0.09)[1]	1.05	***
Type of contract	0.57	***	0.47	**	0.72	**

Logit estimates	Logit estimates	Logit estimates
$N = 1{,}037$	$N = 342$	$N = 1{,}031$
$Chi^2 (20) = 161.77$	$Chi^2 (20) = 40.45$	$Chi^2 (20) = 165.64$
$Prob > chi^2 = 0.0000$	$Prob > chi^2 = 0.0044$	$Prob > chi^2 = 0.0000$
$Pseudo\ R^2 = 0.1513$	$Pseudo\ R^2 = 0.1109$	$Pseudo\ R^2 = 0.1160$
Log Likelihood = -453.7134	Log Likelihood = -162.17917	Log Likelihood = -631.07653
Classification	Classification	Classification
(Positive = $p \geq 0.2$)	(Positive = $p \geq 0.7$)	(Positive = $p \geq 0.5$)
Sensitivity 70.78%	Sensitivity 80.75%	Sensitivity 68.79%
Specificity 68.22%	Specificity 53.25%	Specificity 65.12%
Goodness-of-fit	Goodness-of-fit	Goodness-of-fit
Hosmer-Lemeshow $P > chi^2 = 0.6055$	Hosmer-Lemeshow $P > chi^2 = 0.2733$	Hosmer-Lemeshow $P > chi^2 = 0.4219$

*** significance ≤ 0.001; ** significance ≤ 0.05; * significance approx. 0.10 (Significance level in parenthesis).

1 Controlling for Industry.

Source: CIS, 1994, 2,088. Sub-samples of employed population (calculated by the author).

Our logistic model shows that the probability of taking part in organised strikes or stoppages again depends on firm-level, ideological, and individual-level 'objective' factors. With respect to firm-level factors, the size and the sector of activity of the firm seem to enhance the chances of participation in strikes and stoppages. Workers in the public sector are clearly more likely to participate in strikes and stoppages in their workplaces than those employed in the private-sector. Equally, workers in large firms (more than 500 workers) are more likely to take part in strikes and stoppages at their firms than workers in medium and small firms. Ideological variables also play a key role in explaining why some individuals participate and others do not. The more left wing an individual is and the more positively he or she thinks about trade unions, the more likely it is that s/he takes part in organised strikes and stoppages in the workplace. Finally, three individual objective factors also explain participation in organised collective action at the workplace: gender, class and, again, type of contract. Indeed, our model shows that women, unskilled manual workers and workers on fixed-term contracts are significantly less likely to take part in organised strikes or stoppages.

In order to test whether the experience of temporary work has a differentiated impact on the analysed indicators by occupational class, interaction effects between type of contract and class have been tested for all the models presented in this section. Yet, in none of the three models interactions were significant (results are available for the interested reader). Hence, the experience of temporary work seems to have the same type of consequences on the analysed indicators for workers in all classes. So the models presented on Table 5.5 seem to be the best representation of the data achieved with the CSRSTUA survey. Using the logistic equations provided by these models, I have calculated the different predicted probabilities by class and type of contract for respondents of moderate ideology (i.e. those placed between 4 and 6 in the 1-to-10-left-right-scale) employed in the private sector in firms with fewer than 50 employees. The results of such calculations are presented in Table 5.6.

Table 5.6   Average predicted probabilities of affiliation, vote, and participation in strikes and stoppages by class and type of contract. Values for ideologically moderate respondents employed in small private sector firms as predicted by models (Table 5.5)

Classes	Rate of affiliation		Rate of participation in union elections (if convoked)		Rate of participation in strikes and stoppages	
	Permanent contract	Fixed-term contract	Permanent contract	Fixed-term contract	Permanent contract	Fixed-term contract
Service (I/II)	7.3	4.4	62.3	47.7	48.4	43.0
Intermediate (III)	9.8	5.7	91.0	60.5	40.6	31.6
Skilled manual (V/VI)	14.1	7.8	81.1	71.7	47.0	37.6
Unskilled manual (VII)	15.3	8.9	79.8	62.1	34.6	21.9

Calculated from the models presented in Table 5.5 for respondents of moderate ideology (placed between 4 and 6 in the 1-to-10-left-right scale) who are employed in the private sector in firms employing less than 50 workers.

Source: CIS, 1994, 2,880. Sub-samples of employed population (calculated by the author).

In short, all the regression models presented in Table 5.5 tend to substantiate our thesis. Having a fixed-term contract not only significantly reduces the chances of affiliating to a union, but also reduces the chances of voting in union elections or taking part in organised strikes or workplace stoppages. As expected, the models suggest that a precarious working situation - even for workers sympathetic to the unions - hinders pro-union activity.

Sub-hypothesis 2: A Precarious Working Situation Diminishes Subjective Involvement with the Unions

I have also hypothesised, however, that labour market precarity could reduce subjective involvement in and of itself, eroding workers' sentiments of collective identity with respect to the unions, and generating instead the perception that unions do not represent the interests of outsiders.[94] Workers in the flexible segment of the labour market would thus become increasingly de-identified with trade unions.

The *Spanish Survey on Class Structure, Class Consciousness, and Class Biography* (CSCCCB, 1991) asks respondents to place themselves in a 10-point scale according to their degree of identification with trade unions. The identification scale ranges from 0 ('nothing at all') to 10 ('very much'). Of all other possible indicators found in other surveys, this simple scale seems to be the closest operationalisation of our concept of subjective involvement with trade unions. In order to test the hypothesis that labour precarity produces subjective de-identification with trade unions, I have undertaken two nested robust regressions on this scale, the results of which are shown in Table 5.7. The universe of reference of these models is the economically active Spanish employees. Both models show that, after controlling for class, gender, age, subjective identification with political parties, and class consciousness, being an outsider in the Spanish labour market (i.e. being unemployed or employed on fixed-term contract) significantly decreases the level of identification with unions.

In the regression models presented in Table 5.7, I have considered that union identification depends on two structural variables -occupational class and labour market status - and two ideological variables - subjective identification with political parties and pro-worker attitudes (or class consciousness). Gender and age have also been introduced in the model mainly as control variables. Class has been coded according to the same condensed version of Goldthorpe's class schema used in the previous analyses. The labour market situation variable has been coded with 4 different values. If respondents are employed on permanent contracts, they are coded as value 0, which is the reference category in the model; if they are employed on fixed-term contracts, they are coded as value 1; if they are unemployed due to the termination of their fixed-term contracts, they are coded 2; and if they are unemployed due to the termination of (ex)-permanent contracts, they are assigned value 3. Therefore, value 0 corresponds to insiders in the Spanish labour market, and values 1, 2 and 3 correspond to different forms of being an outsider. The political identification scale is a 1-to-10-scale of self-assessed degree of identification with political parties.

---

[94] Testing attitudinal effects with survey techniques is generally problematic. Individuals' attitudes cannot be measured. What (sometimes) can be measured are the effects of these attitudes on individuals' actual responses to particular survey questions. It is in this transition from *unmeasurable* attitudes to *measurable* responses that potential measurement error is generated. The more complex the attitudinal phenomenon to analyse, the more likely it will be to encounter measurement error, intrinsic variation, and operationalisation problems, and hence the less statistically powerful our models will be.

In placing themselves in this scale, respondents do not have to reveal their party preferences, they only have to state how much they identify with *a* political party. The scale, thus, measures identification with parties as political institutions. It has been included in the model under the assumption that both identification with unions and identification with parties could form part of a common general process of political involvement (Polavieja, 1999b). Finally, the models also include Erik Olin Wright's index of class-consciousness. Wright's index aggregates those items with the most direct class implications in a fairly simple sixteen-point interval scale[95] (Wright, 1985, 146-7, 253). Wright's index shows a Cronbach's Alpha of 0.72.[96]

Model A of our regression analysis shows that identification with unions is related to class, gender, age and ideological factors. Manual workers and men are more likely to show higher identification with unions than service-class professionals and women. Also, the younger the worker, the more s/he identifies with political parties, and the more pro-working-class attitudes s/he holds, the higher his/her identification with unions will be. Finally, and crucially for the validation of our hypothesis, Model A shows that being in the flexible segment of the Spanish labour market reduces identification with unions. Both employed fixed-term workers,

---

[95] The index includes the following Likert-type questions.
1. Corporations benefit owners at the expense of workers and consumers.
2. During a strike, management should be prohibited by low from hiring workers to take the place of strikers.
3. Workers in a strike are generally justified in physically preventing strike-breakers from entering the place of work.
4. Big corporations have much power in Spanish society today.
5. One of the main reasons for poverty is that the economy is based on private property and profit seeking.
6. If given the chance, non-management employees at my workplace could run things efficiently without bosses.
7. It is possible for a modern society to run effectively without the profit motive.
To them, an eighth item is added:
8. Workers are on a strike over working conditions and wages. Which of the following outcomes would you like to occur: (1) workers win their most important demands; (2) workers win some of their demand and make some concessions; (3) workers win only a few of their demands and make major concessions; (4) workers go back to work without wining any of their demands.
Each of these items is coded +1, if the respondent took the working-class position, -1 if she took the pro-capitalist position, and 0 if she said that she did not know or did not answer or, in the case of item 8, if they preferred outcome 2 to occur. The result index is a scale that ranges from -8 (maximally pro-capitalist) to +8 (maximally pro-worker).

[96] It is difficult to establish a standard for judging values of α. However, values lower than 0.70 are usually considered insufficient. Wright's scale therefore shows modest although sufficient reliability (for example: Nunnally and Berstein, 1994, 265; StataCorp., 1999, 22).

unemployed workers coming from fixed-term employment, and unemployed workers coming from (ex)permanent contracts, show lower identification with unions than their permanently employed counterparts. Of the three outsider categories, it is unemployed workers coming from fixed-term employment that show the lower levels of identification with trade unions.

Table 5.7   Robust regressions on index of identification with unions

Explanatory variables	Coefficient	P>$|t|$
Model A		
Class		
(Ref. service)		
Intermediate	-0.05	n.s.
Skilled manual	0.36	***
Unskilled	0.24	* (0.098)
Female	-0.06	**
Age	-0.01	**
Identification with parties (10-point scale)	0.60	****
Working-class consciousness (10-point scale)	0.13	****
Labour market situation		
(Ref. permanent)		
Fixed-term employed	-0.57	****
Unemployed (from fixed-term)	-0.91	****
Unemployed (from permanent)	-0.56	***
Constant	1.38	
Model B		
Class		
(Ref. service)		
Intermediate	-0.07	n.s.
Skilled manual	0.50	**
Unskilled	0.23	* (0.11)
Female	-0.06	**
Age	-0.01	**
Identification with parties	0.60	****
Index working-class consciousness (ICCW)	0.15	****

Table 5.7 Robust regressions on index of identification with unions. Continued

Explanatory variables	Coefficient	P>$\mid$t$\mid$
Labour market situation		
(Ref. permanent)		
Fixed-term employed	-0.41	***
Unemployed (from fixed-term)	-0.64	***
Unemployed (from permanent)	-0.60	**
ICCW * Labour market situation		
ICCW * fixed-term employed	-0.07	**
ICCW * unemployed (from fixed-term)	-0.10	**
ICCW * unemployed (from permanent)	0.01	n.s.
Constant	1.35	

Model's characteristics: n = 2,367; R-squared = 0.4152; Adj. R-sq. = 0.4127; Root MSE = 2.26411.

Model's characteristics: n = 2,367; R-squared = 0.4173; Adj. R-sq. = 0.4141; Root MSE = 2.26151; Likelihood-ratio test; Comparing Model B to Model A; Chi^2 (3) = 8.46; Prob>chi^2 = 0.0375.

**** Significance $\leq$ 0.001; *** Significance $\leq$ 0.01; ** Significance $\leq$ 0.05; * Approx. 0.10 (Significance level in parenthesis).

Source: CSCBBC, 1991 (calculated by the author).

Model A, thus, provides empirical support for our hypothesis that labour precarity has subjective consequences for the levels of identification with Spanish trade unions. Yet, it does not tell us a great deal about the actual functioning of these subjective processes of union disaffection. In order to investigate in detail the subjective mechanisms whereby labour market experiences translate into attitudes towards unions, we should most probably undertake qualitative research. However, multivariate analysis can still be further exploited as a tool that help us identify and illuminate at least *some* of the causal mechanisms of the de-identification phenomenon. Model B in Table 5.7 has been tested with such a goal in mind.

Interaction Effects and the Expectation-disillusion Hypothesis

Notice that Model A assumes that the impact of labour market position on the identification scale is the same for workers holding pro-working-class attitudes and for those without pro-working-class views. However, it seems reasonable to expect that the attitudinal effects of labour market experiences are in fact mediated by ideological aspects. If an outsider worker holds pro-working-class views, she could experience much more of a disillusion with existing unions precisely because her expectations are likely to be higher. Model B tests this hypothesis by looking at the interaction effects between E.O. Wright's index of class consciousness and our labour market position variable. Our findings suggest that this type of mechanism might indeed be taking place amongst both employed and unemployed fixed-term workers, yet it does not seem to be present in the case of the unemployed coming from permanent contracts.

Graphical representation can help us explain the interaction effects shown by Model B. Figure 5.1 below shows graphically the relationship between working-class consciousness and trade union identification for the four different labour market situations considered. Notice that, for all levels of class consciousness, our three types of outsider workers show lower union identification than their permanently employed counterparts (that is why the vectors for fixed-term employed, for unemployed coming from fixed-term work, and for unemployed coming from permanent contracts appear lower in the graph). Notice also that if we compare the linear function of the employed permanent workers with that of the unemployed coming from permanent work, we find identical slopes (i.e. they are parallel). This is because the interaction effect is in this case non-significant, which suggests that the 'distance' between the levels of union identification of insiders and outsiders coming from permanent contracts is the same at each 'level' of class consciousness. That is, both for insiders and for unemployed workers coming from permanent contracts the effects of class consciousness on the identification scale are identical.

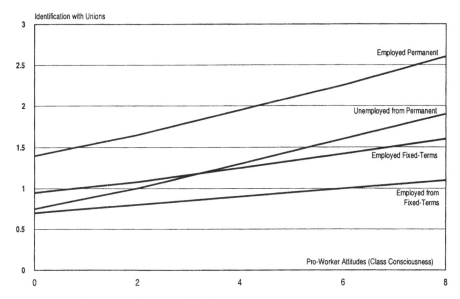

Source: Plotted from model B on Table 5.7.

Figure 5.1 Graphical representation of the effects of labour market position and working-class consciousness on identification with trade unions as shown in model B (Table 5.7)

Yet, if we compare the insiders' vector with those of the employed and unemployed fixed-term workers, we see that the slopes are now different, being flatter in the case of these latter outsider categories. This difference in the slopes is the graphical representation of the significant interaction effects shown by Model B. These effects suggest that the impact of working-class consciousness on union identification is significantly lower in the case of employed fixed-term workers, and even more so in the case of unemployed workers coming from fixed-term work. For these categories of outsiders, working-class consciousness does not seem to have as much impact on union identification. The effect of labour market position on union identification is now greater precisely within the more class-conscious respondents.

I believe that these interaction effects can be interpreted as the result of the *expectation-disillusion mechanism* hypothesised above. Labour market precarity could produce a greater de-identification with unions precisely amongst those workers holding strong pro-working-class views because, for these workers, the distance between the *normative ideal* of what unions *should be like* and the perceptions of, and experiences with, unions as they *are actually like* could provoke ideological disillusion and thus augment de-identification. This phenomenon could bring the mean average score in the union identification scale down for the first two categories of class-conscious outsiders and thus explain the differences in their slopes observed in Model B.

Our data also suggest that expectation-disillusion mechanisms only take place amongst outsiders that have experienced fixed-term work - which are the vast majority of outsiders - but not amongst unemployed workers coming from permanent employment. If we believe these data,[97] we should conclude that the ideological connection between pro-working-class views and union identification is much stronger in the case of outsiders who face unemployment after having experienced long-term stable employment.[98] This is perhaps not that surprising since outsiders coming from permanent contracts are likely to have experienced a rather different face of trade unionism than those coming from fixed-term work. Therefore, the contrast between the normative ideals contained in their pro-working-class views and their own experience with unions might not provoke an intense ideological tension as in the case of those outsiders who have always been in the flexible segment of the Spanish labour market.

In any event, both the main effect and the interaction effect models discussed above give empirical support to our hypothesis that labour market precarity reduces subjective identification with unions. Whilst the former model (Model A) is more parsimonious, the latter (Model B) allows us to identify one possible subjective mechanism of union disaffection and, thus, offer a more complex causal narrative.

---

[97] We should be cautious since the lack of significant interaction effects in the case of unemployed workers coming from (ex)permanent employment could also simply be due to the fact that we have very few cases in this category. Of the 3,341 respondents classified in our labour market position variable, only 147 (4 per cent) correspond to unemployed-(ex)permanent workers. Given the loss of cases that occurs in regression analysis, the actual number of respondents belonging to this particular labour market category in our models is most probably much smaller, which could make unlikely to detect interaction effects in this group.

[98] According to the Labour Force Survey data, the average reported duration in employment of unemployed workers coming from permanent contracts is around ten years (see Part One).

Summary and Conclusions: The Effects of Dualisation on Trade Union Involvement

In this chapter, I have shown that specific characteristics of the deregulation policies implemented in Spain set in motion a particularly intense process of labour market dualisation whereby employment insecurity has been disproportionally concentrated on workers on fixed-term contracts. Labour market dualisation affects workers of all class categories in Spain and constitutes in itself an important source of socio-economic differentiation.

Analysis of data provided by the CSRTUA and the CSCCCB surveys allows us to conclude that labour market dualisation has had clear effects on trade union involvement. Those workers who are unemployed or who are on fixed-term contracts demonstrate significantly lower levels of pro-union behaviour and subjective involvement than workers on permanent contracts. I have shown how a precarious working situation reduces the participation of the worker in union activities. Fixed-term workers affiliate, vote in union elections, and participate in strikes and workplace stoppages significantly less than their permanently employed counterparts. And this happens in all occupational categories, in all industries, both in the public and the private sector, for men and for women, amongst both right-wing and left-wing workers, and both for workers who evaluate unions positively and those with a negative assessment. A precarious working situation, therefore, acts as an 'objective' factor impeding collective action amongst workers. The weakness of their position in the internal and external labour markets ensures that workers in the precarious segment of the labour market (outsiders) are related much more tenuously to union activities.

Furthermore, the data presented in this chapter also tend to confirm the validity of the hypothesis that labour precarity reduces subjective identification with trade unions. Fixed-term and unemployed workers, given their precarious situation in the labour market, are likely to develop the feeling that unions do not represent their interests and, hence, have a weaker identification with unions. Analysis of the interaction effects between E.O. Wright's index of class consciousness and labour market position on a trade union identification scale suggest that the process of union de-identification could be particularly acute amongst workers holding pro-working-class views. This phenomenon has been explained as the result of what I have called *expectation-disillusion* mechanisms.

Perhaps only research of a qualitative kind can further explore these findings and suggest other possible causal narratives that connect labour market experiences to subjective evaluation of trade unions. Qualitative research could also help us answer the important question of whether unions are seen as the offenders or as the failing authorities by outsider workers. Multivariate research on the effects of dualisation on different social and political values has shown that, compared to workers of the same characteristics on permanent contracts, fixed-term and unemployed workers display both higher levels of opposition to employers and the economic system, and higher levels of de-identification with political parties (Polavieja, 1998b, 1999b, 1999c). These findings suggest, in any event, that outsiders do not blame *only* trade unions for their situation.

In any case, on the basis of the data presented here, it can be argued that the process of labour market dualisation has had empirically verifiable repercussions on levels of involvement with the unions. The strength of trade unionism with low affiliation, as in Spain, is based on its capacity to mobilise workers - that is, on its capacity to present itself to workers as the legitimate representatives of their interests. As such, the diminution of the workers' involvement with the unions represents a debilitating trend of very great significance. If a growing segment of the Spanish work force is no longer mobilised by the unions, either because it cannot be, or because it no longer feels represented, then the unions will have lost an important source of their power.

Postscript: Can Unions Bridge the Insider-outsider Divide?

In April 1997, the two main unions, UGT and CC.OO., along with the employers' organisations CEOE and CEPYME, signed a new pact on further labour reform that was hailed by *El País* as *'probably the most important social agreement signed in Spain over the past fifteen years'* (EIRR, 1997, 28). In this pact the unions finally recognised - albeit reluctantly and not without internal dissent - that the perennially stated goal of generating more widespread job security for all may only be achievable by reducing in the long run the levels of security that the insider work force has, up until now, enjoyed. The 1997 pact contained measures to reorganise the institutional setting of collective bargaining as to counter-act insider tendencies, and, most importantly, to promote the use of a new type of open-ended employment contract (which will become the only type of permanent contract as soon as the cohorts of workers with the old type of permanent contract progressively leave the active population). This new contract, which combines an unfixed duration with lower termination costs, is more flexible than old permanent contracts (i.e. cheaper to fire) and less precarious than fixed-term ones (i.e. permanent in nature). The evidence as to whether this new labour market reform has achieved its goal (or might achieve it in the future) is mixed, debatable and inconclusive (Richards and Polavieja, 1997, 1998). But there is little doubt that the pact in itself constitutes a turning point. In agreeing to it, the unions have at least shown themselves willing to incorporate concerns and demands of the outsider work force.

What *is* certain is that greater job security for more workers is the key to removing the barriers that now exist between the unions and large swathes of the outsider work force. If the recent labour market reform does indeed, in the long run, promote more widespread job security, then it will, at the very least, place greater numbers of workers within the realm of trade unionism. If it does *not*, it will only have served to underscore, rather than help to resolve, the severe problems that Spanish unions face in establishing themselves as genuinely representative institutions of Spanish workers as a whole.

6 Union Participation in the Netherlands: Differences Between Traditional and 'New' Employees

SJOERD GOSLINGA AND BERT KLANDERMANS

Introduction

Trade unions are strongly dependent on their membership for their ability to reach objectives and goals. The membership provides the resources that are necessary for a union's success and continued existence. The resources obtained from members, such as union dues, voluntary participation in tasks and activities in or on behalf of the organisation, participation in collective action, etc., are important for the pursuit of collective goals as well as for providing selective goods and services for individual members (cf. Knoke and Wright-Isak, 1982). In order to secure the availability of the necessary resources, trade unions must not only attract members but must also retain them.

As a response to the decline in membership rates during the 1980s, it has been suggested that Dutch trade unions need to adapt to the wishes and demands of the modern employee. A more member-oriented approach has been proposed in order to make union membership more attractive. 'New employees' are said to differ from traditional employees in their motivation for union membership. Instrumental or individual motives for joining and remaining a union member have gradually replaced more ideological or collective motives for union participation (e.g. Van Ham et al., 1985). As a consequence, the unions have started to place much more emphasis on the individual benefits for members and have expanded the range and number of individual services they provide.

The purpose of this chapter is to examine the differences between the more traditional groups of union members and the groups of employees who are relatively new to the labour force and the membership. First we will describe how the composition of the Dutch labour force has changed in the past decades and we will examine how successful Dutch trade unions have been in recruiting and retaining members from the groups of employees who are new to the labour force. In other words, we will examine how the union density rate among traditional groups of employees compares to the union density rate among new groups of employees. In the second part of the chapter we will use data from a survey taken of Dutch union members to examine whether the more traditional groups of union members differ from groups of members that are relatively new to the membership. Our focus will be on differences in satisfaction with and commitment to the union, two concepts that are central to the process of sustained union participation.

Who are the Trade Union Members?

Since the middle of the 1980s the number of union members in the Netherlands has grown by over 2 per cent each year. All together, Dutch labour unions now have more members than they have ever had before. At the end of the 1970s, approximately 1.7 million people were union members. In the early 1980s the total number of members dropped to 1.5 million (Visser, 1995; see also Van den Berg, 1995). In 1995 over 1.8 million people were union members (CBS, 1997). Although membership sizes are growing, union density in the Netherlands has hardly increased over the last decade. From the end of the Second World War until the end of the 1970s, union density was stable at around 37 per cent (percentage of union members in the work force). Because employment growth exceeded membership gains, union density kept decreasing, even when the number of members started to grow again. Union density reached its lowest point (24 per cent) in 1990. In the past few years, employment growth has declined and union density now seems to have stabilised around an estimated 29 per cent (CBS, 1997).

Union density rates differ tremendously between the different sectors of the labour market and between different groups of employees. Union density is much higher among construction workers (±45 per cent) and in the transportation sector (±42 per cent), than union density among employees in sectors such as catering (±11 per cent) and financial services (±10 per cent). Among female employees, union density is 21 per cent, as compared to 35 per cent among male employees. Of the employees aged under 25, only 14 per cent are organised, whereas union density is 45 per cent among employees between the ages of 55 and 64. Union density among full-timers is approximately 32 per cent and among part-timers 18 per cent (Daalder, 1995; Visser, 1995). Moreover, within different sectors of the labour market, different groups of employees are not equally represented. In contrast to several other European countries, however, union members in the Netherlands do not differ much from non-members in terms of socio-economic status variables such as level of income and level of education. Compared to non-members, union members are slightly under-represented among employees with minimum wages or a slightly higher income. As far as level of education is concerned, the membership of the Dutch labour movement reflects the Dutch labour force fairly well (Visser, 1995).

Employment growth in the past two decades has mainly taken place in part-time employment and flexible or atypical employment, and predominantly in the services sectors. The number of part-time jobs (defined as less than 35 hours a week) increased from about 14 per cent in 1975 to 28 per cent in 1995. The number of flexible jobs (employment contracts without fixed hours, for a very short period of time, etc.) also increased and was some 10 per cent in 1995 (CBS, 1997). The Netherlands has also experienced a strong growth in labour supply in the past decades, mainly due to demographic changes and the entry of more women into the labour force. The number of women in the labour force has increased from 22 per cent in 1960 to 38 per cent in 1995. The pressure resulting from this growth in the labour force has been tempered by the exit of older people, longer schooling, labour-time reduction and the shift toward part-time employment (Visser, 1990). Women's participation in the labour force is closely related to the growth of part-time employment: almost 60 per cent of the women in the labour force are working part-time (Niphuis-Nell, 1993; Daalder, 1995).

The changes in the composition of the work force and types of employment contracts have important implications for trade unions. Membership opportunities obviously lie in attracting employees from the groups that are new to the labour force, such as women and part-time workers (Daalder, 1995; Van den Putte and Sips, 1992). But Dutch labour unions have a hard time organising these groups. The membership of Dutch trade unions has changed in the past decades. Possibly the most important shift is that a significant portion of the members no longer belong to the group of traditional employees (male, full-time employed, single wage earner, married with children), whereas in the 1960s almost all union members did belong to this category (see Klandermans and Visser, 1995). Nevertheless, newcomers to the labour force, such as young employees, women and part-time workers are all under-represented in the trade unions. Table 6.1 summarises some of the major differences between the composition of the labour force and the composition of the total Dutch union membership. As mentioned earlier, the table shows women, younger employees and part-time workers to be under-represented among the membership of the Dutch trade union movement. Furthermore, the table shows that the differences between members and non-members are even more pronounced for members of unions affiliated with the National Christian Trade Union Federation, the CNV. With approximately 350,000 members, the CNV is the second largest trade union federation in the Netherlands. These figures are included because we will use data collected among members of the largest unions affiliated with the CNV in the second part of this chapter to look at differences in union satisfaction and union commitment and to analyse the exit behaviour of union members.

Table 6.1   Comparison of the composition of the Dutch labour force and union membership: gender, age and employment status (in %)

	Dutch labour force[1]	Union members[2]	Non-members[2]	CNV member-ship[3]
Men	61.7	72.0	55.0	78.5
Women	38.3	28.0	45.0	21.5
Age				
<25 year	13.6	7.0	17.0	5.1
25-44 year	59.1	57.0	59.0	47.5
44-64 year	27.4	36.0	24.0	47.4
Full-time employment	61.5	82.0	-	83.8
Part-time employment	28.4	18.0	-	14.3
Flexible employment[4]	10.0	-	-	2.0

[1]   Figures 1995 (CBS, 1997).

[2]   Data from Klandermans and Visser (1995).

[3]   CNV panel, 1996 (Goslinga, 1996a).

[4]   Includes employment contracts without a fixed number of hours and/or for a very limited period of time.

Joining and Leaving

So why are the groups of employees that are relatively new to the labour force under-represented in the trade union movement? The number of people who are union members at a certain point in time is the result of two processes: joining and leaving. Joining a union is of course a necessary step, and the under-representation of new employees in the union starts here: women and part-timers are less likely to join a union than their male and full-time counterparts (Daalder, 1995; Van den Putte and Sips, 1992; Visser et al., 1990). But these differences in joining behaviour only account for a part of the differences in density rates between these groups of employees. Even when Dutch trade unions succeed in attracting new members, they do not succeed very well in retaining these members for a longer time. Turnover rates among Dutch trade union members are high; recent figures show that almost half of the people who have joined a union will terminate their membership within five years (Van den Putte, 1995). This study also shows that exit rates among women, part-timers and younger members are much higher (about twice as high) than among men, full-timers and older members.

Satisfaction, Commitment and Exit Behaviour

In order to explain exit behaviour in trade unions, we will use the 'exit, voice and loyalty' framework proposed by Hirschman (1970) as a conceptual model. The present study is not the first to suggest Hirschman's 'exit, voice and loyalty' framework as an explanatory model for the exit behaviour of Dutch union members (e.g. Van der Veen and Klandermans, 1989). To date, however, the model has never been empirically tested within the context of trade union participation.

Hirschman's starting point is that there are three possible reactions to dissatisfaction with an organisation: exit, voice and loyalty. According to Hirschman, members of an organisation who are dissatisfied can either give up their membership in the organisation (exit), express their discontent in an attempt to change the situation and restore the relationship with the organisation (voice), or wait more or less passively for conditions to improve (loyalty). Whether a person will react with a destructive response (exit) or a constructive response (voice, loyalty) depends on the individual's relationship with the organisation (cf. Rusbult et al., 1988). If a person is committed to the organisation, then a constructive response is most probable. If the level of commitment to the organisation is low or non-existent, chances are that a person who is dissatisfied will terminate their membership and leave the organisation. Consistent with the 'exit, voice and loyalty' framework, union satisfaction and union commitment are commonly regarded as being the most important factors in the process of sustained participation in trade unions.

Barling et al. (1992) define union satisfaction as 'an outcome of the extent to which members perceive the union to be meeting their needs' (p. 166). Stated alternatively, union satisfaction results from an evaluation of union performance on issues that are important to individual members. Or, as Fiorito et al. (1988) put it, union satisfaction is a function of the discrepancy between member expectations and perceptions of union performance. As noted previously, it has been suggested that for the new groups of union members the personal benefits of union membership have become more important than the collective or ideological goals of the labour movement. Consequently, union performance might be perceived differently by different groups of members, depending on the issues that are considered most important. If the needs or expectations regarding union membership of new groups of members differ from those of more traditional groups of members, we might expect differences in union satisfaction between the two categories. Research shows that, in general, feelings of commitment to one's trade union stimulate continued participation and voluntary work within or on behalf of the union organisation, whereas lack of commitment can result in defection, i.e. termination of membership (see Barling et al., 1992). Commitment to an organisation can take on different forms, each of which has its own distinct antecedents and consequences. Based on a review of the literature on organisational commitment, Meyer and Allen (1991) make a distinction between three forms of commitment: affective commitment, continuance commitment and normative commitment. All three forms of commitment are viewed as 'a psychological state that (a) characterises the employee's relationship with the organisation and (b) has implications for the decision to continue or discontinue membership in the organisation' (Meyer et al., 1993, 539). Affective commitment refers to an individual's affective attachment to the organisation, which evolves out of a positive exchange relationship between the organisation and the individual. Continuance commitment is based upon the costs associated with leaving, which are determined by the investments in the organisation and the quality of the perceived alternatives to membership. Normative commitment is based on a feeling of obligation to remain in the organisation, which is the result of long-term socialisation processes. A stronger affective commitment thus reflects the *wish* to remain a member of the organisation, a stronger continuance commitment reflects the *need* to remain, and a stronger normative commitment reflects the feeling that one *ought* to remain in the organisation.

Meyer and Allen (1991) developed their three-component model of commitment, to be utilised within the context of a work organisation. They suggested, however, that their conceptualisation could contribute to an understanding of commitment in other domains, such as commitment to one's occupation, employment, management and trade union (Meyer et al., 1993; Meyer and Allen, 1997). Following this suggestion, Goslinga (1996b) modified the three-component model to be used in a union setting. Research conducted among Dutch union members confirmed that the three-component model could be generalised to this domain. The results of this research also revealed that the relative strength of the different union commitment components differs among individual union members. This indicates that some union members continue their membership primarily because they feel an affective attachment to their union, while others stay because they feel they ought to, and still others because they see no other options.

Research Questions

Several specific groups of employees are under-represented in the Dutch trade union movement. Especially among the new and growing groups of employees, such as women, younger employees and part-timers, the union density rates are low compared to the more traditional groups of employees. An significant portion of the under-representation of new groups of employees in the trade union movement is caused by higher exit rates. From our theoretical perspective, this implies that these groups of members are less satisfied with (aspects of) union membership and lack sufficient levels of commitment to their union. This leads us to two general questions that will be investigated in the following part of this chapter using survey data from a sample of union members:
-   Are union members who belong to the groups that are relatively new to the membership less satisfied with and/or less committed to their union? Or, stated differently, to what extent do demographic variables explain differences in union satisfaction and commitment?
-   To what extent can differences in union satisfaction and commitment explain differences in exit behaviour? More specifically, we will investigate to what extent the intention to terminate union membership can be explained by the combination of union (dis)satisfaction and levels of union commitment.

Method

Samples and Data Collection

In this study we use data collected in one wave of a longitudinal panel survey among members of the ten largest trade unions affiliated with the

Dutch Christian Trade Union Federation, the CNV. The unions that belong to the CNV federation have approximately 350,000 members all together, which makes the CNV the second largest trade union federation in the Netherlands. The ten CNV unions included in our study represent over 90 per cent of the total CNV constituency. Among these ten unions are six public sector unions and four private sector unions.[99]

The panel survey was started in 1992 and was conducted ten times in the period 1992-97: once each in 1992 and 1993, and twice a year in the succeeding years. On each occasion, random samples of members of the participating unions were interviewed by telephone. A selected member is asked to participate in three consecutive surveys and is then replaced in the sample. On average, the interviews took about 25 minutes. Before the first interview, each member in the sample group received a letter from his or her union with an explanation of the procedure and purpose of the study and a request to participate. Before the second and third interviews, the members who had already participated once or twice received a similar letter from the researchers. The response rate for the first interview is usually about 70 per cent of the original sample. Of the members who have been interviewed (once or twice), approximately 90 per cent also participate in the next (second or third) round of the panel survey (see also Kerkhof, 1997).

Respondents

For the present study we use data from the members who participated for the first time in the second wave of 1996. The study sample is limited to members with a paid job, only in order to ascertain the influence of job characteristics on union satisfaction, union commitment and exit behaviour. The sample consisted of 423 members of unions affiliated with the CNV trade union federation (78 per cent male, 22 per cent female), all of whom were employed. The mean age of the sample was 42 years, ranging between 19 and 62 years. The average length of union membership was 15 years, ranging between 1 and 40 years. The majority had a full-time job (87 per cent); 13 per cent were employed part-time. Almost one third (27 per

---

[99] The six public sector unions are: CFO, the union for civil servants; ACP, the union for policemen; ACOM, the union for military personnel, *Marechausseevereniging* (MV), the union for military police; KOV, Catholic school teachers union; PCO, Protestant school teachers union. The four private sector unions are: *Hout- en Bouwbond CNV*, the union for construction workers; *CNV Industrie- en Voedingsbond*, the union for the industry and food sector; *Vervoersbond CNV*, the union for the transport sector and *Dienstenbond CNV*, the union for the services sector.

cent) of the sample were single wage earners who were living together with a partner.

Measures

Demographic and work characteristics were assessed in the following manner: level of education and monthly net income were measured on scales ranging from 1 (only primary school) to 7 (university degree) and 1 (less than $f1,000$) to 8 (over $f4,000$), respectively. Full-time employment was scored 1 and part-time employment was scored 2. Members who either had no partner or who were part of a dual-earner couple, were distinguished from the single wage earners. The first group of members were scored as 1 on a variable labelled household income scale, and the second group were scored as 2. We also assessed whether members had a job for a fixed number of hours per week (scored 1), or a job with flexible hours (scored 2).

A one-item measure of union satisfaction was included in the questionnaire. Respondents were asked to indicate how satisfied or dissatisfied they were with their union. Answers were scored on a ten-point scale (1 = extremely dissatisfied to 10 = extremely satisfied).

To measure union commitment, a modified version of Meyer et al.'s (1993) three component operationalisation of organisational commitment was used. The original 18-item scale was translated into Dutch and the wording of the items were changed to fit the union context (e.g. the word 'organisation' was replaced by 'union'). Four items per component that best fitted the union context were selected from the original six reported by Meyer et al. (1993). Thus, the union commitment scale consisted of twelve items: four items for each of the three commitment components (affective, continuance and normative commitment). The answers were scored on 5-point scales ranging from (1) totally disagree to (5) totally agree. Principal components analyses revealed the expected three-factor solution, with all items loading on the expected factors. The factor loadings for all items were above 0.50, except for one item of the continuance scale. This item was therefore discarded, leaving three items in the continuance commitment scale. Reliability analysis yielded coefficient alphas of 0.80 and for affective commitment (e.g. 'I feel a strong sense of belonging to my union'), 0.72 for normative commitment (e.g. 'I would feel guilty if I left my union now') and 0.60 for continuance commitment (e.g. 'Remaining a member of my union is more a matter of necessity than a matter of desire'). For all three-commitment components, scales were constructed based on the unweighted means in such a manner that for every component the scale ranged from (1) low commitment to (5) high commitment.

Turnover intention was measured with a single item asking respondents how often they had considered terminating their union membership in the past six months. The responses were scored 1 = never, 2 = sometimes, 3 = regularly and 4 = very often.

Results

Correlations Between Satisfaction, Commitment and Exit Behaviour

The intercorrelations between union satisfaction, the three union commitment components and the intention to terminate union membership, as well as the means and standard deviations of these variables are presented in Table 6.2. Examination of the correlations between union satisfaction and the three commitment components revealed that union satisfaction was significantly related to all three forms of commitment. The largest of these correlations was between union satisfaction and affective union commitment; the smallest between union satisfaction and normative union commitment. Thus, the stronger the feelings of union commitment, the higher the reported levels of satisfaction with the union.

Affective union commitment was significantly related to both normative union commitment and continuance union commitment. The correlation between normative union commitment and continuance union commitment was not significant.

As expected, the intention to terminate union membership was correlated negatively with union satisfaction. Affective union commitment and continuance union commitment also were negatively correlated with the intention to quit. However, no significant correlation between the intention to quit and normative union commitment was found.

Individual Differences in Satisfaction, Commitment and Exit Behaviour

In order to examine the relationships between personal and work characteristics, on the one hand, and union satisfaction and the three union commitment components, on the other, regression analyses were conducted. The results are displayed in Table 6.3. The analyses showed that only a small part of the differences in union satisfaction was explained by the variables included in the analyses. Demographics and work characteristics only accounted for 4 per cent of the differences in union satisfaction. The only significant predictor in the analysis of union satisfaction was gender, indicating that women were more satisfied with their union than were men.

Table 6.2 Means, standard deviations and intercorrelations among union satisfaction, the three components of union commitment and the intention to terminate union membership

	M	SD	1	2	3	4
1. Union satisfaction	7.08	0.99				
2. Affective union commitment	3.05	0.77	0.52***			
3. Normative union commitment	2.54	0.96	0.24***	0.35***		
4. Continuance union commitment	3.44	0.90	0.38***	0.40***	-0.01	
5. Intention to quit membership	1.32	0.65	-0.49***	-0.42***	-0.07	-0.45***

Correlations

* p<0.05; ** p<0.01; *** p<0.001.

Table 6.3   **Results of regression analyses of personal and work characteristics on union satisfaction and the three union commitment components**

	Union satisfaction	Affective commitment	Normative commitment	Continuance commitment
	ß	ß	ß	ß
Personal characteristics				
Gender	0.13*	0.00	0.01	0.09
Age	0.05	0.15**	0.33***	0.01
Level of education	0.02	-0.01	0.07	0.05
Household income situation	0.04	0.08	0.18**	-0.08
Work characteristics				
Full/part-time work	-0.01	0.02	0.04	-0.01
Net monthly income	-0.12	-0.01	-0.13*	0.02
Flexible working time	-0.01	-0.06	-0.03	-0.04
R^2	0.04	0.04	0.15	0.03
F	2.24*	2.46*	10.45***	1.55
df.	7.415	7.415	7.415	7.415

* $p<0.05$; ** $p<0.01$; *** $p<0.001$.

Similarly, the regression analyses of the three union commitment components showed that only small parts of the variance were explained by the personal and work characteristics. The only significant predictor of affective commitment was age: older members had stronger feelings of affective commitment to their union than had younger members. The personal and work characteristics included in the analyses only accounted for 4 per cent of the differences in affective commitment. Of the differences in normative union commitment, 15 per cent was explained with the variables in the analyses. The beta weights of age, household type and income were significant. Feelings of normative commitment to the union were stronger among older members, among single wage earners and when the net monthly income was lower.

The personal and work characteristics did not explain a significant part of the variance in continuance union commitment and none of the personal and work characteristics had significant beta weights.

Satisfaction and Commitment as Predictors of Exit Behaviour

To determine the contributions of union satisfaction and the three union commitment components to the prediction of the intention to quit, hierarchical regression analyses were conducted. Table 6.4 displays the results. In the first step, the personal and work characteristics were entered in the analysis. These variables did not explain a significant part of the variance in the intention to quit. In the second step, union satisfaction was entered. As is shown in the table, a significant part of the variance (25 per cent) in the intention to quit was explained when union satisfaction was included. In the third step, the three commitment components were entered. This did increase the ability to predict the intention to quit and resulted in a lower beta weight for union satisfaction and in significant contributions for affective union commitment and continuance union commitment. This indicates that the effect of union (dis)satisfaction on the intention to quit is partly mediated by both affective and continuance union commitment.

In the final step, the interaction effects of union satisfaction and the three forms of commitment were examined. Including the three interaction terms' slightly increased explanatory power, the final regression model accounted for 39 per cent of the variance in intention to quit. The interactions between union satisfaction and both affective union commitment and continuance union commitment made significant independent contributions to the prediction. As can be seen, entering the interaction terms did again substantially decrease the contribution of union satisfaction but hardly affected the contributions of affective union commitment and continuance union commitment.

In order to clarify the significant interaction effects that emerged, median splits on the scales for union satisfaction, affective union commitment and continuance union commitment were performed. Based on this categorisation, groups of members were distinguished that had either low or high union satisfaction and either low or high commitment levels. We then determined the percentages of members in the different groups that indicated they had sometimes, regularly or often considered quitting their union membership in the six months previous to the interview.

Table 6.4   Results of hierarchical regression analyses on the intention to terminate union membership (β)

Step	I	II	III	IV
Personal characteristics				
Gender	-0.10	-0.03	-0.03	-0.04
Age	-0.07	-0.05	-0.06	-0.07
Level of education	-0.01	-0.00	-0.00	-0.00
Household income situation	-0.03	-0.02	-0.05	-0.03
Work characteristics				
Full/part-time work	-0.01	-0.00	-0.00	-0.01
Net monthly income	0.03	-0.03	-0.01	0.01
Flexible working time	-0.03	-0.04	-0.05	-0.06
Union satisfaction		-0.49***	-0.33***	-0.23***
Union commitment				
Affective			-0.16**	-0.18***
Normative			0.09	0.09
Continuance			-0.26***	-0.24***
Interactions				
Satisfaction * affective				0.12*
Satisfaction * normative				-0.01
Satisfaction * continuance				0.15***
R^2	0.02	0.25	0.35	0.39
F	0.91	17.01***	19.77***	18.75***
df.	7.415	8.414	11.411	14.408

* p<0.05; ** p<0.01; *** p<0.001.

The interaction effect of union satisfaction levels and affective union commitment levels on the intention to quit is clearly illustrated in Figure 6.1. Of the members who combined low union satisfaction with low affective commitment, 43 per cent had considered terminating their membership, whereas of the members who reported low satisfaction but high affective commitment, only 14 per cent had considered quitting. Only a small percentage of the members with high union satisfaction ratings (independent of their level of affective commitment) had an intention to quit. The same pattern emerged for the combined effects of union satisfaction and continuance union commitment (Figure 6.2). Thus, both affective commitment and continuance commitment prevent dissatisfied members from terminating their membership.

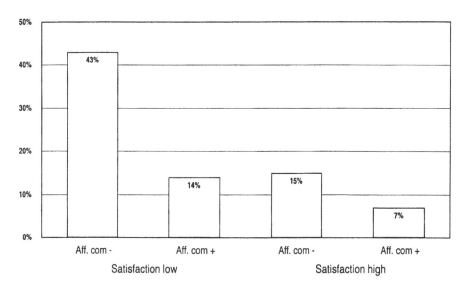

Figure 6.1   Percentage of union members with an intention to terminate union membership as a function of union satisfaction and affective union commitment

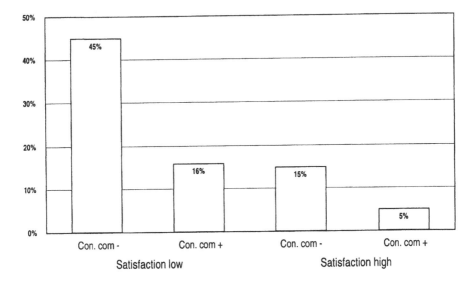

Figure 6.2   Percentage of union members with an intention to terminate union membership as a function of union satisfaction and continuance union commitment

Discussion

Although the number of union members and the union density rate in the Netherlands have increased in the last decade, union density is still lower than before the early 1980s. Especially among the new and growing groups of employees in the labour force, such as young employees, women, part-time employees and partners from dual-earner couples, union density is lower. As for the future of Dutch trade unions, it seems crucial that more employees from these groups should become members. The low-density rates among new groups of employees is only partly due to low entrance rates. Unions are fairly successful in recruiting members, also from these relatively new groups of employees in the labour force. The chances, for example, that women will join a union at the start of their careers are hardly smaller than the chances that men will join at the same point in their life (cf. Klandermans and Visser, 1995). A bigger problem is posed by the exiting of members. The exit rates in general are high and are much higher among members belonging to the new groups of employees than among the more traditional groups of members. Nowadays, retaining members is often more difficult for unions than recruiting new members.

The 'exit, voice and loyalty' framework and the (psychological) literature on organisational turnover suggests that members leave an organisation when they are dissatisfied and lack sufficient levels of commitment to
the organisation. This perspective implies that groups of members with
higher exit rates are either less satisfied with and/or less committed to their
union.

Our study among Dutch union members shows only minor differences
in satisfaction and commitment levels between the more traditional and the
new groups of employees within the membership. Unexpectedly, women
were found to be more satisfied with their union than were men. Moreover,
no differences in either affective, normative or continuance union commitment between men and women were observed. Although women have
higher exit rates than men, this cannot be attributed to differences in either
union satisfaction or union commitment between men and women. The
individual differences that did emerge from the analyses of affective
commitment and normative commitment to the union, however, were
consistent with our expectations. Specific groups of members known to
have higher exit rates were found to be less committed to their union. Both
affective and normative commitment were stronger among older members,
and the normative commitment levels among single wage earners were
above those among members from dual earner couples or members without
a partner. Both affective and normative commitment develop through experience and the socialisation process, either through contacts within the
union organisation (affective commitment) or in the pre-employment stage
(normative commitment). Lower levels of affective and normative commitment thus reflect age and years of union membership. Continuance
commitment is based upon the costs associated with leaving. It appears that
the (quality of the) perceived alternatives for union membership do not
differ between different groups of members.

The results did not reveal any significant relationships between personal
and work characteristics and the intention to terminate membership. Given
the fact that several of the groups of members in our study do have higher
exit rates, this outcome is somewhat puzzling. It could be that our measure
of the intention to quit is not strongly related to - or is not an adequate
predictor of - the actual turnover. Another possible explanation for this
result could be that turnover among new groups of employees is not always
so much a reaction to dissatisfaction with the union, but rather a consequence of an external event, such as a change of jobs, or a temporary
withdrawal from the labour force because of the birth of a child. The
significance of this alternative route to exit behaviour - an external event -
is supported by research among ex-members of Dutch trade unions. The
two most important reasons for membership termination given by ex-

members were dissatisfaction because of a negative experience with the union and falling outside the labour process because of unemployment or injury (Van der Veen and Klandermans, 1989).

The usefulness of the 'exit, voice and loyalty' framework in explaining the exit behaviour of union members is evident from our study. An important part of the differences in the intention to terminate membership was explained by differences in satisfaction and commitment levels. Union satisfaction and union commitment appear to be key variables in the process of sustained participation. Union satisfaction as well as affective and continuance union commitment have unique and direct effects on the intention to quit. The present study is correlational and therefore does not enable us to draw definite conclusions about the causal paths between the variables. The results of our study, however, are supportive of the moderating effect of commitment between satisfaction and the intention to terminate union membership. Indeed, dissatisfied members who were strongly committed to their union had not considered terminating their membership more often than had satisfied members, whereas a substantial percentage of the members who were dissatisfied with their union and felt little commitment to it had considered quitting.

Unions should realise that their performance has important implications for the satisfaction of the membership. Because the labour force - and to a lesser extent also the membership - has become more and more diverse in the past decades, living up to the varied expectations of different groups of members is becoming more difficult. Unions could benefit from research aimed at identifying the work-related needs and expectations of specific groups of employees (cf. Fiorito et al., 1988). At the same time, however, it seems virtually impossible to prevent members from having a dissatisfying experience with their union during their membership. A sufficient general level of union commitment among members is necessary to prevent membership turnover in response to negative experiences with the union. The results of the present study show that both affective union commitment and continuance union commitment moderate the relationship between dissatisfaction and the intention to terminate union membership. A major challenge for the Dutch trade unions lies in enhancing affective and continuance commitment among members in the early stages of union membership. Affective union commitment is based upon a positive exchange relationship between individual members and their union. Such a relationship is shaped by the experiences and contacts members have with their union. The development of affective union commitment takes time, especially among members who are in contact with their union only sporadically. In order to enhance affective union commitment, unions could try to involve members more (actively) in union activities. This would enlarge the number of contacts and experiences members have with their union and, consequently, these experiences would no longer merely depend on situations in which members have a question or problem and contact their union for help. One way to stimulate continuance union commitment, a commitment based upon the costs that are associated with leaving, might be to make it explicitly clear to members what the (short-term) individual benefits of union membership are. Another way may possibly be to expand the number and range of individual services and benefits that are valued by the membership.

7 Models for Industrial Relations in the Private Service Industries

MAURIZIO AMBROSINI

Outline of the Sector

From an economic and employment point of view, the increasing importance of the services sector, and particularly of the market services sector in Europe, is a trend that can be statistically documented and situated in time.

At the end of the 1980s, in all the countries studied, the agricultural and industrial sectors affected employment less than at the beginning of the 1980s; in numerous countries, the employment rate in the services sector had increased to nearly 70 per cent of total employment; only in Germany and Portugal did it amount to less than 50 per cent.

To be sure, the delimitation of the boundaries of the services sector, the demarcation between it and the industrial sector, and the definition of the concept of 'service' itself are problems that are far from resolved. Nevertheless it is important to remember that in 1990 the portion of the EU services sector dealing with sales alone, accounted for 48.2 per cent of the gross national product and 42 per cent of employment, thus representing the single largest sector of economic activity. A substantially increasing trend was reported (10 per cent more of the GNP as compared to 1970), which became especially evident from 1982 onward: an average increase of 0.7 per cent per year, as compared to 0.3 per cent for the previous period (Buigues, 1993).

Each EU country shows different developments in the sector. In Belgium, France, Italy, Luxembourg and Holland, that part of the services sector dedicated to sales produces more than 49.5 per cent of the GNP; in Denmark, Germany, Greece, Ireland, Spain and Portugal, this figure is less than 47.5 per cent; while Great Britain is in line with the average EU figures.

The sales sector's contribution to the GNP therefore is higher than the EU average in countries with higher procapita incomes, even if Germany and Denmark represent notable exceptions to this rule: in Denmark this anomaly can for the most part be explained by the importance of the manufacturing sector, and in Germany by the fact that the greatest development is taking place in the non-sales services sector. Instead of decreasing, the differences became even more pronounced between 1980 and 1990. The increase in the services sector was greater in those countries which, at the beginning of the 1980s, had already manifested greater specialisation in the sector (Buigues, 1993).

If we take a closer look at the contribution of the sector to employment between 1980 and 1990, we see an increase of 10.4 million jobs (which is equivalent to +23.4 per cent) as compared to a loss of 3.6 million jobs (Greece excluded) in the manufacturing sector (which is equivalent to -13.3 per cent).

Nevertheless, the distribution of employment within the different service branches highlights a clear distinction in EU countries between the more developed countries (usually the Northern ones, with the exception of Ireland) and those with lower procapita incomes (in Southern Europe and Ireland) (Ilzkovitz, 1993; see Table 7.1).

In the first group, banking, insurance and communications branches are relatively more important than hotel and commercial distribution branches, which have a less than average impact. On the other hand, the second group presents an employment structure in the services sector where traditional branches, such as hotel (with the exception of Italy) and commercial distribution, are more important, at the expense of more developed and capital-intensive branches.

These data can be explained in terms of two different models of tertiarisation: the first is more oriented towards business service, with higher levels of investment, technological applications and employment qualifications; the second, which involves lower levels of invested capital and technological innovation, is more oriented towards services to individuals and produces more employment, though this employment requires lower qualification levels and is less stable. A third model may be identified with the superiority of the public tertiary sector or, more specifically, with the welfare services that have developed within the socio-economic order of the Scandinavian countries. The high level of tertiarisation in countries such as Sweden and Norway (67-68 per cent) and, to a lower degree, Finland (60.2 per cent), is greatly due to the influence of the public sector. In Sweden, employment in the Welfare State has accounted for 80 per cent of the net growth of employment since 1970. In general, contrary to EU countries, the welfare states of the Nordic countries have expanded social services to the point that this expansion makes up for the reduction in the employment in the private services sectors (Esping-Andersen, 1993, 58).

Nevertheless, our study aims to analyse the private tertiary sector and, as a consequence, it will not be concerned with the specific problems of work and industrial relations in the public sector.

Characteristics of Employment in the Service Industries

An examination of the employment statistics gives us a better picture of the conditions of employment in the service sector. The following characteristics were identified in a European study (Lebrun et al., 1993):

a) The important role that women play in the service sector may be demonstrated by the fact that they presently hold the average of one position out of two compared to an average of one out of four in the industrial sector. In the EU, and in particular in Germany, France, Denmark and Great Britain, women make up 50 per cent of the employees in the service sector. Women play a prominent role in all the countries with retail trade sectors, a hotel sector and other service sectors (especially education, health and welfare, where up to two-thirds of the people employed are women).
In the Scandinavian countries, the percentage of women in the service sector work force is even greater: 71.2 per cent in Norway and 80.5 per cent in Sweden. Women constitute 44.4 per cent of the total work force in Norway and 47.9 per cent in Sweden. The service sector contributes largely to these results.
In Autria and Switzerland, the rates of participation and incidence in the total work force are lower and more similar to average European figures.
b) The high proportion of part-time employment (within the EU, 18.2 per cent of employees in the service sector hold part-time positions, as compared to 5.9 per cent in the industrial sector) is closely related to the great increase in the presence of women in the labour market and is therefore particularly high in countries with a greater presence of women in the labour market. In the Northern European countries, the part-time workers outnumber the full-time workers. Trends vary (rates of increase or pro-rata compared to full-time employment, etc.) from country to country.
c) There is a high rate of self-employment: 16.8 per cent in the EU service sector, as compared to 11.3 per cent in the industries sector in 1990.

The trend is particularly evident in Southern Europe and is concentrated mostly in the trade sector: the top position is held by Greece with non-wage-earners accounting for 34.4 per cent of total employment in the service sector (72 per cent of which is in retail trade); Italy follows with 30.1 per cent, Spain with 24.6 per cent and Portugal with 21 per cent. By contrast, in Northern Europe the percentage of self-employed people is lower: 8.2 per cent in Denmark, 11.1 per cent in Germany, 11.3 per cent in Holland, 11.6 per cent in France and 12.2 per cent in Great Britain. Belgium is an exception with 19.9 per cent. Even in Northern Europe, it is the retail trade sector that contributes most to self-employment with figures ranging from 15.8 per cent in Germany to 25.9 per cent in France, reaching a high of 47.6 per cent in Belgium.

d) The precarious nature of most jobs is due above all to the application of fixed-term contracts and seasonal employment in the different sectors. Trade, individual services, and parts of the banking and insurance sectors are all branches where temporary or seasonal employment practices are common. Apart from the Mediterranean countries such as Greece, Spain and Portugal, where temporary employment is very common in all the sectors of the economy, the phenomenon is also remarkably common in Denmark and Germany. In Germany, 10 per cent of all jobs in the banking sector have a temporary nature, a figure that rises to between 10 per cent and 20 per cent in the retail trade and individual service sectors. Great Britain, Italy, France and Belgium seem to be less affected by this problem. Temporary positions are occupied mostly by women.

e) Industrial relations in the service sector take on very different forms depending on the different branches of industry and the institutional resources that are present in each country. Factors such as average company size, recent developments in the sector, distribution of atypical employment and local union traditions contribute in many cases to produce levels of unionisation and protection that are lower than those in the industrial sector. But where large public or semi-public firms exist, especially if they have a kind of market monopoly (such as communications), then the opposite may be true.

Furthermore, the strong institutional patterns of certain national industrial relations systems, such as the Scandinavian or German systems, have proved to be more efficient in promoting unionisation and joint agreement on working conditions, even in the service sector.

Table 7.1 Sectoral structure of employment in the service sector, 1990 (in %)

Sector	B	DK	D	E	F	IRL	I	L	NL	P	UK	EUR 9*
Transport	9.2	14.9	9.5	11.6	9.6	10.4	12.1	10.6	9.7	11.2	8.2	10.0
Hotels/catering	5.9	5.8	8.7	15.7	8.8	13.7	9.7	9.8	4.6	13.6	12.0	10.4
Banking and insurance	8.2	11.4	8.2	5.3	6.7	10.2	4.3	17.1	6.6	7.0	8.4	7.0
Distribution	34.7	34.0	38.5	41.0	36.1	43.7	40.4	30.6	32.8	51.3	33.4	37.5
Communications	3.9	5.0	4.5	2.9	4.9	6.6	3.1	2.5	2.9	4.1	3.8	3.9
Other services	38.2	28.9	30.6	23.5	33.9	15.4	30.5	29.3	43.3	12.7	34.3	31.3

* EUR 9: Belgium, Denmark, Germany, Spain, France, Italy, Luxembourg, Portugal and United Kingdom.

Source: Eurostat, DG II.

Generally speaking, we can confirm that the sector has a need both for stable rules and active flexibility. It needs the convinced co-operation of the workers, but, at the same time, it has a strong tendency to limit the cost of labour, and these reductions have their greatest effect on the salaries and working conditions of the weaker levels of the work force. The sector offers ample employment opportunities for trained and qualified members of the work force but also creates a demand both for manual labour and for executive personnel, and these two groups still require satisfactory protection. For these reasons, in the perspective of increasing internationalisation of the service sector, the construction of an effective system of industrial relations is a priority, not only for the purpose of protecting workers' interests, but also for promoting balanced economic growth in the European countries.

Characteristics of Work Relations in the Service Industries

The structural characteristics of the private service sector affect employment relations, producing certain specific aspects that we now need to explain.

Plurality of Employment Frameworks and Atypical Work Relations

Relations between management and labour in various sub-sectors of service industries are rendered particularly difficult by a single major factor: the frequency of atypical work relations, meaning arrangements which do not correspond to traditional salaried employment and cannot be identified as strictly self-employment relations. Consequently, the discrepancy with the standard model of employment, based on the manufacturing industries framework, may sometimes be considered emblematic of the service industries.

This peculiarity has become particularly evident in the advanced service branch.[100] Here, on the basis of empirical findings, it can be demonstrated that, besides the common arrangement of employment for an unspecified period of time, there exists a broad range of methods for classifying professional work:

a) professional partners directly employed in the company;
b) professionals employed on an exclusive contract basis;
c) experts employed for occasional or specific tasks;

---

[100] By this term we mean professional services for industries such as consulting, marketing, advertising, finance, data processing, etc. (cf. Regalia, 1990).

d) professionals on a kind of 'vertical' part-time basis (guaranteeing a certain number of working days per year);
e) freelancers;
f) specialised technicians;
g) occasional support personnel.

All these categories compose the menu of human resources and respective types of work relations from which the companies can choose (Regalia and Sartor, 1989).

Such a variety of work relations leads to three consequences. First of all, there is a widespread application of 'forms of collaboration on a self-employed basis', especially in the case of small businesses. Secondly, the companies' organisational profiles become 'systems with comparatively open and fluid boundaries', rendering it in fact impossible to consider the enterprise as consisting solely of partners and employees, without taking into account those who are usually labelled as 'outside' collaborators.

Finally, it is becoming evident that in the advanced service branch knowing the type of contract is not sufficient to identify the bargaining strength and the organisational role of the individuals: external professionals can be more central and influential in the labour process than in-house technicians and professionals.

These forms of management behaviour, aiming to achieve the highest flexibility of labour while minimising the direct and indirect responsibilities arising from traditional employment relations, also satisfy the interests and the aspirations of certain segments of workers who are interested in taking advantage of the multiple opportunities and occasions in order to create their own professional career.

The difficulty implied in regulating and standardising professional work activities stems from the very nature of the work: it is performed on a contractual basis for the purpose of implementing specific projects or solving complex problems, and quite often it is carried out at the client's facilities. This state of affairs generates a series of divergences from the way work is usually arranged in a traditional company. For instance, it is often impossible to set the working hours on a fixed schedule. The prevailing practice, then, is that of the schedule-frame, which allows for time self-management and the making of adjustments between hectic and comparatively calm periods.

Atypical work arrangements are found not only among professionals employed in advanced service industries, however. Even at the opposite extreme of the employment scale, i.e. the unskilled activities of lower service industries, the traditional employment relationship is not the rule. Here, the growing flexibility of the working conditions has led to an employment situation that is increasingly precarious and unstable. This is probably the single area in which market relations have made the greatest gains in importance in recent years, all at the expense, naturally, of the social rights acquired by workers over the course of several decades of conflicts and negotiations. Recently, especially the literature on the economic transformations of metropolitan areas in the direction of the service economy has pointed to the deterioration of the working conditions of the lower service sector workers (Sassen, 1997; Mingione, 1997).

The reaction, as it happens especially in the case of young people, is to consciously assimilate the concept of temporary, discontinuous working arrangements, which then may become compatible with other activities and interests, or may otherwise be considered as a temporary phase, while one is waiting for a better position. In fact, mobility rates among workers in the lower service sectors are generally high. Contrary to the more optimistic analyses, a study I carried out showed that these temporary 'odd jobs' are mainly time-fillers, expedients or temporary activities carried out while the person is waiting for a 'normal', steady job - a goal that is proving to be increasingly distant and difficult to achieve, especially for the less qualified (Ambrosini, 1995).

Moreover, the sub-sectors of the service industries employing the least qualified show some instances of underemployment in terms of discontinuity or restrictions to just a few hours a day. Part-time labour is frequently utilised in sectors such as industrial cleaning or the hotel business, and it often corresponds to socially unappealing portions of the day (early morning, late evening). Usually it has little to do with the workers' preference for flexibility, but rather is largely determined by organisational demands and advantages (the client company, or the company obtaining the contract).

Nevertheless, the flexibility of the working schedule may meet the needs of adjusting paid work with other activities and (mainly) family responsibilities.

The contracting system is associated with a characteristic of many low-skilled jobs: these activities are frequently jobbed out - and thus transferred to 'third-party' service industries - by many companies in various sectors. This trend increased remarkably during the 1980s and 1990s. Sociologically speaking, the most significant consequence of this trend, according to a study by Ruffier (1980), is the fracture, not only of the unity of time, but also of the unity of status and contractual coverage of those workers physically present in the same facility.

Thus in the same workplace and under the co-ordination of a single management structure, we can find workers who are employed by different firms, under different contracts, and under different economic and social conditions. Fragmentation grows, and inequality as well. It becomes harder for unions to harmonise demands and interests, and thus to organise workers.

The jobbing out of activities with little strategic or secondary relevance to the firm's *core business* is clearly part of the same trend.

From the unions' point of view, such a development represents a remarkable step backwards in terms of safeguarding jobs and working conditions, as contract workers are always subject to the risk that their contract will not be renewed. Moreover, there is the risk of a significant difficulty in organising and safeguarding the interests of workers scattered among the various external contractors.

In the international debate, these phenomena have been interpreted as an attempt made by the economic system to counterbalance the success of the so-called 'primary' sector of the labour force in creating stronger protection of the workers' interests, by creating a 'secondary' sector where labour is 'susceptible of being treated just like a mere good' (Goldthorpe, 1984, 335). The result is an 'enlargement of certain areas of the economy where the market forces, and the corresponding relations of authority and control, can work more freely than in others, so as to actually compensate the rigidity prevailing elsewhere' (Goldthorpe, 1984, 329). Apart from the debate about the validity of such a dualistic and schematic approach, there is no denying the growth in the weak and underprotected areas of the labour market of Western economies, of which the employment situation in the service industries is emblematic.

Labour as a Crucial Factor in Quality of Service

The discourse on the problematic working conditions at the lower end of the service industry scale embraces, but is not limited to the pertinence of a reflection on the importance of labour as an organisational factor, an issue which has engaged a conspicuous body of literature (in particular, Norman, 1984; for a critical approach, see Caselli et al., 1993).

In the service industries, the possibility of replacing human labour with technological investments is structurally limited, and the interaction with the outside world (public, clients, users, etc.) is often a key element in the work performance. The role of personnel directly involved with clients and their needs plays a major role in terms of organisation, public relations and the company image that forms in the clients' mind. Furthermore, the intangible nature of service - where 'the merchandise, medium between the producer and consumer, disappears' (Butera, 1988, 66) - and the frequent overlapping of production and supply/consuming of the service itself, tends to focus on the interactive element of service-industry work in the sector, on the basis of which 'the front-office/client relationship is the funnel where the whole process passes through' (Butera, 1988, 65).

It should again be pointed out that the aforementioned recognition of the key role of the human relations factors - thus 'live' work in service industries activity - does not lead to univocal consequences. Within the service industries, a great deal of effort is put into achieving the goal of containing labour costs and reducing the importance of the role of the workers in the service sold to the public. This happens primarily through automation and shifting to self-production and self-service techniques involving a number of simple, repetitive tasks in a broadening spectrum of services: gas pumps, cash machines, free-service sales, etc.

Even in the case of services where the role of personnel is indispensable, company policies aim primarily to economise labour as much as possible: the expanding presence of temporary and atypical work relations belongs to the same strategy. Therefore, the ambivalence implied by the expression 'human resources', particularly underlined by Storey (1992), is even more emphasised in the service industries: labour is considered a 'resource', along with energy, materials and machinery, and thus companies strive to use it as efficiently as possible, avoiding waste, redundancies and added costs.

However, there have also been signs of efforts in the opposite direction, that is towards a greater attention to a positive relationship between labour quality and company results. A German study about sales service showed that: 'There are clear signs, contrary to what happened in the 1960s and 1970s, that the key slogan concerning personnel will no longer be *reduction at any cost*, but instead it will be to give increasing attention to the qualitative development of human resources, and the companies themselves are promising them a better position on the market, based on the growing potential for personnel qualification' (Baethge et al., 1989).

The innovative tendencies appear to be more accentuated in the so-called 'advanced service industries', where 'the work performed, as well as the service produced and visible to the purchaser, frequently represents two sides of the same process' (Regalia, 1989, 12). This is due to the importance of the activities of contact with the client, interaction and problem solving, or else to the combined contribution of specialists.

More than in other already labour-intensive sub-sectors of the service industry, the supply of highly qualified services, partly due to their immaterial nature, tends to be identified with the sale of skills and professional activities supplied by individuals.

Nevertheless, even in the most traditional sub-sectors, as in large chain stores, there is the perception of a contradiction between the orientation of centralised highly bureaucratic company structures towards reducing the costs of labour and their orientation towards innovative policies that inherently involve the valorisation of human resources: the quality of the service, the introduction of commercial innovations (assisted sales, specialised branches), and the very image the clients have of the company are closely related to the behaviour of employees when they are directly in contact with the public (see Negrelli, 1989). The client/supplier relationship, therefore, somehow reflects the very nature of service-industry work, since the supply of a service is an activity involving human relations, where the recipient, the user or the client, becomes a part of the production process.

This explains the companies' efforts to motivate and involve sales personnel through the use of incentives, an effort which is hard to combine with the emphasis on cost reduction, the implementation of atypical and unappealing schedules (such as night and Sunday shifts), and the introduction of large-scale part-time arrangements. It is not a coincidence that in Italy, while attempting to solve this organisational dilemma, the large-scale distribution companies have been among the first to introduce contractual forms of worker participation in the departmental sales profits, long before this type of agreement was introduced in the manufacturing industry (Zito, 1986).

Similar problems have been observed in sectors such as banking, where labour was once considered to be subject to an almost unavoidable trend toward lower job qualifications as a result of the implementation of new technologies. In fact, the increasing competition, on the one hand, and the fact that the routine duties are being absorbed by the new technological resources, on the other, mean that front-line personnel are becoming involved in more dynamic roles such as client counselling and the promotion of new banking products and services (Ambrosini et al., 1989).

The outcome is a situation in which the labour-intensive characteristics of most service industry activities, along with the intensive exposure to the external environment and the coincidence between production and consumption of the product, all together produce two symmetric consequences: on the one hand, there is the considerable power to take advantage of the vulnerability of the workers and the professional groups, and therefore the companies' need to promote the establishment of relations based on collaboration and agreement; on the other hand, where technologies and the market operations allow it to be, there is the tendency to introduce forms of automatisation and to reduce labour costs, even through radical means of employment reduction.

Unionisation Profile of the Sector

It is not easy to synthesise the observations about the state of unionisation in the private service industry. On the whole, the level of unionisation is one of the main factors that contribute to deeply differentiating the European social panorama. This is even more true in the service industry: highly unionised sectors with a strong collective bargaining coverage, such as telecommunication and railways, exist in all the European countries alongside fragmented sectors in which the level of unionisation is very low. Generally speaking, though, the average rate of unionisation is lower in the private services industry than in the manufacturing industry or in public services.

Some of the characteristics of the service labour market serve to explain this trend: the precariousness of the work and the high rate of part-time labour can be identified as conditions that work against unionisation. Almost everywhere, the prevalence of small business induces legal disadvantages and organisational difficulties in reaching and organising workers. Seasonal or temporary workers, with a high-risk of losing their job, are often individually indifferent to union protection or objectively compelled not to unionise. Nevertheless, even in these cases it is not proper to generalise or to formulate hurried and mechanistic conclusions. In countries such as Sweden and Belgium, the unionisation rates have increased, even in a context of growing precariousness and unemployment, due mostly to the fact that the unions manage the unemployment welfare and secure specific services for interested workers.

If there are many who are too weak to be able to organise themselves in a union, there are also the others who express little interest in the various forms of collective protection because they have educational credentials and levels of qualification that induce them to think they can better protect themselves by various forms of individual contract and by voluntary mobility from one job to another (Regalia, 1990).

Another source of complications lies in the history and the forms of organisation of the union movement which are rooted in the large-scale industries. It is there that culture and the various forms of protection of the workers' interests were born, and from there they extended to the rest of the world of labour.

Private service, except in certain cases, is typical for younger sectors without a tradition of unionisation. Workers who enter it, do not frequently encounter any institution or practice of consolidated union action. The same instruments that are applied to industry would probably prove to be unfit for protecting workers in the service industry.

Conflict in the Service Industry

The need expressed by business enterprises to guarantee worker co-operation may be confirmed by analysing the behaviour that emerges when this co-operation does not occur, i.e. by analysing labour conflict in the service industries.

Sub-sectors of the private service industries that provide key community services (banking, air transportation, chain-store distribution) and that have experienced prolonged disputes concerning contract renewals, are being affected by problems of visibility and loss of 'public' popularity tied to labour strikes.

Therefore, according to Accornero (1985), the 'tertiarisation' of labour conflicts should not be interpreted merely as a shift of protests from the industrial sector to the service industries, but should also be seen in terms of the increasing involvement of those who are being *served*, who become accidental hostages, and are ultimately the ones at whom the strikes are aimed. Indeed, it is the service user who most suffers the damage and the inconveniences, and much more directly than the employers, though admittedly the costs are, for the most part, intangible and hard to calculate in economic terms.

Public protest, therefore, becomes a tool to create pressure during negotiations, which will find the company, especially if private and exposed to competition, threatened by a loss of image and customer trust. This explains the principle that 'labour disputes are solved faster, and victoriously, if the users complain' (Pipan, 1989, 118). Moreover, the conflicts tend to gain a social - and even spectacular - dimension: by a spiralling effect, the ability of the conflict to take advantage of vulnerable situations generates attention in the media, and this attention, in turn, increases the visibility and the impact of the strike, to the extent that the 'announcement effect', or the mere 'threat' of a strike, produces the same effect of an actual strike, thus compelling the users, for instance, to give up taking their vacation or using the required service.

Rather than being used to seeking the support of public opinion, the press becomes an instrument for amplifying the perception of the inconveniences caused by the strike. Service industry conflicts have no need for public or external support; rather, they simply claim an audience (Accornero, 1985). At the same time, the easiness of amplifying the echo of the disputes increases the service industries workers' power to take advantage of vulnerability, so that it could even be argued that the discontent stems less from objective conditions than from the mere possibility of the idea of being communicated (Accornero and Marcucci, 1987).

Another peculiar characteristic of recent service-industry conflicts is the analogy with some aspects of contemporary culture, such as the growth of the individual propensity towards personal self-fulfilment, regardless of the consequences for the collective interests. These conflicts seem to lack 'a formulation of values to be shared, as well as collective projects calling for conscious commitment, ideologies, preferences, or activist devotion' (Pipan, 1989, 53).

It is not a coincidence that the feeling against labour unions, both in Italy and France has been identified as a fundamental component of spontaneous groupings, in the dual sense of protest against 'traditional' union activity and a rejection of the principle of general representation of the interests of salaried workers. Indeed, a shared characteristic of the new organisations is the 'claim for the strengthening of a specific workers group, or for a given job category, or simply for a working position, together with the desire to differentiate the group from the rest of the world and from other categories and positions' (Bordogna, 1991, 54; see also Bordogna, 1998).

Furthermore, it may be observed that the new protagonists in the service industry conflicts share certain characteristics with *single-issue* movements, and this may somehow be viewed as being an expression of the post-modern, post-ideological and post-collective culture. They do not pursue goals relating to social progress, nor do they worry about the general political effects of their actions; they do not seek widespread support, explicitly favouring the interests of professional categories or groups that are often locked in competition; they do not involve the public in their protests, and indeed they often use the public as a tool to increase the pressure on the opposite side; within their organisation they are characterised by a low level of organisational structuring, with the result that they may disband after a dispute, only to regroup once again, as soon as new sentiments of discontent arise; they express an intransigent attitude in their demands, and they are little fond of negotiation; they view the social conflict more on a horizontal plain (i.e. versus other categories and groups of workers) than in a vertical one (against the owners of the capital or the dominating classes) (Ambrosini, 1991).

We can attempt to summarise the main differences between the traditional industrial conflicts and the newly emerging service industry conflicts by referring to and broadening the scheme proposed by Accornero (1985) (see Table 7.2 next page).

These potentially disruptive characteristics of service-industry conflicts are evidence of the complex set of interrelations that interweave contemporary society, and of which the service system represents an infrastructure of vital importance, explaining the fragility of its functioning. Nevertheless, they also paradoxically highlight the importance of reaching joint agreement on a set of rules for regulating labour relations and preventing and limiting instances of conflict while guaranteeing the public's rights. If such a system were created, the confederate unions, on the basis of their social concern, which is much deeper than the concern of the individual categories, would be entitled to play a decisive role.

Table 7.2   Differences between industrial conflict and service industry conflicts

	Industrial conflicts	Service industry conflicts
Position in the social organisation	Isolation	Crucial role
Effects on external social solidarity	Positive	Negative
Possibility of taking advantage of third parties' vulnerability	Incidental	Inevitable
Attitude towards the public	Involvement	Indifference
Potential role of the public	Ally	Hostage
Main characters	Confederate unions	Independent unions (wildcat groups)
Goals	Broadened solidarity	Narrow solidarity (professional categories)
Mandate to representatives	Broad	Restricted
Ability to negotiate and achieve agreements	High	Limited
Structure of social conflicts	Vertical	Horizontal

Development of Unionisation in Private Services: Some Research Hypotheses

The study of union relations in the service industry sector must take into account two phenomena which lead to marked distinctions on the international level: first, the peculiar characteristics of the single national systems of industrial relations, which lead to sharp differences in the rates of unionisation and in the organisational procedures of workers' unions (Ferner and

Hyman, 1992), and secondly, the significant differences between production sub-sectors in the private services industry sector.

While specific analyses are generally more widely used (concerning sub-sectors such as banking-insurance, retail sales, telecommunications, etc.), it appears worthwhile to make an overview of a sector which represents a growing proportion of employment, in which old and new demands for the regulation of the use of labour overlap, and in which the traditional forms of union activities have proved to be relatively ineffective in a number of countries.

Our research confirms, first of all, the need for more appropriate, more uniform regulation of working conditions in the sector, by establishing a satisfactory balance between flexibility and minimum threshold guarantees, in the light of the imminent establishment of a more integrated European economic system: just take, for example, the common interest (shared by management forces) in avoiding forms of social dumping and downward spirals in the cost of labour within the European Union itself.

Secondly, even the least skilled professional sectors are not exempt from the problem of raising the quality and the reliability of the service, and they cannot simply continue to compete only in terms of price. In this area, as well in the others, the improvement of personnel stability and motivation is beginning to develop into a goal to be pursued, although the hard economic situation of the early 1990s favoured cost reduction and weakening of the protection of workers' interests (Accornero, 1997; Gallino, 1998).

Furthermore, despite a general picture that is certainly unfavourable to protecting the workers' interests and improving their treatment, there are a number of signs of development in the opposite direction. Even in the low-skilled services, the trend towards a concentration and rationalisation of the services on offer, due in part to the increasing degree of internationalisation, has enlarged the boundaries for union initiatives. Unions are considered protagonists to be dealt with on each occasion. They may or may not prove to be useful, but they cannot be avoided by many of these enterprises that have crossed the threshold of micro-entrepreneurial fragmentation (Caselli et al., 1993). Thus, there could be a development similar to that which took place during the transformation from traditional sales to modern distribution: a transformation which led to increased possibilities for the protection of salaried employees and their organisation into unions.

Obviously, from the unions' point of view, the first step to be taken in the relatively low-skilled services is to demand traditional types of safeguards, emphasising security both in terms of salaries and schedule arrangements. One primary task is the need to control - or at least obtain additional compensation for - the flexibility that has so clearly functioned to serve management's interests. In this case, unions can once again play their relevant role as regulators of the market forces in defending the working man and woman. Additionally, other areas of action, as yet untested and little explored, are appearing on the horizon: for example, the question of professional partnerships; the introduction of forms of minimum protection in the half-hidden world of the black economy, where more decisive action must also be taken by public authorities; the problems generated by the outsourcing of services formerly performed within the industrial enterprises; and the increasing use of different forms of decentralisation and contracting out.

The needs and opportunities for union initiatives in the realm of the advanced service industries are greater than they are usually thought to be. Though there admittedly exists a strong tendency to prefer self-representation on an individualistic basis among the most qualified workers, it should not be forgotten that there are a number of issues that call for collective bargaining: the need for regulatory certainties in terms of defining working relationships, as in the case of insurance and pension issues; the presence of workers holding clerical or relatively unskilled positions, for whom union bargaining will probably remain indispensable; the diffusion of several forms of temporary employment, which can certainly not be treated through the traditional approach used with workers' rights, but which presumably will still benefit from a more specific set of regulations (Regalia, 1990).

Finally, we can identify an area of potential activity which has been relatively ignored by union initiatives: the supply of services to meet individual demands. High career mobility, the need for lifelong learning and a frequently unclear classification falling between salaried and self-employed work are typical of many jobs in the advanced services industries and elsewhere. For such work, there is a growing need for protection that is linked more closely to the forces of the labour market than to the relations with the employer. In addition to this need for protection, highly skilled professionals may be interested in training activities, consulting, and opportunities to meet other professionals in the service industry.

Here a problem arises. The union activity we know varies from country to country and is essentially influenced by experiences in the industrial sector. The question is whether these union activities are able to meet the needs and satisfy the workers' demands in the private services industries? By way of answer, it may be claimed that there has long existed the idea of a 'major' form of union activity, which developed within large industrial enterprises, and that around it proliferated minor, residual groups of workers independently organised - often with many difficulties - to defend their interests, in different areas, and especially in those sectors characterised by production structures dominated by small and medium-sized enterprises: construction, crafts and (an increasingly important area) different sub-sectors of the private service industry.

The underlying idea was to gradually overcome the existing fragmentation and then slowly establish 'modern' approaches to production, based on the rationalisation of production systems and economies of scale and therefore focus on enterprises with more sizeable dimensions.

As a result, the accepted framework of interpretation, even for union activities, was based on developmental dynamics: historical models of initiatives, based on a strong local presence, in attempting to regulate the relationship between the demand and supply of labour, as well as forms of individual defence of the workers' interests, were viewed as relics of the past, the result of dispersion of the production structures and the weakness of salaried employees.

The model then coming to the fore was identified with the collective protection of workers' rights organised according to the style of industrial union activities: unifying the labour demands, undertaking actual labour actions, and introducing forms of company-wide contractual negotiations was considered the model to be achieved and the 'ideal' path for union activities to take.

It is also obvious that union activities manage to develop more effectively where there are processes at work which lead to the concentration of the labour force: the regulation through collective bargaining of the conditions under which the labour force is employed is necessarily accepted in this situation as a rational, equitable and transparent principle for the management of personnel affairs.

Today, we must consider the fact that the production structure includes a persistent, and in some cases increasing, presence of small enterprises, along with a reduction in the size of the average enterprise. Facing such a situation, it is obviously difficult to propose anew the universal implementation of a model for union activities that is essentially taken from the past and involves large industrial concerns.

Furthermore, the mechanisms of the labour market supply shows today a tendency to adopt individualistic attitudes. On the one hand, the prevailing method for improving one's employment conditions at the lower end of the service industries scale is individual mobility within the labour market, which means changing job and company, rather than collective action. On the other hand, in the highly skilled job categories, the establishment of a professional status and the safeguarding of the workers' interests in organised forms, establish a balance which may vary remarkably from case to case.

Thirdly, there is reason to believe that union membership has become a matter that is increasingly subject to negotiation and personal preference, on the basis of a timely offer of service, advice and concrete defence of the workers' interests in monitorable ways. The relationship between member and union is less and less influenced by ideologies and political affiliations. In such a context where union membership has become a personal matter and devoid of ideology, the 'persuasive' role of the union activist would appear to have grown in importance. The quality of the personal relationship between the union officer and the worker, may be seen as the primary resource for restoring the legitimacy of trade union activity in a time of low political and economic expectations.

In terms of the 'professional skills' of the union activist, the need to establish relations with the rank and file, to personally meet them and to discuss their problems - although it may risk becoming a worn-out repetition of an administrative, welfare-type task - may also serve as a stimulation to avoid the ever-present danger of bureaucratic separation between the professionals of the union organisation and the rank and file membership.

However, one can question if this relationship will be company-based. In the most fragmented sectors of the production system, the traditional weapons used in industrial conflict, which make the other side so vulnerable in the large infrastructure service (transportation, communication, etc.), often prove to be useless. In small and very small enterprises, as we have seen, workers are less protected, work relations are more individualised, unions are less influential, and the organisation of industrial actions is much more difficult. Negotiation at the company level, (for enterprises under a certain size), is almost absent.

As a reaction to this situation, we observe in the Italian experience the development of interesting forms of industrial relations at the territorial level that involve several fragmented sectors: some are more traditional and consolidated, as those in the construction sector; others are connected with the industrial districts, and yet others with new laws that tend to support social dialogue in the smallest enterprises (e.g., instituting bilateral bodies in the crafts sector) (Accornero, 1996). This development of territorially-based industrial relations could also produce results in those private services that are fragmented in small and very small production units (distribution, hotels, catering, etc.).

As a matter of fact, the difficulties of organising and representing workers dispersed in a fragmented production system is not quite new in labour union history: before the development of large industries and vertically structured unions (organised by production sectors), the first experiences of the unions, in Italy as in France and in several other countries, took place on site and represented a point of reference for the protection and promotion of workers who, except in the case of restricted workers' aristocracies, generally had weak contractual conditions, were precariously employed and were dispersed in small enterprises. In addition to the first industrial actions, educational and service activities such as the health funds (Paci, 1997) were organised at the territorial level. Some sectors, such as the building industry, still have (both in Italy and other countries) a series of institutions which derive from this historical experience of organising workers who are structurally dispersed over numerous small enterprises, and thus are exposed to precarious conditions: from bilateral bodies for education and industrial accident prevention to financial funds for the management of parts of the salary and of forms of assistance to the individual workers (Filca-Cisl, 1993). Some noteworthy ideas can be inferred from this experience in order to identify new possibilities for developing industrial relations in other sectors with a fragmented production structure, as in most parts of private services.

In the building sector there is an organic relationship between the collective agreements and the management of bilateral bodies: the creation, functioning and organisation of these institutes are defined by collective agreements, both national and territorial. Above all, the commitment of the management of these institutions obliges the social parties to maintain intense relationships, which in turn nourish the development of the collective agreements. In other words, the industrial relations become consolidated through the management of the bilateral institutes.

The constitution of a system of bilateral boards with joint control encourages also the employers and the unions to identify common goals and to entrust their achievement to these boards. Thus, although the parties maintain their organisational autonomy, they are engaged in a constant verification of their capacity and willingness to conciliate divergent interests.[101]

In addition, there is interest of the employers' associations to utilise the building social assurance (*Casse edili*) as an instrument for regulating the local competition, while restraining the possibility of improper reduction of the cost of labour.

The building social funds control the assignment of important shares of the salary (Christmas bonus, holidays and annual leaves, seniority bonus). The system is collectively organised by setting aside the sums paid by the

---

[101] Legislative support has considerably contributed to the institutionalisation of the experience of the bilateral boards. The Italian Law 55 (of 1990) establishes the obligation of the companies, to whom public works have been adjudged, to obey the rules deriving from collective contracts (including the contributions destined to support the functioning of the bilateral boards).

companies and assuring the payment to the workers. Therefore this is an important contribution to the protection of the working conditions and to the transparency and well-functioning of the sector.

An integrated pension fund was established a few years ago thanks to a union agreement. This system of bilateral funding and organisation can be viewed not only as a social protection institution for the individual, but also as a possible tool for economic democracy. One particularly interesting experience was that of the education institutes of the building sector (*Scuole edili*), which are scattered all over the Italian territory. This is an exemplary experience of joint management of professional training by the social actors, which has been diversified into primary training of the youth, programmes for worker re-qualification, post-diploma and post-graduate training, courses aimed at the new segments of the labour force (e.g. immigrants), and training related to the contractual rules for safety.

A more recent field of action relates to the connection between professional training and new work and employment policies. As a result of a protocol of agreement subscribed at the beginning of this decade, worker mobility lists have been introduced in some building trade bilateral boards present in particular territorial areas. A sector with a type of employment structurally subjected to seasonal and economic variations is obviously interested in consolidating the institutions that are apt to reinforce the stability of employment by fostering the matching of labour supply and demand, and - ultimately - the transfer of workers from companies with an employment surplus to companies with an employment demand.

The last area in which the building sector shows interesting experiences of participation at a territorial level is that of safety on the job, where apposite joint committees have been established. Their role ranges from direct on-the-job intervention to informative action, and from fostering contractual agreements to the risk management training of technicians and union representatives.

In Italy, something similar is happening in other fragmented production sectors, such as the artisan sector, where recent legislative interventions, following the example of the building sector, have led to the establishment of bilateral boards consisting of representatives from the unions and from the employers' organisations in the sector. These boards are currently being organised at the territorial level, with great efforts being made to engage in issues of common interest, despite the many difficulties being encountered and with remarkable territorial differences. Again in this case, they are concerned with professional training, health and safety prevention and workers' integrative assistance.

The development of Italian industrial relations towards an increased commitment at the territorial level has been confirmed by the recent introduction of the 'territorial agreements' (Law 341 of 1995). Here, the local government, the economic institutions (chambers of commerce, banks, etc.), the employers and the unions all subscribe to agreements aimed at creating adequate conditions for attracting investments and fostering local development. According to the latest data (Censis, 1998), 109 territorial agreements have already been subscribed to, even though the procedures still seem too slow and complicated.

Nevertheless, in the most prosperous Italian industrial districts experimental co-operative industrial relations programmes have been in operation for years. These are based on the involvement of the local public institutions, the identification of matters of common interest and the supply of services both to the workers and to industry, as Piore and Sabel have already pointed out (1984).

Despite the smaller employers' notorious distrust of union intervention, the pragmatism and flexibility that characterise the search for an agreement lead to a concrete acknowledgement of each other. As Trigilia has observed: 'The agreements and the union's action do not impose rigid obligations with respect to the mobility and flexibility of labour. In exchange, the unions benefit economically and they gain the recognition and respect of the entrepreneurs' (1985, 200).

Also Brusco, referring to the Italian case, has pointed out the importance of territorial agreements and of the intervention of the public institutions in fostering an atmosphere of mutual trust and co-operative industrial relations. The collaboration among public power, entrepreneurial and unions' associations, Chambers of Commerce and universities has made it possible to provide the system with a number of services that the market alone would not have been able to produce. 'By these, there has been an attempt to supply the access to a kind of knowledge and competence otherwise not available to the single company, in fields such as new technologies, data processing, import-export techniques, certification of quality, and high level training' (Brusco and Fiorani, 1998, 176-7). Initiatives for the diffusion of knowledge to companies and workers, through the supply of services linked to the training system, are considered to be important components of the virtuous circle which connects economic development, quality of labour and social integration

As far as I know, the available literature on industrial districts does not yet include a complete study of union participation, although it does offer a series of useful contributions to the understanding of the peculiarities of industrial relations systems within the district context. In this context, particularly noteworthy are: territorial agreements, negotiated flexibility, high social consent, and the involvement of local institutions in the achievement of services that tend to support the competitiveness of the industries and the quality of labour (Perulli, 1989; Trigilia, 1989).

Thus the main lines of a participative approach are emerging, an approach that so far has had its greatest success in economic formations at the district level, but which in the last few years has also been extended (thanks in part to specific legislative interventions) into various fragmented productive sectors:

a) introduction of forms of territorial agreement, especially when there are high levels of product specialisation and widespread production structures in the local areas, as is typical of industrial districts;
b) constitution of bilateral or trilateral boards, with the involvement of local public institutions;
c) creation of research centres that are able to carry out provisional analyses of market trends, of the functioning of the labour market and for the professional needs;
d) interest convergence among the social parties relating to different issues (management of the labour market and reinstatement of surplus workers, professional training for workers and employers, improvement of safety on the job, etc.);
e) supply of services for the workers (in order to consolidate their position in the labour market, improve skills, reinforce social protection) and for industry (research centres for the propagation of innovations, consortiums for the management of the services, creation of trademarks for local products, support to encourage the presence of the industries on the foreign markets, etc.).

As a result, a model of union activity based on a mandate to handle various matters (unemployment, benefits, welfare factors, etc.) when accepted by the public authorities and while attempting to establish convergences and shared interest with the employers, may often prove adequate for achieving the goal of defending the workers' interests and representing labour in the regulation of production systems.

This model of widespread union activity, based on a local presence throughout the territory, on the regulation of the labour market, on the management of certain elements of the social security system, on the supply of individual services, could represent an interesting future perspective for the organisation of workers in the private service industries.

Table 7.3   Comparison of two models of union action

	Industrial model	Extended model
Typical target of initiatives	Company	Territory
Membership and motivation	Class ideology	Pragmatic adhesion, solidaristic attitudes
Type of relationship with members	Collective mobilisation	Representation, offer of service and welfare, personalisation
Forms of action	Collective defence of common interests	Protection of individual interests, regulation of labour market negotiation
Role of the public institutions	Mediator of conflicts	Partner in local development projects
Type of negotiations	National and company level agreements	Industry/territory
Role of union officer	Promoter-negotiator of claims and conflicts	Social consultant, negotiator, development catalyser

Table 7.3 summarises this line of thought by establishing a stylised (and undeniably schematic) comparison between the two models for union action that we have been trying to describe. On the one hand we have the model for union action that is typical of large industrial enterprises, where the unionisation is based on traditional motivations; the identification of common interests on a collective basis is the precondition for establishing a relationship with management based on demands and conflict; the role of government authorities is being a mediator between the two sides; and the 'job' of the union activist consist in following the sequence: claim - incitement of conflict - negotiation - management of agreement - and proposal of new demands.

The second model for union action is less familiar and it is little studied in the relevant literature, being based on the implementation and enrichment (through the addition of new tasks) of the traditional characteristics of union activities in production sectors with fragmented structures

(Ambrosini, 1999). Here the main target of union initiatives is not the company, but it combines the sectorial dimension with the territorial aspect. Ideals and, above all, solidarity are not the main reasons for joining the unions, but the focus is on the pragmatic, utilitarian motives. The relationship with the rank and file is mainly based on the management of specific services and personalised responses to the workers' needs, The management of the labour market, especially in the presence of temporary, discontinuous employment, is a fundamental part of activities designed to promote individual interests, supplementary to the bargaining function. Public authorities are called on to play an active role in relations between the different social forces, especially in terms of promoting joint initiatives for local development (including training, job-creation activities, and job programs for disadvantaged sectors of society). The union is still engaged in negotiations, but it must also become increasingly active as a social consultant and promoter of local economic development.

It seems to me there are several reasons why this second perspective could contribute to the development of industrial relations in private services as well.

a) It is a fragmented sector, in which it is difficult to implement industrial relations at the enterprise level and general rules can only define certain minimal conditions.
b) It is a sector in which employment is often precarious, and therefore the management of the labour market and the outplacement of redundant workers is a strategic function.
c) It is a sector in which several atypical types of workers do not identify with traditional union structures and activities, being more concerned with their own professional improvement rather than with collective action.
d) It is a sector in which voluntary job mobility and individual strategies for career enhancement are widespread, and initiatives that enhance the skills of the workers and match their professional interests are important.

On the basis of this outline, it is possible to formulate a number of observations about the prospects for participatory activities as an emergent form of industrial relations (Baglioni, 1995). As a rule, energies are focused either on centralised negotiations and consultations among unions, management and government (the issues being economic decisions and matters such as the cost of labour, salary indexes and income strategies), or else on participation within the company, with a view to opening up possibilities for joint management on a micro-level of issues involving working conditions in the broadest sense: work organisation, safety, job classifications and management of 'downsizing'.

More specifically, along with Regini's analysis (1991), it may be said that in the most advanced Western countries there has been a movement away from joint, centralised methods of regulating economic policy, which were typical of the postwar decades of development, and towards micro-social forms of regulation based on co-operation at the company level, in which worker support and organisation appears to be a precondition that cannot easily be ignored if processes of restructuring and technological and organisational innovations are to be successfully implemented.

Table 7.4   Possible forms of worker participation

	Centralised	Territorial	Company
Counterparts	Government, associations	Local business associations	Medium and large-sized firms
Negotiations	Between confederations	Territorial	At company level
Organs	Joint agreements	Bilateral bodies	Mixed committees
Issue	Macroeconomic decisions relating to income policies	Services, environment, management of local labour market, solution of welfare disputes	Company policies, organisational innovation, work conditions
Main goals of participation	Social peace	Quality of labour, development	Internal co-operation
Public sector entities	Central government	Local government bodies	-

In the industrial relations studies, less attention is given to the possibility of an intermediate level of participation involving the local territory, which appears particularly well-suited as a forum for establishing dialogue and co-operation between the various social forces (Brusco and Solinas, 1997) and for identifying issues of common interest which can be managed outside the company, but which are tied to its operations, as well as being themselves the subject for active intervention by the local governmental bodies: these issues include the regulation of the labour market, the settlement of disputes, forms of income support to be provided in case of job interruption, professional training activities, supplementary social security benefits, prevention of on-the-job-accidents, and other similar issues (Table 7.4).

For the above reasons, the establishment of bilateral institutions - like those already active in Italy in a number of industrial districts or in fragmented sectors of production, such as graphics, and particularly construction - may also be considered a possible element that can contribute to the reformation of industrial relations in other sectors with fragmented structures or with seasonal variations in employment, as in the case of different types of private service industries.

Although the fact cannot be ignored that there are institutional differences between the individual European countries, the following list is provided as an example of the tasks and the responsibilities that would be assigned to such a hypothetical bilateral institution:

a) management of supplementary social security benefits for job-related accidents or illness;
b) creation of a system for the stabilisation of seasonal employment, possibly including controlled forms of manpower leasing;
c) contribution to the setting of training standards for the most skilled sectors and monitoring of the initiatives undertaken;
d) organisation and supervision of training initiatives for workers in a given sector;
e) promotion of a research observatory concentrating on a specific sector and drawing on experts selected by the management and the social partners, and aiming to analyse the trends which could effect the labour market;
f) playing a mediatory role in settling individual or collective disputes and administering the resulting contracts or agreements;
g) managing an information system relating to the labour supply/demand.

Naturally this is a hypothetical set of guidelines, which are only partially valid under the present conditions in the individual countries and which all have their own institutional and regulatory frameworks. Moreover, there are many management forces that are more concerned with defending their company's flexibility and independence than with promoting transparent, jointly established procedures of labour market regulation or promoting the quality of service by increasing the quality of labour.

There exists a weak, widely dispersed work force that is frequently compelled to accept sub-standard treatment and that not infrequently tends to have an intermittent relationship with the labour market, either for subjective or structural reasons. But it is precisely as a response to these restrictions that the union organisations must undertake an organising and cultural effort in order to formulate new participatory activities.

The potential goals to be achieved in pursuing this course of action include: succeeding in defending the interests of the weaker segments of the labour market; creating more opportunities for establishing direct dialogue with workers, and for listening to what they have to say; playing a more active role in the economic development of the surrounding territory and in the stabilisation of employment; making an effort to increase the level of professional skills and the overall quality of labour by organising and monitoring the labour market; supplementing union activities with associated service structures (professional training institutes, assistance organisations, research structures).

Naturally, the unions themselves must do all they can to achieve these goals, (something that has happened many times already), but this in itself is hardly enough. Contributions by governmental institutions to promoting the development of the social dialogue in terms of the specific characteristics of the private service industries would not only be a very positive development, but will, most likely, also be a very necessary one.

8 Urban Centredness as a Source of Variation in Middle-Class Formation: Evidence from North London

TIM BUTLER

Introduction

Not unsurprisingly, sociologists have conflicting views about the middle class (Butler and Savage, 1995).[102] These can be dichotomised into two camps: those following the position originally identified by Goldthorpe (1982) as against Savage's (Savage et al., 1992). The first sees the middle class as essentially a single service class whose (privileged) position is an outcome of the specific employment relations of its members which are characterised by 'trust' and 'autonomy'. This analysis has not changed in substance over the intervening years and Goldthorpe (1995) has recently restated this position and that internal divisions (fractions, *situses*, etc.) are of marginal significance in relation to the position of this class in the overall class structure. It is, in Goldthorpe's view, an essentially conservative (small c) group which anxiously patrols its borders with subordinate social classes in order to maintain its 'service' class relation to ruling groups. Savage's analysis (Savage et al., 1992; Savage and Butler, 1995;

---

[102] I would like to thank my colleagues Aidan Kelly and Paul Watt as well as an anonymous referee who read an earlier draft and made invaluable comments. Needless to say all the mistakes are my responsibility. I would also like to acknowledge the contribution of the research committee of the Department of Sociology and Anthropology at the University of East London who provided some remission from teaching which enabled me to undertake the follow-up research in 1997.

Longhurst and Savage, 1996) draws on Bourdieu (1986) and Wright (1985).[103] Savage argues that there are three dimensions to the middle class,[104] all of which are dependent on the possession of 'assets'. These three dimensions are the *entrepreneurial* whose assets are property in some form, the *managerial* which trades on its organisational position and finally the *professional* whose major asset is its possession of cultural capital. There are therefore, he suggests, different bases for class formation and this in turn affects the ideological and political consciousness of the middle class (for example: Heath and Savage, 1995). At the same time there have been important structural changes that have seen an increase in the profile of the professional middle class at the expense of the managerial. The nature of 'professional' has also been changing from the narrow 'credentialism' of the traditional credentialed 'profession' to a wider range of occupations - so-called 'knowledge workers'. In what follows more emphasis is given to Savage's conceptualisation of the contemporary middle class.

Savage's re-evaluation of both his own work, and of approaches derived from Bourdieu in general, identifies two broad shortcomings in this approach (Longhurst and Savage, 1996). These are first the non-contextualisation in the 'everyday' of many market research style studies of (individual) consumption, and second an insufficient interest in axes of similarity, as well as differentiation, within the middle classes.[105] Taking the second point first, Longhurst and Savage (1996) observe that middle-class individuals may exhibit more complex and contradictory forms of consumption than the attribution to them of straightforward habitus-types allows for. It is argued that Bourdieu's focus on patterns of variation leads him to overlook commonalties across apparently differently structured groups. The caution here is against simply setting up in the business of habitus-mapping, as the 'search for variation needs to be placed in direct relationship to the related need to examine patterns of commonality' (Longhurst and Savage, 1996, 287). This leads on to the second point about connections with everyday experience. Variations may not in themselves

---

[103] This dichotomization of work on the middle class ignores the significant contribution of John Urry (Abercrombie and Urry, 1983; Lash and Urry, 1987) on the middle class and later the role of the service class in 'disorganizing' capitalist class formation. Crudely it could be said that Goldthorpe is, and has consistently been, interested in the issue of class structure whilst Urry and his co-authors were more concerned with that of class formation. In a sense Urry has moved on from the debate (e.g. Lash and Urry, 1994) whilst Savage has attempted to develop an analysis which incorporates both issues of class formation and class structure.

[104] Interestingly, the few previous studies of the middle class have also proposed a similar tripartite structure (Roberts, 1977; Lewis and Maude, 1949).

[105] This auto critique is considered more fully in Robson and Butler (1999).

be of any particular significance. The crucial point is not simply to establish that variation exists but to 'bring out the relational character of such variation or, in other words, that the existence of tastes is directly related to the absence of given tastes elsewhere' (Longhurst and Savage, 1996, 288). A focus on the questions of everyday life is therefore thought important in order to gauge the significance of cultural practices in their context. The call here is for analyses of consumption more sensitive to the interplay between subjectivity and context, more sophisticated and flexible in their rendering of consumption practices and exploring this field in ways which are less concerned to base such practices in occupational class divisions. The interactive dynamics of households, particularly where gender relations are concerned (Crompton, 1995; Breugel, 1996; Massey, 1995a; Warde, 1991), and the collaborative, unintended and 'subversive' uses to which consumed products might variously be put, constitute this sense of the everyday. The authors are, in short, suspicious of the attempt to derive straightforward correlative connections between class and culture.

A research programme for studying change in the middle class and evaluating its significance cannot therefore be separated from the study of class relations generally. In this respect it is useful to return to the original debate, of nearly a generation ago, about the embourgeoisement of the working class. Lockwood's (1960; and Goldthorpe and Lockwood, 1963) seminal contribution was to try and think through what it might mean to suggest that social classes had converged. Lockwood and Goldthorpe argued that there were three dimensions to an embourgeoisement process. For this to be proved it had to occur across all three dimensions which they identified as being the *economic*, the *relational* and the *normative*. They claimed that, in so far as the case for embourgeoisement had been argued at all, it had been an argument solely in economic terms. In other words, contemporary theorists were arguing that *if* the working class had attained similar economic capabilities to those traditionally possessed by the middle class *then* they had become middle class (e.g. Zweig, 1961). Goldthorpe and Lockwood's subsequent study of Luton (Goldthorpe et al., 1968; 1969) using data drawn from an explicitly *a*typical section of the working class, set out to investigate this hypothesis. They were able to show that what was occurring was a degree of fragmentation within the working class. They had found evidence, amongst the 'affluent' working class of Luton, of the emergence of a 'privatised' group whose work relations were 'instrumental' (determined broadly by the 'cash nexus') and whose non-work life was 'home centred'. No evidence was found that this group was any less politically radical although its reasons for voting for the Labour party and joining trade unions were more instrumental than ideological. This led Lockwood (1966) to the conclusion that there were 'variations in working-class images of society' and that the 'sources' for these variations lay in the work/community context of different working-class groups - three were identified: the traditional proletarian, the traditional deferential and the new privatised worker. This typology has been the inspiration for much empirical work and also debate (Bulmer, 1975). Lockwood demonstrated that it was possible to hold on to the concept of class whilst accepting variation in class-consciousness and fragmentation in class structure.[106]

Lockwood (1995) proposes a similar approach to studying middle-class formation to the one he adopted towards the working class nearly forty years ago (Lockwood, 1960). The class formation of the middle class might be investigated in relation to the extent to which change has taken place along three same dimensions: the economic, relational and normative. Goldthorpe and Lockwood (1963, 135-6) summarised this hypothesis as follows:

> The chief sociological implications of the argument that the more prosperous of the country's manual wage workers are being assimilated into the middle class would appear to be as follows:
> a) that these workers and their families are acquiring a standard of living, in terms of income and material possessions, which puts them on a level with at least the lower strata within the middle class. Here, one refers to certain of the specifically *economic* aspects of class stratification;
> b) that these workers are also acquiring new social perspectives and new norms of behaviour which are more characteristic of middle class than working-class groups. Here, one refers to what may be termed the *normative* aspects of class;
> c) that being essentially similar to many middle-class persons in their economic position and their normative orientation, these manual workers are being accepted by the former on terms of social equality in both formal and informal social interaction. Here, one refers to what may be called the *relational* aspect of class.

In their evaluation of the data, they concluded that:

> the treatment of the economic aspect of class in the thesis of *embourgeoisement* is then unconvincing because it is incomplete. In regard to what we have called the relational aspect of the problem, however, the neglect is more or less total (Goldthorpe and Lockwood, 1963, 138).

The key issue for embourgeoisement to be 'proved' turned on a change in attitudes (the 'normative'). From this they propose that different *images* of

---

[106] Massey's (1995b) *Spatial Divisions of Labour* is important in this context because it provides a spatial explanation for this variation in working-class formation.

society are held by different class fractions (Goldthorpe and Lockwood, 1963, 145). This leads them to the now familiar model which ultimately emerged - via the 'Luton studies' - in Lockwood's (1966) article 'sources of variation in working-class images of society'. What relevance does this have for the study of intra-class divisions in another social class in different social, spatial and economic circumstances? One important difference is that there was an external referent for the process of working-class embourgeoisement - the middle class. In studying divisions within the middle class, the external referent is rather different. On the one hand there is the fear of dilution from below or of downward social mobility (Ehren-reich, 1990). There is also the need (at least according to the Goldthorpe prescription) to retain the trust of the ruling class. Nevertheless, Lock-wood's three-stage methodology can be used to investigate what changes might be occurring within the contemporary middle classes and this is the subject of this chapter.

Lockwood's own tentative evaluation of the data presented in Butler and Savage's (1995) collection is that it is 'too early to call' what the *economic* consequences of restructuring have been for the contemporary middle classes particularly in relation to the vexed question of permeability between managerial and professional occupations. As far as the *relational* aspects are concerned he is also unclear in what direction the evidence points in respect of the association between - for instance - higher and lower and professional and managerial sections of the middle class. The main evidence is Goldthorpe's (1980) claim that most members of the service class draw their friends from within the service class. Lockwood (1995, 7) indicates that there may now be evidence of a spatial division between what he terms the 'urban centred' and 'urban fleeing' middle classes. Finally, in relation to *normative* aspects of class formation, again the evidence is sparse but he suggests that, for example, professionals and managers do have different lifestyles and consumption habits. This is probably clearest in relation to 'party affiliation, voting and related socio-political attitudes' (Lockwood, 1995) for which self-selection is the major probable cause:

> ... whereby certain kinds of employment are sought by people who have retained or acquired left wing, collectivist or altruistic values and beliefs as a result of their social origins, their choices of subjects in further or higher education or their choice of spouse or partner. Such orientations are most prevalent in the 'cadet' service class of caring professionals in health, education and the social services, which taken together make up a large proportion of the service class as a whole (Lockwood, 1995).

The weakness perhaps of Lockwood's position is in his attachment to what Pahl (1989) has termed the 'structure-consciousness-action' (SCA) mantra. Pahl criticises the unquestioning manner in which sociologists have accepted the direction of causality in terms of understanding social action. However, Lockwood (1995) demonstrates that he is at least open to being convinced with his discussion of the role played by 'social milieus' in contemporary German sociology which sees the sources of social (in)equality as multi-sourced and by no means necessarily linked to questions of social class or occupation (Lockwood, 1995, 8). Although Lockwood clearly has reservations about this approach because it lacks any structural anchoring, nevertheless, despite his own misgivings, he identifies this as being a potentially fruitful approach. In what follows, I investigate these three dimensions of class formation in the context of an 'urban centred' middle-class group. In particular, I am interested to investigate whether differences in relational and normative dimensions are related to differences in economic dimensions. My working hypothesis is that 'urban centredness' may be more important than economic differences in determining relational and normative differences. The post second world war middle class was, in Lockwood's terminology, 'urban fleeing' (to the suburbs and beyond), I am interested to see what might constitute 'urban centredness' amongst a middle-class group who appear to have demonstrated a remarkable affinity for living in the inner city of London. Put another way, the choice to live in Hackney (as opposed to elsewhere in or outside London) may be an outcome of prior values acquired, for example, as a consequence of higher education. If this is so, economic interests are secondary to other values.

The Evidence from Hackney

The remainder of this chapter draws upon data from two surveys undertaken in the London borough of Hackney in 1988 and 1997 with the same group of respondents. Whilst care needs to be taken in generalising from this limited data source, it permits a longitudinal picture to be built up of life amongst a group of urban centred middle-class people. The study began in 1988 with some 245 respondents who were interviewed in two areas of the London Borough of Hackney - approximately 125 middle-class homeowners in each area were interviewed.[107] A largely fixed-response questionnaire for each respondent was completed by the interviewer. A smaller subset was then interviewed in greater depth as a follow-up. Of course, this approach means that it cannot show how Hackney has changed in the intervening period because it does not include new middle-class inhabitants, nevertheless it is able to investigate a group who have shown a continued desire to live in the city.

In 1997, I attempted to contact all of those who I had interviewed in 1988 to find out what had happened to them in the meantime. I was eventually successful in contacting 117 of the original sample of 245. 105 questionnaires were returned and processed. 21 per cent of those who completed questionnaires had left Hackney in the intervening period and a further 48 letters were returned indicating that approximately a further 20 per cent of the original respondents had moved. The characteristics of the samples were remarkably comparable in terms of their gender, age and education. Males and females were equally represented. The mean age of respondents in 1997 was 48.2 years with a standard deviation of 8.6 years. All respondents were home owners and 84 per cent had gained a university degree, 70 per cent having gone to university straight from school or after a 'gap year' and the remainder as mature students.

Hackney is an inner London borough situated immediately to the north of the 'City' of London - the capital's financial district. Since the deregulation of financial services in 1985, there has been rapid growth in jobs in that sector and related industries. Hackney has become an increasingly attractive place to live for the financial and cultural intermediaries working in these industries. It offers not only large, and often stylish, houses but prices are also considerably lower than in neighbouring Islington - which is within comparable travelling distance from the City. Hackney is deeply

---

107 The overall take-up rate was approximately 35 per cent, which is similar to that obtained in other investigations (e.g. Saunders, 1990). The difficulties in constructing sampling frames in London are now well known: there is no publicly available record of property ownership which means that researchers have to rely on voter registration data ('the electoral register') which are notoriously inaccurate. Local authorities, which are responsible for updating the register annually, have neither the resources nor the incentive to do more than a token trawl for changes. This was particularly the case in the early 1990s because of a government decision to change the basis of local taxation to one based on the number of people living in a house which meant that there was widespread non co-operation. The high turnover arising out of the active housing market in the 1980s together with these problems meant that the electoral register was particularly inaccurate in 1988 and Hackney Council's notorious administrative inefficiency probably compounded this. The letter requesting an interview was worded to exclude non homeowners. This, taken together with the high and probably unreported turnover in homeownership in the selected areas, meant that the real take-up rate was probably much higher than the 35 per cent reported.

polarised socially and economically: it is one of the poorest local authority areas in the United Kingdom (Rix, 1996). The 'gentrification'[108] of Hackney has been confined to a few 'wards'[109] in the west of the borough, and even in these wards there are high levels of deprivation.

The research was centred on two areas in this western side of Hackney: De Beauvoir and Stoke Newington (Butler, 1997). The areas are rather different. Half of De Beauvoir was knocked down during the early 1970s as part of a comprehensive redevelopment programme and rebuilt with municipally owned high rise blocks; the remainder, which was spared the bulldozer, is known as De Beauvoir Town. This was a nineteenth century development and much of the freehold is still owned by the family of the original developers (the Benyon Trust). The layout and architecture are unfamiliar by London terms: the streets are in a grid plan and the houses low and wide with many semi-detached 'villas' in contrast to the ubiquitous tall and narrow north London terrace. Gardens are large but public open space is limited. Stoke Newington comprises the more familiar terraced housing and there is more public open space - particularly Clissold Park which is in the centre of the area. Both areas have been subject to gentrification since the 1970s.

In what follows, I draw upon both surveys in an attempt to identify the dimensions of diversity amongst their middle-classes. The aims of this chapter are twofold: firstly, to investigate any distinctive features of the middle class living in Hackney, which has implications for the single service class argument, and secondly to identify possible sources of cleavage within the Hackney middle class. I will look at the evidence under the three headings proposed by Lockwood: *economic, relational and normative*.

Economic

Have economic fissures opened up in Hackney which indicate internal divisions within the middle class? Lockwood's (1995) conclusion is that there are not yet sufficient data to prove the thesis one way or another. Whilst there might be clear economic distinctions between the public and private sector, it is less clear what the significance of these might be and

---

[108] Gentrification is a well-known concept for describing the resettlement of the inner city by middle-class people. For a sociological discussion of the term, see Butler (1997), Ley (1996) and Smith (1996). For a recent discussion of this literature, see Hamnett (1998).

[109] Wards are local authority voting districts - the smallest agglomeration in the electoral geography of urban Britain.

also what degree of 'leakage' there is between the various *situses* e.g. managers and professionals. Within the group that I interviewed in Hackney there were some clear distinctions which *might* support Lockwood's hypothesis (1995, 7) about a distinction between the 'urban centred' and 'urban fleeing' middle class. Approximately two thirds of the middle class, according to Goldthorpe's (1980) data, do *not* come from middle-class families of origin. Approximately two thirds (62 per cent) of the respondents who I interviewed in Hackney came from families where the father's last job was classified as Higher or Lower Professional using Goldthorpe's scale of social status (Goldthorpe and Hope, 1974). 36 per cent of those remaining in Hackney in 1997 came from a *Higher* Professional family background which was almost the same percentage as in 1988. Approximately 80 per cent went to university and a fifth of them graduated from Oxford or Cambridge universities.

There was a tripartite division between those working in the public sector (29 per cent), the private sector (25 per cent) and self-employment (29 per cent of whom 7 per cent work as partners in professional employment as accountants, solicitors and barristers).[110] 8 per cent work in the voluntary sector and 10 per cent have become economically inactive mainly through retirement. These proportions have remained fairly stable between 1988 and 1997 and there has been remarkably little job mobility. Half the respondents in 1997 had worked for his or her current employer for five or more years and nearly one third had worked for the same employer for over ten years. This suggests that there are relatively high measures of job security coupled with high job satisfaction. Only 13 per cent of respondents in 1997 had been made redundant in the last ten years, most of whom had taken voluntary redundancy or early retirement. The figures on redundancy are interesting because the last ten years has witnessed a major restructuring in the services sector in London and the southeast, from which respondents appear to have been largely immune. The numbers staying in their jobs might of course be a response to recession, in that opportunities were not there for moving and people felt best to stay where they were. Nevertheless, the figures are very similar to those I discovered for 1988 when, at the height of the boom, only 8 per cent had changed jobs in the previous year and just under half had been with the same employer for over five years. In contrast, Savage et al. (1988), in a study of managers and technocrats in the Berkshire high-tech belt, found

---

[110] I retain this category of own account professional in many of the tables which follow because it is an important group in the sense that it appears to have many of the characteristics of both private and public sectors. It retains the tax advantages of self-employment together with the salary increases of the private sector, yet in many cases retains the ideological identifications of the public and voluntary sectors.

that over 50 per cent of their respondents had changed jobs in the previous year. It might be expected that those who had moved, would have also changed their job but the figures were remarkably similar between those who had stayed in Hackney and those who had left.

One third of respondents had jobs that could be classified - using the Registrar General's Socio-Economic Groups classification (SEG) - as 'managerial', whilst just under two thirds were 'professional'. Most of the remainder were routine non-manual or technical. Using the alternative Wright (1985) classification for the 1988 sample - which uses the assets based around capital, skill and organisational position brought to the job - the largest group (45 per cent) were 'credentialed employees', followed by the 'self-employed' (29 per cent) and 'credentialed managers' (18 per cent). The Hackney middle class does therefore appear to be atypical - in 1997 only one person worked in manufacturing! The most significant divide *economically* is between the private and public sectors. This can be demonstrated in two ways: firstly by trade union membership and secondly by income.

Table 8.1   Trade union membership

TU member 1997	TU member 1988					
	Yes		No		Total	
	%	n	%	n	%	n
Yes	59	26	4	2	30	28
No	41	18	96	47	70	65
Total	100	44	100	49	100	93

In 1997, 30 per cent of respondents were trade union members compared to 47 per cent in 1988.[111] Of the 44 people who had been trade union members in the first survey 41 per cent had dropped out of membership by 1997. In 1988 approximately two thirds of trade union members lived in Stoke Newington rather then De Beauvoir which accorded with them being less well paid, more likely to work in the public sector and more likely to

---

[111] This compares to 40 per cent overall of the respondents in the first survey who were trade union members, which implies those who ate union members were slightly more disposed to staying in Hackney or at least to answering the questionnaire!

support the Labour Party (Butler, 1997, 95). This pattern was repeated in the 1997 survey and is summarised in Table 8.2. This shows that those who left Hackney are less likely to be trade union members.

Table 8.2   Trade union membership in 1997 by area of residence

	Trade union member		Total	
	%	n	%	n
De Beauvoir	30	9	40	39
Stoke Newington	53	16	39	38
Moved from Hackney	15	5	21	21
Total	100	30	100	98

Of the 105 respondents who completed the questionnaire in 1997, about one third claimed in 1988 to have belonged to a trade union for reasons of principle and this had fallen to 26 per cent by 1997. Two other reasons were given for membership in 1988: instrumental reasons connected with job security or collective bargaining (30 per cent) and collective pressure from colleagues (35 per cent). By 1997, 30 per cent still gave instrumental reasons, nobody mentioned collective pressure from colleagues but 19 per cent said they remained members out of habit and 22 per cent said it was for professional reasons. It is interesting that the concept of peer pressure appears to have disappeared whereas those of professional membership and lethargy were not mentioned previously.

Table 8.3   Comparison of trade union membership of individuals, 1988 and 1997

TU membership	Public		Private		Self-employment		Voluntary		Total	
	%	n	%	n	%	n	%	n	%	n
1988	90	29	24	9	27	6	100	3	47	47
1997	60	19	11	3	6	1	62	5	30	28

The decline in union membership took place across occupational sectors (Table 8.3); the largest percentage point change (ppc) was in the public sector where union membership declined from approximately 90 per cent to approximately 60 per cent, whereas in the private sector it declined from 24 per cent to 11 per cent. The most significant finding, however, is that private sector trade union membership more than halved to 11 per cent in comparison to the public sector which, despite a drop in density, remains highly unionised. Amongst the self-employed, trade union membership was almost eliminated, declining from 27 per cent to 6 per cent. There is therefore an overall trend away from trade union membership including in the public. Two fifths of respondents gave up their union membership. This occurred amongst a group that had experienced a very low rate of redundancy and tended to stay with the same employer for a long period of time. The economically inactive are excluded from these figures but in fact only one of those who had become economically inactive by 1997 had been a trade union member in 1988. The reasons for this fall are not clear. Trade union members were less well paid, earning on average £27,083 compared to £40,198 for non-union members and overall average annual salary for respondents in 1997 of £35,968. Union members, however, saw their real pay (nominal pay deflated by inflation) increase by 41 per cent compared to 32 per cent for non-union members. There are, however, too many extraneous factors to argue that union membership was necessarily causal here.

Some of the changes in union membership may be explained by changes in employment sector by individuals. Whilst the majority of people have stayed in their sector of employment, there has been some leakage particularly from the private sector with the voluntary sector showing some growth (Table 8.4). It is of course entirely possible that these figures reflect movements either from their previous address or out of Hackney which may well have been more likely by those working in the private sector - Table 8.2 demonstrated that those who left were more likely not to be union members. None of these movements could explain, of themselves, the downward shift in trade union membership, but they do reflect the general reduction in trade union membership in Britain - even in the public sector. One possible explanation for this, other than another ten years of anti-union rhetoric from employers, could be that individuals have been promoted into so-called managerial positions which have become increasingly incompatible with trade union membership. Whilst more respondents said they would vote Labour in a hypothetical general election in 1997 compared to 1988 (53 per cent compared to 46 per cent), the percentage of these who were trade unionists declined by nearly half (from 63 per cent to 32 per cent). This would suggest that the association

Table 8.4   Employment sector membership, 1988-97

Employment sector 1997	Employment sector 1988									
	Public		Private		Self-employed		Voluntary		Total	
	%	n	%	n	%	n	%	n	%	n
Public	75	21	13	3	11	3	14	1	33	28
Private	7	2	75	18	33	9	43	3	37	32
Self-employed	19	5	13	3	56	15	14	1	28	24
Voluntary	0	0	0	0	0	0	29	2	2	2
Total*	100	28	100	24	100	27	100	7	100	86

* The missing figures are largely explained by retirement (including early retirement) and withdrawal from the labour market.

between union membership and voting intention has undergone some change. Given the restrictions imposed by the data, it is unfortunately not possible to explain the causes of this decline in trade union membership in any greater detail.

Table 8.5 Salary change for individuals and households, 1988-97

| Salary per annum | Respondent | | | | Household | | | |
| | 1988 | | 1997 | | 1988 | | 1997 | |
	%	n	%	n	%	n	%	n
Less than £10k	19	19	0	-	11	11	0	-
£10-15k	29	29	17	17[1]	15	16	8	8[1]
£15-20k	23	23	16	16	12	12	7	7
£20-30k	18	18	22	22	18	19	15	15
£30-40k	7	7	12	12	20	21	9	9
£40-50k	2	2	11	11	8	8	11	11
£50-60k	3	3	6	6	5	5	15	15
More than £60k	0	0	7	7	12	12	20	20
More than £100k	0	-	7	7[2]	0	-	13	13
Totals[3]	100	101	100	98	100	104	100	98

[1] In 1997 the lowest category was 'less than £15,000'.

[2] In 1997 an additional category of higher than £100,000 was introduced.

[3] There are persistent rounding errors, all columns should total to 100.

The second area that I wish to look at in 'economic' terms is levels of pay (Table 8.5). The figures are not directly compatible, because in 1988 I did not ask about incomes in excess of £100,000, however, by 1997 14 per cent of households had an income in excess of £100,000 as did 7 per cent of individuals. These are high incomes particularly in one of the United Kingdom's poorest areas. Care needs to be taken in drawing inferences from the household income because of changes in individual household formation and the high number of single person households. This is not to argue that household income is not of great importance. This is likely to be especially so for those working in the public sector where there is a trade off between lower incomes but generally more favourable conditions of employment for working parents with childcare responsibilities.[112]

As I show later, there is a suggestion that men working in the private sector are more likely to have partners working in the public sector and childcare could be one reason that might account for this (Crompton and Harris, 1998). Although the modal category for individual income in 1997 is £20-30,000, it is £60-100,000 for household income, which bears out the suggestion that there is a combination of high and low earners in the household.

A mean annual income was calculated by taking the midpoints of the categories. Unadjusted for inflation, mean income in 1988 was £19,948 and had risen to £35,924 by 1997 - an increase of 80 per cent. The retail price index over the same period rose by 50.7 per cent, individual incomes therefore rose by approximately 30 per cent over prices during the period. Taking into account the caveats expressed above, respondents' mean household incomes rose from £30,673 to £53,698 which represents a 75 per cent increase which is still comfortably above the rate of inflation.

Table 8.6   Income changes 1988-97, 1988, employment sector

Sector	Mean 1988 £	Coefficient of variation[1]	Mean 1997 £	Coefficient of variation[1]	Increase[2] %
Public	14,286	42	26,429	60	43
Private	24,797	49	46,397	59	44
Self-employed	20,673	95	34,891	101	35
Total	19,949	68	35,924	76	41

[1] Calculated as SD/mean*100.

[2] Deflated by inflation 1988-97 of 50.7 per cent.

Although the percentage increases for those in private and public sector employment were very similar taking into account price inflation (44 per cent and 43 per cent respectively), there was nearly £20,000 a year (up from £10,000 in 1988) difference in the annual salaries for individuals in

---

[112] This of course is mitigated by high income earners being able to employ full-time (and often live in) childcare.

these two sectors. Although the real salary increase is lower for those in self-employment (35 per cent), the coefficient of variation for this group is by far the largest. This is accounted for by large rises for those working in professional partnerships and consultancies, on the one hand, and at the other end, those working at home in marginal employment.

The main conclusion in relation to the economic dimension of the middle class in Hackney remains a public-private division. Respondents employed in the private sector, on average, continue to earn nearly twice as much as the former. The growth in the coefficient of variation also suggests a growing disparity within employment sector. Next, I turn to the relational aspects in order to see whether these economic divisions map on to social ones.

Relational

The evidence on relational aspect of class is harder to find from questionnaire data since it involves looking at friendship networks, intermarriage and patterns of leisure and association. My starting point is the economic differences between the private and the public sector and whether this extends into the 'private' domain of personal relationships?[113] Approximately half the respondents provided information about their partner's employment sector. Table 8.7 shows the odds for respondents of their partner being in the same occupational sector.

---

[113] In more recent and as yet incomplete follow-up interviews, I have been asking people about their circles of friends. It seems clear that, for the most part, these comprise people going back a long way - often to university - and that they do not necessarily work in the same sectors of employment or live nearby.

Table 8.7   Employment sector of respondents and their partners

Respondents' employment sector	Number of partners in same sector	Number of respondents	Probability ratio
Public/voluntary	13	23	0.57
Private	5	15	0.33
Self-employed	4	18	0.22

Only in the public sector is the ratio greater than 0.5, although if those in professional practice are abstracted from the self-employed, then the ratio for that sub group increases to 0.6. It appears that only those in the public (and voluntary sector) and self-employed professionals cluster together. The private sector and the self-employed tend to live with partners in a wider range of sectors. In the private sector, nearly as many respondents had partners in the public sector as the private and for those in self-employment (excluding professional practice partnerships), there were more with partners in the private sectors. Great care should be taken about generalising from such a small sample. Nevertheless, it might be suggested that in the public sector there does appear to be a degree of elective affinity and the same is the case *between* those in the private sector *and* the public or self-employed sectors. In other words there is not a social polarisation that maps on to the economic one suggested in the previous section. One reason for this might be that there is less of an ideological divide amongst Hackney residents between the not-for-profit and for-profit sectors than might be the case more generally. It may also be that the need for dual family incomes and more flexible working patterns for childcare are important considerations. This may account for at least one partner working in the not-for-profit sector which probably remains more family-friendly in terms of employment practices (Crompton and Harris, 1998). This implies that there is a gendered pattern to these associations. There is a strong association between gender and sector - men are more likely to work in the private sector and women in the public and voluntary sectors with the self-employed being equally divided.[114]

---

[114] In fact, there is a systematic gender divide in self-employment which reflects the income pattern commented on above, with men earning high salaries at the top usually in some form of private practice and women working in more routine, badly paid occupations often from home.

Table 8.8   Respondents' employment sector by gender

Gender	Male		Female	
	%	n	%	n
Public/voluntary	30	13	51	24
Private	39	17	17	8
Self-employed	32	14	32	15
Total	100	44	100	47

A more detailed analysis of these relationships within the household was undertaken of all 245 respondents with the 1988 data. It was found that generally speaking men had higher salaries than their partners and that, whilst men in the private sector tended to have partners in the public sector, the opposite did not occur (Butler, 1997, 96-7). Although more men worked in the private sector and more women in the public in 1988, the association was not statistically significant. Two thirds of respondents working in the public sector had partners working in the public sector, with no significant variation between the sexes. Men working in the private sector lived with partners who were evenly distributed across the sectors, whereas the (male) partners of female respondents working in the private sector were much more likely to work in the private sector or to be self-employed. Nearly two thirds of women who were self-employed had self-employed partners. In other words, women working in the private sector are less likely to have partners working in the public sector. I was unable to confirm these findings in 1997 because there were too few cases, but there seem no grounds for doubting that this gender-sectoral association has continued.

I believe that there is some significance in these complex findings for the overall argument which is that, whilst the employment status of both members of the household is important, it remains structured by dominant gender relations. Using Goldthorpe's class schema (Goldthorpe and Hope, 1974), the 1988 data showed that half of the (female) partners of male respondents in social class One[115] were in social class Two and only 15

---

[115] Social class was measured using the Hope Goldthorpe Scale and social classes One and Two comprise what they term the 'service class'. Social class One includes senior managers, professionals and administrators and social class Two is what they term the 'cadet' section and includes more routine professionals and semi-professionals such as school teachers and social workers.

per cent were in social class One. However, only one male respondent in social class Two had a partner in social class One. The position for female respondents is rather different; of those in social class One, 44 per cent had partners in social class One and of those in social class Two, 15 per cent had social class One partners. Two thirds of female respondents had partners in the same class. Gender differences within relationships correspond to the broader pattern of gender inequality; it was relatively rare that women had a higher social class position than their male partners. 85 per cent of men in social class Two had partners in social class Two, whereas 66 per cent of women in social class Two had partners in social class Two.

The in-depth interviews undertaken in 1988 suggested that interactions with similar people - 'people like us' - was a major reason for moving into the area and then for staying there and this was confirmed by those still living there ten years later. Reasons for choosing Hackney in particular and London in general included not only the existence of similar people but also the cultural and consumption infrastructure that this engendered (Butler, 1997). It has been suggested that there is an association between the disproportionately high number of second generation middle-class people, the concentration in the credentialed professions and issues of gender amongst the middle class in Hackney (Butler and Hamnett, 1994). The most important reason for this was the large number of female graduates who entered the labour market in the 1970s and then began having children. The wish, or the economic necessity for many households, to maintain two earners ensured that they remained living in inner London rather than living in the suburbs and commuting. Savage et al. (1992) have shown that women are disproportionately likely to have entered the professional middle class from a similar class background through higher education.

It therefore seems reasonable to suggest in relational terms that this is an inclusive group and that economic divisions (for instance between public and private sector employment) do not replicate themselves in terms of household formation. This does, however, appear to be asymmetrical and possibly structured by gender. Where both partners are in public sector employment, the need for them both to continue in full-time employment is an economic necessity for the household. This is less the case where the major breadwinner is in the private sector or a well paid self-employed professional; a number of female respondents, living with such men, had in fact given up paid work since 1988. The boundary between the public and private sector is however also becoming more opaque. There are two reasons for this: firstly, with the changes that have taken place in the public sector over the last twenty years and the introduction of a market mechanism, the distinction between the non-profit and for-profit sectors has lessened as a source of 'cleavage'. Secondly, the fact that many households had members working in the private and public sector was perhaps cause as well as effect in mitigating against a sectoral polarisation in beliefs. Returning to the focus of this chapter, which is whether there are distinctive divisions within the 'middle class' and what they might be, the conclusion to be drawn from this section is that economic divisions are mitigated by cross sectoral household patterns of association. The critical factor is likely to turn on normative factors, i.e. are there distinctive sets of beliefs and values that these people hold and what is their nature? It is to this that I turn next.

Normative

The key variable that I will use to discuss the normative dimension of middle-class formation in Hackney is that of respondents' voting intention. In Britain, voting intention has traditionally been one of the best determinants of class identification and the direction of political affiliation and ideological stance more generally (Marshall et al., 1988). It was argued that this relationship had broken down during the 1980s leading to the so-called 'class dealignment thesis' - which was largely about how the working classes were deserting their 'natural' party, the Labour Party (Dunleavy, 1980; Heath et al., 1985; Saunders, 1990). This was to be explained by change taking place in the working class and in the Labour Party (and politics in general). In relation to the former, a combination of a growth in the non-manual work force and a shift away from manufacturing to service employment was held to be responsible for a breakdown of traditional forms of collective working-class organisation. This was nothing new, as Goldthorpe et al. (1968) had shown in the 1960s, and this did not necessarily work to the Labour Party's disadvantage. It was argued that there was now a shift away from production towards consumption and towards the privatisation of previously collectivised forms of consumption notably housing (Saunders, 1990; Burrows and Butler, 1990). The 1980 'right to buy' legislation was held to have seduced many working-class home-owners from being Labour to Conservative voters. The Conservative Party has always relied on a significant proportion of the working class voting for them - the so-called deferential voter in an earlier round of explanation for cross-class voting. The supply side of the argument revolved around whether the parties had (or had not) changed their policies and appeals to particular groups. The Conservatives' success was, in part, a consequence of the Labour Party's failure to adapt to changed circumstances. This, it was claimed, had alienated traditional supporters of the Labour Party, some of whom were also attracted by the raw populism of Mrs Thatcher's governments in the 1980s. The formation of the Social Democratic Party, formed by a right-wing breakaway from the Labour Party, which split the centre left vote was a further complicating factor.

The middle class tend, on the whole, to support the Conservative Party although this is mitigated by university-level education and working in the public sector (Dunleavy and Husbands, 1985). Crewe's (1987) data from the 1987 general election showed that 60 per cent of managers and professionals supported the Conservative Party. Marshall et al. (1988) showed that a similar proportion of those in social class one (top managers and professionals) voted along the same lines. Savage (1991) has argued that the managerial/professional distinction is important in understanding the middle-class vote and that professionals, especially those working in the public sector, are less likely to vote Conservative and more likely to vote for the Liberal Democrats or even Labour. The group most favourable to Labour, according to Crewe, is university graduates of whom, in terms of the three party vote, 34 per cent are likely to vote Conservative, 36 per cent Liberal Democrat and 29 per cent Labour. Amongst the 245 respondents interviewed in Hackney in 1988 the distribution of the three-way vote was: Conservative 16 per cent, Liberal Democrat 27 per cent and Labour 68 per cent. In other words, the Conservative vote is half the national figure and the Liberal Democrats about two thirds, whereas the Labour vote is over twice as great. Clearly caution needs to be exercised about these figures given the relative sample sizes and the non-random nature of the Hackney sample, nevertheless it is suggestive of a normative consensus amongst the middle class in Hackney. This trend is confirmed by the 1997 findings which show that, 'if there were to be a general election tomorrow', 62 per cent would have voted Labour, 14 per cent Conservative, 15 per cent Liberal Democrat and 10 per cent for other parties (mainly Green). Compared to how they actually voted in May 1997, the Labour vote increased by 8 per cent at the expense of the Liberal Democrats and others (the data were gathered during July and August 1997). 32 per cent of respondents claimed to have changed their vote since the 1992 election with the biggest change being from Liberal Democrat to Labour. As Table 8.9 shows, the Hackney vote is in some way related to class but other factors - living in Hackney apparently - seem more important.

Table 8.9   Voting and social class[1] in Hackney and nationwide 1988 (in %)

Voting intention	Hackney 1988 %		Marshall et al. 1987 %	
	Social class 1	Social class 2	Social class 1	Social class 2
Con	37	11	57	50
Lab	39	80	18	25
Alliance[2]	24	10	25	25
N (100%)	62	114	98	193

[1]   Social class One is 'higher professional' and social class Two is 'lower professional' according to the Hope Goldthorpe scale.

[2]   The Liberals and the Social Democrats pursued an electoral alliance before finally merging into the Liberal Democrats, this accounts for the no-doubt infuriating changes of names. I have called them what they called themselves at the time.

The voting figures for the 1997 election were cross-tabulated against employment sector - the voluntary sector has once more been collapsed into the public. The voting figures are for the three-way vote.

Table 8.10   Vote in 1997 general election by employment sector

	Public sector		Private sector		Self-employed	
	%	n	%	n	%	n
Conservative	6	2	10	2	30	7
Labour	75	24	67	14	44	10
Liberal Democrat	19	6	24	5	26	6
Total	100	32	100	21	100	23

Chi Square = 8.41; Cramer's V = 0.235; Sig = 0.08.

The lack of significance in the relationship between voting and sector indicates that sector is *not* the major determinant of voting intention. Only eleven respondents voted Conservative and the only sector in which it had any strength was amongst the self-employed and, even there, more respondents supported Labour. This is an important finding, because it shows that, although there are clear economic divisions between those working in the public and private sectors, this is not reflected at the level of normative consciousness. We can only speculate about the reasons for this, but they are probably a consequence of decisions and choices entered at university or earlier. These choices are symbolised by deciding where to live and what work to follow and, in some measure, are probably the outcome of a general political/ideological orientation (Bagguley, 1995). In recent years, with a shift from a manufacturing to a knowledge-based economy, the divisions between the public and private sector, particularly the advanced services sector of the private sector, have also become more opaque. Working in the private sector now has more to do with skills and knowledge and less to do with a managerial direction of labour which many young middle-class people felt uneasy about, whilst the public sector has become more managerial.

Respondents were asked to agree with a set of questions about why they had voted the way they had in 1997 (see Table 8.11). The most important reasons cited were those concerning 'quality of life' and 'social inequality', however when respondents were separately asked which was the single most important, 'social inequality' was ranked first by 38 per cent of respondents. This social concern was not entirely altruistic in the sense that the issue of 'quality of life' was related to the downside of social deprivation, high rates of crime, poor educational performance in local schools, etc. This was reinforced by responses to questions about local authority services. The local authority is not often seen as an efficient manager of resources, yet only 36 per cent expressed dissatisfaction whilst 60 per cent expressed satisfaction with its management of services. When asked whether the authority prioritised services most effectively towards those in most need, the most common response was 'don't know' - those for and against the proposition were equally balanced at about one quarter of all respondents. Only 20 per cent answered a hypothetical question about whether they would be willing to pay more tax for better services by saying they wouldn't. By contrast, 23 per cent were prepared to give an open ended commitment to paying more taxes for local services, 26 per cent depending on which services would be improved and 32 per cent if they were more efficiently delivered. Hypothetical questions are indicative of a general set of values and attitudes and in this case reinforce the message from the data about voting intention by pointing to a general concern about social inequality and justice. These are reinforced by the prioritisation of local services in which respondents were asked to rank the importance they gave to a number of locally provided services (Table 8.12, next page).

Table 8.11   Reasons for voting in 1997

Reason for voting	%*
Concerned about quality of life	73
Concerned about social inequality	72
Time for a change	54
Management of the economy	51
Always voted for this party	42

* In other words, how often the respondent indicated that it was an important factor; for instance 54 per cent of respondents said that 'time for a change' was amongst their reasons for voting for their chosen party.

These findings, together with the voting intentions and reasons expressed for them, suggest a high degree of altruism and social concern as well as an antipathy to the individualisation of welfare provision. Newspaper readership reinforces this - 42 per cent read the 'liberal' leaning *Guardian* with the only other significant paper being *The Independent* (13 per cent). Taken together these indicators suggest that there is a highly specific normative consciousness concentrated in Hackney, of which 'the arts' and culture form an important part. 44 per cent gave a generally 'cultural' pursuit such as theatre, music or reading as their major leisure activity compared to 17 per cent for sport in one form or another. Although half the respondents did some form of keep fit or sport, my impression was that in most cases this was for the good of their health, rather than for enjoyment!

Table 8.12   Priorities for local service provision*

Per cent top ranking given service	%
Education	88
Housing	43
Social services	37
Environmental services	34
Leisure services	10

* The percentage of respondents ranking the services indicated in the table shows those who gave each service a top priority ranking - they could rank all five top if they so chose.

Table 8.13 Those regularly going to a form of cultural entertainment

	% attending regularly
Art gallery or exhibition	75
Cinema	71
Theatre	56
Concert or other live music	55

Nearly three quarters of all respondents went to the cinema or visited art galleries and over half also went to the theatre or a concert regularly. This reinforces the reasons given by people for wanting to live in London; the two most important factors quoted (both by 80 per cent of respondents) was London's cultural facilities and the fact that friends lived in the capital.

Conclusions

The findings from this paper only relate to Hackney but nevertheless do, I believe, indicate that there may be a section of the middle class whose identity is significantly 'urban'.[116] This notion of urbanity, which to all intents and purposes means living in North London, appears to be of greater importance to their self-identity than for example the sector of the economy in which they are employed. They are however set apart from the middle-class nationally by their occupational location, their very high level of formal education and their political/ideological orientation. Gouldner (1979) refers to this group as having a particular form of 'speech community' based around what he calls a 'careful and critical discourse' which is acquired during higher education. Another way in which they are set apart is in terms of gender roles, which although I have not discussed in detail here, are important. The argument on this is set out elsewhere (Bondi, 1991; Warde, 1991; Butler and Hamnett, 1994; McDowell, 1997), and is that dual earner professional households have a particular affinity to living in inner city areas. At a more abstract level, what is being identified here is the emergence possibly of a new class grouping which has been the subject

---

[116] These findings are generally supported by initial findings from a current research project being undertaken by the author as part of the ESRC, *Cities: Cohesion and Competitiveness* Programme (Grant L130251011). Support can also be found for them in Ley (1996) and Lyons (1996). See also Phillips (1993) on rural gentrification.

of more discussion in North America than in the UK. This has been termed the 'cultural new class' (Brint, 1984; Ley, 1996). Ley has made the clearest analysis of the association between this group of liberal professionals, working in a range of public sector occupations or independent professions, and gentrification.

The conclusion which I draw from the evidence presented here is that it suggests that, although there are clear income inequalities within the Hackney middle class, these fail to mitigate the normative and relational dimensions which show a high measure of convergence. Respondents' voting behaviour, their attitudes to social justice, inequality and culture show little consistent divergence either by employment sector or income. These findings offer tentative support for Lockwood's proposal, quoted earlier, about the significance of a shared socialisation experience especially during the long years of elite higher education. These, it appears, might manifest themselves as 'urban centredness' and require the cultural and personal support infrastructures offered by inner London. It might therefore be argued that they therefore share a common experience of class formation which has influenced their choice of career and lifestyle and has a powerful influence on their material circumstances rather than the other way around. The extent to which they work in occupations which are open to women is also a common identifying factor. The factor of dual career - or indeed single person - households is probably one of the most distinctive features of this group. The direction of this common culture is important and those who, by their income or sector of work, might be expected to vote either Conservative or Liberal Democrat support the Labour party. One important factor here might be that these households live in an inner city borough with one of the highest levels of material deprivation in the UK. The choice to live in the city and particularly in Hackney is therefore indicative of a sense of self-identity, which moves beyond that traditionally associated with the middle class, which was not only assumed to be 'urban fleeing' but also politically conservative.

Whilst however there is a 'leftwards' tendency in terms of voting intention, this does not carry across to the key indicator of occupational collectivism, trade unionism. This is an important issue given the focus of the book. In the data presented here, there is no evidence of great enthusiasm for trade union membership, nor that it influences political attitudes. When asked what their reasons were for belonging, people often said rather disparagingly 'the usual'. Trade union membership did not appear to have any causal effect on any of the dependent variables such as voting intention, party identification or general social, political or cultural attitudes. It did however seem associated with relative low pay, but also with effective cost of living increases and professional interests. The latter is probably related to the need to be protected against professional negligence which has become increasingly salient in professions such as teaching or social work. Trade unionism is not therefore a major influence on the lives of these middle-class people and it has declined over the last ten years even in the public sector - despite its economic effectiveness in maintaining real wages for the less well paid. It may well be the case that on receiving promotion, individuals now leave their trade union.

We thus have a situation where employment sector and income is associated with trade union membership but not with voting pattern and trade union membership appears to have little effect on voting intention. Those who might not be expected to support the Labour party tend to, whilst a third of those who traditionally belonged to trade unions have left them over the last ten years. This suggests that there is a degree of complexity to contemporary middle-class life which cannot be explained by employment or class factors alone; values and social networks appear to be an important element in such people's construction of their lives and the meanings they give to them. Political progressivism may remain associated with voting for the Labour party, but not apparently with trade union membership, nor with social class.

Lockwood, whilst retaining a commitment to the 'structure-consciousness-action' mantra articulated by Pahl (1989), appears to accept that the degree and direction of causality amongst contemporary social groups is a matter for empirical investigation. In this respect, his three dimensional strategy for assessing class formation is helpful in identifying areas of convergence and divergence amongst the middle class. In Hackney there appears to be a normative and relational convergence despite an economic divergence amongst the middle class. Goldthorpe and Lockwood (1963) suggested that the 'relational' factor was likely to prove crucial in accepting or rejecting an embourgeoisement thesis on the grounds that it would measure whether sections of the working class were being accepted into the middle class. In the case of the middle class in Hackney, where the field of investigation is intra class differences, normative factors are likely to prove the most important particularly if they 'counteract' economic divergence. This appears to be what is happening in Hackney. It may, or may not, be being repeated across a wider geographical scale. One possibility, which I am currently investigating, is whether there is a spatial representation and amplification of these normative identifications. It is also not clear whether or not this is an urban/non urban dichotomization such as hinted at by Lockwood and quoted earlier in this chapter.[117] Urbanism does nevertheless suggest itself as a source of variation in the middle-class images of society and of self. The contrast however may not be between urbanism and rurality but with the suburbanism which constituted the place of many of 'my' respondents' upbringing.

---

[117] The author is currently carrying out further research in a number of middle-class locations in London to investigate how much there is an 'urban loving' set of attitudes and values. See Robson and Butler (1999) which gives our preliminary approach to this project.

9 Class, Collective Action and the Countryside

MARTIN PHILLIPS

Introduction: Unions and Rurality in Britain

This chapter will examine the issue of trade unionism and socio-economic differentiation indirectly through a consideration of the formation of collective action in rural Britain and its association with class. Connection between trade unionism and the countryside within Britain has for many years been seen as a rather difficult story to tell. Prior to the twentieth century many rural areas had a clear trade union history, being areas of social unrest, radical political activity and sites of early struggles to establish trade unions (Hobsbawn and Rudé, 1969; Mingay, 1989; Newby, 1980; Adamson, this volume). However, by the second half of the twentieth century a rather peculiar situation has emerged relative to trade unionism and the countryside. Notably, the major organisation with clear rural connections and the word union in its title is an employers organisation - the National Farmer's Union - while people working on rural land are seen to be amongst the workers with the least collective organisation along class lines (Armstrong, 1988; Danziger, 1988; Newby, 1977). Furthermore, many rural areas are being extensively 'colonised' by affluent middle-class groups, many of whom are seen to be highly individualistic in orientation (Cloke and Thrift, 1990). It has also been suggested that much of the economic growth in rural areas which, in part, accounts for rural in-migration has occurred because of the weak levels of unionisation in these areas (Massey, 1984; Massey and Painter, 1989). For these reasons, studies of trade union activity have tended to focus, almost by default, largely on urban populations.

It is possible, however, to suggest that the relations between trade unionism and rurality requires more attention than it has hitherto received. In particular, rather than viewing the inter-relation of trade unionism and rurality as some peculiar derivation from the norm, it may be seen as a harbinger of a more general future for the trade unions. In particular, with studies documenting the widespread presence of such phenomena as de-unionisation (Edwards et al., 1986; Marting et al., 1993) and weakening class identification (Bauman, 1982; Gorz, 1982; Maffesoli, 1996), and suggestions that collective action is increasing more a feature of capital than labour activity (Crompton, 1993; Hoggart, 1998), then perhaps rural areas may be viewed as exemplars of modern, or maybe 'post-modern', societies in which collective action does not revolve around stable and production centred articulations of class interests, but instead appear as diasporic, rhyzomatic, fleeting and localised actions. This is not to say that future of trade unionism will ever involve a simple expansion of some rural past. Rather, my point is simply that there may well be some valuable lessons to be learnt even from the peculiar and rather tangential intercon-nections which can be drawn between trade union activity and the country-side.

As already stated, in this chapter attention will be focus on the broad issue of the formation of collective action, of which trade unionism can be seen as one particular instance. The chapter will begin by empirically exploring the character of collective action in rural areas by drawing on the results of three research projects addressing the causes and consequences of socio-economic changes in six areas of Britain, namely Berkshire, the Cotswolds, Gower, Leicestershire, Norfolk and Warwickshire.[118] This material will then be connected into a more theoretical discussion of the constitution of collective action, and its connections to class, which will draw on the work of Eder (1993).

---

118 The research projects on which this chapter are based are: (1) an ESRC funded study of 'Local economic impacts of the middle class in rural areas' (R000231209) conducted in 1989-1991 under the direction of Paul Cloke and Nigel Thrift; (2) a study of 'Recent social change in the Leicestershire and Warwickshire Countryside' conducted in 1992-1995 with Jenny Agg, funded by Coventry University and undertaken in collaboration with the Leicestershire and Warwickshire Community Councils; and (3) an ESRC Research Fellowship examining 'The processes of rural gentrification' (H53627500695).

Class and Collective Activity: Impressions from Five Rural Areas

The research projects on which this chapter draws, all paid attention to both the extent and character of social-economic change in a range of rural localities and the implications of these changes for how people act in, and upon, these rural spaces. Here particular attention will be paid to the formation of collective action, understood as actions involving the co-ordinated actions of more than one person and orientated to a significant extent towards some common purpose.

A number of studies have recently been published on the formation of collective action in rural areas, particularly by Cloke and Little (Cloke, 1990; Cloke and Little, 1990; Little, 1986) and Marsden and Murdoch (Abram et al., 1996; Marsden et al., 1993; Murdoch, 1995; Murdoch and Marsden, 1994). Particular stress is placed in much of this work on action centred around the formal planning system, it being suggested that this forms a 'critical arena for middle-class activity' (Abram et al., 1996, 355) and 'an active force' within class formation (Murdoch and Marsden, 1994, 28). The planning system is clearly an important network of power and arena for collective action, but it is not the only one. In the studies which form the basis of this chapter, questions were asked on both involvement in formal politics and governance and also on less explicitly political forms of collective action, including both workplace based activity and participation in local community organisations, events and activities.

This emphasis on collective action, focused on the planning system may be to stem in part from a widespread academic acceptance of the notion that there may be some peculiarity in social action within the countryside. In particular, it has been argued that in the modern countryside there is little evidence of either workplace centred consciousness or recognition of economic inequality (Cloke et al., 1995; Newby, 1977; Newby et al., 1978), although the latter conclusion has been recently critiqued by the Rural Lifestyle Project (Cloke, 1996; Cloke et al., 1995; Cloke et al., 1994, 1997).

The research projects on which this chapter will draw, shed some interesting light on the issue of workplace-centred consciousness amongst the contemporary rural population. In the study of four villages in Berkshire and Norfolk it was found that just over 20 per cent of the respondents in remunerative employment were members of a trade union. By contrast just under 40 per cent of the same people stated that they belonged to environmental and recreational organisations such as the Council for the Protection of Rural England, the National Trust or the Royal Society for the Protection of Birds. Hence it may be said that leisure and environmental interests are stronger motivators for collectivisation than the workplace, although this is probably much too strong a reading of these results. So, for example, in other work I have outlined the significance of the work and career to some rural residents (Phillips, 1999). As other chapters in this volume have argued, declining trade unionism may not reflect a decline in the significance of workplace relations, but rather is the product of new workplace relations which stress competitive, horizontal, worker to worker, relations; as opposed to vertical, hierarchical, worker to manager relationships (Savage, this volume). It should also be noted that there was a clear preponderance in the samples of people who could be classified as middle class, or even 'service class', where such relationships may be at their strongest although, as argued elsewhere, (Cloke et al., 1995, 1998, forthcoming; Phillips, 1993, 1998) it was possible to discern major differences within the class categories. Many respondents clearly adopted highly individualistic outlooks and rejected the validity of notions of class. Below are some illustrative comments, while the annexe of this chapter (p. 275) shows brief details of the class position of these respondents, and of other people quoted subsequently in this text, as indicated by the classifications of the Registrar General, Goldthorpe (1992) and Wright (1978), together with a composite class classification established in Cloke et al. (forthcoming):[119]

> you mean what sort of class? Oh how dreadful (Rebecca).

> [The people I work with are] not in any particular 'position', not in any particular class (Peter).

> I don't categorise people into groups, that is not working class, middle class, upper class (Matthew).

Many people, however, still saw some salience in class differences and indeed some of those who denied their validity, used the term class elsewhere in their conversations. There was also clear recognition of

---

[119] The Registrar General's classification is the social class schema used currently by the UK's 'Office of Population Censuses and Survey's. The schema was applied by following the procedures outlined in the three volume *Standard Occupational Classification* (Office of Population Censuses and Surveys, 1991). The classification of Goldthorpe was applied using the methods outlined in Goldthorpe et al. (1980), in conjunction with Goldthorpe and Hope (1974), while Wright's classification was derived using the methods outlined in Wright (1978). The classification of Cloke et al. (forthcoming) was derived particularly to allow for the differentiation of managers and professionals as emphasised in the work of Savage et al. (1991) and Esping-Andersen (1993), as well as allow for the recognition of ownership and non-ownership of the forces of production within the so-called service class. Hence one has the differentiation of both 'capitalist professionals' and a 'service proletariat'. For further details see Cloke et al. (forthcoming).

differential working conditions and inequality in the workplace, even amongst the new middle classes, although concern over environmental issues was clearly of more general concern (see Table 9.1). Interestingly notions of inequalities in domestic work were much less widely recognised, a feature which reinforces arguments about the patriarchal gender order of many rural areas (Agg and Phillips, 1998; Phillips, 1993, 1999).

Table 9.1   Perceptions of injustice

Classes	Percentage of each class perceiving injustice			
	In workplace	In home	In use of environment	Total no. Respondents
Capitalist and small employers	50.0	25.0	25.0	5
Petit bourgeoisie	0.0	0.0	80.0	6
Corporate executives	100.0	0.0	100.0	7
Top managers	100.0	0.0	86.7	15
Middle managers	41.7	9.1	73.3	15
Technocrats	44.4	17.6	75.6	42
Line supervisors	20.0	22.2	44.4	11
Semi-autonomous employees	22.2	0.0	62.5	16
Proletariat	51.7	16.9	52.2	69
All classes	44.7	14.3	65.9	186
Men	45.3	7.7	75.6	83
Women	44.0	19.1	57.3	103

Notes: Based on survey conducted in five villages in Leicestershire and Warwickshire. Class classification derived from Wright E. (1978).

With reference to formal politics and governance, questions centred around four issues: (1) direct participation in the formal institutions of governance through election as a member of a council or parliament, most generally at local government level;[120] (2) interaction with, and thereby potential influence upon, the formal institutions of local governance through personal contacts with councillors and officers within local authorities; (3) participation in the electoral system of public will formation; and (4) participation in discursive networks of public will formation through membership of, and active involvement in, pressure and interest groups.

Table 9.2 summarises information on participation in all these forms of governance, with the exception of electoral voting. The patterns of participation appear to be generally quite supportive of arguments of middle-class bias in involvement in the institutions of governance. So, for example, it appears that significant proportions of the capitalist, professional capitalist, petit bourgeoisie and professional classes, and slightly numbers of the marginal managers and technocratic middle class, were members of an elected council. The capitalist class, petit bourgeoisie, professionals and managers were also quite likely to be acquainted socially with people on local council planning committees, and there seems to be a general decrease in acquaintanceship with councillors as one progresses towards the more proletarianised, less capitalised and credentialled classes. The capitalist professionals appears to have been heavily involved in local organisations, both as members and as active campaigners, with the professional, managerial and technocratic class also seeming to be highly active campaigners. The capitalist class, although having high levels of membership of local groups, had low levels of involvement in terms of campaigning.

However, as well as being some evidence of class differentiation, there are also some pointers towards gender differences being significant. In particular, men appear to be much more likely to have become councillors than did the women, and to have had more social contacts both with councillors and planning officials. In part, this may be connected to class differences: the capitalist, professional and managerial classes were all heavily masculinised in their composition. Having said this, this leaves open the question as to the precise relationship between gender and class within the constitution of participation within formal governance. While existing studies have highlighted how certain classes may or may not have the necessary cultural competence to gain access into local government, it may also be that there is a gendering of this competence as well.

---

[120] In Britain local government is generally organised within rural areas into three levels: County Councils, District Councils and Parish or Community Councils. County and District Councils have statutory functions to execute, including the creation of development control plans. Parish Councils are encouraged to play an advisory role in development control, although they have no statutory powers over development planning.

Table 9.2   Participation in national and local organisations

| Classes | National economic, environmental, charitable, political organisations | | | Percentage of each class | | | | |
| | | | | Local economic, environmental, charitable, political organisations | | | | |
	Member	Position of responsibility	Active campaigner	Member	Position of responsibility	Active campaigner	School governor	Church
Capitalist	36.4	18.2	9.1	54.5	27.3	18.2	10.0	40.0
Capitalist professional	22.2	11.1	11.1	66.6	55.6	44.4	22.2	22.2
Petit bourgeoisie	20.0	3.3	10.3	51.7	28.6	37.9	11.1	37.0
Professional middle class	53.6	11.1	22.2	62.1	25.9	42.8	7.4	24.1
Managerial middle class	28.1	9.4	12.5	56.3	31.3	34.4	7.1	19.4
Marginal managers	20.0	6.7	0.0	33.3	20.0	20.0	0.0	20.0
Technocratic middle class	38.7	8.1	17.7	57.4	29.5	41.0	5.7	30.5
Labour supervisors	22.2	0.0	11.1	44.4	22.2	33.3	0.0	22.2
Service proletariat	26.7	1.3	10.7	42.9	16.0	28.8	3.0	26.8
Working class	14.3	7.1	7.1	42.9	15.4	28.6	16.7	38.5
All classes	30.4	6.3	12.7	51.1	25.0	34.0	6.5	27.8
Men	30.3	10.4	15.0	49.4	27.6	29.6	8.6	22.1
Women	27.6	1.7	9.8	53.4	21.8	39.7	5.7	33.1

Table 9.2   Participation in national and local organisations. Continued

Classes	Percentage of each class			Total number of respondents
	Participation in local government		Know planning committee	
	Member of council	Know local councillors		
Capitalist	22.2	54.5	45.5	11
Capitalist professional	22.2	44.2	12.5	9
Petit bourgeoisie	21.4	50.0	27.6	30
Professional middle class	20.0	57.1	39.3	29
Managerial middle class	8.0	45.2	28.1	32
Marginal managers	16.6	53.3	14.3	15
Technocratic middle class	15.7	43.3	21.3	62
Labour supervisors	0.0	44.4	22.2	9
Service proletariat	3.5	36.0	10.7	77
Working class	6.7	35.7	21.4	15
All classes	12.7	44.3	21.9	289
Men	19.8	49.0	28.3	142
Women	6.8	40.6	17.3	147

Notes: Based on surveys conducted in villages in Berkshire, Cotswold and Gower.
Details of class classification provided in Cloke et al. (forthcoming).

There is further evidence of the significance of gender within the context of membership of, and active involvement in, national and local pressure and interest groups. With regard to national organisations there is a significant bias in participation towards men, particularly with regard to positions of responsibility. However, with regard to local organisations, rather more women than men were members and a significantly higher proportion saw themselves as being active campaigners, although once again there appears to be an under representation of women within positions of responsibility. These findings would seen to support the argument of Burgess (1990) that women are more concerned about local issues and men about national.

As well as pointing to gender differences in involvement with national and local pressure and interest groups, Table 9.2 also suggests that there are some class differences. In particular it is clear that the professional middle class was heavily involved in both sets of organisations. It also appears that people in the capitalist class, capitalist professions, and the managerial and technical middle classes were also quite likely to be involved within local organisations. Given that these classes are quite masculine in their composition, then it is clear that gender divisions in participation do not necessarily correspond to class differences. It is also important to note that although people classified within capitalist and capitalist professions appear quite likely to have joined local organisations, these classes were numerically quite small within the study villages. Hence in absolute terms, local organisations may well be dominated by other classes, particularly male managers and professionals, a female service proletariat and a technocratic class of both genders (see Figure 9.1). There are also clearly important differences in membership of particular organisations with, for example, membership of church organisations being significantly high amongst the working class, as well as amongst the capitalists and petit bourgeoisie and, in accordance with the findings of other studies (e.g. Seymour and Short, 1994), higher among women than men.

Turning to participation in electoral politics (see Table 9.3), it is clear that at the time when the interviews were conducted, the Conservative Party enjoyed majority support amongst all the designated social classes, with the exception of the working class. The capitalist class and the marginal managers, many of whom worked in the private sector, were the most Conservative classes. The professional middle class had significantly more divergent voting behaviour than the other classes, with similar proportions voting for each of the three main parties. Capitalist professionals also appear to have been significantly more likely to vote Liberal and Labour than did the capitalist class. These findings would support those, such as Savage et al. (1992), who have suggested that there is a significant divergence in political preferences between the professional middle class and the entrepreneurial and managerial middle classes. Some further weight is arguably lent to this claim by the relative parity between Liberal and Labour support amongst the technocratic class, in comparison with the clear aversion to the Labour Party amongst the managerial middle class. Savage et al. relate these differences to the significance of the state in securing the assets of each set of classes: for professionals the state is highly significant through its role in the reproduction of cultural assets, while for those classes centred around property assets, the state has a much lesser significance, and indeed there may be some antipathy towards state activity. In connection with this last point, quite a significant proportion of the capitalists and petit-bourgeoisie did not exercise their right to vote, which may be seen as a indicator of a rejection of the efficacy and/or legitimacy of the state.

Overall, it appears that there is some evidence of a concern of economic injustice and some degree of alignment between participation in forms of governance and the social classes identified on the basis on position within productive relationships. It has, however, also been shown that this alignment is not always evident and that in some instances there is more of an alignment with gender than with class, although there is also a fair degree of interconstitution of gender and class. These findings would suggests some grounds for suspecting that there may be a class connection to the formation of collective action in the countryside, but that there may well also be other factors at work. Having said this, it is also important to heed Longhurst and Savage (1996) call for analysts to pay attention both to practices which differentiate groups from one another and the degree to which there are shared identities. In particular, while there are differences in levels of participation in collective activities, it is important to note that a large proportion of people within all classes was not involved actively in formal politics, governance or interests groups, and a sizeable proportion did not participate in electoral politics even by voting. It would appear that collective action was in many ways the exception rather than the norm across all classes, and that rather than thinking in terms of a general relation between some classes and collective action, attention needs to be paid to why, in some instances and for some people, issues of class become connected to issues of collective action.

Table 9.3 Voting in general election by class position

Classes	Conservative	Liberal	Labour	Green	Other	Non-voter	Total no. Respondents
			Percentage of each class				
Capitalist	72.7	0.0	0.0	0.0	0.0	18.2	11
Capitalist professional	55.6	22.2	22.2	0.0	0.0	0.0	9
Petit bourgeoisie	55.2	13.8	3.5	6.9	0.0	20.7	30
Professional middle class	29.6	22.2	22.2	7.4	0.0	11.1	29
Managerial middle class	50.0	30.0	10.0	3.3	0.0	6.7	32
Marginal managers	71.4	14.3	14.3	0.0	0.0	0.0	15
Technocratic middle class	41.8	21.8	21.8	1.8	3.6	9.1	62
Labour supervisors	55.5	11.1	11.1	11.1	11.1	0.0	9
Service proletariat	51.4	22.9	11.4	0.0	0.0	12.9	77
Working class	21.4	14.3	42.9	0.0	0.0	21.4	15
All classes	48.7	20.4	15.5	3.0	1.1	11.3	289
Men	49.3	21.1	14.1	1.4	2.1	12.0	142
Women	49.7	17.6	15.8	3.6	0.6	12.7	147

Notes: Based on surveys conducted in villages in Berkshire, Cotswold and Gower.
Details of class classification provided in Cloke et al. (forthcoming).

Class and Collective Action: A Theoretical Reprise and Elaboration

The connections between class and collective action have been the subject of considerable debate in recent years, with a wide range of positions being advanced (Bagguley, 1992). In earlier works with Paul Cloke and Nigel Thrift (Cloke et al., 1995, 1998), I have suggested that Klaus Eder's (1993) *The new politics of class* provides interesting ideas on the inter-connections, and differences, between collective action and class. In particular, we highlight Eder's claims that collective actions no longer cleave unambiguously and universally to class differences but have become 'decoupled' largely through the establishment of 'culture' as an intervening variable. Culture, understood as the 'cultural textures' of values, identities and knowledge (Cloke et al., 1995, 224), is seen to have ceased to act as a 'direct bridge' between class and collective action and instead have become 'an 'intervening' variable in a real sense' (Eder, 1993, 2). In other words, while traditional class analysis, and arguably traditional class societies, embrace what Pahl (1989) calls the 'mantra' of structure-consciousness-action, whereby people actions are seen to stem from their class-consciousness which in turn stems from their class position; Eder proposes that cultural values, identities and knowledges do not necessarily flow from class structure and may not lead to particular actions. He argues that culture textures develop through their own particular logics and suggests that contemporary modern societies are undergoing 'paradoxical development' (Eder, 1993, 2) in that class structures are becoming more and more complex but starkly differentiated, while cultures have developed independently of class and have complex and fluid boundaries.

While Eder clearly resists reducing culture to class structure and collective activity, he does not, however, consider them to necessarily totally divorced from one another. He argues, for example, that class, which he conceives of in terms of the distribution of equality and inequality of life-chances, is often a key element in the development of culture, in that it is a subject about which people reflect and interpretations and judgements are formed. Eder adds that the subject of class can be interpreted in a variety of ways and identifies three common forms of interpretation: namely an 'individualistic ethos', an 'achievement ethos' and a 'consumption ethos' (see Figure 9.1). In the 'individualistic ethos' social inequalities are seen to be the outcome of inherent difference between people and their abilities to succeed in social and economic life. In the 'achievement ethos' social inequalities are seen to be the outcome of the differential activity of people: the people who succeed are those who work hard. In the 'consumption ethos', social inequalities are seen to stem from the unequal distribution of control over resources.

Interpretative schema	Cognitive form	Type of lifeworld
1. Individualistic ethos of personal and of the potential equality among man.	Idealistic fallacy: what counts is the culture one has.	Predominance of life interests in the cultural, political and public spheres.
2. The ethos of achievement, recognition of inequality between man.	Ecological fallacy: what counts is the culture one has achieved.	Predominance of life interests in the private sphere (family).
3. The ethos of maximising the chances of consumption, recognition of the division of society into social classes.	Materialistic fallacy: what counts as culture is the goods one has.	Predominance of life interests in the sphere of work, especially the workplace.

Source: Eder (1993, 98).

Figure 9.1   Eder's typology of class specific culture

In the previous studies, we have argued that elements of these interpretations of class, together with other 'cultural textures', can be identified within the lifestyles and collective actions of some village residents. In this chapter I want to elaborate these arguments in more detail, with particular emphasis on the constitution of collective action within, and on, rural space. Attention will return to issues of trade unionism, class and collective issues at the end of the chapter. However, as a starting point, I will take a representation of the interaction of collective action, class and culture which appears towards the end of Eder's *The new politics of class* (see Figure 9.2).

There are at least four points which can be made about this diagram and Eder's accompanying arguments. First, the diagram very much re-iterates the point made above, namely that Eder sees culture as constituting a variable which is distinct from, although interacting with, both collective action and class structure. Second, Eder reiterates his argument that social inequalities and the class structure are an important theme within cultural textures. Indeed he proposes the notion of a 'cultural opportunity structure' which may be seen to be concerned with the linkage of class structure with cultural textures. Third, Eder argues that collective action is connected into class because the later acts as the 'social opportunity structure' for the former: class 'structures' collective action in the sense that it encompasses the distribution of resources which enable/disable certain forms of action. On the other hand, the collective action also 'structures' class in that it is 'the basic mechanism that changes the boundaries between classes and shapes class relationships' (Eder, 1993, 176). Finally, there is in Eder's formulation a clear area of interaction between 'cultural textures' and 'collective action', an area of study which he describes as a concern with 'culturally defined actions spaces' and 'the cultural logic of action spaces' (Eder, 1993, 9-10).

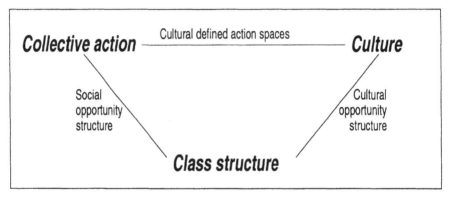

Source: Based on Eder (1993, 150-84).

Figure 9.2   Eder's conception of the interactions between collective action, culture and class

In Cloke et al. (1995) particular attention was effectively paid to points two and four. The 'cultural opportunity structure' was addressed, for example, when it was argued that middle class 'rural lifestyles' - that is the way people were living in, and making sense of the way they were living in, the countryside - could be see to embody aspects of Eder's 'class specific cultures' (see Figure 9.3). Those adopting a 'gentry' identity and lifestyle, centred around being intergenerationally part of the village community, were seen to draw on an 'individualistic ethos of personal identity', and to a lesser extent on evaluations of 'achievement' and 'consumption'. Others, described as 'moving in and joining in', drew primarily on an 'achievement ethos' together with a similar ethos of personal identity which characterised the village gentry.

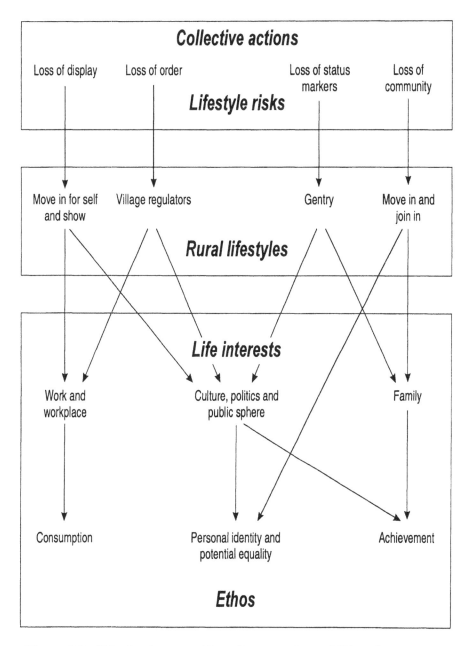

Figure 9.3   Eder's class specific cultures and rural lifestyles

A third category of people appeared to display more of a 'consumption ethos', often associated with an ethos of achievement. This lifestyle strategy was described as 'move in for self and show'. Finally, a group of 'village regulators' was identified, whose concerns seemed to be quite legalistic and aesthetic and who appeared to draw again of the ethos of consumption and naturalistic constructions of identity and difference.

It was further argued, in Cloke et al. (1995, 1997), that while these lifestyle strategies did align to some extent with the 'class cultural textures' identified by Eder, they: (a) did not draw exclusively on one such texture; (b) drew upon other 'cultural textures', including those of rurality; (c) connected into different forms of collective actions; and (d) were sometimes, but not always, associated with the class relations associated with cultural capital, bureaucracy and strategies of economic accumulation. Returning to Eder's diagrammatic conception of the interactions between collective action, culture and class (Figure 9.2), these arguments both elaborated further aspects of the 'cultural opportunity structure' - for instance, highlighting the possibility of people combining 'class schema', the significance of non-class cultural textures, and the inter-connection between workplace competencies and the adoption of particular cultural textures - and gave pointers towards the significance of 'culturally defined action spaces', where cultural textures and collective action are constituted and interact.

In the following section these arguments will be further elaborated drawing on the results of the research in five rural areas. Particular emphasis will, however, be paid to the constitution of collective action in association with culture textures.

Collective Action and Culture Textures

Cultural textures may be see to provide a basis for empirical, normative and risk assessments of people and places: that is they act to enable the articulation of attitudes and the formation of action orientated towards the current, desired and likely future states of societies located in particular activity spaces. In the following section the empirical, normative and risk assessments associated with the four rural lifestyle strategies will be

Table 9.4 Rural lifestyle, cultural textures and collective action

Rural lifestyle	Primary cultural texture of class	Cultural textures of rurality	Social boundary assessments	Utopian ideal	Risk assessment	Typical collective action
Village gentry	Personal identity ethos	Localism and ruralism	Conservative identity politics	Traditional hierarchical village society	Loss of tradition and social recomposition	Participation in village and local history societies; preservation groups
Move in and join in	Achievement ethos	Communalism	Politics of participation and adherence to a work ethic	Participatory community	Loss of community stemming from social recomposition and modernisation	Participation in community organisations; preservation and rural development groups
Move in for self and show	Consumption ethos	Pastoralism and recreationalism	Politics of consumption	Material affluence and private status	Loss of value and status	Individualistic/market activity; preservation groups
Village regulators	Personal identity	Modernist pastoral	Rationalistic politics	Orderly society	Loss of order	Enrolment of planning, legislative and policing systems

explored, together with their impact on the formation of collective action. It will be suggested that each of the lifestyle strategies has discernible class and rural cultural textures and that these may well motivate particular forms of collective action related to socio-economic and cultural changes which are seen to place the various lifestyles at risk (see Table 9.4 for a summary). It should be noted, however, that these lifestyle strategies do not necessarily equate with distinct social grouping, in that people may, first, adopt elements of two or more of the lifestyle strategies, and, second, shift between the lifestyles in relation to different contexts of social interaction.

The Village Gentry Lifestyle

People adopting the village gentry lifestyle strategy may be seen to evaluate people on basis of what Eder calls the 'individualistic ethos of personal identity' in which people are viewed as having inherent differences. This ethos can be seen to lead to a social conservative politics of identity, which suggests that currently recognised differences need to be respected even if they are associated with social inequality, and which tends to view new forms of social identity as morally and culturally suspect. Within the rural context, this identity politics often coheres around the cultural textures of what Bell (1986, 1994) identifies as 'localism' and 'ruralism', whereby the former refers to the length of association to a particular locality, while the latter refers to a person's association with a rural locality. A series of identities are constructed through these cultural textures, such as 'locals' and 'incomers', 'country people' and 'non-country people'.

Such identities have a currency beyond the 'village gentry' (Bell, 1994; Phillips et al., forthcoming), but they are given particular weight by some rural residents. Being born in a country area, being born in the local area, and being born within the village, were all seen as marks of identity and status:

> We wanted to live in Gower ... my wife's from here ... there are strong family connections (Henry).

> We moved because my husband was born in the Swansea valley (Marion).

> It has always been my village since as long as I can remember. My grandparents were here and therefore my roots are here (Eryll).

The last quote highlights how localism and ruralism often involved establishing connections back beyond the point of birth. At an open meeting of village residents held as part of one of the projects, for example, it was stated that people were only considered to be 'locals' if they had 'three generations in the graveyard'.

The construction of identity and value through localism and ruralism was a source of anguish and conflict for many people. One woman who attended the open meeting was offended when asked by another village resident if she was representing the 'newcomers' because she had lived in the village for twelve years. In another village, a woman complained that certain family groups tried to 'maintain their hold' on the village and that the Rural Community Council was,

> not representative of people here, especially me! They meet every month to no avail. I could have some say, but they like the village to stay as it was. They don't like incomers, although this is not true of all the Community Council (Rosemary).

Concern and anxiety were, however, also expressed frequently by adherents to the village gentry lifestyle. As noted earlier, this lifestyle draws on an 'ethos of personal identity' which is socially conservative in that it constructs socio-economic inequality as natural and beneficial. In other words, it is characterised by what Eder terms the 'idealistic fallacy'. For those adopting this world view, a clear and stable social hierarchy forms the preferred social order and processes, events and people who seem to threaten this are the subject of concern. Notions of a 'traditional rural community' with a clear social hierarchy are frequently evoked, and not only by people who might situate themselves at or near the top of the hierarchy. For both people who might position themselves as part of village gentry and those who position themselves on lower rungs of a village hierarchy, changes to this form of community are seen to be putting the rural at risk. Collective activities connected to this lifestyle included participation in village and local history societies which promoted notions of local and rural heritage, and involvement in groups orientated to the preservation of the social structure of the traditional rural community.

The Move in and Join in Lifestyle

Notions of a rural community can be seen as central to the cultural textures of rurality invoked and performed by those adopting a 'move in and join in' lifestyle. These people often invoke quite similar notions of a 'traditional rural community', but they tend to construct these less in terms of a clear and stable hierarchy and more in terms of a heterogeneous mix which is seen to establish some form of social equilibrium or balance:

> The village has a complete cross section of society - judge to ploughman. It is a very pleasant, egalitarian set-up. Most people know everybody else, but do not know everybody elses' businesses (Gareth).

The 'move in and join in' see community as a more fragile accomplishment, something that has to be created, rather than something that is somehow 'in the natural order of things':

> ..., it develops when you get a group of like-minded people, and they must be like-minded to the sort of say, I want to live in a village. You wouldn't normally go and choose to live in a village if you didn't have some feeling for the idea ... [Y]ou're making a commitment and when people are making a commitment to being there, you get community from that ... I feel quite strongly, that if you choose to come and live in a village, and you really want to be there, and you like the village, then you should try and show a bit of interest ... I feel it is incumbent upon one to show a bit of interest in where you live, a bit of concern ... Otherwise villages will die, won't they, the whole idea of what villages are will go (Phillipa).

In this focus on creating a community, this group can be seen to enact and reproduce Eder's ethos of achievement. This group tended to value participation both within and outside the village community. They tended to have a strong work ethic and see the reproduction of a community as a task well worth working for. However, as evident in the quote above, they also frequently expressed concern over the loss of community. Sometimes they saw their community as being threatened by the activities, or more precisely the inactivity, of other village residents. It was also sometimes expressed in terms of being the outcome of a disruption of social balance stemming from the actual or potential arrival of the wrong sort of person, with the social assessment of people's value focusing on their likely ability to participate in the community. Attention was also drawn to the impact of village growth and aspects of the modernisation of village life which might make participation in community harder:

> The major problem is securing a balance between the size of the community and its village character. Binfield still has a village atmosphere ... that is a community feeling, that is friendliness in the streets, people are very approachable (Nigel).

> I think the more professional people are the more they ... tend to leave things in their village for others to see to ... forty years ago ... almost everybody was part of the village. They lived in the village and gained their living from it. But now, of course, there's so many percentage of people who are just not active in the village at all. I mean [they] just come here and sleep (William).

The fear of growth and modernisation motivates some of the 'move in and join in' group to join the rural preservation groups frequented by the village gentry. However, many of the 'move in and join in' were active within both rural community organisations and in campaigns to widen access to rural housing markets, arguing that schemes to promote, for instance, new housing may act to give the balance that they see as necessary for a functioning rural community.

The Move in for Self and Show Lifestyle

While the notion of community is of central importance for both village gentry and for those who move in and join in, for other residents the countryside was viewed largely in terms of being a space of consumption with an emphasis being placed upon the house, the land and rural leisure pursuits, rather than on attachment to a locality or to presence of a communal public sphere. Adherents to this 'move in for self and show' lifestyle tended to view the village and surrounding countryside as an aesthetic backdrop to dwellings and a vista to be gazed upon, often from the privacy of their own property. Illustrative of this perspective are the comments of one middle class resident who stated that he and his wife had moved to Maiden's Green in Berkshire because they wanted 'a bigger house and a nicer environment', that the village 'does not really feel like a village' because it has 'no real community', and they 'don't think of ourselves as villagers, we just live here', but they like living there 'because we can see for miles and feel freer and it can be quiet' (Carl). Another resident, Kathleen, who moved to the same village because it was 'ideal for horses', argued that 'the country should be used for leisure' and that they liked the village because 'it is countryside ... that is, fields, trees, peace and quiet'.

For some people consumption was a purely personal affair, orientated towards the nurturance of the self in within what was often seen as an unsettling world, while for others consumption could be seen as orientated to social display (Cloke et al., 1995, 1997; Halfacree, 1997; Phillips, forthcoming). Both those concerned with 'self' and those concerned with 'show' can, however, be seen to broadly adhere to Eder's 'consumption ethos' in that they saw social inequalities as stemming from control over material resources, which is seen as inevitably unequally distributed, either due to 'external forces that cannot be changed by individual chance' (Eder, 1993, 97) or, drawing on the 'achievement ethos', they explain as a consequence of an individual's effort. For both the 'inconspicuous' and 'conspicuous' consumers, the major lifestyle risks were threats on their consumption power, either through changes in their general economic circumstances or through developments in rural space, such as new house construction, which might undermine their ability to consume. Given their emphasis on private accumulation and consumption, this group tended to be less involved in collective village activities and often espoused individualistic responses to threats to their lifestyles:

> Planning and pressure and money and people's need for housing are greater than many, many things. At the end of the day, you're very worried because you have no real control over it. I mean, if you take the Green Belt policy and White Land policy which has been operating for many years now, you would think that they had, you know, driven a horse and cart through the whole thing ... Everybody doesn't want it on their own doorstep. So everybody pushes it around ... But, having said that, fortunately Bracknell's got a lot of land around it ... [so] you're not going to have, hopefully, a housing estate at the back of you. It'd totally ruin it, but then again, loads of other peoples' houses are being ruined, why should I be so special? ... [If it happened], well to be honest with you, I would hope that I would call my house 'main entrance' ... and say, 'well OK, then fine ..., take the lot as well, and I'll bugger off somewhere else!' (John).

Where this group was involved in village organisations and collective activity, the group members tended to be either reluctant participants or explain their involvement as an investment which would yield personal, or household, rewards. One resident, for example, who was a governor in a local school, explained that he had moved to the village in part because he felt it was the best place to bring up children and that he was involved in the school because 'you get out what you put in' (Peter). A resident in another village, Nicholas, explained the formation of the village preservation society as the outcome of 'self-interest' pulling people together in order to protect the value of their properties being undermined by further house building.

'Village Regulators'

The defence of property values has often been cited as the motivation for middle-class activity within the local planning system (Abram et al., 1996; Lowe, 1977; Murdoch and Marsden, 1994) and it is certainly a concern which extend beyond the consumption orientated 'move in for self and show group'. However, the connection of rurality and the planning system may not simply revolve around the protection of economic values but may, as a number of studies have highlighted (e.g. Gryffydd, 1994; Matless, 1990; Murdoch and Pratt, 1993), involve a broader concern with order and the processes of ordering. A concern with ordering was clearly evident among some rural residents, who can be characterised as 'village regulators'. This group saw themselves as protectors of quite abstract notions of village space and were concerned that the regulations and policies through which this space was delimited should be implemented both efficiently and comprehensively. One illustration was a respondent who was a 'reluctant' member of the village preservation society and complained of:

> the rather lax, unplanned, developments that's taking place ... its a classical no-man's-land between agricultural land and an urban area so you only have to have an area of land to put up a goat farm and under current legislation you call yourself an agricultural dwelling and you shove up a barn and you convert it into accommodation and low and behold you have a property which you have acquired on agricultural land at agricultural value and where there is no planning at all. So really the basis of the preservation society is either 'plan it' or 'stop it', but don't get caught half pregnant (Nicholas).

Another example was a resident who complained that there was 'very little planning regulation applied to agriculture' which he suggested 'leads to blights on the landscape' such as 'dilapidated farm buildings, incongruous buildings, for example, with red rood tiles or modern bungalows' (Julian).

This respondent also complained that a major problem was the style of house construction with people 'getting away' with building 'unsympathetic buildings', leading in places to the 'blight' of 'mini-suburbia'. He argued that planning controls should be strengthened by 'making them applicable to agricultural buildings, insisting on architectural conformity ... (and) restricting buildings to well defined village envelopes'. His desire for aesthetic order clearly influenced his evaluation of rural areas: he suggested that although he liked the village in Gower where he was living, because it had 'a sense of community and some visual interest', it also had 'some misfits' and did not have the 'unity' of a Cotswold village (Cloke et al., 1998).

Many of village regulators because of their abstract concept of rurality tended to have a naturalistic view of social difference seeing it as part of some 'natural order'. There was, however, also evidence of difference amongst the cultural textures of village regulators with some adopting a more achievement focus ethos and others very much adopting a materialist focus. For this group, however, the main lifestyle risk was a loss of order and the principal forms of collective action were connected to instruments of disciplinary power, such as the planning system, legal regulation and policing of behaviour.

Conclusion

This chapter has addressed the issue of collective action and its relationships with class and culture, in the context of the British countryside. It was suggested that while this issue is sometimes ignored or considered solely in terms of middle-class protection of property interests, rather more in-depth consideration might be in order. It was argued, for instance, that while trade union membership appears to be low, particularly in comparison with membership of recreational and environmental groups, many rural residents do express concerns over workplace centred inequalities and injustices. It was further argued that there is some alignment between levels of participation in forms of governance and the social classes identified on the basis on position within productive relationships. It was, however, suggested that this alignment was far from clear-cut and a persistent feature across all classes was a high-level of non-participation in collective activity, or at least those forms of it identified in the research. This is of clear concern to trade unionism, particularly if the rural situation is seen as a potential harbinger of a more general future.

Moving to more theoretical issues, it was claimed that attention needs to be paid to what connects class and collective action, and here attention moved to the work of Klaus Eder and his suggestion that attention need to be paid to the role of cultural textures in formation, and non-formation, of collective action. On the basis of research conducted in five rural areas in Britain, four lifestyle strategies were identified, along with associated cultural textures of class and rurality.

It was suggested that these lifestyle strategies might be associated with particular forms of collective action including participation in village preservation, heritage and community organisations, as well as in attempts to enrol the more general institutions of regulation and discipline. Given that these lifestyles involve, at least in part, cultural constructions of class, then they may well also be a constituent of trade union involvement as well. It should be noted, however, that these lifestyles are not necessary completely distinct: indeed commonalties in the cultural constructions of class and in possible forms of collective activity were highlighted. An individual person might adopt one or more of the lifestyle strategies, either switching between them or creating some longer term hybrid lifestyle. However, it was also suggested that these lifestyle strategies would, in some instances at least, connect with class relations, practices and assets associated with the workplace and strategies of economic accumulation, or what Eder terms the 'social' and 'cultural opportunity structures'. So for instance, those respondents quoted here as expressing the 'self and show' lifestyle were all involved in occupations which placed particular emphasis on market relations: these respondents were all either self-employed or involved in the managing private sector buildings. By contrast the quoted village regulators were drawn from the public sector. However this is not to say that the rural lifestyles can be simply reduced to class positions: quotes expressing a 'move in and join-in' lifestyle, for example, were made by people variously classified as capitalist, managers, technocrats and service proletariat. It should also be noted that the relationship between lifestyle strategy and collective action is contingent in the sense that the collective action is seen to stem from a lifestyle risk assessment. While people such as Beck (1992, 1995) and Giddens (1991) portray modern societies as being populated by people feeling at risk, it may be that many of those living in rural Britain feel relatively low levels of risk and as a result are, at present and in the five areas studies here, not engaged in collective actions in support of their lifestyles. As one respondent explained it:

> I've not done anything ... because it's not a personal priority, although it should be I suppose ... I ... just live here (Carl).

This suggests that collective action, and lack of it, is conditioned by wider cultural and social settings and associated notions of risk.

In the introduction it was stated that this chapter would address the issue of trade unionism and class indirectly, via a discussion of class, culture and collective action. As a final part of the conclusion it is perhaps therefore incumbent on me to consider quite directly what implications might be drawn from this discussion with regard to the current and future states of trade unionism. Perhaps the most immediate issue of concern, if not surprise, is the level of trade union membership amongst the sampled rural population. Clearly a large majority of the people questioned were not members of a trade union. It has, however, also been shown that this does not mean that these people were unaware or unconcerned about inequalities. Rather, what does seem to vary is how people make sense of these inequalities and how they respond to them. Many people appeared to interpret them in a naturalistic manner - as a universal, unchangeable element of social life - or as a product of the effort that people have put into their lives. These interpretations may not be particularly conducive to collective activity such as trade union involvement. It may be useful therefore to turn back to Figures 9.1 and 9.2, and to consider how trade unionism may be constituted and resisted in the 'cultures of class' of Eder's individualistic ethos, achievement ethos and consumption ethos.

So, for example, the trade unionism of Hobsbawm's (1989) 'classic labour movement' can be seen as drawing on and reproducing Eder's 'consumption ethos' in that the trade union is seen as a way of addressing inequalities in the material resources at peoples' disposal. This form of trade unionism has also been frequently seen as clearly centred in a 'cultural opportunity structure' related to class position: trade unionism is seen as a facet of class-consciousness. This trade unionism may also be seen to draw on Eder's individualistic ethos in the sense that certain people were seen to be 'naturally' part of, or not part of a trade union, by virtue of the socialisation processes operating in their own social and geographical milieus.

However, as is documented by many other chapters in this book, trade unionism is undergoing change in both its character and extent. In particular it has been suggested that trade unions may be under threat from rising 'individualisation' whereby people are seen to describe themselves in individualistic rather than collective terms and to act in less collectivist ways. The notion of individualisation can be seen to have clear connections with Eder's 'achievement ethos' in that social inequalities are connected with individual performativity: people who are able and work hard 'become' rich, those who are unable or lazy 'stay' poor. A rise to social hegemony of such a 'cultural texture' may be seen to have clear implications for trade unionism, ranging from complete rejections of trade unionism as a denial of individuality and meritocracy to the incorporation of performativity into trade unionism as in, for example, the negotiation of productivity and performance-related-pay agreements. Such agreements do not, however, necessarily stem from a cultural internalisation of the values of individualism, but may have more structural causes relating to the balance of power between employers and unions. Indeed, just as in this chapter the discussion of rural lifestyles and associated collective action is seen to connect, albeit in far from clear cut ways, with class structures; so the analysis of trade unionism and class cultures needs to recognise how class may still structure culture and collective action, even if it no longer unites them.

Appendix 9.1 Class position of respondents quoted in text

Name	Registrar General	Classified class positions Goldthorpe (1980)	Wright (1978)	Composite classification
Carl	II Managerial and technical	I Higher grade professional	Top manager	Professional
Eryll	I Professional	Not codeable	Technocrat	Technocratic middle class
Gareth	I Professional	Not codeable	Top manager	Manager
Henry	II Managerial and technical	I Higher grade professional	Capitalist	Capitalist
John	II Managerial and technical	IVa Small proprietor with employees	Small employer	Petit bourgeoisie
Julian	I Professional	II Lower grade professional	Proletariat	Service proletariat
Kathleen	II Managerial and technical	IVa Small proprietor with employees	Top manager	Marginal manager
Marion	No paid employment	No paid employment	No paid employment	No paid employment
Matthew	I Professional	I Higher grade professional	Capitalist	Capitalist
Nicholas	II Managerial and technical	I Higher grade professional	Top manager	Managerial middle classes

Apendix 9.1   Class position of respondents quoted in text. Continued

Name	Registrar General	Classified class positions		Composite classification
		Goldthorpe (1980)	Wright (1978)	
Nigel	I Professional	II Lower grade professional	Semi-autonomous employee	Technocratic middle class
Peter	II Managerial and technical	I Higher grade professional	Capitalist	Capitalist
Phillipa	II Managerial and technical	II Lower grade professional	Proletariat	Service proletariat
Rebecca	II Managerial and technical	IVa Small proprietor with employees	Small employer	Petit bourgeoisie
Rosemary	II Managerial and technical	II Lower grade professional	Technocrat	Technocratic middle class
William	III M-Skilled manual	I Higher grade professional	Capitalist	Capitalist

Notes: The names listed in this table are all pseudonyms so as to respect agreements made with interviewees that would not be directly identifiable. Details of the composite classification, which also uses information generated though the OPCS's 'Socio-economic group' categorisation and the class classifications of Wright et al. (1982) and Wright (1985), are provided in Cloke et al. (forthcoming).

10 Building Again? Trade Unions and Formalisation in the British Construction Industry

IAN ROBERTS AND TIM STRANGLEMAN

Introduction

The British construction industry is an industry that often seems, on the one hand to be beset with perpetual crises, and on the other to display a number of irresolvable paradoxical conundrums. Cyclical and seasonal fluctuations in demand have always produced problems for workers who identify themselves as building workers. Historically workers have displayed high levels of occupational and craft identity yet this is allied to relatively weak union organisation. Both the structure of demand for the products of the building industry and its institutional organisation have ensured that for employees, instability of employment patterning (although not always of employment per se) has characterised the experience of working in a context of either famine or feast.

What we shall be arguing in this chapter is that whilst the industry has historically been characterised by instability, the way in which that instability has been dealt with owes much to a relatively orderly social reproduction of the labour force accruing from the wider context of the patterning of social class. In more recent times however we will suggest that cyclical crises in the industry have been exaggerated by several secular trends resulting from the increasing intensity of the permeation of market forces into the industry and wider contextual changes in the labour market for manual labour. Such trends include changes in both class structures and processes, which have served to create an exaggerated crisis in the social reproduction of the labour force. At the level of the workers at the point of production these changes have served to pose questions about the viability of occupational commitment and meaning, most graphically represented in

275

a reordering of relations between generations in a shift from what Mead (1978) has called a post-figurative to a co-figurative culture.[121] If this analysis is correct then the emerging situation presents problems for both capital and labour. For the former the availability of a flexible and suitably skilled work force is compromised, in part as a result of new training regimes with the avowed aim of promoting a flexibly skilled work force. For the latter problems of meaning at work combined with those social status within the community are brought into question within a context in which the structural opportunity to even out cyclical fluctuations in demand for labour are declining.

We would maintain that many of the problems of the British construction industry are to be located within the class relations and dynamics of British capitalism. In a situation in which class certainly does still divide we shall go on to tentatively suggest a way which building workers can attempt and move towards industrial citizenship.[122] We do this not in the expectation that such moves will produce an unproblematic harmony, but rather in the expectation that the limitation of such a strategy may produce a basis around which at least this fragment of the working class can possibly unite.

The empirical evidence drawn on in this paper is from a three-year study into the engineering and construction industries in the Northeast of England. Methodologically the research deployed a triangulation of primarily qualitative methods in order to understand the process of changes occurring in these industries in a way that could contribute towards the generation of grounded theory (Glaser and Strauss, 1967). The empirical research produced 44 individual life and work histories, 5 intensive case studies of organisations studied over a two and a half year period. Semi-structured interviews with representatives from three trade unions, Union of Construction, Allied Trades and Technicians (UCATT), Transport and General Workers Union (TGWU), Amalgamated Engineering and Electri-

---

[121] A post-figurative culture is one in which there is an orderly reproduction between generations, where experiential learning is valued as a way of coming to know technique and values. A co-figurative culture is one that is subversive in respect to the experience of previous generations. As Mead (1978, 49) suggests, in such cultures: 'The essential mark of the post-figurative culture - the reversal in an individual's relationship to his own parents - disappears. The past once represented by living people, becomes shadowy, easier to abandon and to falsify in retrospect.'

[122] T.H. Marshall (1950) saw the development of industrial citizenship as parallel with, and supplementary to, the system of political citizenship. Historically, the working class had forged industrial citizenship. This was represented through the movement from individual to collective action, whereby the trade union movement began to exercise civil rights collectively on behalf of their members and that this was used as a basis for claiming social rights and enhancing workers social and economic status.

cal Union (AEEU) were carried out with representatives at national, regional, local and site levels. In addition, both authors regularly attended local UCATT branch meetings in County Durham. The triangulation of these different sources of material was pursued using the twin approaches of thematic congruence and dissonance. Particular weight was given to the experience of shop-floor workers as constituted within their life and work histories where they constructed coherent narratives, these were then situated organisationally within the case studies where individual coherence was often challenged in the face of differences in the work force based primarily upon age.

The British Construction Industry

The building industry is clearly not an homogenous whole, there is under the umbrella term of construction several relatively distinct and specialised markets. Thus domestic house building is rather different from civil engineering both in terms of the labour process and the structure of market demand within the industry. This paper will be primarily concerned with the domestic house building sector. This sector is itself divided between labour forces in the public and private industry. Nevertheless, what unites both the public and private sectors is a common skill requirement and similar features of the labour process. Moreover the market position of the public sector has become more akin to that of the private sector since the advent of competitive tendering and the squeeze on public spending over the past two decades.

The labour process historically bears the hallmarks of all construction industries, notably a relatively high dependence on skilled labour as a consequence both of the existence of non-standard products and geographic mobility, the need even with standard designs to ensure that they can be erected in a non-standard environment. Once we acknowledge these conditions we are immediately presented with the specificity of the construction labour force. Namely that whilst on aggregate building workers have constituted a significant proportion of the manual labour force they do not constitute a factory proletariat in the way that Marx spoke of (Marx, 1959). Even large sites involving the agglomeration of workers are usually existent for a short duration. In terms of a collective worker this presents problems not only for the routine organisation of union structures but also presents fertile grounds, in the absence of a single site of work for the intrusion of competing loyalties of place within the fragmented and geographically dispersed work force. Such fragmentation is partly why those associated with the industry tend to describe it as displaying anarchic tendencies both at the level of its structural organisation and in terms of the attitudes and orientations of the workers within it. One reason perhaps, why it is often seen as a traditional industry that has not modernised (Ball, 1988, Rainbird and Syben, 1991). Added to these intractable features of the labour process has been a further fragmenting tendency observable over the last forty years and that is the move towards labour only subcontracting (known as lump working) within the industry (Austrin, 1980; Clarke, 1992).

Given a description of the weakness of the trade unions and the fluctuating demand for labour it may be asked why anyone, with a choice would continue to work in such an industry? Yet many of the features that serve to weaken collective organisation also impact upon the ability of capital to directly control labour. It is true that the building industry does not facilitate a fixed occupational community[123] akin to those described by Alfred Marshall (1922) as 'industrial districts'. Nevertheless the existence of dispersed small firms often means that openings into the industry are not only available within a given locality but are also embedded (Granovetter, 1985) within working-class communities and institutions. One worker interviewed gives an account of how he came to be working in the industry.

> ... there weren't many jobs anyway - but my mum was a Methodist she'd been to chapel in Crook to a big service and she got talking to some people who she knew, and he was a small builder, and she says I was leaving school and whatever. He said: 'right, the first Monday after he leaves school he can start for me, I need an apprentice' (Tape, 134).

It is interesting to compare the relatively smooth transition from school to work of this respondent with his rather more problematic attempts to join the union.

> ... my dad (who was a miner) always encouraged me to join the union. In fact as soon as I started work he said: 'Can I give you a bit of advice son, before you start. There's two things I would like you to remember in your life, they'll stand you in good stead.' He says: 'the first thing is to pay your union money, and the second thing is to pay your rent.' He says: 'in that order.' He says: 'if thou doesn't pay your union money you's little likely to get enough money to pay the rent. That's why I put it in that order.' For about a year I never joined, I couldn't really find it (i.e. the union branch),

---

[123] A fixed occupational community in this sense refers to the creation and sustenance of a local community around a single dominant industry such as steel, shipbuilding or coal. Whereby the dominance of the industry can be mapped very directly onto the social relations of the community in both the work and non-work contexts.

because there were some lads that were in, but they were in different branches, and eventually my dad says: 'I'm going to take you along, I've met a lad who's a bricklayer.' You had to be nominated then to get into a branch, to verify that you were an apprentice. So he arranged for this chap to nominate me, and that's how I became a union member (Tape, 134).

There are a number of interesting points about this account. Firstly, is the embedded nature, or nexification of recruitment strategy, not the imperso-nal ties of the cash nexus within the labour market. The small firm nature of the industry is clearly attested to and is significant in relation to the inability to organise union branches around units of capital, i.e. the firm itself. This presents problems not only in finding the union branch, but also given the non-economic ties around recruitment, being a union member can itself be seen as problematic in a small firm where the social distance between employer and employee is not as great as in larger firms. In an inversion of the implications of the flexible specialisation thesis the rela-tive social closeness of employer and employee produces a situation in which union membership is more likely to be taken personally by the employer as implying treachery and disloyalty in the face of such a personal relationship (Scott et al., 1989). Also of importance is the inter-generational sponsorship of the young worker, the legacy of work being handed down through, unusually in this case (religious) connections of the mother and a trade union legacy (albeit from a different industry) of the father.

In this one example then we can identify several paradoxical features of the social reproduction of labour within the building industry. It is an in-dustry, which is enduringly local in terms of the base of firms. However given that most firms in the industry remain small they do not provide a centre of gravity around which union organisation can form. Added to this the geographical dispersion of work projects produces a constantly chan-ging locus of work together with, as a consequence of the varying size of projects, a usually short-term shifting combination and recombination of the collective worker. In short what we are arguing is that it has always been relatively problematic for class to unite in a structural sense within the construction industry. The great wonder is that at times collective action such as that in the national building workers strike of 1973 has been taken.

What Does Unite?

To understand how the industry and the work force have been successfully reproduced historically we need to look at processes which are embedded within experience. To use a conception of class akin to that promoted by the Marxist historian E.P. Thompson who saw class as a process not a structure. In this sense the importance of class can only be evidenced through events occurring in time. Further this approach avoids the problem of the essential attribution of consciousness on the basis of static structural location, the consciousness that workers or employers 'should' have given their position. Rather this approach sees class as:

> ... a historical phenomenon, unifying a number of disparate and seemingly unconnected events, both in the raw material of experience and in consciousness. I emphasise that it is a historical phenomenon. I do not see class as a 'structure' nor even as a 'category', but as something which in fact happens (and can be shown to have happened) in human relationships (Thompson, 1968, 3).

Rather than allowing static theory to tell us how the proletariat should think we are guided to the historical and empirical study of the workers and the industry. In an industry that has some real disadvantages for the labour employed the relative satisfactions tend to accrue as the reverse side of the disadvantages. If the insecurity and constantly changing location and terrain can be seen as a disadvantage they can at times, especially when labour is in short supply be used as advantageous to individual workers. As the *Financial Times* reported recently in discussing the revival of the housing market in the Southeast of England:

> Top bricklayers in Southeast England have almost doubled their earnings in the last 12 months with the housing market at its strongest for a decade, according to one of the country's most successful developers. Berkley Group, the house-building and property concern ... said skill shortages were starting to push up construction costs in what is the country's best performing regional housing market (*Financial Times*, 27/6/1997).

'Top bricklayers' in this sense are those who display both qualitative skill and quantitative speed and thereby make high bonus earnings. The relative fluidity of the industry can be used by individuals and small squads to maximise earnings in the short-term. However such times of plenty are for the majority of workers in the industry often offset by leaner periods, what keeps them in the industry?

For many of the workers interviewed in this research the idea of a choice of career, freely made and rationally arrived at was a myth. Rather the reality of working-class communities was that restricted ranges of occupations were deemed real work and most information and eventual 'choice' of career followed from direct personal contacts. As one roofer told us:

> ... 1969, that's when I left school. So I left school and straight into a job really, local roofing contractor at Consett ... I got it through a friend actually, one of my pals was working there and he got me a job there (Tape, 14).

The importance of the personal connection in obtaining a particular kind of work was emphasised more generally by an employee of the Construction Industry Training Board (CITB)[124] who we interviewed:

> I mean usually that's your first question (when interviewing a prospective trainee) when you talk about the trade, 'you put bricklaying as your first choice, why do you want to do bricklaying?' Usually sixteen year old, nervous as hell, ... 'Well do you know somebody who is a bricklayer?' ... 'Oh yes my uncle is a bricklayer' (Tape, 11).

The overwhelming view to emerge from our interviews with workers and employers alike is that the 'decision' of a youth to seek employment within the construction industry is as an embodied and tangible example of the kind of work that is 'open to someone like me'. As important as the kind of work is the ability to point to a significant other, either relative or friend, who does this kind of work. In this sense the 'choice' of building work is as much an aspiration to be akin to the type of person that one knows as it is to opt for a particular kind of work. This is not to deny that the work itself either is seen as important, or just as likely, becomes so once employment is undertaken. Clearly the explanatory power of prior orientations to work needs to be supplemented by what is often an emerging elective affinity between the characteristics of the job and what is valued by the worker him/herself. At the level of discursive consciousness to avoid making such connections is to live a life of total alienation and, an anathema to a skilled worker to submit to a conception of deskilled debasement.

What we are trying to suggest here is that career choice for working-class youth has historically taken place within a particular structure of opportunity, the access to which is grounded in concrete exemplification. As such career choice is in no way less rational than for those attempting to pursue a professional career, rather sources of information emanate from different communities and become expressive of and further reproduce a particular habitus (Bordieu, 1990). What is valued about such a career choice becomes articulated not only in instrumental terms, but also often implies a form of the interpenetration of rationality's outlined by Munch

---

[124] The Construction Industry Training Board is an organisation funded in part by Government and in part by a levy on participating construction firms its mission statement is, 'The mission of CITB is to support in-scope employers in obtaining an adequate supply of people trained to appropriate standards to meet the needs of the Construction Industry.' It does this through the development of training policies and the awarding of training grants to participating firms.

(1987). In other words what is valued about skilled manual work is not only the high pecuniary rewards relative to unskilled work, but also the total lifestyle and respectable status that comes from such an occupational identity built as it is upon deferred gratification. Perhaps we should attempt to exemplify some of these claims.

The appeal to the type of work as lifestyle is in oral accounts often a complex compendium of distinct elements that includes negative comparison with other types of work particularly where greater levels of direct control are evident. Added to this is the estimations that are usually forthcoming involving evaluations of examples of good and bad craftsmen, the terminology implies not only objective skill levels but is at times inseparable from moral association, the good craftsman is a model for life. Consider the following account that is worth quoting at length.

> ... the building industry is in a way ... not rigidly regimented like a factory environment. It has an anarchistic streak, and that I think appealed to me. I don't know whether since then it's moulded me ... but it was that kind of flexibility that I quite liked. For example, ... we worked way out at Harperley and we were refurbishing a very old house, I hadn't been on all that long, it was late summer. We used to do our stint and then the bricklayer would say, 'Dave go and get some blackberries for the wife will you ... knock us some stuff up, we've done this, nip away out, maybe 2 o'clock, get yourself back here for four'. So that was brilliant, that was part of my apprenticeship. You used to nip away out, quickly fill a few bags and then have a laze in the sun.
>
> It was that kind of flexibility. The other thing, even when you got into a very highly productive kind of element when you worked on site and it was payment by results, everybody was motivated into selfishness and greed if you like. There was still elements where that kind of anarchistic thing came in. If you wanted to go to the fish shop you never asked anybody, you just buggered off and got it, or somebody would come round the site and do a collective thing, so we would stop and have a bit crack (i.e. conversation).
>
> So it wasn't that rigid, regimental production process that you would get, for example in Nissan or any other factories. There was always that kind of flexibility, and provided you met your target, which you wanted to anyway, because it was part of your earnings then the gaffer wasn't worried (Tape, 134).

Such accounts of the benefits of working in industries of a construction nature are widespread (Roberts, 1993). What a succinct example they provide of a class process at work. The problem of the closure of the employment relationship for the employer, the transformation of labour power into labour, the reduction of the porosity of the working day are themes that have preoccupied classical and contemporary sociology. (Marx, 1959; Baldamus, 1961; Braverman, 1974; Brown, 1992). It is these aspects of construction work, autonomy and freedom from direct control which are almost universally valued by workers. Added to these features of the labour process is the value that workers put upon the skills and the personalities of older workers. Emphasis is given both to the way in which older workers promoted 'leisure in work' (Brown et al., 1973) and yet also disciplined younger workers into what was acceptable and what was not, as one roofer recalled,

> These fellows were just great, they'd been, like the ones I worked with had been at it all their lives and they were really great craftsmen. Some of the tricks they used to get up to used to be horrendous ... 'go and get us a sky hook and glass nails and stuff like this'. But they were really great to work with, really good ... Well I mean, I would be a kid about 16, 17 year old and these fellows would be in their fifties but they didn't take no cheek or anything off you in them days, you done what you were told and if they thought you were slacking off, like I say you used to get the boot, real tyrants but they were great blokes. Like on a Saturday they used to take you to the bar at dinnertime, used to have some great times (Tape, 14).

What all of this speaks of is the social reproduction of labour which owes at least as much to the agency of the workers as it does to capitalist organisations in which they work. In this sense what appealed to the workers that we spoke to was the relative satisfactions of the work that the construction industry could offer them allied to and inseparable from, an embedded working-class culture at the point of production, which asserted itself in terms of desubordination with respect to those in higher supervisory positions. Yet it was not a culture that disavowed legitimate authority as invested in older and more skilled craftsmen. The significant defences that had been erected on the unfriendly terrain of capitalist industry were a product of collective endeavour with historical antecedents, they were a product of the agency of past generations as well as the vigilance of those in the present. As such British construction industries involving the craft administration of labour and collective sectionalism constituted an extreme example of resistance to the expropriation of control at the point of production (Lorenz, 1983; Kendall, 1975). What the shop-floor existence in the construction industry offered was an identity not only in a community of practice (Hargreaves, 1997) but also within a living cultural inheritance based on the principles of post-figuration (Mead, 1978).

The processes by which such post-figuration proceeded we have analysed in detail elsewhere (Strangleman and Roberts, 1996; Roberts and

Strangleman, 1997). However of importance is not only what Penn (1986) has called 'the socialisation into skilled identities' but also the institutional recognition of that form based upon craft apprentice training. The decline in this form of training has been well documented,

> Since the war, and especially from the 1960s, the number of apprenticeships has declined sharply and there has been a failure to maintain traditional craftsmen/apprenticeship ratios, even when the reduction in overall craft training is accounted for ... Reproducing skills has tended to become an ad-hoc process ... This tendency is reflected in changes in the nature of apprentice training. Traditionally, apprenticeship meant being an organic member of an industry and a trade and maintaining standards. Specific materials and knowledge's made up different, but not every, domain of construction work and provided the criteria for apprenticeships relating to the maintenance of collective skills. Through the powers of indenture, those who served apprenticeships belonged to the qualified stable workforce of the country, protected by labour legislation. In this way workers potentially had access to all the skills of the trade for craftsmen co-operated in passing these on. The cost of apprenticeship was repaid for the rest of a worker's life, often through a 'loyalty' to the firm he trained with and worked for (Clarke, 1993, 10).

In the construction industry the decline of apprentice training was linked primarily to the fragmenting market structure as a result of the increasing rise of subcontracting, i.e. a way in which to hedge off the costs of the reproduction of labour onto labour itself. Allied to which, in the context of a rapidly worsening training crisis the relative expense of apprentice training was avoided by firms still undertaking training provision. In other words it was the intensity of the penetration of market forces into the industry where at the level of the individual firm, training was seen as a cost rather than an investment that has lead to the demise of apprentice training not the efficacy or the 'old fashioned' nature of apprenticeship itself. Thus by 1992 only 5 per cent of first year trainees entered the industry by way of the traditional apprenticeship system, whereas 68 per cent of year 1 trainees were accounted for by the youth training (YT) route, a government funded scheme offering low cost training. Figures on relative costs of training in the construction industry show that whilst traditional apprentice training produces a net cost to an individual employer of £6,826 over the first three years of training (that is when gross cost is offset against productivity benefits and training grants). The comparable net figure for an individual employer partaking in a YT foundation Training Scheme is a benefit of £1,665 over the first three years of training.

The immediate market logic is undeniable and yet it is also widely recognised that such training involved not only impoverished skills but also produced a huge drop out rate,

> ... of those who joined during its first 18 months, just over half who were actually referred to the scheme completed their initial assessment period and, among those who stayed, more than two thirds left early. The latest evidence shows that this ambivalence has persisted, and by March 1992 only 41.2 per cent of trainees were completing their agreed training programme (Mizen, 1995, 17).

What this scheme did not and could not provide was the socialisation into skilled identities that had been so prominent a part of the traditional apprenticeship system. The largely college based training did not provide trainees with the depth of skill that working on site over the prolonged period of apprenticeship did. Neither did it furnish them with the social skills to cope the objective demands of life on a building site or indeed with time served craftsmen who had earned the right to be called craftsmen within the community of practice.

Such problems remain in the new training initiative, the Modern Apprenticeship,[125] in which the return to the discourse of apprenticeship is no coincidence. However this language game is likely to founder on the way in which skill is being redefined as competency. There are then several respects in which these recent training initiatives differ from previous systems in relation to both structures and processes of training and the way in which such training relates to the division of labour in the workplace. Firstly, consequent upon a conception of the progressive accumulation of competencies the structural divisions that have traditionally existed between skilled, semi-skilled and unskilled work are to be replaced by a gradation of competence accredited levels (which are seen as horizontal modules, not vertically accumulating skill. Roberts and Corcoran Nantes, 1994), for example National Vocational Qualification (NVQ) levels.[126] At the level of the work force this represents a diminution of the collective labourer insofar as traditional collective divisions between skill

---

[125] The Modern Apprenticeship system was introduced across a number of industries, including construction, in the mid-1990s. It differs from the traditional apprenticeship in being competence based, rather than time based. The length of training to reach NVQ level 3 is two years, effectively halving the time that traditional apprentices were trained for.

[126] National Vocational Qualifications (NVQ's) were introduced in Britain in the late 1980s. They comprise of a series of competence based attainment levels which are said to have an equivalence to either more academic qualifications or earlier types of vocational qualification. Thus NVQ level 3 is said to be comparable with trained apprentice status.

levels become replaced by more individuated competence certification. The literature produced by the National Council for Vocational Qualifications (NCVQ) makes it clear that the only legitimate collective body it is concerned with are companies, workers are seen merely as individuated units of human capital which can be progressively empowered within the firm or the labour market.

> Within companies, NVQ's can assist in improving business performance and results; create a more flexible and motivated work force; and introduce a targeted and systemic approach to training, resulting in a more economic use of resources to meet business objectives. NVQ's are by their very nature relevant to companies' objectives and human resources development strategies ... For individuals, an NVQ provides the clearest possible evidence that the holder can make a contribution to effective business performance. NVQ's encourage not only more and better learning opportunities, but also higher levels of participation and achievement. Certification can be progressive throughout the unit structure of an NVQ (NCVQ, 1995).

Whilst there was some gradation of 'achievement' in the traditional apprenticeship system these were not reflected at the point of production where the craft identity was the 'master status' and skill was seen to reside both at the level of individual competence but also at the level of the collective worker. Similarly where individual wage packets did vary this was usually as a result of special payments and bonuses which accrued to individual jobs, rather than to differences within the basic rates for a particular class of labour. Insofar as the new training schemes emphasise the accumulation of competencies that is then mirrored in the division of labour at work they represent an attenuation of collective structural division and thereby a weakening of the focus for collective identity. If the traditional divisions around the axis of skill were divisive (Lane, 1976) the newer forms of individuated 'achievement' are positively fragmentary.

Underlying such developments is a changing conception of what is implied in the notion of a skilled work force. There is a move away from seeing skills of the work force as residing within the collective worker to a concern with measurable individual competence. Surely then there is a manifest concern to render the training process and the subsequent division of labour more instrumentally rational when viewed from the position of capital. Yet what all of this neglects is the embedded nature of the division of labour within construction, the autonomous working-class space that has been created at the point of production. Insofar as capital has been successful in doing damage to this they have exacerbated the crisis in the construction industry. As a former worker in the industry put it,

... sub-contractors tend to focus purely on the financial return, which is not a great motivator ... it's the dignity that's gone. If you take away the dignity - some men can hang onto it in the face of overwhelming odds and adversity ... Dignity, pride, internalised values ... However you just got a feel for it. And what they do get, which they don't get now, is a feel for the spirit, the ethos of the industry they're in, the camaraderie, the characters - and every industry has them; and without that how can you bond towards that industry; you can't bond towards it. If all you've got is an NVQ on a bit of paper in a sterile college environment, where's the bonding, where's the camaraderie, where's the mining spirit - there isn't any, and it is there ... This is the one thing, the one part of the industry that overrides the dismal wages ... you'll still get people saying, 'yes, I like this work, I know its outdoors, I know its rough, I know its wet, I like sitting on a warm cement bag on Friday afternoon eating my fish and chips with a cup of tea that would take the enamel off your teeth', that sort of thing, and it feels good to them because it feels real, its not isolated ... We're not producing that; the modern apprenticeship won't do it, the NVQ won't do it (Tape, 131).

To recap then, what is being argued to this point is that the development of the division of labour in the British construction industry is characterised by processes that have involved the generational transmission of skills and culture which are inscribed within a process of social class. Whilst these processes are best characterised as collective sectionalism, thereby reflecting the hierarchical inequality within capitalism, they nevertheless have been productive of a high degree of strategic power at the point of production. Part of the durability of this power has been its embedded nature and ability to mobilise moral force in the defence of standards of skill and autonomy. These standards have been respected by past and present generations of workers, whose models of maturity are to a large extent cast upon the preceding generation. What we have witnessed in recent years owing to the intensity of the penetration of market forces upon the industry is a lost generation in terms of a collapse of apprenticed training. This has produced, from the point of view of capital, far from a more flexible work force, but rather a work force in which skills have degraded. Rather than even providing a more pliable work force, what we have seen is a younger work force that is far more easily detached from the industry than their older colleagues. What has been destroyed in the rush towards increased preoccupation with cost efficiency has been the ability of the industry to reproduce a work force with any semblance of responsible autonomy. The inability of the employers to grasp the specific class culture of the work force emanating from the respectable working class has produced a disorganisation suggestive of anomie (Durkheim, 1933). A tendency exaggerated through recent changes to the historical specificity of the British labour market (Inui, 1993). In this setting it could be argued that the unifying possibilities of class have been dissolved on the terrain of class society, a result that has produced problems for both capital and labour. The disorganising tendencies of the market have produced a crisis of the social reproduction of labour for capital, with an associated disorganisation of labour (Allen, 1988) for the workers.

Towards Reorganisation?

In many ways the construction industry appears to exemplify the process that Polanyi (1944) described as the differentiation of market economies. In this view initial forms of embeddedness are jettisoned in favour of the domination of the market, only to produce a situation where integration becomes problematic because of the very processes that the market itself unleashes. He goes on to suggest that what typically occurs in such situations is that a new form of embeddedness develops in order to meet the limitations of the rule of the market. At the level of society as a whole he suggested that the development of welfare states involving a degree of social protection for the vulnerable re-emerges to take precedence over market independence. Is it possible to envisage such a shift within the construction industry? On the one hand the prospects do not look good. The 1980's demonstrated one example after another where British manufacturing industry was either left to collapse, or actively liquidated by employers or the State (Lorenz, 1991; Roberts, 1993). However, the fact that construction is by definition linked to locality means that it can not be closed down wholesale as in the case of the shipbuilding industry for example. Moreover there are indications that building employers are increasingly aware that the disorganisation of the industry is ultimately unsustainable in the long-term. This view is fuelled by an immediate skills shortage in several areas.

What then are the prospects for unification of the work force? Again we would point to the unevenness of the industry as suggesting that attempts to overtly organise around the issue of craft exclusivity and a return to a traditional apprenticeship system are likely to be less than successful. Let us be clear about the reasons for this. The collapse of traditional apprenticeship training in most British manufacturing industry follows firstly the restructuring of industry, away from manufacturing and towards services. Secondly, as a response to increased levels of competition arising in part from more volatile product markets brought about through the retreat of the state from Keynesian economic management strategies and more general deregulation of markets, employers have defined training as a cost and sought out cheaper alternatives to apprenticeship. Thirdly, employers have identified the power of the workgroup implied in a craft division of labour as a cause of inflexibility. They have thus further sought to destroy this system as, at least in part, as a reassertion of 'management's right to manage'. All of these issues have been felt with a particular severity within the construction industry. The principle and practice of craft exclusivity has been breached and with this the moral order of craft divisions of labour have been largely destroyed.

However one particular area that is being pursued by rank and file activists may involve, as an unintended consequence in relation to other parties, the possibility of a degree of labour market closure. This is the issue of health and safety. It should not be thought that activists have neglected this issue in the past, far from it, some of the most active struggle has taken place on this terrain. However much of that struggle has been reactive and about securing financial compensation after incidents as settlement of individual cases often without acceptance of liability by employers (see Elvin, 1995). The increasingly disorganised nature of the industry has had the effect of making such claims harder for workers. For example on a visit to one UCATT branch we heard of an accident that had taken place in a local quarry, where a dump truck driver had gone over the top of the quarry wall and had been seriously injured. The quarry wall had not been fenced off or even indicated with warning markers. There were two witnesses to the accident. However when the secretary of the branch approached these men he found that both had been employed unofficially and were also claiming social security. As a consequence they refused to give evidence and went on to threaten the secretary, in one case turning a dog on him. The discussion that followed in the branch made it clear that such contexts were not unusual. Also what was interesting was the decision that the branch would not report these two workers to the authorities for unofficial working, it seemed that whilst class may not unite all it certainly did bind some. In a return visit to this branch some two years later the same case was again discussed. The worker concerned had been in a coma for over a year and whilst he had regained consciousness he would never work again. The legal disputes were still continuing in the context where no witnesses could be produced.

For the industry as a whole the issue of health and safety of employees is a difficult one to handle. The locus of responsibility for the health and safety of workers has become complicated by the system of labour only sub-contracting and self-employed status of many individual operatives. However recent changes in health and safety regulations have moved responsibility towards the main contractor. Allied to this is the development of a scheme using 'smart card' technology, promoted by the

Construction Industry Training Board (CITB). The Construction Skills Certification Scheme represents not only an attempt to register experience and skills of individual workers but also includes a mandatory period of health and safety training before a worker can go on site (CSCS, 1996). If not in terms of experience and skills, which in this early phase of the scheme can be registered in retrospect, then certainly in terms of health and safety training this scheme, if successful, could enact a degree of labour market closure. As a Construction Safety Unit (CSU) publication (1996) points out:

> What the major contractors are saying
>
> Amec, Balfour Beatty, Trollop and Colls, Edmund Nuttall, Sheperd Construction, Barrett, John Kennedy (civil engineering) Ltd, Chatterton (Building Services) Ltd. have said publicly that they will in future require their craftsmen and operatives to be registered under the CSCS. In addition they will expect their specialist subcontractors to require the same of their employees.

The importance of the process of this training was evidenced at one of the CITB training sessions that we attended. The trainers involved where time served craftsmen who had worked a number of years on site. What they were communicating was not only abstract training from written material but they were locating this in the context of what were clearly the shared assumptions of the trainees. For example the idea that when push comes to shove most employers will disregard safety issues in order to maximise profitability. The group of trainees included workers of all ages, a context in which the prospects for the continuation of a post-figurative culture were maximised, the older workers clearly had more experience to draw on.

The importance of this new initiative then is its ability to unite non-formal concerns of the shop-floor workers with an evolving formal structure that implies a degree of labour market closure. Health and safety within the construction industry is an issue of particular importance given the past historical legacy of working with substances such as asbestos as well as the sometimes precarious work locations. In other words the practical importance of health and safety to such a working-class occupation is paramount. Yet the basis of the health and safety issue is a one that at least on the face of it transcends class sectionalism and ultimately can be located within claims for industrial citizenship (Marshall T.H., 1950). It is at this level that workers in the British construction industry, and indeed other industries, have not been as formally successful as their European counterparts. The unification and power of British trade unionism has shown itself largely in its historical capacity to resist the expropriation of control at the point of production. What the last two decades have shown is that unless that power is institutionalised within a wider context it cannot always be successfully reproduced. Part of the answer to this question must be located in the move towards a system of positive rights within industry, rather than the more negative exemptions from common law which have historically characterised the British case.[127]

In other words, whilst the British system of trade unionism has historically been very good at retaining power at the level of the workgroup it has been rather weaker at the more macro level of institutional provision legislated for by the State. There has never been an equivalent in Britain of *the collective agreement statute* in Germany, or the framework of *commissions paritaires* in Belgium. Whilst such institutions can become overly bureaucratic and out of touch with the rank and file, nevertheless their legal status ensures that labour at least in theory will have a seat at the negotiating table. In Britain the balance of power between employers and employees has been more directly based on prevailing economic conditions than on institutional embeddedness with the only medium to longer term mediating influence being the power of the workgroup based upon claims to specific and unique skills. With the decline of the craft division of labour it seems to us that the area of health and safety is a particularly useful one to attempt to start this change. The issue of health and safety is important as it lends itself to struggle for provision at the macro legislative level and, simultaneously at the more micro level of the shop-floor. Moreover it is an issue that can unite workers irrespective of skill designation, age or gender. It is a universalising issue but one which, rather than moving beyond class, can illustrate the realities of specific class and occupationally defined existence. The call for a healthy environment underpins the assertion of a common human dignity and appeal that cannot be directly denied

---

127 The historical legacy, at least until relatively recently, of the relationship between trade unions and the law in Britain has been one of abstention. As Otto Kahn-Freund wrote in 1954:

'There is perhaps, no major country in the world in which the law has played a less significant role in the shaping of [industrial] relations than in Great Britain.'

(Quoted in H.A. Clegg (1979), *The Changing System of Industrial Relations in Great Britain*, Basil Blackwell.)

Insofar as the law has been implicated there has been a very slow development of positive rights for trade unions, rather a system of immunities to the operation of the common law is more characteristic. Thus limited immunities to prosecution for picketing were given under the 1875 Conspiracy and Protection of Property Act. These were extended in the 1906 Trade Disputes Act, only to be repealed in part in the 1982 Employment Act. It would appear that even negative recognition (i.e. immunity) is harder to establish in more recent times.

within a liberal democratic society. Yet insofar as it is at odds with the lived reality of much manual labour it provides a challenge and an opportunity for organising workers both officially and unofficially. Its problematic nature confronts liberal democracy with an immanent critique: the right of manual workers to a healthy environment equal to others. The class basis lies in the counterfactual reality, which demands a reply from the philosophical universalism of the liberal State.

Conclusion

What we have argued in this chapter is that the British construction industry represents some of the paradoxes of a peculiarly British pattern of development. Historical strength at the point of production within the labour process combined with exclusion at the strategic level of the industry. One result of this pattern has been the way in which the logic of the market has come to dominate both the structure and process of the industry. As such the industry represents a sector which has become differentiated and disembedded in Polanyi's sense. The result of this, is a situation akin to anomie, where no one sees it as in their individual interest to continue widespread training and the orderly social reproduction of the labour force. The result of this for workers in the industry is demoralisation and for those not yet in the industry discouragement to joining. The satisfactions of working in the industry have historically been those arising from freedom from direct control and an actively created and reproduced class based culture. This is seen to be breaking down in the shift from a post-figurative culture to a co-figurative culture emphasising individuation. Allied to this, movement in the broader labour market and wider society has arguably led to a decline in the status and relative material rewards accruing to skilled manual work. All of these secular trends have served to further problematise occupational unity in an industry whose very structure militated against stable aggregation.

In a more optimistic tone what we have gone on to suggest is that an elective affinity appears to be gathering between employers who are realising that the disordered nature of the industry is unsustainable, the technology of smart cards, which whilst clearly is not without danger for workers (one employer suggested to us that sickness records of workers could also be recorded) nevertheless would enable certain valued criteria in relation to training to be used as a form of labour market closure. Further we have singled out the health and safety issue as one that would serve both the specific occupational hazards existent in the industry and yet the basis for appeal is that of industrial citizenship, a concept which should appear to transcend sectional or class based concerns. The importance of this however is not only to be gauged in its instrumental moment, but also insofar as it provides a structure for the continuation of a post-figurative culture emanating from the shop-floor. Thus health and safety should not be seen as a version of single issue trade unionism. Rather it is to be seen as a focus through which an appeal to all workers, whatever their age or skill status, can be made. Class can perhaps still unite but it needs to do so in both formal and non-formal contexts, as structure and experience.

11 For-itself but not In-itself: Class and Democracy in Post-communist Europe

DAVID OST

When the Solidarity movement came to power in Poland in 1989, it seemed to many that a genuine working-class organisation had come to head the state. Business circles, excited about the beginning of the opening of the Soviet bloc, were wary of the presumed power of the Polish working class. To an outsider, and even to many insiders, Solidarity looked like a movement that took its working-class roots seriously. It was founded in 1980 as a result of militant strikes by shipworkers. Intellectuals latched onto them, seeing in the workers' movement a chance to advance the struggle for political democracy, but in style and in substance the battles of the first Solidarity period had an unmistakable working-class character. Workers behind factory gates were the recurring image of 1980-81. The entire movement was personified by the Gdansk electrician Lech Walesa, whose proletarian origins were as evident from his language and demeanour as Eliza Doolittle's were from hers. When martial law was imposed in December 1981, workers took the lead in fighting against it, staging strikes in mines and factories, and suffering the casualties of the ensuing repression. After martial law, while opposition to the new authorities was widespread throughout Polish society, the road to the Round Table negotiations of 1989 that ended the communist monopoly of power again went through workers' protest: a series of militant strikes in 1988 left the authorities convinced that the only way they could bring about the market reforms they now desired was to win the co-operation of the workers. They opened negotiations with Solidarity, and brokered the political deal that led to the elections of 1989 that Solidarity won decisively. The close affiliation of Solidarity's parliamentary candidates with the workers' movement was evident by their main bit of electoral propaganda for the 1989 electoral campaign: a personal photo of each candidate next to Lech Walesa.

Observers, in other words, could be forgiven for seeing class as the decisive identity for Polish workers as they headed into the new capitalist era. No wonder business circles saw the fall of the Berlin Wall, and not Solidarity's triumph, as the moment when socialism really fell.

As we know, however, the post-communist era has not been a time of workers in control. Indeed, from the point of view of the previous decade, the years since 1989 have been a time of unprecedented working-class defeat. Just when it seemed that they could pursue their interests with unencumbered commitment, workers have watched passively, even approvingly, as former benefits and rights have been progressively whittled away. Job security and employee governance were the first to go. Hundreds of thousands lost once-secure jobs. Prices skyrocketed and real wages plummeted. Work force participation quickly eroded, with employee councils abolished as enterprises became privatised. New private-sector jobs often lack basic health and safety conditions, and are frequently outside the legal economy altogether. Social benefits paid for by factories have eroded dramatically, as enterprises change from being social institutions to economic agents. Moreover, the losses have not been compensated by corporatist structures at the national level, which were slow in coming and still have little impact. Union membership plummeted, and even activists were not interested in recruiting. Overall, workers have taken a beating.

Moreover, it is not just at the economic level that workers have suffered, but at the cultural and symbolic level as well. Whereas workers in the 1980s were lionised as the great democratic revolutionary agent (see, for example, Andrzej Wajda's anticommunist agitprop film *Man of Iron*), the proclaimed hero of the 1990s is the 'middle class', a term usually used to denote budding capitalists rather than professionals.

The irony of all this, however, is that this economic and cultural transformation has been overseen by Solidarity. It is not a question here of a workers movement doing the dirty work and then losing power to the economic elite. Rather, it is Solidarity itself that has introduced these changes. A Solidarity government introduced the economic changes, Solidarity newspapers promoted the cultural transformation, and all these developments were strongly supported by Solidarity trade unionists. At the union's first National Commission meeting after the formation of a Solidarity government, Walesa (in Lawinski, 1989) argued that the union's first goal should be to support the reforms, not unionism. 'We will not catch up to Europe if we build a strong union', he said.

The point, therefore, is that the undermining of working-class power was carried out not by an alien ideology but by a workers' ideology. Solidarity, from 1980 into the 1990s, was operating very much with a notion of class. But the notion of class denotes something very different in the communist context than in the capitalist context. Workers who become class conscious in communist society embrace a notion of class that refers quite literally to everyone. And while that is its great strength (allowing a movement like Solidarity where all of society was united behind a trade union - something about which Western unionists can only dream), it is also its great weakness. For since 'working class' in the communist framework refers to everyone, it does not refer to workers *per se*. In the communist era, this was not much of a problem, since workers' basic economic interests were largely addressed by the Party, for whom the establishment of a comprehensive welfare state with strong protections for workers in the workplace was a matter of basic policy. In the post-communist era, however, when the new market economic system offers workers as workers no special privileges, then this broad notion of working class became detrimental to workers, who suddenly had no one to look out for their own interests. More: workers *themselves* were not assertive of their own interests, because they understood their interests as politically and not economically. When Lech Walesa argued that 'we cannot have a strong trade union until we have a good economy', he was speaking for most union leaders in the early 1990s.[128] So - does class unite? The problem is that in the communist context it united too many - so many, in fact, that it was unable to unite workers on their own.

What are the political implications of this weakness of class identity in post-communist society? Many political democrats welcomed the weakness of labour, and even said it was necessary. Adam Przeworski (1991), calling himself a social democrat, argued that workers posed the greatest threat to the consolidation of a liberal market democracy because they were likely to be so militant in defence of their class interests that they would prevent the implementation of necessary market reforms. The reality, however, has been quite different: workers have been so *lax* in asserting their own economic interests against those of the rising 'middle class', and so distant from a notion of class that refers to industrial workers and wage labourers alone, that they have found themselves extremely alienated from the new democratic political system and unable to find their place within it. It is not the demands for inclusion that has weakened democracy in the post-communist era, but the *lack* of demands for inclusion. As workers find themselves increasingly excluded, yet uncertain what to do about this, they

---

[128] Interview with *Gazeta* Wyborcza, cited in *Tygodnik Solidarnosc*, No. 20, October 20, 1989, p. 23. On the moderate and even anti-union tendencies among lower-level Solidarity activists, see Ost and Weinstein (1999).

become open to illiberal, 'populistic' appeals that challenge the basic principles of democracy.

Indeed, this is precisely what has happened in Poland. In 1996, after years of feeling excluded by the governments and parties it once helped create, Solidarity the trade union finally organised its own political representation. Explicitly claiming to be a right-wing organisation, Solidarity brought together numerous other right-wing parties (including one that had openly called for new laws drastically reducing the role and influence of trade unions), and ran for office on a program promising to increase the role of the Church and take tough action against the continued presence of 'communists' in public life. Its economic program consisted of a call for a 'pro-family' wage and taxation policy (partly aimed at reducing the role of women in the work force), the acceleration of privatisation, and benefits to workers as shareholders rather than as workers. Solidarity appealed to workers for their votes, but the appeal was directed not along class lines - not directed against a rising capitalist class - but along religious, cultural, and political lines, against secularists, liberals, communists, and other 'aliens'. Since coming to power (in a coalition with liberals) in September 1997, this new Solidarity has pursued its religious and political agenda, not its economic one. In other words, the danger to political democracy is coming not from workers asserting their class demands, as Przeworski and others feared, but from workers being unable and unwilling to assert their class demands, and turning their class anger into illiberal identity-based anger.

The problem, in other words, is that workers are experiencing hardships due to the emergence of a capitalist, class-based society, but they lack a language of class in which to make sense of them. As a result, many workers and unions are latching onto non-class identities, such as religion or nationality, as a way of explaining the new problems they face. Organising social conflicts in this way, however, conflicts with the tenets of political democracy, which insist that everyone is an equal citizen regardless of ascriptive characteristics.

Class and the Organisation of Anger

The conflicts natural to a liberal market economy can never be suppressed. A stable democracy requires that conflicts be minimal. But it also requires that conflicts be expressed, rather than lie latent waiting to blow up. Consolidating democracy depends not on avoiding conflicts, which is impossible, but on structuring conflicts in the most democratic way.

How, then, *should* antagonisms be organised? If the aim is a democratic political outcome, then conflicts must be structured in an inclusive way. Political cleavages ought to be shaped in a way that accepts everyone as part of the community. Democratic politics depends not on the elimination of anger and the suppression of conflicts, but on the structuring of social anger in a way that does not treat particular groups or individuals as enemies because of what they think or believe or because they are members of a different ethnic or racial group. Only cleavages that accept the fact and the permanence of difference will ultimately respect the principle of tolerance central to political liberalism.

The experience of Western democracies shows that 'class' is the optimal political cleavage - not of socialism but of liberalism. Class cleavages are most compatible with liberal democracy because the proffered enemy is an impersonal economic system, and not an ethnic, political, or religious other slated for expulsion from the community. Class conflicts lead to democratic outcomes because they seek to resolve conflicts through bargaining among different groups of people, all of whom are accepted as citizens of the same state. Such cleavages lead to a more inclusive polity, and are thus conducive to liberal politics, precisely because they target their enemies on an abstract rather than concrete basis. Unlike nationalist, communitarian, religious, racial, or ethnic antagonisms, which exclude whole categories of people from citizenship on the basis of attributes one can do nothing about, class-based antagonisms target only an abstract distributional arrangement as the problem. Thus, they can be resolved by adjusting the economic system, rather than, say, by expelling Moslems from Bosnia. Unlike the enemy of nationalist and fundamentalist politics, the class enemy is represented by a citizen just like you.

Of course, the argument against this view is that not all class conflicts have been organised in such a way. In communist practice, if not always in theory, 'class' has been interpreted in a tragically concrete way. Stalin identified the 'class enemy' not as a system, which had allegedly been abolished, but as specific individuals said to be imbued with its values. Various concrete groups took their turns of being the official class enemy: engineers in the late 1920s, peasants ('kulaks') in the 1930s, Volga Germans or Crimean Tartars in the 1940s, and all political oppositionists during the entire Stalinist period. These were the ones who soon filled the Gulag. In China, Maoists identified as the 'treacherous class enemy' anyone with a tiny plot of land, anyone able to hire even one agricultural worker, and the 'evil felons' were put to death by the hundreds of thousands. The Khmer Rouge, of course, also used the language of class in order to kill millions. Clearly, class is not always a democratic demarcation.

These, however, are all examples of governing communist regimes using the language of class in order to suppress opposition. In capitalist systems, parties advocating class conflicts have almost always pushed for the political inclusion of all minority groups, opposed distinctions based on race or ethnicity, and promoted a broad-based idea of community, just as liberal democracy commands. And it is this that has led communist and socialist parties to consistently speak out against racisms and other ascriptively-based hatreds. Long before Stalinism, early Russian Marxists fought labour's tendencies to think in ethnic rather than class terms. When strikes turned to pogroms, Bolsheviks and Mensheviks alike admonished workers for attacking the wrong enemy (see Wynn, 1992). In America, communists were consistently among the leaders in the fight for full racial integration precisely because they saw class as the only legitimate cleavage. In Western Europe, socialists and social democrats have played the crucial role, appealing to the notion of class inclusion in order to introduce comprehensive inclusive welfare states in the postwar era. Promoting the organisation of anger along class lines implies discouraging it along other lines, and that has usually led to the inclusiveness characteristic of democracy.

Market economies create class-based conflicts in which the interests of labour run contrary to the interests of capital. A democratic system in a market economy requires that conflicts be expressed in a way that taps the underlying causes of the conflict, because only then can the conflict be resolved. Cleavages based on non-class criteria, such as religion, gender, or ethnicity, are incommensurable with democratic systems not only because they entail the persecution of a minority but because their proposed substitute satisfactions are incapable of solving the problems that led to the social anger in the first place.[129] Class conflicts in market societies mitigate antagonisms by being able to challenge and ameliorate the sources of anger. Building a liberal political system requires the organisation of antagonisms along class lines because only in this way can the majority of people win a stake in the economy, and thus become defenders of the lib-

---

[129] In multi-ethnic societies, of course, some workers can become included at the expense of other workers. Downwardly mobile workers in the nineteenth century United States secured inclusion through denying class benefits to Blacks and Asians, and Afrikaner workers in South Africa gained a piece of the British-controlled prosperity by excluding black workers through apartheid. But these, of course, are not democratic outcomes. In each case, democracy became consolidated only when the racial cleavages were abandoned for economic ones (see Roediger, 1991; Sparks, 1991).

eral system that maintains that economy.[130] Democracy is endangered when workers fight against economic problems in other than economic ways.

Of course, this argument does not mean that class cleavages are the only ones present in democratic systems. The point is only that in the conflict that emerges naturally in a capitalist workplace, in the conflict between workers and managers/owners, class ought to be the dominant cleavage, because this is the cleavage that leads to compromise, not exclusion. Second, my argument does not mean that democrats must continually press for greater and greater class conflicts in order to make democracy ever more secure. The point, again, is only that the underlying economic conflict should be *based* on class. It is this, I claim, that allows these conflicts to be managed peacefully and democratically. Neocorporatist systems have been democratic not because they continually promote more and more class conflict, but because they *assume* class conflict as the foundation of the system, and in this way serve to manage and reduce the social anger that class tensions otherwise produce. Such systems seem to have a minimal degree of class conflict precisely because they are openly based on the existence of class conflict, and in this they keep it under control.

In the sections that follow, I want to, first, discuss the peculiar communist construction of class that leaves workers in post-communist society weak and uncertain. Then, I will more fully discuss the political implications of organising social conflict along class cleavages or identity-based cleavages through a comparison of the Polish and Czech situations.

The Communist Construction of Class

Perhaps the key reason why workers in post-communist society latch onto non-class identities, such as religion or nationalism, as a way of explaining the problems they face is that they lack a language of class. Class identities are weak in post-communist society due to the structural and ideological framework of communism, as well as to the nature of the struggle against communism.

---

[130] This is not a completely new argument. Gregory Luebbert (1991) has argued that European political systems evolved differently depending on how and by whom the working class was incorporated. Political democracy (either liberalism or social democracy) was possible when working class anger was addressed and redressed by either liberal or social democratic parties. Political democracy resulted when parties and unions were able to incorporate workers as a class into the capitalist economy that had so threatened and alarmed them. Political democracy, therefore, was based on class compromise.

We can best understand why the Polish working class moved from being a militant actor during the communist era to being so hesitant and confused, often acting against its own interests, in the post-communist era, by asserting a paradox: in the communist era, Polish labour indeed acted as a class-for-itself. The problem, however, is that it never was a class-in-itself.

In Marxist theory, of course, class-in-itself is non-problematic, referring only to workers' objective status in the economic system. 'In-itself' is assumed, and only 'for-itself' remains a question mark, as it refers to labour's appearance on the political stage, aware of its clout and asserting its interests. For Marxists, class-for-itself without class-in-itself makes no sense at all.

As for so many social science concepts, however, this one too refers only to a *capitalist* system. When a self-proclaimed working-class party comes to power and nationalises all industry, the meanings of 'in-itself' and 'for-itself' change radically. In such a system, everyone objectively becomes a member of the working class, as employees of the owner-state. Moreover, everyone can claim subjective membership as well, as 'working class' becomes an honorific, the equivalent of the liberal democratic 'citizen'. (Thus, intellectuals who wanted to transform the communist system always did so in the name of the working class.[131]) In the public realm of communism, it is impossible to say who exactly belongs to the working class. And the point is that this is a problem not just for the social scientist but for the labour activist, who never did know whom exactly he had in mind when speaking of the working class. Labour activists certainly did use the term, and always evoked the image - the standard, traditional image of the male, manual, industrial labourer. But every time labourers armed with this image moved into the public realm, and sought directly to transform politics, they invariably raised general systemic demands aimed at democratising the system politically, not improving the conditions of workers economically. In communist society, workers appeared in politics not as workers but as citizens.[132] They were, in other words, condemned to

---

131 In their well-known work, George Konrad and Ivan Szelenyi (1971) argue that communism allowed intellectuals to come to power precisely because it allowed them to appear as workers, and thus as members of the official universal class.

132 I am adopting a notion of class-consciousness developed by Victoria Hattam (1993, esp. pp. 137-8 and Conclusion) in her history of unionism in the United States. For Hattam, working-class consciousness entails recognition of labour's role as the subordinate class in a relationship between labour and capital. In other words, a recognition of class-in-itself comes first. In this view, workers developed class-consciousness when they gave up illusions about changing capitalism and devoted their efforts to getting a better deal within it. They become class conscious when they finally started organising as workers, rather than as 'producers'.

be a 'universal class'. But in so doing they lost sense of their own particularity.

Class divisions make sense when one social group defines itself and its interests against those of another social group. In Poland, as in other communist countries, everyone defined themselves solely in relation to the state. No strikes in communist Poland, or anywhere else in communist societies for that matter, were ever directed at managerial targets alone. Workers saw not managers but the state as their real enemy. Similarly, managers had no gripes with labour. It would not get more money by cutting workers' wages; there was no conceivable sense of a zero-sum game here. When professionals began to organise politically, they identified the same enemy that labour did: the state that monopolised everything.[133] Without social others that could be construed as antagonists, the concept of class barely makes sense. The term was used, however, because the communist state insisted on it. But it never did refer to just workers.

Workers went on strike in 1956 for better conditions, but were soon displaced by a movement, which many workers bought into, calling for self-management. In 1980-81, economic issues again were the initial cause of the strike. But again, the central demand quickly became independent trade unions, and when workers won, they immediately reduced demands on bread-and-butter issues, fighting for political ones instead. My point here is not to criticise the choices of Polish workers, but to point to the way that class demands were regularly occluded in favour of civic ones. It was communism itself that facilitated the satisfaction of class demands - that is, it created a comprehensive welfare state with real, if constrained, on-the-job bonuses. But it did so only through non-political means, either at the workplace or through non-formal bargaining with the Party (the so-called 'social contract' entailing a steadily increasing standard of living in return for political quiescence).[134] When the state retreated on providing class benefits, it is no surprise that labour chose political struggle instead. But in doing so, it lost its class-specific identity. By opting for the political route and seeking to articulate the democratic demands of all, labour did nothing to secure specific benefits for itself. The right to have an independent union would of course help labour win its rights in the future, but only in a future in which it had no specific claim on state power, only in a future in which it had *less* privileges than before. Politics was needed only for the introduction of non-class demands, and this is where workers ultimately got stuck. Labour was adopting a strategy and policy that would leave it

---

[133] On engineers and social class in Poland, see Kennedy (1991). On the ambiguity of class in communist society, see Ost (1993, 453-85).

[134] On collective bargaining in socialist societies, see Sabel and Stark (1982, 439-75).

vulnerable at the very moment of success. The ostensible and symbolic class militance of Solidarity was being deployed in favour of alternative class interests.

The point is that sustained workers' protests during the communist era led not to the articulation of workers' interests as workers, but to movements aimed at benefiting all. Politically, workers did not and could not think of themselves as a particular class within civil society, but only as a universal class. They did not fight politically for their own interests but for everyone's interests.

Polish workers tended to follow the line intellectuals laid out for them. Oppositionist intellectuals, however, never had a specifically working-class program. They readily identified themselves as workers, particularly during the Solidarity era, but for them the only real aim of workers was to win the right of independent organisation. Of course, this was important to industrial workers too, but for the latter the right to organise is needed for workers to defend their economic interests, while for the intellectuals organisation is the end in itself. Workers embraced the program as theirs. They were so used to economic issues being resolved through non-political means, either at the workplace or through non-formal bargaining with the Party, that they believed the addition of political rights would be pure gain. What they did not see is that the institutionalisation of political freedom meant the end of the era of special privileges for workers. The latter, in the workers' experience, was a given. During the Solidarity era, few intellectuals spoke loudly about eroding workers' special rights, though none denied that this loss would follow from freedom's gain. So workers embraced the intellectuals' program, and that was their problem. Because when they won, they no longer saw a need to defend themselves. Ironically, of course, this was just the time when it became necessary to defend themselves, because this was precisely the time that a working class-in-itself was finally being constituted.

In communist society, therefore, the problem is that class 'united' people all too well - turning workers into citizens, but preventing the crystallisation of their separate identity as workers. The irony is that in communist society class only unites 'all', but does not unite workers.

Class and Politics

What are the political consequences of this understanding of class? We can best answer this through a comparison of Poland and the Czech Republic.

If Poland has been a place where a strong labour movement under communism has generated weak labour outcomes in the post-communist era, in the Czech Republic we have a weak labour movement under communism leading to a stronger post-communist outcome. For all of its reputation as the country in which 'capitalism' has gone farthest, both individual workers and organised labour alike emerged in a more advantageous position than in Poland (Orenstein, 1996). Czech unemployment has hovered at about 3-4 per cent, compared to about 15 per cent in Poland. Czech unions won early representation on a prominent nationwide Tripartite Council, something denied to Polish unions until 1994, after the pattern of neglect had already been established.

Benefits for labour entailed more than just low unemployment. Although the privatisation program did not allow direct employee ownership, a universal voucher program distributed property to the citizenry at large (in contrast to Poland, which emphasised sales to individual investors). Labour also gained here by the government's bankruptcy policy, which reduced the fear of unemployment in privatised firms. In the workplace, meanwhile, Czech unions won limited codetermination rights in privatised firms (again in contrast to Poland, where Solidarity sanctioned the withering away of the powerful Employee Councils). All in all, labour's better deal derives not from any 'natural' advantages enjoyed by the Czech economy but by policy worked out in an arrangement between government and unions.

Why should the country with the stronger labour movement end up in a worse place than the one where this labour movement had for so long been so dormant? The answer seems to lie in the nature of the opponent against which union organised. Whereas Polish unions defined themselves in the struggle against communism, independent Czech unions emerged at the time of nascent capitalism. Whereas 1989 in Poland appeared to mean that labour had finally won, in Czechoslovakia it meant that labour had to start organising. The Czech situation was different because workers did not get politically mobilised until after the fall of the communist system. They positioned themselves not against communism but against nascent capitalism.

That process began in November 1989.[135] With the press still in the hands of the Party, the actual organising of the strike had to be done by hundreds of individual activists, including young workers drawn to militance by the new images of freedom, and savvy older union bureaucrats bent on survival. After the communist system toppled, only weeks after the strike had ended, this motley group of November activists went on to become the new union leaders, taking over the old official unions' institutions and assets.

---

[135] An excellent account of Czech unions from 1989-92 is Myant (1994).

Now that they had control, they still had to gain legitimacy. What were unions to do in the new epoch? They could not simply relinquish decision-making authority to the government, because, unlike in Poland, neither historical, institutional, nor personal ties linked them to the new government. Perhaps more important, they could not do so because the government didn't have a plan, either. Market thought had not developed in Czechoslovakia to the extent it had in Poland. And so, whereas the latter country was ready to introduce the new economic programs already in 1990, the Czechs used 1990 to discuss what that program should be.

This gave the union (CSKOS) its great opportunity. Instead of simply sanctioning a reform package, as in Poland, it helped create one. The union needed to consolidate its position among its members precisely at the moment when fundamental discussions about the new economy were taking place, and when the new government needed legitimacy as much as the unions did. With no pro-market legacy to fall back on, and with hard-line communists (who had formed a rival union) pressing from the outside, CSKOS had to define itself by its actions to protect workers against the coming of the market. CSKOS first gave notice of its influence in November 1990, when it called a national strike alert to protest government plans outlawing political strikes and denying unions a say in dismissals. As a result, the government backed down. The new union leaders needed to win concessions and the new government leaders needed to win popular support. An organisational logic pushed the Czech unions into opposition, and the political ambitions of Klaus' - the Czech Prime Minister - led him to compromise. This scenario gave labour the clout it lacked elsewhere. In this way, Czech workers won benefits because they were able to assert their particular class interests, and they were able to assert those interests because they defined themselves against a nascent capitalist system, rather than against the old communist one.

What do the different ways in which labour has been integrated into the new system mean for politics? The answer is that it has helped consolidate democracy in the Czech Republic while jeopardising democratic stability in Poland. In 1996, while Czech unions have stayed in the democratic political mainstream, Solidarity has embarked on an extended flirtation with the illiberal right.

While labour in the Czech Republic may be in a better position than in Poland, that does not mean that Czech workers are satisfied with their lot. Low wages might help maintain employment but that does not make them popular. Moreover, in the last couple of years Klaus has renewed his campaign against labour, citing budgetary problems to justify cutbacks in key areas, leading to a huge hospital strike in March 1996 and general dissatisfaction with the direction of reform. Nevertheless, the achievement of

Czech 'social liberalism', as Orenstein calls it, has been to ensure that dissatisfaction with current policies is expressed within an established liberal democratic framework. When Czech voters turned away from Klaus' Civic Democratic Party in the June 1996 elections, they did not embrace the ex-communists, as in Poland, but turned instead to authentic reformist social democrats. Although the hard-line left and right did gather about 20 per cent of the total vote, suggesting increasing anger as hardships continue, organised labour remains firmly behind the committed democratic parties.

In Poland it's another story, as the liberals' complete disregard for labour has finally led labour to disregard the liberals. Unfortunately, this has meant not just a rejection of economic liberalism but very often a rejection of political liberalism as well.

The first to move in that direction was the Solidarity leader in Szczecin, Marian Jurczyk, who broke off in 1989 to form his own union, provocatively called 'Solidarity '80'. While Solidarity '80 attacked the effects of shock therapy, its proclaimed target was not the market but the 'aliens' (*obcy*) who were allegedly distorting it. The market is a good thing, Jurczyk said, if run by 'real Poles'. The problem is that it is dominated by 'communists' (in their new role as 'capitalists'), foreigners, and Jews.

By 1992, three years of experience with shock therapy left workers susceptible to any apparently anti-market appeals. In the summer, both Solidarity '80 and the old 'official' union (OPZZ) organised a series of strikes demanding higher pay, an end to the crippling wage tax, and a bigger role for workers in deciding economic policy. Solidarity stood at a crossroads: either join the discontented and break with the government, or risk marginalisation itself. It decided on the former path, inaugurating a chaotic process that is still not over.

This process began in earnest in 1993, when Solidarity led a massive strike campaign of teachers and hospital workers and then forced the ouster of the government of Prime Minister Hanna Suchocka, despite that government's Solidarity pedigree. When new elections produced a government led by ex-communists but essentially following the economic policy of the Solidarity liberals before them, the union moved to a new vision of politics in which communism and liberalism are seen as two sides of the same coin. What joins the two, says Solidarity today, is their lack of concern with 'the Polish nation'. In Solidarity's new view, both communists and liberals care only about the elite - that is, about themselves - and 'real Poles' are left to wallow in the gutter.

Although mobilised to militance by the economic crisis, Solidarity is so tied to its anticommunist past that it has not been able to give up faith in communism's putative enemy, the market.[136] Paradoxically, it attacks the liberals and ex-communists for not being pro-market enough. In a 'real' market economy, says Solidarity, workers are treated fairly and are rewarded for their work, whereas Polish elites, who are not 'real Poles', are rewarded for their connections. Unable to develop any compelling anti-market narrative, Solidarity seeks substitute enemies through a new nationalism.

The most extreme representative of this new tendency in Solidarity is Zygmunt Wrzodak, from the powerful Ursus Tractor Plant in Warsaw. Wrzodak combines a populist, proudhonian faith in small enterprises owned by workers with a strong belief in the need for a strong state run on Christian principles to protect 'the nation' against being bought out by the enemies. And the enemies (again defined as 'aliens') are all over the place: they are the communists, capitalists, Russians, Americans, Europeans, foreigners, and the Jews. Wrzodak has led a number of militant demonstrations, including the first violent ones of the post-1989 era, in which the government is denounced for selling out the interests of the nation. At one anti-government march in 1995, Wrzodak supporters chanted 'To the Gas!' as the names of government leaders, none of whom were Jewish, were read from the podium.

Solidarity president Marian Krzaklewski has criticised Wrzodak as extreme, even 'proto-fascist'. Yet even Krzaklewski sees himself squarely on the political right, and he has recently organised a successful 'right-wing' coalition that came in first in the recent parliamentary elections. He plays to the same kind of themes as Wrzodak, though without the aggressiveness or open bigotry. Nationalist, anti-communist, masculinist (anti-abortion rights, family wages for men), and even 'tough-on-crime' themes play an important part in this new right coalition.

On specifically union issues, Solidarity has had some interesting ideas. It calls for a reversal of the privatisation process (described as booty for nomenclature thieves) and the introduction of a program of 'universal ownership', whereby workers would receive, one-time only, a voucher worth several thousand dollars to invest where they choose. Yet this proposal shows the same fundamental problem mentioned earlier: a reluctance to think of union members as 'workers' rather than 'citizens'. For even if workers thereby get some capital, they would still be workers, and Solidarity's proposal does nothing at all to address problems of low wages, precarious or non-existent contracts, unemployment, unsafe working condi-

---

[136] On workers' generally pro-market beliefs, see Ost and Weinstein (1999), and Gardawski and Zukowski (1994). Also, Gardawski et al. (1994). For evidence that the weakness of unions has persisted even through the end of the decade, see Pankow et al. (1999).

tions, and the numerous other problems its members face because of their role as workers. Solidarity is still living out its existential crisis: shaped so intrinsically by the struggle against communism, it is unable to think of workers as a class and so still does not know how to wage normal union battles against capital.

When the Solidarity-sponsored 'right-wing' government came to power in October 1997, it did so with a program calling for more privatisation, quicker market reform, and a greater role for Catholicism and the Church in public life. A cross was hung in parliament as the new Sejm met for the first time. As for union issues and union rights, the new Solidarity government has had little to say. Still unable to think in class terms, Solidarity offers substitute satisfactions as a way to divert class anger.

In Poland, Solidarity was so committed to civic struggle as opposed to class struggle that it has been unable to defend workers in the post-communist era, and has turned to a dangerous nationalist-religious framework to explain the problems. In the Czech Republic, labour re-emerged in struggle not against communism but against nascent capitalism, forcing upon it a class sensibility that has benefited both workers and democracy.

Social anger produced by a market economy must be organised in some way. If it is not organised along class lines (abstract), it will be organised along identity lines (concrete), which often lead to an exclusionary ethos that is contrary to liberal democratic principles. The structure of communist society and the legacy of anticommunist resistance led to a particular construction of class in Poland whereby workers are unable to forcefully defend their interests. 'Class' does not yet unite in Poland. It needs to if political democracy is to be secured.

12 Can Class Still Unite: Lessons from the American Experience

SHERRY LINKON AND JOHN RUSSO

The question of whether class unites has, historically, been different for the United States and Europe. The discussion of class in America has always been paradoxical - stressing both classlessness and a vision of 'middle-class' as synonymous with 'American'. At the same time, polls show that almost 50 per cent of Americans define themselves as working class, but only a small percentage of workers belong to working-class organisations such as trade unions (Navarro, 1992, 361). Meanwhile, women and people of colour have often felt barred from full membership in the working class and its institutions, which have linked whiteness and maleness with privilege for some and exclusion of others. Consequently, when class has not been ignored or denied in the US, it has often been perceived as divisive.

American culture has frequently downplayed the idea of class as a meaningful aspect of identity or a source of social movement organising. In early American culture, democratic government and agrarianism suggested distinct differences from European patterns of inherited wealth and privilege. In America, because land was abundantly available and political positions were based on popular elections, social leaders argued that a 'meritocracy' would supplant the aristocracy of Europe. Class identity would not be inherited but created, and therefore a matter of individual effort. In the nineteenth century, the immigrant dream of making a better life in the 'land of opportunity' gained prominence, and it remains powerful even as many Americans support limitations on immigration. This 'American dream' combines with ideas about individualism to create a national culture that defines individual success and upward mobility as equally available to all. A common American fantasy, re-enacted every four years during presidential campaigns, suggests that anyone can 'pull himself up by his bootstraps' and rise to a position of power and wealth. Given this ideology, it's not surprising that many Americans see being working-class as a sign of personal failure rather than as a source for activism. The apparent absence of a self-conscious American working class has been exacerbated in the twentieth century. While unions have sometimes used traditional notions of class conflict as tools for organising and mobilising workers, they have also worked hard to provide industrial workers with incomes that enabled them to acquire the trappings of middle-class life: suburban home-ownership, college education for their children, two cars, and other consumer goods. Especially in the postwar era, class has been increasingly defined around consumption, and many industrial workers don't see them-selves as having common interests with service workers or the unem-ployed.

While historically class has functioned differently in the US than it has in Europe, today the imperatives of global capitalism, immigration, and economic restructuring have led to a convergence of economic and social conditions, and so class, identity, and multiculturalism are being re-exam-ined in both the US and Europe (Modood and Werbner, 1997). This re-examination provides an opportunity to reassess our understanding of class and gain fresh insight into its potential as an organising principle, espe-cially for labour solidarity in a multicultural, global economy. In the US, this process is proving controversial and has sparked debate and divisions from the shop-floor to the lecture hall, and its outcome remains uncertain. We want to begin with a few examples and trends that highlight some key aspects of the current American situation and that will have resonance for the European trade union movement.

The American labour movement has witnessed a significant demo-graphic shift in recent years. In 1996, for the first time in American labour history, there were more women and people of colour in American labour unions than there were white men (United States Department of Labor, 1997). In part, this is the result of economic restructuring, downsizing, and de-unionisation in the traditionally male-dominated unionised manufactur-ing and construction industries. The trend has also been influenced by increasing opportunities for employment and labour organising in the traditionally female- and minority-dominated retail, service, healthcare, and public sectors and by population shifts resulting from immigration and relatively higher birth rates among people of colour as compared with whites. This demographic shift is reflected in the leadership of international unions and the AFL-CIO, where more attention to diversity by the union and in class issues among workers have led to increased organising of women and people of colour. AFL-CIO Director of Education, Bill Fletcher (1998) argues that unions must focus on building class consciousness among new members, but he points out that this class consciousness cannot be 'narrowly economic' nor can it pretend 'that issues of racist oppression, male supremacy, and homophobia don't exist'.

These demographic changes have shifted the locus of power within the labour community. White male dominated unions, such as those in the building trades, have lost power to unions in the service sectors whose membership reflect these changes. This has led to a backlash within some parts of the labour community. For example, at the AFL-CIO Convention this past fall, many conservative and former labour leaders were reported to have been carping that if the labour movement continued on its present course it would soon be composed of 'strawberry pickers and chicken pluckers' (Wypijewski, 1997, 4) and vowed a fight over the leadership and future direction of the AFL-CIO at the next convention.

The divisions have been intensified by recent trends in the nature of work - what and where it is, who has access to jobs, how jobs are structured - which, paradoxically, create both another source division and potential opportunities for social movement mobilisation. As work is increasingly divided hierarchically between secure, 'good' jobs and less certain low-wage part-time and temporary jobs, and as companies continue to move the work to where workers are cheaper and less 'demanding', divisions within the working class are being complicated.

The conflict within traditionally class-based institutions like labour unions is mirrored in a growing debate among American left intellectuals. For example, Todd Gitlin (1995), a former leader of Students for a Democratic Society and a professor at New York University, has argued that the American left failed because it abandoned 'commonality' and class struggle in favour of narrowly defined politics of identity focused on race, gender, ethnicity, and sexuality. Gitlin is correct that this focus on identity has led to a backlash against the left within working- and middle-class communities. Yet, as critics such as black labour historian Robin D.G. Kelley (1997) and philosopher Iris Young (1997) have argued, such arguments privilege class over other categories and ignore the importance of anti-racist and anti-sexist struggles to the universalist themes of class struggle.

Differences among identity-based social movements are not unexpected, as Tim Jordan (1995, 680) has argued: 'Each social movement creates its definitions of society from its members' perspective and so ... it can be expected that these definitions will be different and contradictory'. Jordan's statement reminds us that we cannot simply wish away divisions between social movements. Rather, if class is to unite, we must learn how to link these movements without asking participants to deny their own frames of reference. Here, recent social movement theory can augment traditional approaches to class. As we will argue later, using the 1997 UPS strike, frame analysis may be helpful in developing strategies for building coalitions that incorporate divergent perspectives.

American Experience of Class Division

As European trade unions increasingly face changing demographics and economic restructuring, the American experience may offer several useful lessons. First, don't underestimate the complexity of increasing work force and trade union diversity. The increasing diversity of the American labour movement sounds like an unqualified step in a direction that is both appropriate politically and inevitable as the demographics of the US population make whites less and less the dominant group in terms of numbers. Yet, as the conflicts within the AFL-CIO and the academic left suggest, the diversity of labour is far from simple. In the US, a racially and ethnically diverse working class has been divided along a boundary of 'whiteness', which operated as an alternative to class as a primary source of identity for white ethnic workers. As David Roediger (1991) argues in his important book *The Wages of Whiteness*, white workers have found psychological and economic benefits in identifying themselves as white rather than as working-class. By eliding ethnic and religious identities, these workers created a coalition that gave them political clout while also excluding African Americans and other people of colour as well as women. While these 'others' could and did join unions, unions did not embrace them as legitimate members whose voices and experiences were taken seriously, nor did the white male majority usually feel compelled to protect their rights as workers. Yet, as Roediger argues, policing the boundaries of their whiteness kept white men from fully recognising the connections between class and community that make class-based movements possible. Emphasising whiteness meant that the working class could not create the truly broad-based coalitions required to foster significant economic and social change.

Similarly, from the other side of the political spectrum, the rise of identity politics has contributed to the fracturing of any potential working-class coalition. While advocates of identity politics do not reject the notion of working-class coalition building (any more than the white male working class ever *explicitly* rejected it), they call for recognition and organising around other categories of identity, primarily race, gender, and sexuality. The roots of identity politics can be traced at least as far back as the civil rights movement in the 1960s, as African Americans claimed a special authority in dealing with the problems of racism, and women asserted their unique understanding of the personal and public politics of gender. Such arguments have some validity, of course; experience is an important element of critical understanding. However, when defined either in terms of basic requirements, such as the idea that only black people can validly discuss the experiences of black people, this approach can divide would-be allies. When organisations operate on the assumption that shared identity equals shared experiences, as when women's groups suggest that all women struggle to balance home and work life, they can overlook diversity within groups.

Further, in recent years identity politics has been at the heart of a growing division within the American left, as activists and academics argue about the best way to organise for social change. While the debate raises important issues about organising, identity, and class, it also sharply divides the left and leads those involved to turn inward, fighting with each other about what works rather than fighting for the rights of workers. Examples of the growing divide have surfaced in numerous articles in progressive magazines, several widely-discussed books, and discussions at recent conferences. For example, the debate surfaced at the inaugural meeting in Washington of Scholars, Artists, and Writers for Social Justice (SAWSJ) in April 1998. The purpose of the conference was to attempt to close divisions between different interest groups and create new progressive coalitions. But while the conference included keynote speeches by leading African-American scholars and activists, such as Julian Bond and Kimberle Crenshaw, Robin D.G. Kelley lambasted SAWSJ for have too many white male leaders, whom he called 'neoconservative white guys in left clothing', and for focusing too 'narrowly' on class and labour organising instead of giving more attention to racist oppression (Alterman, 1998, 10). The most troubling aspect of this debate is that it has claimed so much energy and attention within the left, detracting from the 'real' politics of union organising, crafting public policy, or becoming involved with the electoral process. Thus, not only is the American working class split over issues of identity, it is also hampered by a politics of theory that accomplishes little and undermines the very coalition building with which it claims to be so concerned.

Second, recent changes in the structure and nature of work make traditional ideas about class unstable and create another significant source of division especially among the working class. Traditional notions of work and non-work as well as other concepts that help shape class identity, such as place, time, and employer, are all increasingly fluid and fractured. For example, as Arlie Hochschild (1997) argues in *The Time Bind: When Work Becomes Home and Home Becomes Work*, full-time workers, while attaining a measure of job and economic security, are being overworked to the point where work has replaced the home as the centre of daily life. In other words, the workplace becomes one's home and the employer becomes part of one's family. The relationship between worker and employer is even more problematic for those who are statistically 'fully employed' while working multiple jobs where working conditions may vary widely.

Other fractures can be seen in the secondary labour market, where job and economic insecurity are rampant as employers increasingly use part-time, temporary, and contingent workers who have little loyalty and commitment to their employers. Most of the heralded job growth in the US over the last five years has been in industries that support part-time low-wage employment. In 1996, there were more than 30 million Americans working part-time, most of whom were in the fast-growing service and retail sectors (Nifong, 1997, 3). The average yearly earnings of these workers was under $20,000 (Bellah, 1996, 755). It is no surprise that the fastest growing sector of the economy is the temporary worker industry or that industry leader Manpower, Inc. has become the nation's largest employer replacing both GM and IBM. For more and more workers, this secondary labour market has become their primary work site. People who once were sure of where they stood have become unsure. Workers whose jobs once exemplified the differences between white- and blue-collar labour (divisions that often stand in for working- and middle-class identities) find themselves in work situations that don't fit the old models, raising questions about whether divisions based on the colour of one's collar matter anymore.

Work and work conditions are key elements in most definitions of class, and when these lines are blurred, class identities and affiliations become fluid. This can be seen in the new class terminology that has emerged, with the 'overclass', 'underclass', and 'virtual class' replacing the more familiar middle and working class. Thus, the instability in the structure and nature of work is mirrored discursively in the instability of class language. Such language makes class position seem relativistic, fluid, and elusive, which contributes to individual and collective ambivalence about class identity.

Economic restructuring not only creates uncertainty for individual workers, it also creates a fracture within the working class. While some theorists might expect economic restructuring to generate stronger class commitments, in the US such changes are often seen as part of a 'natural' economic order. Thus, individuals worry about losing their middle-class status, what Barbara Ehrenreich (1989) calls 'fear of falling', but they see the problem largely as a matter of individual failure rather than as part of a global threat to their class. So instead of creating solidarity, economic changes can often turn workers against one another. The experiences of full-time workers who have good working conditions (normally the result of a union contract) with one employer differ significantly from those of 'fully employed' temporary workers, and in many cases, the two groups see themselves in competition with each other. Thus, the working class is divided not only by issues of race, gender, and sexuality but also by hierarchies within the labour market itself. These work divisions often dovetail with and thus underscore other demographic differences. For example, 62 per cent of those working part-time were women, and approximately 50 per cent were under the age of 24 or over 55 (Nifong, 1997, 3). Historically, such divisions have led to accusations that a labour aristocracy existed, in which full-time unionised workers in the primary labour market were largely unsympathetic to 'lower class' workers in the secondary labour market.

The alterations in employment are intimately related to economic globalisation and corporate restructuring. In both Europe and North America, changes in communications, transportation, and especially capital mobility have blurred national borders and resulted in the movement of jobs to low wage countries with 'business friendly' governments and weak labour movements. This has acted as a brake on wages and forced domestic employers to use various labour market strategies to compete with low-wage foreign subsidiaries of corporations.

In this increasingly global economy, national boundaries that once seemed absolute become more uncertain, as so-called 'American jobs' and the ubiquitous middle-class lifestyle they (supposedly) supported move into a global marketplace. One result is that nationalism, racism, and anti-immigrant sentiments are running high in the US (as they are in Europe). During the recent contentious debates over the extension of the North American Free Trade Agreement (NAFTA) and affirmative action, tensions between the white, Latino, and African-American working and middle classes have undermined diversity and coalition building as class has been put in opposition to race. It should not be surprising that some of the most ardent supporters of affirmative action and NAFTA in recent years have come from the corporate sector, which in the global economy increasingly sees the support of diversity as in its self-interest. In 1997, corporations spent significant sums to help defeat an initiative to repeal affirmative action in Houston, Texas. Obviously, the NAFTA and affirmative action debates have generated class confusion, as working-class movements and labour unions have been faced with the difficult challenge of fighting unfair free trade agreements while continuing to organise non-white workers and promoting international labour and working-class solidarity. At the same time, they have also found themselves defending affirmative action programs often without the support of their traditional white male constituency.

Hopeful Signs

Yet, as two final examples from the American situation suggest, there is reason to believe that class can still unite. Unions have begun to form multi-identity coalitions that are creating more inclusive leadership and incorporating identity-based issues into union practices. For example, AFL-CIO President John Sweeney's focus on women helped him win election, and he, in turn, added more women to the executive council and other leadership positions, including Linda Chavez-Thompson as executive vice president. And while the organisation's recent convention included all too many 'old style' unionists who, as JoAnn Wypijewski (1997, 4) wrote in *The Nation*, 'cut the deals, sell out the members, ... [and] hate the left', the convention also featured Jesse Jackson's claim that rather than having a national discussion on race, which President Clinton declared as a central goal for his administration, it's time to talk about 'the Grand Canyon of American life, ... the vertical gap between wealthy and workers, between rich and poor, the canyon between haves and have-nots'.

It has not gone unnoticed by advocates of identity politics that, while income gaps between blacks and whites and women and men have declined over the last twenty years, inequality within racial and gender groups has grown. Labour organisers and left academics are beginning to understand how class is lived through race and gender and therefore how important it is to organise in a multicultural context. In a recent article in *Working USA*, Manning Marable (1997) argues that while people of colour and women have good reasons to be sceptical about white male leftists who argue for a broad-based working-class coalition, they also have much to gain from such an effort.

The UPS strike in 1997 provided another hopeful sign when it generated stronger than expected broad-based support both nationally and internationally for the protection of part-time workers. Despite the inconveniences of the strike, the relatively high wages of UPS workers, and the company's efforts to capitalise on the old image of the International Brotherhood of Teamsters (IBT) as corrupt, the majority of Americans supported the union's position. While some in the media have argued that this is largely a matter of customers having positive relationships with their UPS drivers, that hardly seems a complete explanation. Rather, the IBT reasoned that to gain support for the strike it was necessary to emphasise issues with which people could identify. Consequently, it chose part-time employment - a class/work issue that transcends lower/middle-class divisions. That strategy paid off, helping the union win public support and undermining UPS's anti-union rhetoric. As the president of UPS told CNN, if he had known that it would become a national referendum on part-time employment, UPS would not have precipitated the strike.

The IBT also put together an international coalition that many believed was as essential as the part-time work social justice campaign. While UPS knew that its 80 per cent market share of the small package business in the US made it strong enough to withstand a long strike, its European business was much more vulnerable. In the last three years, UPS had spent more than one billion dollars to upgrade its European facilities and to launch a full-scale attack on its European competitors. UPS's investment in its European corporate operations was threatened when the IBT gained international support (through both direct and indirect actions) from its international trade secretariat and independent unions. No doubt, international organising and working-class solidarity contributed to the early resolution of the strike. The UPS case indicates the potential for international labour solidarity in the global economy when organising around work-related issues.

These developments demonstrate the importance of linking workplace issues with other social and psychological factors influencing individuals' participation in social movements. Erving Goffman (1974, 21) approaches this through the study of 'frames', which he defines as 'schemata of interpretation' through which people understand their own lives and the world around them. In order to mobilise support for social movements, the frames of participants must be aligned through the processes of frame bridging, amplification, extension, and transformation (Snow et al., 1986). This approach can help explain how the IBT garnered so much support, not only from unionists but also from the general public.

The first step in building support for the strike was a year-long internal campaign among UPS workers, highlighting the significance of part-time employment as a threat to job security. This was a form of frame amplification, which helped intensify union members' existing attitudes. Second, the IBT had to develop a mass media campaign to generate support among those in the general public who shared the strikers' concerns about part-time employment. They also used direct interpersonal and intergroup networks to reach out to international unions as well as to women's and African-American organisations that have traditionally been concerned with employment issues for women and minorities. These are both examples of frame bridging, which creates links between 'ideologically congruent but structurally unconnected frames' (Snow et al., 1986, 467). Third, the IBT had to extend existing frames for both its members and the public by expanding the narrow definition of the strike to allow it to be seen as a broader social justice campaign. This, too, they accomplished primarily through their mass media efforts as well as the involvement of figures who are identified nationally as representing social justice movements, such as Jesse Jackson. In the process, the Teamsters transformed existing frames, jettisoning old beliefs about what labour unions were and reframing the meaning of 'working class' to include not just industrial workers but all workers, regardless of their race or gender, who are threatened by economic restructuring.

Conclusions

To conclude, what specific lessons can be drawn from the American experience as to the potential for class to unite in a period of rapid economic, social, cultural, and technological change?

First, if class is to unite, we have to change the way we talk about class. Theories that depict class as a universalist structure or in static terms of social stratification or that cast labour politics only in terms of industrial relations are clearly insufficient. In fact, such theories can be misleading in developing and understanding the potential of both organised and unorganised segments of the working class and their political behaviour. Rather, behaviours and interests are determined not only by economic position but by a confluence of factors salient to an individual's social, political, and economic life of which class is but one factor. Not only race and gender but also job-related differences, issues of place, and public discourse about class and work affect how people see themselves and how they respond to organising efforts. Clearly, class theory must account for all of these elements if we are to develop viable organising strategies.

Several recent examples of scholarship on class and work demonstrate how important such theoretical shifts can be. Anthropologist Kathryn M. Dudley's (1994) research on the closing of an auto plant in Kenosha, Wisconsin emphasises the way public discourse constructs ideas about class and, in turn, people's experiences and beliefs. Cultural geographer Don Mitchell (1997) argues that landscape is a site of class conflict in his reading of worker housing and the landscape of farm labour. Rick Fantasia (1988) analyses the cultural moments that make solidarity possible, arguing that working-class consciousness doesn't exist as a static or predetermined condition but is created by specific experiences and situations. In addition, as our brief frame analysis of the UPS strike suggests, class theory must consider the psychological and social factors that influence whether individuals perceive themselves as members of the working class and how they act on that identification. Contemporary theories of social movements, such as frame analysis, draw our attention to these social and psychological factors and how they intersect with structures and organisations. All of these projects move beyond traditional class theories to suggest new ways of approaching questions about class identity, consciousness, and action.

Second, spending time worrying about who is more oppressed or arguing about whether to privilege class over race, race over gender, or sexuality over the other social categories will not produce more active social movements. Rather, we need to understand how race, gender, class, and sexuality are structurally interconnected, while at the same time exploring how organisations can effectively build support and participation through frame bridging, amplification, extension, and transformation. Organisations must learn to pay more attention to participants' perspectives in order to develop strategies to build coalitions that encompass frames based on racial, gender, sexual, ethnic, and class perspectives. As Manning Marable (1997, 48) suggests, organised labour must 'develop the capacity to address class and racial issues simultaneously' rather than be caught up in the debate about which should dominate the discussion. Iris Young (1997, 69) puts it another way: 'Unity and understanding for a new people's movement will not come from pretending that group differences do not matter, but rather from understanding precisely how they do matter, and so forging an inclusive picture of our social relations'.

Third, class will unite when it is understood that capitalism can not exist without class and that, while capital may be winning the battle over the restructuring of work and workplaces at the moment, it has not won the class war. Perhaps, as the UPS example shows, the best hope for greater equality in the future is the development of inclusive, international, multiracial labour and working-class movements organised around specific work-related issues. If Europeans and Americans can incorporate these three lessons, surely class can still unite.

13 Does Class Still Unite? Concluding Remarks

BERT KLANDERMANS

'Does class still unite?' This question, which has been the focal point of this anthology and of the conference it originated from, implies that once upon a time class did unite. I propose that we relegate this implicit message to the realm of fairy tales, where it belongs, and formulate a different question, namely, 'Did class ever unite?'.

The two questions - 'Does class still unite?' and 'Did class ever unite?' - are basically empirical questions. For decades, sociologists have been investigating class as a unifying factor that establishes and maintains the various segments of society that are internally homogeneous in terms of wealth and hardship or that generate homogeneous mindsets among people in the same objective situation. Questions about the homogeneity of people's mindset - often phrased in terms of the absence or presence of class-consciousness - also relate to class as a determinant of collective action. Thus formulated, these questions concern the participation of the working class in labour unions and industrial action in the past and in the future. Empirical questions can be answered by empirical research, provided that we manage to agree on how to define and operationalise concepts such as 'class' and 'unity'. Unfortunately, such agreement remains wishful thinking. Moreover, we often forget that differences in the institutional arrangements between countries may give supposedly identical measures and indicators a different meaning. It would be much easier to answer questions such as those formulated here if we had put more time and energy into the development of comparable measures and indicators.

Behind the question about class unity there seems to be the tacit normative assumption that class should unite, or at least the expectation that people in similar adverse circumstances will react collectively and in unison to their circumstances. In my view there is little reason to take such a reaction for granted. In fact, in my view, a theory of class and collective action should focus precisely on the question of 'Why should class unite?'. With this third question, I want to direct our attention to the possible determinants of the unity of class.

In the remainder of this concluding chapter I will further elaborate on these three questions. Inevitably, my considerations will have a social psychological emphasis, but such an approach still provides enough room to formulate some fundamental questions.

Does Class Still Unite?

The question of whether class still unites is, of course, inspired by the changes in industrial relations we have witnessed over the last few decades in the industrialised countries. I have neither the space nor the expertise to give an exhaustive treatment of those changes, but I will summarise the basics, which are discussed in much more detail in several of the papers in this volume.

While the traditional blue-collar sectors have declined, both the service sector and the public sector - and for that matter also the white-collar sector - have showed a dramatic growth. At the same time, the gender composition of the work force has changed and the work force has become culturally and ethnically ever more diverse. In the mean time, the work force has also had to become increasingly flexible (part-time jobs, temporary employment) and we have witnessed a growing division in the labour market between secure, full-time jobs and insecure, low-paid, part-time jobs. All this has been accompanied by a growth in the numbers of long-term unemployed and workers on disability benefits, and the development of a so-called 'underclass'.

Changes like these have produced what in some of the papers in this volume is called the 'crisis of representation'. Labour unions, by many scholars seen as the manifestation of class solidarity or unity, have lost their strongholds in the traditional blue-collar sectors and have failed to recover these losses with membership gains in the growth sectors of the economy. Indeed, some of the authors in this volume fear that the unions will never be able to regain their strength. Although there is much to be said in support of that claim, I am less pessimistic than some scholars, as I will argue in the answer to my third question. But as for the first question, yes, unions do seem to be caught in a vicious circle of decline and this raises serious questions about class as a unifying principle. In order to explain what I mean by this observation, I must elaborate on the process of membership turnover. I will draw on research on union participation we conducted some years ago with a group of Dutch scholars (Klandermans and Visser, 1995). These data are inevitably limited by Dutch peculiarities, but they can serve to illustrate an argument that I believe to be relevant for other countries as well. In fact, the papers in this volume confirm this view.

In the Netherlands most people who become a member of a union join the organisation within five years after they have entered the labour market. Chances that they will become a member after five years decline rapidly, and become very much dependent on critical events such as a strike, a conflict, or a personal problem. However, people enter the labour market with a certain pre-existing inclination to join a union. Processes of socialisation at home, in school, among peers and through the mass media generate a more or less positive attitude toward labour unions and therefore a stronger or weaker inclination to join a union. Such processes of sociali-sation create the first vicious circle: as the unions decline, fewer people grow up in a union environment. Having parents who are union members was and still is a factor that predisposes to union membership. But less and less individuals have parents who are union members. The more union membership declines, the more this will be the case. The same holds for schools and peer groups: unions are increasingly absent in such environ-ments. Finally, the declining overt ideological orientation of the mass media in general has led to a situation in which the union-oriented media have typically lost their ideological direction. All these influences together have been responsible for the fact that people's readiness to join a union upon entrance to the labour market has declined.

Whether individuals entering the labour market actually do become a union member depends on the presence and presentation of the union in the company they enter and on the industrial relations climate in that company (whether or not union friendly). These factors make for the second vicious circle. People are entering the labour market increasingly in sectors where the unions are weak: in temporary jobs, via temp agencies, in the service sector, and so on. As a consequence, the chances that they will encounter strong and effective unions are declining, which considerably reduces their chances of becoming a member.

Half of those who become a member leave again within five years and, what is more serious, the chances are very small that they will ever become a union member again. Keeping members is apparently just as problematic as recruiting members. Contacts with the union or the lack thereof and the evaluation of these contacts play a crucial role in membership loss. This creates a third vicious circle. Membership loss will be greater in those sectors where the unions are weak. In a way, this makes sense. If you are working in a company where the union is almost invisible, then why bother being a member?

The combined effect of these three vicious circles is that unions continue to have difficulties strengthening their position in those companies and sectors where they are weak, while at the same time the companies and sectors where they used to be strong have declined. As a consequence, unions have lost much of their capacity to unify the working class. Hence, on the one hand, the working class has crumbled and become much more heterogeneous during the last decades. On the other hand, the actors that must unite this ever more heterogeneous class - the unions - have become weaker. This legitimates the question as to whether class still unites. But before I formulate an answer to this question I would like to turn around and raise the more fundamental question: 'Did class ever unite?'.

Did Class Ever Unite?

The question of class unity in the past is echoed in some of the papers in this volume, but admittedly not very loudly or clearly. Obviously, each industrialised society has its historical examples of mass industrial action, but instances in the past where class did not unite abound as well. In this context, it is an interesting coincidence that the conference which produced this volume was held in Belgium, a country where as long as unions have existed there have been always been both catholic and socialist unions. In Holland, there is still a Christian Union Federation and one will encounter ideologically diverse unions in France, Italy and Spain. In South Africa white workers are defending their privileges vis-à-vis blacks and in many other societies labour unions are bulwarks of white male workers who have difficulties with changes in favour of female workers or workers from different ethnic backgrounds. Strikes have failed because of lack of support or because of the use of strike-breakers, and workers have crossed the picket lines. Indeed, labour history is full of examples where class, in fact, has *not* united. Some of these are referred to in the papers in this volume.

Indeed, I want to argue that class as such never did unite, but that there are always additional identifiers involved that explain spells of unity. In the classical study of Kerr and Siegel (1957), it was the working-class community or more precisely the mining community that provided additional constituents of identification. Often it is the company. For example, Rick Fantasia in his *Cultures of Solidarity* (1988) demonstrates that already existing 'cultures of solidarity' which have developed over the years explain why the work force of a company reacts in a united way. Alternatively, it might be 'suddenly imposed grievances' that come *with* a collective identity. For example, the work force of a company or an industry is threatened by mass lay off, company closure, wage cuts, or the like. On other occasions, it is the members of a union who follow their union when it calls them on strike. I could go on and give many more examples, and there are yet more examples cited throughout the papers in this volume. *Note however*, that in all these examples the additional identifiers, be it a neighbourhood, a company, the fact of being affected by some decision of management, or of being mobilised by one's union narrows class down considerably to a much smaller subset defined by the additional identifier(s). Sometimes these smaller subsets may even compete or conflict with one another, other, or fail to support each other. For example, cases in which the work forces in two different plants of the same company have played against each for which plant was going to lose jobs. Or workers in the same company who have secure positions versus workers who have insecure positions.

My argument here is that this has always been the case. The working class has always been subdivided in smaller subsets of solidary members who share an additional identifier, be it a company, a department, a profession or occupation, a community, or membership in a specific union. What I am referring to is in the social psychological literature known as the inclusiveness or exclusiveness of social groups (Brewer, 1991). People tend to identify less with inclusive groups than with exclusive groups, and the more exclusive the group, the stronger the identification that is to be expected. Class is a highly inclusive category, much more inclusive than the company, the department, the professional group or whatever, to which a person belongs. As a consequence, we may expect a person to identify more strongly, for example, with the department in which he or she works than with his or her class. This is exactly what the literature on organisational commitment (Meyer and Allen, 1991) and commitment to social movements (Klandermans, 1997) tells us. The more exclusive the group (sector vs. company vs. shop or movement vs. movement organisation vs. local branch of the organisation), the stronger the commitment one will encounter. It is not even unusual to find these identifications to be in conflict with one another. For example, the workers in company X may find it difficult to participate in a national strike because they identify with their company and feel that they do not want to do any damage to 'their' company.

In short, class is too inclusive a category to spontaneously generate high levels of identification. Within the broad category there are too many more exclusive categories that workers tend to identify more strongly with. Hence, I totally agree with Richards (in this volume), who argues that 'sectionalism and solidarity are points on a continuum and that historically solidarity has been constructed'. Labour history has demonstrated that 'solidarity' has had to be constructed, often with blood, sweat and tears on the part of the organisers. This brings me to my third and final question.

Why Should Class Unite?

The question as to why class should unite, relates to the fact that people can be categorised in many different ways: class, gender, age group, religion, ethnic background, nationality, and so on. There is no reason why any of these categories should a priori be more than any other and thus should be more the focus of unity or solidarity than any other. In my view, students of class, gender or ethnicity in such sub-disciplines as class studies, women's studies and ethnic studies often make the mistake of working from the assumption that the category they capitalise on (class, gender or ethnicity, respectively) is the most fundamental social category in society. I will argue that people have multiple identities and can and in fact often do identify with different categories, depending on the social context.

The various identities people maintain are hierarchically organised (Stryker, 1997). We know, however, from history and identity literature that there is no fixed hierarchy of identities. A few examples may help to illustrate the argument. Class and gender are identities that have conflicted in the past: witness the dilemma of many a woman whether to identify with the women's movement or with the labour movement. In a similar way, class and ethnic background have also raised conflicts of identification. Class and nationality have always been identities that are difficult to reconcile, as the international labour movement discovered to its shame when World War I broke out. And finally, class and religion have traditionally existed in an uneasy marriage with one another. After all, the opponents in the class struggle could be and in fact often were members of the same religious community. The early socialists saw religion as the opium of the people and church and capital as allies in the suppression of the working class. Indeed, at the turn of the twentieth century many a Catholic and Christian labour union was established to take the wind out of the socialist union sails (Windmuller et al., 1983).

These examples illustrate that, to be sure, an individual's various identities *are* hierarchically organised, but that these hierarchies are context dependent. That is to say, different contexts and changing times may produce diverging hierarchies, even in the same person. In one situation, the person's identity as a women may be more important than her identity as a worker or a mother. In another situation, her identity as a mother may be the most important. This brings me to one of the key points I want to make with regard to identification or to 'people's willingness to act as a member of a group or category' (Kelly and Breinlinger, 1996), namely, the context dependence of identification. For our subject, the context dependence of identification implies that with contexts and times changing, different identifiers - and thus different subsets of the working class - may become prominent. But first I need to explain the process of identification.

The process of identification. Identification is a process that has three different aspects: the *cognitive*, that is, the classification of oneself as a member of a category; the *evaluative*, that is, the assessment of the situation of this category in comparison with other categories, and, the *affective*, that is, the emotional bonding with other members of this category (Ellemers, 1991). Obviously, classifying oneself as a member of a social category does not necessarily mean that one identifies with this category. A positive evaluation might strengthen group identification, and a negative evaluation might weaken it. In fact, the social psychological social identity theory (Tajfel and Turner, 1986) predicts that a negative evaluation reduces group identification. Reduced identification in turn leads to social mobility, that is, to attempts to leave the group. This will not come as a surprise to students of social mobility. After all, generations of workers have tried with more or less success to leave the working class. The affective component appears to be the strongest predictor of willingness to act as a member of a group or a category.

According to social identity theory, a negatively evaluated situation of the group or category someone identifies with (which evaluation is deemed to be illegitimate), combined with the perception that one cannot leave the group, stimulates collective action to improve the group's situation. None of these perceptions come about automatically. Rather, they are socially constructed in interpersonal interaction, by union organisers, in public discourse, and so on. Note that an identity can be imposed on a person by others. Others can treat a person as if they were a member of a certain category (which is the typical experience of women and ethnic minorities). And the more others do so, the more prominent this category will become. The more a person is treated as a member of the group 'women' or 'Moroccan', for example, the more the person's 'membership' in such a category will become a significant aspect of their self-identity. Let us now return to the question of the context dependence of identification and, more specifically, to the question of the prominence of class and other categories as identifiers.

The context dependence of identification. Whether class will unite, depends on processes of identification. In this respect, class is no different from any other social category. Class is one of the many social categories that people belong to. Depending on the context, any of these categories may gain prominence and, as these things go, categories other than class might very well become the most important. But the context may also make class the most prominent. It may indeed impose class membership upon a person. If everyone treats a person as a member of the working class, then class will inevitably become a more important aspect of the person's identity. However, most of the time class on its own is too diffuse and too broad a category for class identity to develop. As a consequence, additional sources of identification that single out smaller subsets of the working class are required. It is my argument that this has always been the case. The point, however, is that with the times and contexts changing, the additional identifiers that may serve to create solidarity among some subset of the working class have also changed. Hence, it is not so much that class no longer unites, but rather that class never did unite and, in any case, that many of the traditional additional identifiers are no longer effective.

What we are witnessing today is that some of the additional sources of identification that traditionally have served to create solidarity among subsets of the working class have disappeared or become insignificant, as for example the working-class neighbourhood, or being a socialist. Other sources of identification have become more prominent in society, as for example gender, ethnic background, nation or region, but these do not necessarily replace those that have vanished. Paradoxically, in the context of industrial relations, one of the additional sources of identification left is the company. In fact, in the Netherlands the company has grown in importance as a source of identification for workers, both because of modern human resource management techniques and because industrial relations are becoming decentralised. But the extent to which the unions (as the organisational representation of class unity) are able to make identification with the company work to their advantage depends on their strength in the company. As a consequence, unions must put more and more emphasis on making themselves present and visible in the companies. At the same time, the company is the context in which unions are not necessarily at their strongest - as we indicate in the opening section of this chapter. Moreover, identification with the company can only serve as an additional source of identification for the working class if identification with the union and identification with the company are not mutually exclusive.

The strategy of counting on identification with the company has serious drawbacks as well. In the first place, it excludes important groups. Temporary workers (a growing proportion of the work force), the unemployed, and people on social security and disability benefits are obviously not part of any company. Thus far, the Dutch labour unions have not been very successful in organising these groups. Against this background, it is of interest to mention that Dutch labour unions have recently succeeded for the first time in negotiating a collective agreement with temp agency associations. Secondly, the labour movement may breakdown into an archipelago of company unions that do not coördinate and sometimes even compete. The more the unity is defined at the company level, the higher the risks that the unions disintegrate, unless the unions are able to maintain master frames that glue these different collectives together.

There are other identifiers than company identification, and they could possibly serve to unite. Much depends on the extent to which the unions are able to reconcile multiple sources of identification, not only as far as company identification is concerned, but with regard to other sources of identification as well. The studies done by Sharon Kurtz (forthcoming) and by Silke Roth (1997), who studied the interface of gender, ethnicity and class as sources of identification, are of interest in this regards. Both studies demonstrate that the multiple identities can be successfully combined in collective action and interest representation. For that matter, the fact that Dutch unions are increasingly successful in organising women points in the same direction.

In Conclusion

In and of itself, class does not unite. Common fate has seldom been a sufficient condition for solidarity to develop. However, solidarity can nonetheless be constructed on the basis of common fate. It has been constructed many times in the past, and will continue to be constructed in the future. Such constructions will always concern a subset of class as a category defined by some additional source of identification. I have argued that the company has currently become an important additional source of identification. This is not to say that class is irrelevant. On the contrary, without the shared grievances generated by class relations there would have been no conflict in the first place. It is the secondary sources of identification, however, that generate the group solidarity needed to transform such discontent into collective action. Which secondary source of identification becomes prominent depends on the context in which the process of identification occurs. These processes are not random. They are influenced and constructed by social actors such as unions, management, political parties, and government.

This brings me to a final remark. The unions are not the only actors in the arena. Attempts to understand the processes of identification must always take into account that other actors are trying to have an influence. People not only belong to many different categories, but they are also linked to different actors. Actors that are competing for people's hearts and minds.

Bibliography

Abercrombie, N. and Urry, J. (1983), *Capital, Labour and the Middle Classes*, George Allen and Unwin, London.

Abram, S., Murdoch, J. and Marsden, T. (1996), 'The Social Construction of 'Middle England': the Politics of Participation in forward Planning', *Journal of Rural Studies*, Vol. 4, No. 12, pp. 353-64.

Accornero, A. (1985), 'Conflitto, 'terziario' e terzi', in *Giornale di diritto del lavoro e di relazioni industriali*, A. VII, No. 25, pp. 17-52.

Accornero, A. (1996), 'La piccola impresa e le relazioni industriali', in *Giornale di diritto del lavoro e di relazioni industriali*, A. XVIII, No. 72.

Accornero, A. (1997), *Era il secolo del lavoro*, Il Mulino, Bologna.

Accornero, A. and Marcucci, F. (1987), 'Ancora sul conflitto terziario', in *Politica ed economia*, No. 7-8.

Ackers, P. (1995), 'Change in Trade Unions since 1945: A Response to Heery and Kelly', *Work, Employment and Society*, No. 9, pp. 147-54.

Adamson, D.L. (1988), 'The New Working Class in Welsh Politics', *Contemporary Wales*, No. 2, pp. 7-28.

Adamson, D.L. (1991a), *Class Ideology and the Nation. A Theory of Welsh Nationalism*, University of Wales Press, Cardiff.

Adamson, D.L. (1991b), 'Lived Experience, Social Consumption and Political Change in Wales', in G. Day and G. Rees (eds), *Nations and European Integration: Remaking the Celtic Periphery*, University of Wales Press, Cardiff.

Adamson, D.L. (1995), 'The Spatial Organization of Difference and Exclusion in a Working-Class Community', in Ken Coates (eds), *Full Employment. A European Appeal*, Bertrand Russell Peace Foundation, London, pp. 141-52.

Adamson, D.L. (1996), *Living on the Edge. Poverty and Deprivation in Wales*, Gomer, Llandysul.

Adamson, D.L. (1997), 'Communities of Resistance: Social Exclusion, Community Development and Economic Regeneration', *British Sociological Association Annual Conference, Power and Resistance*, University of York.

Adamson, D.L. and Jones, S. (1996), 'The South Wales Valleys: Continuity and Change', *Regional Research Programme*, University of Glamorgan, Pontypridd.

Agg, J. and Phillips, M. (1998), 'Neglected Gender Dimensions of Rural Social Restructuring', in M. Boyle and K. Halfacree (eds), *Migration into Rural Areas: Theories and Issues,* Wiley, London.

Alba, A. (1991), 'Fixed-Term Employment Contracts in Spain: Labour Market Flexibility or Segmentation?', Working Paper, pp. 91-2, Universidad Carlos III de Madrid.

Alba, A. (1997), 'How Temporary is Temporary Employment in Spain?', Working Paper, pp. 97-14, Universidad Carlos III de Madrid.

Albarracín, J. (1990), 'La Política Económica y el Empleo', Paper presented at the II Jornadas de Economía Crítica, Madrid.

Allen, C.S. (1990), 'Trade Unions, Worker Participation, and Flexibility. Linking the Micro to the Macro', *Comparative Politics,* No. 22, pp. 253-72.

Allen, J. (1988), 'Fragmented Firms, disorganised Labour', in J. Allen and D. Massey, *The Economy in Question,* Sage, London.

Alterman, E. (1998), 'Making One and One equal Two', *The Nation,* Vol. 19, No. 266, p. 10.

Althusser, L. (1977), *Ideologie und ideologische Staatsapparate,* Berlin.

Ambrosini, M. (1991), 'Il caso francese', in G.P. Cella (eds), *Nuovi attori nelle relazioni industriali,* F. Angeli, Milano.

Ambrosini, M. (1995), *La fabbrica dei giovani. Il lavoro dei giovani tra necessità e progetto,* Ediz. Solidarietà, Rimini.

Ambrosini, M. (1996), *L'impresa della partecipazione,* F. Angeli, Milano.

Ambrosini, M. (1999), 'Una nuova prospettiva per la partecipazione sindacale: il livello territoriale', in M. la Rosa and D. Meda (eds), *Il problema del lavoro, il lavoro come problema. Un confronto italo-francese sui temi del futuro del lavoro, dell'occupazione e della partecipazione,* F. Angeli, Milano.

Ambrosini, M., Colasanto, M. and Gasparini, G. (eds) (1989), *Tecnologia organizzazione e lavoro. Uno studio di casi nel settore creditizio assicurativo,* F. Angeli, Milano.

Anthias, F. (1998), 'Rethinking Social Divisions: some Notes towards a theoretical Framework', *Sociological Review,* Vol. 3, No. 46, pp. 505-35.

Antolín, P. (1995), 'Movilidad Laboral, Flujos de Desempleo,Vacantes y Comportamiento en la Búsqueda de Empleo en el Mercado de Trabajo Español', *Moneda y Crédito,* No. 201, pp. 49-85.

Argentaria (1995), *La Desigualdad en España. Síntesis Estadística (II Simposio sobre Igualdad y Distribución de la Renta y la Riqueza),* Fundación Argentaria, Madrid.

Armstrong, A. (1988), *Farmworkers: a Social and Economic History 1770-1980,* Batsford, London.

Aronowitz, S. (1983), *Working Class Hero. A New Strategy for Labor,* The Pilgrim Press, New York.

Austrin, T. (1980), 'The 'Lump' in the UK Construction Industry', in T. Nichols (ed.), *Capital and Labour,* Fontana, Glasgow.

Baethge, M. (1989), *Technological Change and Human Resources Development in the Service Sector: the Case of the Federal Republic of Germany,* SOFI, Göttingen (mimeo).

Baethge, M. (1991), 'Arbeit, Vergesellschaftung, Identität - Zur zunehmenden Subjektivierung der Arbeit', in W. Zapf (eds), *Die Modernisierung moderner Gesellschaften,* Campus, Frankfurt am Main.

Baethge, M., Denkinger, J. and Kaditzke, U. (1995), *Das Führungskraefte-Dilemma. Manager und industrielle Experten zwischen Unternehmen und Lebenswelt,* Campus, Frankfurt am Main.

Bagguley, P. (1992), 'Social Change, the Middle Classes and the Emergence of 'new Social Movements': a Critical Analysis', *Sociological review,* No. 40, pp. 26-48.

Bagguley, P. (1995), 'Middle class radicalism revisited', in T. Butler and M. Savage (eds), *Social Change and the Middle Classes*, UCL Press, London, pp. 293-309.

Baglioni, G. (1995), *Democrazia impossibile? I modelli collaborativi nell'impresa: il difficile cammino della partecipazione tra democrazia ed efficienza*, Il Mulino, Bologna.

Bahrdt, H.P. (1962), 'Die Angestellten', 'Die Industriearbeiter', 'Die Beamten', in M. Feuersenger (ed.), *Gibt es noch ein Proletariat?*, EVA, Frankfurt am Main.

Bain, G.S. and Price, R. (1972), 'Who is a White-Collar Worker?', *British Journal of Industrial Relations*, No. 10, pp. 325-39.

Bain, G.S. and Price, R. (1980), *Profiles of Union Growth. A Comparative Statistical Portrait of Eight Countries*, Basil Blackwell, London.

Baldamus, W. (1961), *Efficiency and Effort*, Tavistock, London.

Ball, M. (1988), *Rebuilding Construction*, Routledge, London.

Bardacke, F. (1988), 'Watsonville: A Mexican Community on Strike', in M. Davis and M. Sprinker (ed.), *Reshaping the US Left. Popular Struggles in the 1980s*, Verso, London, New York, pp. 149-82.

Barling, J., Fullagar, C. and Kelloway, E.K. (1992), *The Union and its Members: a Psychological Approach*, Oxford University Press, New York.

Bauman, Z. (1982), *Memories of Class*, Routledge, London.

Bauman, Z. (1988), *Freedom*, Open University Press, Milton Keynes.

Beaumont, Ph.B. (1987), *The Decline of Trade Union Organisation*, Wolfeboro, NH, Croom Helm, London.

Beck, U. (1983), 'Jenseits von Klasse und Stand? Soziale Ungleichheit, gesellschaftliche Individualisierungsprozesse und die Entstehung neuer sozialer Formationen und Identitäten', in R. Kreckel (ed.), *Soziale Ungleichheiten (Soziale Welt, Sonderband 2)*, Otto Schwartz & Co, Göttingen.

Beck, U. (1986), *Risikogesellschaft. Auf dem Weg in eine andere Moderne*, Suhrkamp, Frankfurt am Main.

Beck, U. (1992), *Risk Society: towards a new Modernity*, Sage, London.

Beck, U. (1995), *Ecological Politics in an Age of Risk*, Polity, Cambridge.

Beck, U. and Beck-Gernsheim, E. (1996), 'Individualization and 'Precarious Freedoms': Perspectives and Controversies of a subject-orientated sociology', in P. Heelas, S. Lash and P. Morris (eds), *Detraditionalization*, Basil Blackwell, Oxford.

Beck, U., Giddens, A. and Lasch, S. (1994), *Reflexive Modernization*, Polity Press, Cambridge.

Becker, U., Becker, H. and Ruhland, W. (1992), *Zwischen Angst und Aufbruch. Das Lebensgefühl der Deutschen in Ost und West nach der Wiedervereinigung*, Econ, Düsseldorf.

Bell, D. (1973), *The Coming of post-industrial Society. A Venture in Social Forecasting*, Basis Books, New York.

Bell, M. (1986), 'The Fruit of Difference: the Rural-Urban Continuum as a System of Spatial Identity', *Rural Sociology*, Vol. 1, No. 51, pp. 65-82.

Bell, M. (1994), *Childerley: Nature and Morality in a Country Village*, Chicago University Press, Chicago.

Bellah, R.N. (1996), 'The Neocapitalist Employment Crisis', *Christian Century*, Vol. 23, No. 113, pp. 754-56.

Benn, T. (1985), 'Who Dares Wins', *Marxism Today*, No. 29, pp. 12-5.

Bentolila, S. and Dolado, J.J. (1994), 'Labour Flexibility and Wages: Lessons from Spain', *Economic Policy*, No. 18, pp. 54-99.

Bentolila, S., Segura, J. and Toharia, L. (1991), 'La Contratación Temporal en España', *Moneda y Crédito*, No. 193, pp. 225-65.

Berger, P.A. (1986), *Entstrukturierte Klassengesellschaft? Klassenbildung und Strukturen soziler Ungleichheit im historischen Wandel*, Westdeutscher Verlag, Opladen.

Berger, S. and Broughton, D. (eds) (1995), *The Force of Labour: the Western European Labour Movement and the Working Class in the Twentieth Century*, Berg, Oxford.

Beynon, H. (1975), *Working for Ford*, Penguin, Harmondsworth.

Bilbao, A. (1993), *Obreros y Ciudadanos: la Desestructuración de la Clase Obrera*, Trotta, Madrid.

Blauner, R. (1964), *Alienation and Freedom. The Factory Worker and his Industry*, Chicago-London.

Bondi, L. (1991), 'Gender divisions and gentrification: a critique', *Transactions of the Institute of British Geographers*, NS, Vol. 16, pp. 190-98.

Bordogna, L. (1988), 'Arcipelago Cobas: frammentazione della rappresentanza e conflitti di lavoro', in P. Corbetta and R. Leonardi (eds), *Politica in Italia*, Il Mulino, Bologna.

Bordogna, L. (1991), 'Il caso Italiano', in G.P. Cella (eds), *Nuovi attori nelle relazioni industriali*, F. Angeli, Milano.

Bordogna, L. (1998), 'Le relazioni sindacali nel settore pubblico', in G.P. Cella and T. Treu (eds), *Le nuove relazioni industriali. L'esperienza italiana nella prospettiva europea*, Il Mulino, Bologna.

Bordogna, L. and Provasi, G.C. (1998), 'La conflittualità', in G.P. Cella and T. Treu (eds), *Le nuove relazioni industriali. L'esperienza italiana nella prospettiva europea*, Il Mulino, Bologna.

Boreham, P. and Hall, R. (1994), 'Trade Union Strategy in Contemporary Capitalism: the Microeconomic and Macroeconomic Implications of Political Unionism', *Economic and Industrial Democracy*, No. 15, pp. 313-53.

Borland, J., Fevre, R. and Denney, D. (1992), 'Nationalism and Community in North-West Wales', *The Sociological Review*, No. 40, pp. 49-72.

Bourdieu, P. (1982), *Die feinen Unterschiede*, Suhrkamp, Frankfurt am Main.

Bourdieu, P. (1984), *Distinction. A Social Critique of the Judgement of Taste*, Routledge & Kegan Paul, London.

Bourdieu, P. (1990), *The Logic of Practice*, Polity, Cambridge.

Bourdieu, P. (1992), 'Ökonomisches Kapital - Kulturelles Kapital - Soziales Kapital', in P. Bordieu, *Die verborgenen Mechanismen der Macht*, VSA, Hamburg.

Bourdieu, P. (ed.) (1993), *La misère du monde*, Éditions du Seuil, Paris.

Boyer, R. (1986), *La théorie de la régulation: une analyse critique*, La Decourverte, Paris.

Brand, K.W., Buesser, D. and Rucht, D. (1983), *Aufbruch in eine andere Gesellschaft. Neue soziale Bewegungen in der Bundesrepublik*, Frankfurt am Main.

Braverman, H. (1974), *Labor and Monopoly Capitalism*, Monthly Review Press, New York.

Breen, R. and Rottman, D. (1995a), 'Class Analysis and Class Theory', *Sociology*, Vol. 29, No. 3, pp. 453-73.

Breen, R. and Rottman, D. (1995b), *Class Stratification: a Comparative Perspective*, Harvester Wheatsheaf, New York.

Breugel, I. (1996), 'Gendering the Polarisation Debate: a Comment on Hamnett's 'Social Polarisation, Economic Restructuring and Welfare State Regimes'', *Urban Studies*, Vol. 33, pp. 1431-40.

Brewer, M.B. (1991), 'The Social Self: On Being the Same and Different at the Same Time', *Personality and Social Psychology Bulletin*, No. 17, pp. 475-82.

Brint, S. (1984), ''New class' and Cumulative Trend Explanations of the Liberal Political Attitudes of Professionals', *American Journal of Sociology*, Vol. 90, pp. 30-71.

Brody, D. (1980), *Workers in Industrial America. Essays on the 20th Century Struggle*, Oxford University Press, New York, Oxford.

Brody, D. (1992), 'The Breakdown of Labor's Social Contract. Historical Reflections, Future Prospects', *Dissent*, pp. 32-41.

Brody, D. (1994), 'The Future of the Labor Movement in Historical Perspective', *Dissent*, pp. 57-66.

Brown, R.K. (1992), *Understanding Industrial Organisations*, Routledge, London.

Brown, R.K., Brannen, P., Cousins, J. and Samphier, M. (1973), 'Leisure in Work: the Occupational Culture of Shipbuilding Workers', in M. Smith, S. Parker and C. Smith (eds), *Leisure and Society in Britain*, Allen Lane, London.

Brusco, S. and Fiorani, G. (1998), 'Competitività, partecipazione e condizione operaia nelle piccole imprese emiliane', in M. Ambrosini (eds), *La partecipazione dei lavoratori nell'impresa: realizzazioni e prospettive*, F.Angeli, Milano ('Sociologia del lavoro', 68, 1998).

Brusco, S. and Solinas, G. (1997), *Competitività e partecipazione*, Il Mulino, Bologna.

Buechler, S.M. (2000), *Social Movements in advanced Capitalism. The Political Economy and Cultural Construction of Social Activism*, Oxford University Press, Oxford.

Buerklin, W. and Rebenstorf, H. et al. (1997), *Eliten in Deutschland. Rekrutierung und Integration*, Leske + Budrich, Opladen.

Buigues, P. (1993), 'Market services in the Community economy', in *European Economy - Social Europe Reports and Studies*, Commission of the European Communities, No. 3.

Bulmer, M. (ed.) (1975), *Working-Class Images of Society*, Routledge and Kegan Paul, London.

Burgess, J. (1990), 'The Production and Reception of Environmental Meanings in the Mass Media: a Research Agenda for the 1990s', *Transactions, Institute of British Geographers*, New series, Vol. 2, No. 15, pp. 139-61.

Burrows, R. and Butler, T. (1989), 'Middlemass and the Pit: a Critical Review of Peter Saunders' Sociology of Consumption', *Sociological Review*, Vol. 37, pp. 338-64.

Butera, F. (1988), 'I paradossi del service management', in *Sviluppo e organizzazione*, No. 105, pp. 63-74.

Butler, T. (1997), *Gentrification and the Middle Classes*, Ashgate, Aldershot.

Butler, T. and Hamnett, C. (1994), 'Gentrification, class and gender: some comments on Warde's 'Gentrification as consumption'', *Environment and Planning D: Society and Space*, Vol. 12, pp. 477-93.

Butler, T. and Savage, M. (eds) (1995), *Social Change and the Middle Classes*, UCL Press, London.

Campbell, B. (1995), *Goliath. Inside Britain's Dangerous Places*, Methuen, London.

Carabaña, J. et al. (1993), 'Encuesta Estructura Consciencia y Biografía de Clase: Informe Técnico', *IESA/CSIC*.

Caselli, L. et al. (1993), *Le attese dei lavoratori dei servizi. Indagine sul ruolo del sindacato nel terziario che cambia*, Quademi Sindnova, Edizioni Lavoro, Roma.

Castells, M. (1996), *The Network Society*, Basil Blackwell, Oxford.

CBS (1997), *Statistisch Jaarboek 1997*.

Cella, G.P. (eds) (1991), *Nuovi attori nelle relazioni industriali*, F. Angeli, Milano.

Cella, G.P. and Treu, T. (eds) (1998), *Le nuove relazioni industriali. L'esperienza italiana nella prospettiva europea*, Il Mulino, Bologna.

Censis (1998), *32° rapporto sulla situazione sociale del paese - 1998*, F.Angeli, Milano.

CERC (1991), *Les bas salaires dans les pays de la Communauté économique européenne*, Communauté européenne.

Chamberlayne, P. (1997), 'Social Exclusion: Sociological Traditions and National Contexts', in SSIRSWP (eds), *Social Exclusion in Risk Societies*, Centre for Biography in Social Policy, London.

Chiesi, A.M. (1988), 'I lavoratori emergenti del terziario arretrato', in *Prospettiva sindacale*, A. XIX, No. 69, pp. 23-35.

Cinnéide, M.Ó. and Grimes, S. (1992), 'Planning and Development in Marginal Areas', Centre for Development Studies, Social Sciences Research Centre, University College Galway, Galway.

CIS (1994), 2,088, DATASET.

Clark, T. and Lipset, S.M. (1991), 'Are Social Classes dying?', *International Sociology*, No. 6.

Clarke, J. and Hall, S. et al. (1979), *Jugendkultur als Widerstand. Milieus, Rituale, Provokationen*, Syndikat, Frankfurt am Main.

Clarke, L. (1992a), *Building Capitalism*, Routledge, London.

Clarke, L. (1992b), 'The Building Labour Process', Occasional Paper, No. 50, The Charted Institute of Building, London.

Cloke, P. (1990), 'Community Development and Political Leadership in Rural Britain', *Sociologia Ruralis*, 30 (3-4), pp. 305-22.

Cloke, P. (1996), 'Rural Lifestyles: Material Opportunity, Cultural Experience and how Theory undermined Policy', *Economic Geography*, No. 7, pp. 433-49.

Cloke, P. and Little, J. (1990), *The Rural State? Limits to planning in Rural Society*, Oxford University Press, Oxford.

Cloke, P. and Thrift, N. (1990), 'Class Change and Conflict in Rural Areas', in T. Marsden, P. Lowe and S. Whatmore (eds), *Rural Restructuring*, David Fulton, London, pp. 165-81.

Cloke, P., Goodwin, M., Milbourne, P. and Thomas, C. (1995), 'Deprivation, Poverty and Marginalization in Rural Lifestyles in England and Wales', *Journal of Rural Studies*, Vol. 4, No. 11, pp. 351-65.

Cloke, P., Milbourne, P. and Thomas, C. (1994), *Lifestyles in Rural England*, Rural Development Commission, London.

Cloke, P., Milbourne, P. and Thomas, C. (1997), 'Living lives in Different Ways? Deprivation, Marginalisation and changing Lifestyles in Rural England', *Transactions, Institute of British Geographers*, Vol. 2, No. 22, pp. 210-30.

Cloke, P., Phillips, M. and Thrift, N. (1995), 'The new Middle Classes and the Social Constructs of Rural Living', in T. Butler and M. Savage (eds), *Social Change and the Middle Classes*, UCL Press, London, pp. 220-38.

Cloke, P., Phillips, M. and Thrift, N. (1998), 'Class, Colonisation and Lifestyle Strategies in Gower', in M. Boyle and K. Halfacree (eds), *Migration to Rural Areas*, Wiley, London, pp. 166-85.

Cloke, P., Phillips, M. and Thrift, N. (forthcoming), *Moving to Rural Idylls*, Sage, London.

CNEL (1992), *Prospettive dei sistemi europei del lavoro terziario* (documenti di base del seminario), Roma (mimeo).

Coates, K. and Topham T. (1994), *The making of the Labour Movement. The Formation of the Transport and General Workers' Union 1870-1922*, Spokesman, Nottingham.

Cobble, D.S. (1994), 'Labor Law Reform and Postindustrial Unionism', *Dissent*, pp. 474-80.

Cochran, B. (1977), *Labor and Communism. The Conflict that shaped American Unions*, Princeton University Press, Princeton.

Codara, L. (1988), 'Lavoratori manuali non operai: un problema ad una risorsa per il sindacato?', Intervista ad alcuni dirigenti sindacali, in *Prospettiva sindacale*, A. XIX, No. 69, pp. 37-62.

Coggins, J. et al. (1989), *Trade Unions of the World 1989-1990*, St. James Press, Chicago and London.

Colasanto, M. (1993), *Paradigmi dello sviluppo*, Vita e pensiero, Milano.

Comisiones Obreras and UGT (1989), *Propuesta Sindical Prioritaria*, PSP, Madrid.
Comisiones Obreras and UGT (1991), *Iniciativa Sindical de Progreso, ISP,* Madrid.
Comisiones Obreras and UGT (1993), *Bases para un Acuerdo sobre el Empleo,* Madrid.
Comisiones Obreras and UGT (1994), *Alternativas de los Sindicatos sobre la Reforma Laboral,* Madrid.
Commissione delle Comunita' Europee (1994), *Crescita, competitività, occupazione,* trad. it. 'Il Saggiatore', Milano.
Community Enterprise Wales (1995), *Community Enterprise in Wales. Baseline Study,* CEW.
Contarino, M. (1995), 'The Local Political Economy of Industrial Adjustment. Variations in Trade Union Responses to Industrial Restructuring in the Italian Textile-Clothing Sector', *Comparative Political Studies,* No. 28, pp. 62-86.
Conze, W. (1966), 'Vom 'Pöbel' zum 'Proletariat'', in H.-U. Wehler (ed.), *Moderne deutsche Sozialgeschichte,* Westdeutscher Verlag, Köln-Berlin, pp. 111-36.
Cooke, P. and Rees, G. (1981), *The Industrial Restructuring of South Wales,* Dept. of Town Planning, Cardiff, UWIST.
Crewe, I. (1987), 'A new class of politics', *The Guardian.*
Crompton, R. (1993), *Class and Stratification. An Introduction to Current Debates,* Polity, Cambridge.
Crompton, R. (1995), 'Women's Employment and the 'Middle Class'', in T. Butler and M. Savage (eds), *Social Change and the Middle Classes,* UCL Press, London, pp. 58-75.
Crompton, R. and Harris F. (1998), 'Gender Relations and Employment: the Impact of Occupation', *Work, Employment and Society,* Vol. 12, pp. 297-317.
Crouch, C. (1986), 'The Future Prospects for Trade Unions in Western Europe', *Political Quarterly,* No. 57, pp. 5-17.
Crouch, C. (1992), 'The Fate of Articulated Industrial Relations Systems: a Stock-taking after the 'Neo-Liberal' Decade', in M. Regini (ed.), *The Future of Labour Movements,* Sage, London, pp. 169-87.
Crouch, C. (1995), 'Exit or Voice: Two Paradigms for European Industrial Relations after the Keynesian Welfare State', *European Journal of Industrial Relations,* No. 1, pp. 63-81.
CSCCCB (1991), *Encuesta Estructura Consciencia y Biografía de Clase,* DATASET.
CSCS (1996), *Construction Skills Certification Scheme: Scheme Booklet,* CSCS, London.
CSU (1996), *Free Safety Training for Construction Workers,* CSU, London.
Daalder, A. (1995), 'Participation in Trade Unions in The Netherlands: Women and part-time Workers', in L.E. Tetrick and J. Barling (eds), *Changing Employment Relations: Behavioral and Social Perspectives,* APA, Washington D.C., pp. 255-72.
Dahrendorf, R. (1957), *Soziale Klassen und Klassenkonflikt in der industriellen Gesellschaft,* Stuttgart.
Danziger, R. (1988), *Political Powerlessness: agricultural Workers in post-war England,* Manchester.
Davis, M. (1986), *Prisoners of the American Dream. Politics and Economy in the History of the US Working Class,* Verso, London, New York.
Day, G. and Murdoch, J. (1993), 'Locality and Community: coming to terms with place', *Sociological Review,* No. 41, pp. 82-111.
Dennis, N. and Erdos, G. (1992), *Families without Fatherhood,* Institute of Economic Affairs, London.
Deppe, F. (1971), *Das Bewußtsein der Arbeiter,* Pahl-Rugenstein, Köln.
Détraz, A. (1965), 'L'ouvrier consommateur', in L. Hamon (ed.), *Les nouveaux comportements politiques de la classe ouvrière,* Paris.
Devine, F. (1992), *Affluent Workers Revisited,* Edinburgh University Press, Edinburgh.

Devine, F. (1998), 'Class Analysis and the Stability of Class Relations', *Sociology*, Vol. 32, No. 1, pp. 23-42.

Dudley, K.M. (1994), *And the End of the Line: Lost Jobs, New Lives in post-industrial America*, The University of Chicago Press, Chicago.

Dunleavy, P. (1980), 'The Political Implications of Sectoral Cleavages and the Growth of State Employment: Part 1, the Analysis of Production Cleavages; Part 2, Cleavages, Structures and Political Alignments', *Political Studies*, Vol. 28, pp. 364-83 and pp. 527-49.

Dunleavy, P. and Husbands, C. (1985), *British Democracy at the Crossroads*, George, Allen and Unwin, London.

Durkheim, É. (1893/1902), *Über soziale Arbeitsteilung*, Suhrkamp, Frankfurt am Main.

Durkheim, É. (1933), *The Division of Labour in Society*, The Free Press, New York.

Ebbinghaus, B. and Visser, J. (1997), 'When Labour Institutions matter: Union Growth and Decline in Western Europe, 1950-1990', *Paper presented at European Sociological Association Conference, University of Essex*.

Eder, K. (1993), *The New Politics of Class. Social Movements and Cultural Dynamics in advanced Societies*, Sage, London.

Edwards, A.J. (1985), 'Manufacturing in Wales: a Spatial and Sectoral Analysis of Recent Changes in Structure, 1975-1985', *Cambria*, No. 12, pp. 89-115.

Edwards, R. (1979), *Contested Terrain. The Transformation of the Workplace in the Twentieth Century*, Basic Books, New York.

Edwards, R., Garonna, P. and Todting, F. (1986), *Unions in Crisis and beyond: Perspectives from six Countries*, Auburn House, Dover, Massachusetts.

Ehrenreich, B. (1989), *Fear of falling: the Inner-Life of the Middle Class*, Pantheon Books, New York.

EIRR (1997), *European Industrial Relations Review*, No. 280.

Ellemers, N. (1991), *Identity Management Strategies. The Influence of Socio-Structural Variables on Strategies of Individual Mobility and Social Change*, Ph.D. Dissertation, Rijksuniversiteit Groningen.

Elvin, A. (1995), *Invisible Crime*, Ann Elvin, London.

Erikson, R. and Goldthorpe, J.H. (1992), *The constant Flux: a Study of Class Mobility in Industrial Societies*, Clarendon Press, Oxford.

Erikson, R., Goldthorpe, J.H. and Portocarero, L. (1979), 'Intergenerational Class Mobility in three Western European Societies', *British Journal of Sociology*, No. 30, pp. 415-41.

Esping-Andersen, G. (1993a), 'Le classi sociali in una prospettiva comparata', in M. Paci (ed.), *Le dimensioni della disuguaglianza*, Il Mulino, Bologna.

Esping-Andersen, G. (1993b), *Changing Classes. Stratification and Mobility in post-industrial Societies*, Sage, London.

Esping-Andersen, G. (1995), 'Welfare States without Work: the Impasse of Labor Shedding and Familialism in Continental European Social Policy', *CEACS, Instituto Juan March de Estudios e Investigaciones, Estudios/Working Papers, No. 71*.

Esping-Andersen, G. (1998a), 'The Effects of Regulation on Unemployment Levels and Structure. The Evidence from Comparative Research', *Unpublished Paper, Dipartamento di Sociologia e Ricerca Sociale, Universita di Trento*.

Esping-Andersen, G. (1998b), 'Conclusions and Policy Implications', *Unpublished Paper, Dipartamento di Sociologia e Ricerca Sociale, Universita di Trento*.

Ester, P., Halman, L. and De Moor, R. (1993), *The Individualizing Society. Value Changes in Europe and North-America*, Tilburg University Press, Tilburg.

European Commission (1996), 'Social and Economic Inclusion through Regional Development - The Community Economic Development Priority in European Structural Funds Programmes in Great Britain', Office for Official Publications of the European Communities, Luxembourg.

Evans, G. (1992), 'Is Britain a class-divided Society: a Re-analysis and Extension of Marshall et al.'s Study of Class Consciousness', *Sociology*, Vol. 2, No. 26, pp. 233-58.

Evans, G. (ed.) (1999), *The End of Class Politics. Class Voting in Comparative Context*, Oxford University Press, Oxford.

Eyerman, R. and Jamison, A. (1991), *Social Movements: a Cognitive Approach*, Cambridge University Press, Cambridge.

Fantasia, R. (1988), *Cultures of Solidarity. Consciousness, Action, and Contemporary American Workers*, University of California Press, Berkeley.

Fantasia, R. (1995), 'From Class Consciousness to Culture, Action and Social Organisation', *Annual Review of Sociology*, No. 21, pp. 369-87.

Fernández, F., Garrido, L. and Toharia, L. (1991), 'Empleo y Paro en España. 1975-1999', in F. Miguélez y C. Prieto (eds), *Las Relaciones Laborales en España*, Siglo XXI, Madrid.

Ferner, A. and Hyman, R. (eds) (1992), *Industrial Relations in the New Europe*, Basil Blackwell, Oxford.

Feuersenger, M. (ed.) (1962), *Gibt es noch ein Proletariat?*, EVA, Frankfurt am Main.

Filca-Cisl (1992), *Partecipazione e nuova contrattazione*, Atti del seminario nazionale, Torino.

Fiorito, J., Gallagher, D.G. and Fukami, C.V. (1988), 'Satisfaction with Union Representation', *Industrial and Labor Relations Review*, No. 41, pp. 294-307.

Fiske, M.J. (1996), *Home Truths. Issues for Housing in Wales*, Gomer Press, Llandysul.

Flaig, B.B., Meyer, T. and Ueltzhoeffer, J. (1993), *Alltagsästhetik und politische Kultur*, Dietz, Bonn.

Fletcher Jr., B. (1998), A presentation to the University and College Labor Education Association/AFL-CIO Education Conference in San Jose, CA.

Fosh, P. (1993), 'Membership Participation in Workplace Unionism: The Possibility of Union Renewal', *British Journal of Industrial Relations*, No. 31, pp. 577-92.

Fowler, B. (1996), *Pierre Bourdieu and Cultural Theory*, Sage, London.

Friedrich-Ebert-Stiftung (ed.) (1993), *Lernen für Demokratie. Politische Weiterbildung für eine Gesellschaft im Wandel*, 4 Bde., Friedrich-Ebert-Stiftung, Bonn.

Fulcher, J. (1991), *Labour Movements, Employers and the State*, Clarendon Press, Oxford.

Galbraith, J.K. (1952), *American Capitalism. The Concept of Countervailing Power*, Houghton Mifflin, Boston.

Galbraith, J.K. (1958), *The Affluent Society*, Penguin, Harmondsworth.

Galbraith, J.K. (1992), *The Culture of Contentment*, Boston.

Galenson, W. (1986), 'The Historical Role of American Trade Unionism', in S.M. Lipset (ed.), *Unions in Transition. Entering the Second Century*, Institute for Contemporary Studies, San Francisco, pp. 39-73.

Gallie, D. (1994), 'Are the Unemployed an Underclass? Some Evidence from the Social Change and Economic Life Initiative', *Sociology*, No. 28, pp. 737-57.

Gallino, L. (1997), *Se tre milioni vi sembran pochi*, Einaudi, Torino.

Gardawski, J. and Zukowski, T. (1994), *Robotnicy 1993: Wybory Ekonomiczne i Polityczne*, Friedrich Ebert Stiftung, Warsaw.

Gardawski, J., Gilejko, L., and Zukowski, T. (1994), *Zwiazki Zawodowe w Przedsiebiorstwach Przemyslowych*, Friedrich Ebert Stiftung, Warsaw.

Gardemin, D. (1998), *Mentalitäten der neuen Mitte'. Forschungsbericht*, Agis, Hannover.

Geiger, T. (1932), *Die soziale Schichtung des deutschen Volkes*, Enke, Stuttgart.

Geiger, T. (1949), *Die Klassengesellschaft im Schmelztiegel*, Kiepenheuer, Köln und Hagen.

Geiling, H. (1996), *Das andere Hannover. Jugendkultur zwischen Rebellion und Integration in der Großstadt*, Offizin, Hannover.

Geissler, R. (1998a), 'Kein Abschied von Klasse und Schicht. Ideologische Gefahren der deutschen Sozialstrukturanalyse', *Kölner Zeitschrift für Soziologie und Sozialpsychologie*, Vol. 48, No. 2, pp. 319-38.

Geissler, R. (1998b), 'Das Mehrfache ende der Klassengesellschaft. Diagnosen sozialstrukturellen Wandels', in J. Friedrichs, M.R. Lepsius and K.U. Mayer (eds), *Die Diagnosefähigkeit der Soziologie*, Westdeutscher Verlag, Opladen, pp. 207-33.

Geissler, R. (ed.) (1994), *Soziale Schichtung und Lebenschancen in Deutschland*, Enke, Stuttgart.

George, K.D. and Mainwaring L. (eds) (1988), *The Welsh Economy*, University of Wales Press, Cardiff.

Giddens, A. (1987), *Social Theory and Modern Sociology*, Polity Press, Cambridge.

Giddens, A. (1990), *The Consequences of Modernity*, Polity, Cambridge.

Giddens, A. (1991), *Modernity and Self-Identity*, Polity, Cambridge.

Giddens, A. (1994), *Beyond Left and Right*, Polity, Cambridge.

Giddens, A. (1999), *Der dritte Weg - die Erneuerung der sozialen Demokratie*, Suhrkamp, Frankfurt am Main.

Gilbert, D. (1992), *Class Community and Collective Action. Social Change in two British Coalfields, 1850-1926*, Clarendon Press, Oxford.

Gitlin, T. (1995), *The Twilight of Common Dreams: why American is Wracked by Culture Wars*, Metropolitan Books, New York.

Glaser, B. and Strauss, A.L. (1967), *The Discovery of Grounded Theory*, Aldine Publishing, London.

Goffman, E. (1974), *Frame Analysis: an Essay on the Organization of Experience*, Northeastern University Press, Boston.

Goldthorpe, J. (1982), 'On the Service Class, its Formation and Future', in A. Giddens and G. Mackenzie (eds), *Social Class and the Division of Labour*, Cambridge University Press, Cambridge, pp. 162-85.

Goldthorpe, J. (1984), 'The End of Convergence: Corporatist and Dual Tendencies in Modem Western Societies', in J. Goldthorpe (ed.), *Order and Conflict in Contemporary Capitalism*, Clarendon Press, Oxford.

Goldthorpe, J.H. (1988), 'The Intellectuals and the Working Class in Modern Britain', in D. Rose (ed.), *Economic Restructuring and Social Change*, Hutchinson, London.

Goldthorpe, J. (1995), 'The Service Class revisited', in T. Butler and M. Savage (eds), *Social Change and the Middle Classes*, UCL Press, London, pp. 313-29.

Goldthorpe, J.H. (1996), 'Class Analysis and the Re-orientation of Class Theory: the Case of Persisting Differentials in Educational Attainment', *British Journal of Sociology*, No. 45, pp. 481-505.

Goldthorpe, J.H. (1997), 'Social Class and the Differentiation of Employment Contracts', *Paper presented at the European Consortium for Sociological Research, Conference on Rational Action Theories in Social Analysis: Applications and new Developments, Stockholm*.

Goldthorpe, J. and Hope, K. (1974), *The Social Grading of Occupations: a New Approach and Scale*, Clarendon Press, Oxford.

Goldthorpe, J. with Llewellyn, C. and Payne, C. (1980), *Social Mobility and the Class Structure*, Clarendon, Oxford.

Goldthorpe, J. and Lockwood, D. (1963), 'Affluence and the British Class Structure', *Sociological Review*, Vol. 11, pp. 133-63.

Goldthorpe, J., Llewellyn, C. and Payne, C. (1980), *Social Mobility and the Class Structure in modern Britain*, Oxford University Press, Oxford.
Goldthorpe, J., Lockwood, D., Bechhofer, F. and Platt, J. (1968), *The Affluent Worker: Political Attitudes and Behaviour*, Cambridge University Press, Cambridge.
Goldthorpe, J., Lockwood, D., Bechhofer, F. and Platt, J. (1969), *The Affluent Worker in the Class Structure*, Cambridge University Press, Cambridge.
Goldthorpe, J.H. and Marshall, G. (1992), 'The Promising Future of Class Analysis. A Response to Recent Critiques', *Sociology*, No. 26, pp. 381-400.
Gordon, D., Edwards, R. and Reich M. (1982), *Segmented Work, Divided Workers: the Historical Transformation of Labor in the United States*, Cambridge University Press, Cambridge.
Gorz, A. (1965), 'Work and Consumption', in P. Anderson and R. Blackburn (eds), *Towards Socialism*, London.
Gorz, A. (1980), *Abschied vom Proletariat. Jenseits der Sozialismus*, EVA, Frankfurt am Main.
Gorz, A. (1982), *Farewell to the Working Class*, Pluto Press, London.
Gorz, A. (1991), 'The New Agenda', in R. Blackburn (ed.), *After the Fall. The Failure of Communism and the Future of Socialism*, Verso, London, New York, pp. 287-97.
Goslinga, S. (1996a), *CNV-panel: voorjaar 1996*, Onderzoeksprogramma CNV/VU, Amsterdam.
Goslinga, S. (1996b), 'Voor wat hoort wat: een ruiltheoretische benadering van vakbonds-binding', *Paper presented at the WESWA Congress, Rotterdam, The Netherlands*.
Gottschall, K. (2000), *Soziale Ungleichheit und Geschlecht*, Leske + Budrich, Opladen.
Gouldner, A. (1979), *The Future of Intellectuals and the Rise of the New Class: a Frame of Reference, Theses, Conjectures, Argumentation and an Historical Perspective*, Macmillan, London.
Gramsci, A. (1971), *Selection from the Prison Notebooks*, Lawrence & Wishart, London.
Granovetter, M. (1985), 'Economic Action and Social Structure: the Problem of Embeddedness', *American Journal of Sociology*, Vol. 3, No. 91.
Green, F. (1992), 'Recent Trends in British Trade Union Density: how much of a Compositional Effect?', *British Journal of Industrial Relations*, No. 30, pp. 445-58.
Green, H.S. (1990), *On Strike at Hormel: the Struggle for a Democratic Union Movement*, Temple University Press, Philadelphia.
Green, J.R. (1980), *The World of the Worker. Labor in Twentieth-Century America*, Hill and Wang, New York.
Grusky, D. (ed.) (1994), *Social Stratification: Class, Race and Gender in Sociological Perspective*, Westview press, Boulder.
Grusky, D. and Sörensen, J. (1998), 'Can Class Analysis be salvaged?', *American Journal of Sociology*, Vol. 103, No. 5, pp. 1 187-234.
Gryffydd, P. (1994), 'Back to the Land: Historiography, Rurality and the Nation in interwar Wales', *Transactions, Institute of British Geographers*, Vol. 1, No. 19, pp. 61-77.
Gubbay, J. (1997), 'A Marxist Critique of Weberian Class Analysis', *Sociology*, No. 31, pp. 73-89.
Güell-Rotllan, M. and Petrongolo, B. (1998), 'The Transition of Workers from Temporary to Permanent Employment: the Spanish Case', Working Paper, pp. 98-81, Universidad Carlos III de Madrid.
Halfacree, K. (1997), 'Contrasting roles for the post-productivist countryside: a post-modern Perspective on Counterurbanisation', in P. Cloke and J. Little (eds), *Contested Countryside: Otherness, Marginalisation and Rurality*, Routledge, London, pp. 109-22.
Halford, S., Savage, M. and Witz, A. (1997), *Gender, Careers and Organisations: current Developments in Nursing, Local Government and Banking*, MacMillan, Basingstoke.

344 *Can Class Still Unite?*

Hall, P. (1987), 'European Labor in the 1980s', *International Journal of Political Economy*, No. 17, pp. 3-25.

Hamann, K. (1998), 'Spanish Unions: Institutional Legacy and Responsiveness to Economic and Industrial Change', *Industrial and Labour Relations Review*, No. 51, pp. 424-44.

Hamnett, C. (1998), 'Review of Recent Books on Gentrification', *Transactions of the Institute of British Geographers*, NS, Vol. 23, pp. 412-16.

Hancké, B. (1991), 'The Crisis of National Unions: Belgian Labor in Decline', *Politics and Society*, No. 19, pp. 463-87.

Hancké, B. (1993), 'Trade Union Membership in Europe, 1960-1990: Rediscovering Local Unions', *British Journal of Industrial Relations*, No. 31, pp. 593-613.

Hargreaves, D. (1997), 'Equipped for Life', in *ESRC - Future Britain - Revitalising Policy Through Research*, ESRC, Swindon.

Hartmann, M. (1998), 'Homogenität und Stabilität - Die soziale Rekrutierung der deutschen Wirtschaftselite im europäischen Vergleich', in P.A. Berger and M. Vester (ed.), *Alte Ungleichheiten - neue Spaltungen*, Leske + Budrich, Opladen.

Harvey, D. (1989), *The Condition of Post-Modernity*, Basil Blackwell, Oxford.

Hattam, V. (1993), *Labor Visions and State Power: The Origins of Business Unionism in the United States*, Princeton University Press, Princeton.

Heath, A. and Savage, M. (1995), 'Political Alignments within the Middle Classes', in T. Butler and M. Savage (eds), *Social Change and the Middle Classes*, UCL Press, London, pp. 275-92.

Heath, A., Jowell, R. and Curtice, J. (1985), *How Britain votes*, Pergamon Press, Oxford.

Hedges, B. (1994), 'Work in a Changing Climate', in R. Jowell, J. Curtice, L. Brook and D. Ahrendt (ed.), *British Social Attitudes. The 11th Report*, Dartmouth, Aldershot, pp. 37-50.

Heery, E. and Abott, B. (2000), 'Trade Unions and the insecure Workforce', in E. Heery and J. Salmon (eds), *The Insecure Workforce*, Routledge, London, pp. 155-80.

Heery, E. and Kelly J. (1995), 'Conservative Radicalism and Nostalgia: a Reply to Paul Smith and Peter Ackers', *Work, Employment and Society*, No. 9, pp. 155-64.

Hirschman, A.O. (1970), *Exit, Voice and Loyalty: Responses to decline in Firms, Organizations and States*, Harvard University Press, Cambridge, Mass.

Hobsbawm, E. (1978), 'The forward March of Labour halted?', *Marxism Today*, No. 22, pp. 279-86.

Hobsbawm, E. (1989), 'Farewell to the Classic Labour Movement?', *New Left Review*, No. 173, pp. 69-74.

Hobsbawm, E. and Rudé, G. (1969), *Captain Swing*, Lawrence and Wishart, London.

Hochschild, A.R. (1997), *The Time Bind: when Work becomes Home and Home becomes Work*, Metropolitan Books, New York.

Hofmann, M. (1995a), 'Die Leipziger Metallarbeiter', in M. Vester et al., pp. 136-92.

Hofmann, M. (1995b), 'Die Kohlearbeiter von Espenhain', in M. Vester et al., pp. 91-135.

Hoggart, K. (1998), 'Rural cannot equal Middle Class because Class does not exist?', *Journal of Rural Studies*, Vol. 3, No. 14, pp. 381-86.

Hoggart, R. (1959), *The Uses of Literacy*, Chatto and Windus, London.

Holmwood, J. (1997), 'The Problem of Inequality and Class in Contemporary Debates', Paper presented to Cambridge Stratification Seminar, Clare College, Cambridge.

Homms, N. and Ueltzhoeffer, J. (1991), 'The Internationalisation of Ebery-Day-Life-Research: Markets and Milieux', in ESOMAR-Kongressbericht, Stockholm.

Hradil, S. (1987), *Sozialstrukturanalyse in einer fortgeschrittenen Gesellschaft. Von Klassen und Schichten zu Lagen und Milieus*, Leske + Budrich, Opladen.

Hradil, S. (ed.) (1992), *Zwischen Bewußtsein und Sein. Die Vermittlung 'objektiver' und 'subjektiver' Lebensweisen*, Leske + Budrich, Opladen.

Huebinger, W. (1996), *Prekärer Wohlstand. Neue Befunde zu Armut und sozialer Ungleichheit*, Lambertus, Freiburg im Breisgau.
Hyman, R. (1985), 'Class Struggle and the Trade Union Movement', in D. Coates, G. Johnston and R. Bush (ed.), *A Socialist Anatomy of Britain*, Polity Press, Cambridge, pp. 99-123.
Hyman, R. (1990), 'Trade Unions, the Left and the Communist Party in Britain', *Journal of Communist Studies*, No. 6, pp. 143-61.
Hyman, R. (1999), An Emerging Agenda for Trade Unions? www.labournet.de/diskussion/gewerkschaft/hyman.html.
Hyman, R. and Ferner, A. (eds) (1998), *Changing Industrial Relations in Europe*, Basil Blackwell, Oxford.
Hyman, R. and Price, R. (eds) (1983), *The new Working Class? White-Collar Workers and their Organizations*, Macmillan, London.
IILS (1999), *Network on Organized Labor in the 21ste Century: Progress Report*, IILS Publications, Geneva.
ILO (1998), *World Labour Report: Industrial Relations, Democracy and Social Stability 1997-1998*, International Labour Office, Geneva.
Ilzkovitz, F. (1993), 'Sectoral Country Dimension', in Commission of the European Communities, *European economy: Social Europe Reports and Studies*, No. 3.
Inglehart, R. (1977), *The Silent Revolution. Changing Values and Political Styles among Western Publics*, Princeton.
Inglehart, R. (1990), *Culture Shift in advanced Industrial Societies*, Princeton University Press, Princeton.
Instituto Nacional de Estadística (1991), *Encuesta Experimental de Salarios*, DATASET.
Inui, A. (1993), 'The Competitive Structure of School and the Labour Market: Japan and Britain', *British Journal of the Sociology of Education*, Vol. 14, No. 3.
Iriso Napal, P.L. (1993), *Sistemas de Negociación Colectiva y Acción Sindical. Sindicatos y Trabajadores en la Empresa*, CEACS, Instituto Juan March de Estudios e Investigaciones, Madrid.
Istance, D., Rees, G. and Williamson, H. (1994), *Young People not in Education, Training or Employment in South Glamorgan*, Education Training and Labour Markets Research Unit, School of Social and Administrative Studies, University of Wales Cardiff, Cardiff.
JAGNET (1994), *Proposals for the Construction Industry Training Scheme for Craft and Operative New Entrants*, CITB, London.
Jenkins, R. (1991), *Pierre Bourdieu*, Routledge, London.
Jimeno, J. and Toharia, L. (1992), 'Productivity and Wage Effects of fixed-term Employment: Evidence from Spain', *FEDEA, Documento de Trabajo*, pp. 92-11.
Jimeno, J. and Toharia, L. (1994), *Unemployment and Labour Market Flexibility: Spain*, International Labour Office, Geneva.
Jones, H. (eds) (1997), *Towards a Classless Society?*, Routledge, London and New York.
Jones, R.M. (1973), ''The Miners' next Step. Being a Suggested Scheme for the Reorganisation of the Federation', in *Reprints in Labour History*, Pluto Press, London.
Jordan, T. (1995), 'The Unity of Social Movements', *The Sociological Review*, Vol. 4, No. 43, pp. 675-92.
Jordana, J. (1996), 'Reconsidering Union Membership in Spain, 1977-1994: Halting Decline in a Context of Democratic Consolidation?', *Industrial Relations Journal*, No. 27, pp. 211-24.
Joyce, P. (ed.) (1995), *Class*, Oxford University Press, Oxford.
Katz, H.C. (1993), 'The Decentralization of Collective Bargaining: a Literature Review and Comparative Analysis', *Industrial and Labour Relations Review*, No. 47, pp. 3-22.

Katznelson, I. & Zolberg, A.R. (ed.) (1986), *Working-Class Formation. Nineteenth-Century Patterns in Western Europe and the United States,* Princeton University Press, Princeton.

Kay, J. (1993), *The Foundations of Corporate Success,* Routledge, London.

Kazin, M. (1988), 'A People not a Class: rethinking the Political Language of the Modern US Labor Movement', in M. Davis and M. Sprinker (ed.), *Reshaping the US Left. Popular Struggles in the 1980s,* Verso, London, New York, pp. 257-86.

Kelley, R.D.G. (1997), 'Identity Politics & Class Struggle', *New Politics,* Vol. 4, No. 6, pp. 84-96.

Kelly, C. and Breinlinger, S. (1996), *The Social Psychology of Collective Action,* Taylor and Francis, Basingstoke.

Kelly, J. (1988), *Trade Unions and Socialist Politics,* Verso, London.

Kendal, W. (1975), *The Labour Movement in Europe,* Allen Lane, London.

Kennedy, M. (1991), *Professionals, Power, and Solidarity in Poland,* Cambridge University Press, Cambridge.

Kerkhof, P. (1997), *Van mediabericht naar politieke opvatting: een onderzoek naar de opvattingen van CNV-leden over de verzorgingsstaat,* Unpublished dissertation, Vrije Universiteit, Amsterdam.

Kern, H. and Sabel, C.F. (1991), 'Trade Unions and Decentralized Production: a Sketch of Strategic Problems in the West German Labor Movement', *Politics and Society,* No. 19, pp. 373-402.

Kern, H. and Schumann, M. (1970), *Industriearbeit und Arbeiterbewußtsein,* EVA, Frankfurt.

Kern, H. and Schumann, M. (1982), 'Arbeit und Sozialcharakter: alte und neue Konturen, Vortrag bei 21. Deutschen Soziologentag', in SOFI-Mitteilungen, No. 7.

Kerr, C. and Siegel, A.J. (1957), 'The Inter-Industry Propensity to strike: an International Comparison', in A. Kornhauser, R. Dubin and A.M. Ross (eds), *Industrial Conflict,* McGraw-Hill, New York, pp. 189-212.

Kessler-Harris, A. and Silverman, B. (1992), 'Beyond Industrial Unionism. Into Politics, into the Communities', *Dissent,* pp. 61-6.

Kirkland, L. (1986), 'It has all been said before ...', in S.M. Lipset (ed.), *Unions in Transition. Entering the Second Century,* Institute for Contemporary Studies, San Francisco, pp. 393-404.

Klandermans, B. (1997), *The Social Psychology of Protest,* Basil Blackwell, Oxford.

Klandermans, B. and Visser, J. (eds) (1995), *De vakbeweging na de welvaartsstaat,* Van Gorcum, Assen.

Kluegel, J.R., Csepeli, G., Lolosi, T., Orkeny, A. and Nemenyi, M. (1995), 'Accounting for the Rich and the Poor: existential Justice in Comparative Perspective', in Kluegel et al. (eds), pp. 63-81.

Kluegel, J.R., Mason, D.S. and Wegener, B. (eds) (1995), *Social Justice and Political Change: Public Opinion in Capitalist and post-communist States,* de Gruyter, New York.

Knoke, D. and Wright-Isak, C. (1982), 'Individual Motives and Organizational Incentive Systems', *Research on the Sociology of Organizations,* No. 1, pp. 209-54.

Koelble, Th. (1992), 'Recasting Social Democracy in Europe: a Nested Games Explanation of Strategic Adjustment in Political Parties', *Politics and Society,* No. 20, pp. 51-70.

Konrad, G. and Szelenyi, I. (1971), *Intellectuals on the Road to Class Power,* Harcourt Brace Jovanovich, San Diego.

Krueger, H. (2000), 'Ein espandierender Arbeitsmarkt mit sieben Siegeln', in Frankfurter Rundschau, p. 11.

Kurtz, S. (forthcoming), *All Kinds of Justice: Labor and Identity Politics,* University of Minnesota Press, Minneapolis.

Kwik, Ph. and Moody, K. (1988), 'Dare to struggle: Lessons from P-9', in M. Davis and M. Sprinker (ed.), *Reshaping the US Left. Popular Struggles in the 1980s*, Verso, London, New York, pp. 133-48.

La Botz, D. (1990), *Rank-and-File Rebellion. Teamsters for a Democratic Union*, Verso, London, New York.

Labour Force Survey/Encuesta de Población Activa (1987), DATASET.

Labour Force Survey/Encuesta de Población Activa (1991), DATASET.

Labour Force Survey/Encuesta de Población Activa (1993), DATASET.

Labour Force Survey/Encuesta de Población Activa (1995), DATASET.

Labour Force Survey/Encuesta de Población Activa (1997), DATASET.

Lane, Ch. (1989), 'From 'Welfare Capitalism' to 'Market Capitalism', a comparative Review of Trends towards Employment Flexibility in the Labour Markets of three major European Societies', *Sociology*, No. 23, pp. 583-610.

Lane, T. (1976), *The Union Makes Us Strong*, Arrow Books, London.

Lange, A. (1993), "Man muß eben der beste draus machen, Kopf in'n Sand stecken hilft nicht' - Strategien der Bewältigung der 'Wende' am Beispiel von zwei Brandenburger Facharbeiterinnen', in P. Frerichs and M. Steinruecke (ed.), *Soziale Ungleichheit und Geschlechterverhältnis*, Leske + Budrich, Opladen, pp. 117-44.

Lash, S. and Urry, J. (1987), *The End of Organized Capitalism*, Polity Press, Cambridge.

Lash, S. and Urry, J. (1994), *Economies of Signs and Spaces*, Sage, London.

Lawinski, P. (1998), 'Ile Wytrzymacie?', in *Tygodnik Solidarnosc*, No. 18, p. 2.

Layard, R. and Nickell, S. (1987), 'The Labour Market', in R. Dornbusch and R. Layard (eds), *The Performance of the British Economy*, Clarendon Press, Oxford.

Layard, R., Nickell, S. and Jackman, R. (1991), *Unemployment*, Oxford University Press, Oxford.

Lazear, A.P. (1995), *Personnel Economics*, MIT Press, Cambridge, Mass.

Lebrun, J.F., Petit, P. and Winter, C. (1993), 'Employment Dimension', in Commission of the European Communities, *European Economy: Social Europe Reports and Studies*, No. 3.

Leisink, P. (1997), 'New Union Constituencies call for Differentiated Agendas and Democratic Participation', *Transfer*, Vol. 3, No. 3, pp. 534-77.

Leisink, P., Van Leemput, J. and Vilrockx, J. (1996), *Challenges to Trade Unions in Europe*, Edward Elgar, Cheltenham.

Lepsius, M.R. (1973a), 'Parteiensystem und Sozialstruktur: zum Problem der Demokratisierung der deutschen Gesellschaft', in G.A. Ritter (ed.), *Deutsche Parteien vor 1918*, Kiepenheuer & Witsch, Köln.

Lepsius, M.R. (1973b), 'Wahlverhalten, Parteien und politische Spannungen', in *Politische Vierteljahresschrift*, pp. 295-313.

Lewis, R. and Maude, A. (1949), *The English Middle Classes*, Phoenix House, London.

Ley, D. (1996), *The New Middle Class and the Remaking of the Central City*, Oxford University Press, Oxford.

Lindbeck, A. and Snower, D. (1988), *The Insider-Outsider Theory of Employment and Unemployment*, The MIT Press, Boston.

Lipset, S.M. (1962), *Soziologie der Demokratie*, Luchterhand, Neuwied/Berlin.

Lipset, S.M. (ed.) (1986), *Unions in Transition. Entering the Second Century*, Institute for Contemporary Studies, San Francisco.

Little, J. (1986), 'Social Class and planning Policy: a Study of two Wiltshire Villages', in P. Lowe, T. Bradley and S. Wright (eds), *Deprivation and Welfare in Rural Areas*, Geo Books, Norwich.

Locke, R.M. (1990), 'The Resurgence of the Local Union: Industrial Restructuring and Industrial Relations in Italy', *Politics and Society*, No. 18, pp. 347-79.

Lockwood, D. (1958), *The Black Coated Worker*, Allen & Unwin, London.

Lockwood, D. (1960), 'The 'new' Working Class', *European Journal of Sociology*, Vol. 1, No. 2.

Lockwood, D. (1966), 'Sources of Variation in working-class Images of Society', *Sociological Review*, Vol. 14, pp. 249-63.

Lockwood, D. (1989), *The Blackcoated Worker. A Study in Class Consciousness*, Second Edition, Clarendon Press, Oxford.

Lockwood, D. (1992), *Solidarity and Schism*, Clarendon, Oxford.

Lockwood, D. (1995), 'Marking out the Middle Classes', introduction to T. Butler and M. Savage (eds), *Social Change and the Middle Classes*, UCL Press, London, pp. 1-12.

Longhurst, B. and Savage, M. (1996), 'Social Class, Consumption and the Influence of Bourdieu', in S. Edgell, K. Hetherington and A. Warde (eds), *Consumption Matters: the Production and Experience of Consumption*, Basil Blackwell, Oxford, pp. 274-301.

Longhurst, B. and Savage, M. (1996), 'Social Class, Consumption and the Influence of Bourdieu: some Critical Issues', in S. Edgell, K. Hetherington and A. Warde (eds), *Consumption Matters: The Production of Experience and Consumption*, Basil Blackwell/Sociological Review, Oxford.

Lorenz, E. (1983), *The Labour Process and Industrial Relations in the British and French Shipbuilding Industries from 1880-1970: Two Patterns of Development*, Ph.D. Thesis, University of Cambridge.

Lorenz, E. (1991), *Economic Decline in Britain*, Clarendon Press, London.

Lovering, J. (1997), 'Wales 2010 three years on. We need a New Pattern of Economic Development', *Agenda. The Journal of The Institute of Welsh Affairs*, pp. 29-32.

Lowe, P. (1977), 'Access and Amenity: a Review of Local Environmental Pressure Groups in Britain', *Environment and planning A*, No. 9, pp. 35-58.

Lucas, E. (1976), *Arbeiterradikalismus*, Roter Stern, Frankfurt.

Lucas, E. (1983), *Vom Scheitern der deutschen Arbeiterbewegung*, Roter Stern, Frankfurt.

Luciano, A. (1989), 'Nuove professsioni: la formazione di un soggetto collettivo', in *Impresa & Stato*, No. 6.

Lucio, M.M. (1990), 'Trade Unions and Communism in Spain: the role of the CCOO in the Political Projects of the Left', *Journal of Communist Studies*, No. 6, pp. 80-99.

Luebbert G.M. (1991), *Liberalism, Fascism, or Social Democracy*, Oxford University Press, New York.

Lyons, M. (1996), 'Employment, Feminisation and Gentrification in London, 1981-1993', *Environment and Planning A*, Vol. 28, pp. 341-56.

MacInnes, J. (1987), *Thatcherism at Work: Industrial Relations and Economic Change*, Open University Press, Milton Keynes, Philadelphia.

Maffesoli, M. (1996), *The Time of the Tribes*, Sage, London.

Mahieu, L. (ed.) (1995), *Social Movements and Social Classes. The Future of Collective Action*, Sage, London.

Maksymiw, W., Eaton, J. and Gill, C. (1990), *The British Trade Union Directory*, Longman, Harlow.

Mann, E. (1988), 'Keeping GM Van Nuys Open', in M. Davis and M. Sprinker, *Reshaping the US Left. Popular Struggles in the 1980s*, Verso, London, New York, pp. 183-209.

Mann, M. (1970), 'The Social Cohesion of Liberal Democracy', *American Sociological Review*.

Mann, M. (1973), *Consciousness and Action amongst the Western Working Class*, MacMillan, London.

Marable, M. (1997), 'Black Leadership and the Labor Movement', *Working USA*, Vol. 3, No. 1, pp. 39-48.

Marcuse, H. (1964), *One Dimensional Man. Studies in the Ideology of Advanced Industrial Society*, Routledge & Kegan Paul, London.

Markovits, A.S. and Otto, A. (1992), 'German Labor and Europe '92', *Comparative Politics*, No. 24, pp. 163-79.

Marsden, T., Murdoch, J., Lowe, P., Munton, R. and Flynn, A. (1993), *Constructing the Countryside*, UCL Press, London.

Marshall, A. (1922), *Principles of Economics*, Macmillan, London.

Marshall, G. (1988), Some Remarks on the Study of working-class Consciousness', in D. Rose (ed.), *Economic Restructuring and Social Change*, Hutchinson, London.

Marshall, G. (1997), *Repositioning Class. Social Inequality in Industrial Societies*, Sage, London.

Marshall, G. and Rose, D. (1988), 'Proletarianization in the British Class Structure?', *British Journal of Sociology*, No. 39, pp. 498-518.

Marshall, G., Newby, H., Rose, D. and Vogler, C. (1988), *Social Class in Modern Britain*, Hutchinson, London.

Marshall, T.H. (1950), *Citizenship and Social Class, and other Essays'*, Cambridge University Press, Cambridge.

Martín Valverde, A. (1991), *European Employment and Industrial Relations Glossary: Spain*, Sweet & Maxwell/Office for Official Publications of the European Communities, London/Luxembourg.

Martin, R., Sunley, P. and Wills, J. (1993), 'The Geography of Trade Union decline: Spatial Dispersion or Regional Resilience?', *Transactions, Institute of British Geographers*, Vol. 1, No. 18, pp. 36-62.

Martinez Lucio, M. (1993), 'Spain: Constructing Institutions and Actors in a Context of Change', in A. Ferrer and R. Hyman (eds), *Industrial Relations in Europe*, Basil Blackwell, Oxford.

Martinez Lucio, M. and Blyton, P. (1995), 'Constructing the Post-Fordist State? The Politics of Labour Market Flexibility in Spain', *West European Politics*, No. 18, pp. 340-60.

Marx, K. (1959), *Capital: volume one*, Lawrence and Wishart, London.

Marx, K. and Engels, F. (1848), 'Manifest der Kommunistischen Partei', in *Marx Engels Werke*, Bd. 4, Dietz, Berlin.

Marx, K. and Engels, F. (1977), 'Manifest der kommunistischen Partei', in K. Marx and F. Engels, *Ausgewählte Werke*, Vol. 1, Dietz, Berlin, pp. 415-51.

Massey, D. (1984), *Spatial Divisions of Labour: Social Structures and the Geography of Production*, Macmillan, London.

Massey, D. (1995a), 'Reflections on Gender and Geography', in T. Butler and M. Savage (eds), *Social Change and the Middle Classes*, UCL Press, London, pp. 330-44.

Massey, D. (1995b), *Spatial Divisions of Labour: social structures and the geography of production*, 2nd edition, Macmillan, Basingstoke.

Massey, D. and Painter, J. (1989), 'The changing Geography of Trade Unions', in J. Mohan (ed.), *The political Geography of Contemporary Britain*, Macmillan, London.

Matless, D. (1990), 'Definitions of England, 1928-1989: Preservation, Modernism and the Nature of the Nation', *Built environment*, Vol. 3, No. 16, pp. 179-91.

McDowell, L. (1997), 'The new Service Class: Housing, Consumption and Life Style among London Bankers in the 1990s', *Employment and Planning A*, Vol. 29, pp. 2061-78.

Mead, M. (1978), *Culture and Commitment*, Doubleday, New York.

Meiksins, P. (1997), 'Same as it ever was? The Structure of the Working Class', *Monthly Review*, Vol. 49, No. 3, pp. 31-45.

Meiksins-Wood, E. (1986), *The Retreat from Class. A New 'True' Socialism*, Verso, London.

Melucci, A. (1989), *Nomads of the Present. Social Movements and Individual Needs in Comtemporary Society*, Temple University Press, Philadelphia.

Melucci, A. (1996), *New Social Movements*, Cambridge University Press, Cambridge.

Mény, Y. and Wright, V. (eds) (1986), *The Politics of Steel: Western Europe and the Steel Industry in the Crisis Years*, W. de Gruyter, Berlin.

Merleau-Ponty, M. (1965), *Phänomenologie der Wahrnehmung*, de Gruyter, Berlin (*Phénoménologie de la Perception*, Gallimard, Paris, 1945).

Mershon, C. (1989), 'Between Workers and Union. Factory Councils in Italy', *Comparative Politics*, No. 21, pp. 215-35.

Meyer, J.P. and Allen N.J. (1991), 'A Three Component Conceptualization of Organizational Commitment', *Human Resource Management Review*, No. 1, pp. 61-89.

Meyer, J.P. and Allen, N.J. (1997), *Commitment in the Workplace: Theory, Research and Application*, Sage, Thousand Oaks.

Meyer, J.P., Allen, N. and Smith, C. (1993), 'Commitment to Organizations and Occupations: Extension and Test of a three-component Conceptualization', *Journal of Applied Psychology*, No. 78, pp. 538-51.

Meyer, J.W. (1994), 'The Evolution of modern Stratification Systems', D. Grusky (ed.), *Social Stratification: Class, Race and Gender in Sociological Perspective*, Westview Press, Boulder, pp. 730-37.

Milgrom, P. and Roberts, J. (1992), *Economics, Organization and Management*, Prentice-Hall, London.

Miliband, R. (1964), 'Socialism and the Myth of the Golden Past', in R. Miliband and J. Saville (ed.), *The Socialist Register 1964*, Monthly Review Press, New York, pp. 92-103.

Mingay, G. (1989), *The unquiet countryside*, Routledge, London.

Mingione, E. (1997), *Sociologia della vita economica*, Nis, Roma.

Miracapillo, M. (1992), 'Relazione', in Filca-Cisl, *Partecipazione e nuova contrattazione*, Atti del seminario nazionale, Torino.

Mitchell, D. (1997), *The Lie of the Land: Migrant Workers and California Landscape*, University of Minnesota Press, Minneapolis.

Mizen, P. (1995), *The State, Young People and Youth Training*, Mansell, London.

Modood, T. and Werbner, P. (1997), *The Politics of Multiculturalism in the New Europe: Racism, Identity, and Community*, Zed Books, London.

Mooser, J. (1983), 'Abschied von der 'Proletariat'. Sozialstruktur und Lage der Arbeiterschaft in der Bundesrepublik in historischer Perspektive', in W. Conze and M.R. Lepsius (eds), *Sozialgeschichte der Bundesrepublik*, Klett-Cotta, Stuttgart, pp. 143-86.

Mooser, J. (1984), *Arbeiterleben in Deutschland 1900-1970*, Suhrkamp, Frankfurt am Main.

Morgan, K.O. (1995), *Modern Wales: Politics, Places and People*, University of Wales Press, Cardiff.

Morris, J. and Wilkinson, B. (1995), 'Poverty and Prosperity in Wales: Polarization and Los Angelesization', *Contemporary Wales*, No. 8, pp. 29-45.

Mueckenberger, U., Schmidt, E. and Zoll, R. (eds) (1996), *Die Modernisierung der Gewerkschaften in Europa*, Westfälisches Dampfboot, Münster.

Mueller, D. (1990), *Zum Typus der neuen Arbeiterinnen*, Arbeitspapier, Hannover.

Munch, R. (1987), *Theory of Social Action*, Routledge and Kegan Paul, London.

Murdoch, J. (1995), 'The Spatialization of Politics: Local and National Actor Spaces in Environmental Conflict', *Transactions, Institute of British Geographers*, Vol. 3, No. 20, pp. 368-81.

Murdoch, J. and Marsden, T. (1994), *Reconstituting Rurality: Class, Community and Power in the Development Process*, UCL Press, London.

Murdoch, J. and Pratt, A. (1993), 'Rural Studies: Modernism, post-Modernism and the 'post-Rural'', *Journal of Rural Studies*, Vol. 4, No. 9, pp. 411-27.

Murray, C. (1989), 'The Emerging British Underclass', in *Charles Murray and the Underclass*, Institute of Economic Affairs, Health and Welfare Unit, London.

Myant, M. (1994), 'Czech and Slovak Trade Unions', in M. Waller and M. Myant (eds), *Parties, Trade Unions, and Society in East-Central Europe*, Frank Cass, Essex.

Myrdal, G. (1974), *Ökonomische Theorie und unterentwickelte Regionen*, Frankfurt am Main.

Nairn, T. (1978), 'The English Working Class', in R. Blackburn (ed.), *Ideology in Social Science*, Fontana, Glasgow.

Navarro, V. (1992), 'Excluding the others: the Middle Class - a useful Myth', *The Nation*, Vol. 11, No. 254, pp. 361, 381.

NCVQ (1995), *NVQ criteria and Guidance*, Employment Department, London.

Negrelli, S. (eds) (1989), *Le relazioni sindacali nel commercio*, F. Angeli, Milano.

Newby, H. (1977), *The deferential Worker*, Allen Lane, London.

Newby, H. (1980), *Green and pleasant Land? Social Change in rural England*, Penguin, Harmondsworth.

Newby, H., Bell, C., Rose, D. and Saunders, P. (1978), *Property, Paternalism and Power: Class and Control in Rural England*, Hutchinson, London.

Nickell, S. and Wadhwani, S. (1990), 'Insider Forces and Wage Determination', *The Economic Journal*, No. 100, pp. 496-509.

Niethammer, L. (ed.) (1983), *Lebensgeschichte und Sozialkultur im Ruhrgebiet*, 3 vols., Dietz, Berlin-Bonn.

Nifong, C. (1997), 'How Part-Timers fare in US Economy', *The Christian Science Monitor*, online: http://www.csmonitor.com/durable/1997/08/14/us/us.3.html.

Niphuis-Nell, M. (1993), *De 'nieuwe werknemer'*, Osmose, No. 19, pp. 9-10.

Noble, B.P. (1993), 'Reinventing Labor: an Interview with Union President Lynn Williams', *Harvard Business Review*, pp. 115-25.

Normann, R. (1984), *Service Management: Strategy and Leadership in Service Business*, Wiley and Sons, Chichester.

Nunnaly, J.C. and Berstein, H. (1994), *Psychometric Theory*, McGraw-Hill, New York.

OECD (1988), *Employment Outlook*, OECD, Paris.

OECD (1991), *National Accounts*, OECD, Paris.

OECD (1993), *Employment Outlook*, OECD, Paris.

OECD (1995), *Employment Outlook*, OECD, Paris.

OECD (1997), *Employment Outlook*, OECD, Paris.

Offe, C. (1985), *Disorganized Capitalism. Contemporary Transformations of Work and Politics*, Polity Press, Oxford.

Office for National Statistics (1997), *Social Trends*, The Stationery Office, London.

Orenstein, M. (1996), *Out of the Red: Building Capitalism and Democracy in post-communist Europe*, Ph.D. dissertation, Yale University.

Ost, D. (1993), 'The Politics of Interest in post-communist East Europe', in *Theory and Society*, No. 22, pp. 453-85.

Ost, D. and Weinstein, M. (1999), 'Unionists against Unions: towards Hierarchical Management in post-communist Poland', in *East European Politics and Societies*.

Paci, M. (1997), *Welfare State. Chi ha beneficiato dello Stato sociale, a chi andrà la nuova solidarietà*, Ediesse, Roma.

Pahl, R. (1989), ''Is the Emperor naked', some Questions on the Adequacy of Sociological Theory in Urban and Regional Research', *International Journal of International and Urban Research*, Vol. 13, pp. 709-20.

Pahl, R. (1993), 'Does Class Analysis without Class Theory have a Promising Future? A reply to Goldthorpe and Marshall', *Sociology*, No. 27, pp. 253-58.

Pakulski, J. and Waters, M. (1996), *The Death of Class*, Sage, London.

Pankow, W., Gardawski, J., and Gaciarz, B. (1999), *Rozpad Bastionu?*, Institute for Public Affairs, Warsaw.

Parenti, M. (1995), *Democracy for the Few*, sixth Edition, St. Martin's Press, New York.

Parsons, T., 'How are Clients Integrated in Service Organizations?', in W.R. Rosengren and Lefton, M. (eds) (1970), *Organization and Clients: Essays in the Sociology of Services*, Charles Merrill Publ., Ohio.

Pateman, C. (1990), *The Sexual Contract*, Polity, Cambridge.

Payne, J. and Payne, C. (1994), 'Recession, Restructuring and the Fate of the Unemployed: Evidence in the Underclass Debate', *Sociology*, No. 28, pp. 1-19.

Payne, P. (1996), 'Investing in Class Analysis Future', *Sociology*, Vol. 30, No. 2, pp. 339-54.

Penn, R. (1986), 'Socialisation into Skilled Identities', *Paper presented at Aston/UMIST labour process conference, Birmingham.*

Pérez, S.A. (1999) forthcoming, *The Resurgence of National Social Bargaining in Europe: Explaining the Italian and Spanish Experiences, Estudio/Working Paper, Instituto Juan March de Estudios e Investigaciones, Madrid.*

Pérez-Díaz, V. (1987), 'Unions' Uncertainties and Workers' Ambivalence. The Various Crises of Trade Union Representation and their Moral Dimension', *International Journal of Political Economy*, No. 17, pp. 108-38.

Perulli, P. (1989), 'Il distretto industriale di Modena', in M. Regini and C. Sabel (eds), *Strategie di riaggiustamento industriale*, Il Mulino, Bologna.

Phillips, M. (1993), 'Rural Gentrification and the Processes of Class Colonisation', *Journal of Rural Studies*, Vol. 9, pp. 123-40.

Phillips, M. (1998), 'Investigations of the British Rural Middle Classes: Part 2, Fragmentation, Identity, Morality and Contestation', *Journal of Rural Studies*, Vol. 4, No. 14, pp. 427-43.

Phillips, M. (1999), 'Gender Relations and Identities in the Colonisation of Rural 'Middle England'', in P. Boyle and K. Halfacree (eds), *Gender and Migration in Britain*, Routledge, London, pp. 238-60.

Phillips, M. (forthcoming), 'Consuming ruralities', *Paper submitted to Sociologia Ruralis.*

Phillips, M., Fish, R. and Agg, J. (forthcoming), 'Putting together Ruralities: towards a symbolic Analysis of Rurality in the British Mass Media', *Journal of Rural Studies.*

Piore, M. and Sabel, C. (1984), *The second industrial divide*, Basic Books, New York.

Pipan, T. (1986), 'Verso le metamorfosi del conflitto industriale', in *Sociologia del lavoro*, No. 29, pp. 151-64.

Pipan, T. (1989), *Sciopero contro l'utente*, Bollati Boringhieri, Torino.

Polanyi, K. (1944), *The Great Transformation*, Reinehart, London.

Polavieja, J.G. (1998a), 'The Dualisation of Unemployment Risks. Class and Insider/Outsider Patterns in the Spanish Labour Market', Estudios/Working Papers, 1998/128, CEACS, Instituto Juan March de Estudios e Investigaciones.

Polavieja, J.G. (1998b), 'Efectos Valorativos de la Dualización del Mercado de Trabajo en España', Paper presented at the seminar Clase y Política, Universidad Nacional a Distancia, Madrid.

Polavieja, J.G. (1999a), 'Labour Market Dualisation and the Two-Tier System of Industrial Relations: the Effects of fixed-term Work on Wages and Working Conditions', *Typescript*, Nuffield College.

Polavieja, J.G. (1999b), 'The Effects of Labour Market Dualisation on Trade Union Involvement and Political Attitudes in Spain', Paper presented at the Harvard-Oxford-Stockholm Graduate Conference, Harvard University.

Polavieja, J.G. (1999c), 'Political Effects of Labour Market Dualisation in Spain: an Analysis of the Causal Mechanisms that link Labour Market experiences to Attitudinal Outcomes', Estudios/Working Papers, 1999/142, CEACS, Instituto Juan March de Estudios e Investigaciones.

Popitz, H., Bahrdt, H.P., Jueres, E. and Kesting, H. (1957), *Das Gesellschaftsbild des Arbeiters*, Mohr, Tübingen.

Poulantzas, N. (1975), *Classes in Contemporary Capitalism*, New Left Books, London.

Poulantzas, N. (1980), *Politische Macht und gesellschaftliche Klassen*, Frankfurt.

Przeworski, A. (1991), *Democracy and the Market*, Cambridge University Press, Cambridge.

Rainbird, H. and Syben, G. (eds) (1991), *Restructuring a Traditional Industry*, Berg Publishers, London.

Raschke, J. (1985), *Soziale Bewegungen. Ein historisch-systematischer Grundriß*, Campus, Frankfurt am Main.

Reay, D. (1998), 'Rethinking Social Class: Qualitative Perspectives on Class and Gender', *Sociology*, Vol. 2, No. 32, pp. 259-75.

Recio, A. (1991), 'La Segmentación del Mercado de Trabajo en España', in F. Miguélez and C. Prieto (eds), *Las Relaciones Laborales en España*, Siglo XXI, Madrid.

Rees, G. and Rees, T. (1983), 'Migration, industrial Restructuring and Class Relations: an Analysis of South Wales', in G. Williams (eds), *Crisis of Economy and Ideology. Essays on Welsh Society, 1840-1980*, SSRC/BSA Sociology of Wales Study Group, London.

Regalia, I. (1989), 'Tra mercato, contrattazione e identificazione professionale', in I. Regalia and M.E. Sartor, 'Le relazioni di lavoro nelle imprese del terziario avanzato', Ires/Papers 'Ricerche', No. 21, pp. 2-16.

Regalia, I. (1990), *Al posto del conflitto. Le relazioni di lavoro nel terziario*, Il Mulino, Milano.

Regini, M. (1991), *Confini mobili*, Il Mulino, Bologna.

Regini, M. (1992), 'Introduction: the Past and Future of Social Studies of Labour Movements', in M. Regini (ed.), *The Future of Labour Movements*, Sage, London, pp. 1-16.

Rhodes, M. and Wright, V. (1988), 'The European Steel Unions and the Steel Crisis, 1974-1984: a Study in the Demise of Traditional Unionism', *British Journal of Political Science*, No. 18, pp. 171-95.

Richards, A. (1995), 'Down but not Out: Labour Movements in late Industrial Societies', Estudios/Working Papers, 1995/70, CEACS, Instituto Juan March de Estudios e Investigaciones.

Richards, A. and Polavieja, J.G. (1997), 'Trade Unions, Unemployment and Working Class Fragmentation in Spain', Estudios/Working Papers, 1997/112, CEACS, Instituto Juan March de Estudios e Investigaciones.

Richards, A. and Polavieja, J.G. (1998), 'Unemployment and Working Class Fragmentation in Spain: The Dilemmas of Contemporary Spanish Trade Unionism', Paper presented at the seminar Desempleo, Desigualdad y Educación, Universidad Internacional Menéndez Pelayo.

Richards, A.J. (1995), 'Down but not Out: Labour Movements in late Industrial Societies', Estudio/Working Paper 1995/70, Instituto Juan March de Estudios e Investigaciones, Madrid.

Richards, A.J. (1996), *Miners on Strike. Class Solidarity and Division in Britain*, Berg, Oxford, New York.

Richards, A.J. and García de Polavieja, J. (1997), 'Trade Unions, Unemployment, and wor-king-class Fragmentation in Contemporary Spain', *Estudio/Working Paper 1997/112, Instituto Juan March de Estudios e Investigaciones, Madrid.*

Rigby, M. and Lawlor T. (1994), 'Spanish Trade Unions 1986-1994, Life after National Agreements', *Industrial Relations Journal*, No. 25, pp. 258-71.

Rink, D. (1994), 'Das Leipziger Alternativmilieu zwischen alten und neuen Eliten', in M. Vester et al. (1995), pp. 193-229.

Rix, V. (1996), 'Social and Demographic Change in East-London', in T. Butler and M. Rustin (eds), *Rising in the East? The Regeneration of East-London*, Lawrence and Wishart, London, pp. 20-60.

Roberts, I. (1993), *Craft, Class and Control: The Sociology of a Shipbuilding Community*, Edinburgh University Press, Edinburgh.

Roberts, I. and Strangleman, T. (1997), 'Workplace Culture contested? The reshaping of Generations and Moral Orders', Paper presented at the British Sociological Association Conference, York.

Roberts, K. and Corcoran-Nantes, A. (1994), 'TQM, the new Training and Industrial Rela-tions', in A. Wilkinson and H. Willmott (eds), *Making Quality Critical*, Routledge, London.

Roberts, K., Cooke, J., Clarke, A. and Semeonoff, E. (1977), *The Fragmentary Class Structure*, Humanities Press, Atlantic Highlands NJ.

Robinson, F. and Gregson, N. (1992), 'The 'Underclass': a Class apart?', *Critical Social Policy*, No. 34, pp. 38-51.

Robson, G. and Butler, T. (1999), 'Plotting the Middle Classes in London', Departmental Working Paper available from the author.

Roediger, D.R. (1988), ''Labor in White Skin': Race and working-class History', in M. Davis and M. Sprinker (ed.), *Reshaping the US Left. Popular Struggles in the 1980s,* Verso, London, New York, pp. 287-308.

Roediger, D.R. (1991), *The Wages of Whiteness. Race and the Making of the American Working Class*, Verso, London, New York.

Rojo Torrecilla, E. (1990), 'El Sindicalismo ante los Cambios en el Mercado y la Composi-ción de la Clase Trabajadora', *Política y Sociedad*, 5, pp. 31-44.

Room, G. (1995), 'Poverty in Europe: competing Paradigms of Analysis', *Policy and Poli-tics*, No. 23, pp. 103-13.

Rose, D. (1998), 'Once more unto the Breach: in Defence of Class Analysis yet again', *Work, Employment and Society*, Vol. 12, No. 4, pp. 755-67.

Rosenblum, J.D. (1995), *Copper Crucible: how the Arizona Miners' Strike of 1983 recast Labor-Management Relations in America*, ILR Press, Ithaca.

Rostow, W.W. (1948), *British Economy in the Nineteenth Century*, Oxford.

Roth, S. (1997), *Political Socialization, Bridging Organization, Social Movement Interac-tion: the Coalition of Labor Union Women, 1974-1996*, unpublished Dissertation, University of Connecticut.

Ruffier, J. (1983), 'Mort du taylorisme et recul des syndicats', in *Economie et humanisme*, No. 259, pp. 50-7.

Rupp, J.C.C. (1995), 'Les classes populaires dans un espace social à deux dimensions', in *Actes de Recherche en Sciences Sociales*, No. 109, pp. 93-98.

Rupp, J.C.C. (1997), 'Rethinking Cultural and Economic Capital', in J.R. Hall (ed.), *Reworking Class*, Cornell University Press, Ithaca (N.Y.), pp. 221-41.

Rusbult, C.E., Farell, D., Rogers, G. and Mainous III, A.G. (1988), 'Impact of Exchange Variables on Exit, Voice, Loyalty, and Neglect: an integrative Model of Responses to declining Job Satisfaction', *Academy of Management Journal*, No. 31, pp. 599-627.

Rutherford, T. (1991), 'Industrial Restructuring, Local Labour Markets and Social Change: The Transformation of South Wales', in G. Day and G. Rees (eds.), *Contemporary Wales*, University of Wales Press, Cardiff.

Sabel, C. and Stark, D. (1982), 'Planning, Politics, and Shop-Floor Power: Hidden Forms on Bargaining in the Soviet-imposed State-Socialist Societies', in *Politics and Society*, No. 11, pp. 439-75.

Sabel, C.F. (1987), 'A Fighting Chance. Structural Change and New Labor Strategies', *International Journal of Political Economy*, No. 17, pp. 26-56.

Sabia, D. (1988), 'Rationality, Collective Action, and Karl Marx', *American Journal of Political Science*, No. 32, pp. 50-71.

Said, E. (1978), *Orientalism*, Penguin, Harmondsworth.

Salvatore, N. (1992), 'The Decline of Labor. A grim Picture, a few Proposals', *Dissent*, pp. 86-92.

Sassen, S. (1997) (ediz. orig. 1994), *La città nell'economia globale*, Il Mulino, Bologna.

Saunders, P. (1990), 'Left write in Sociology', *Network*, No. 44, pp. 3-4.

Saunders, P. (1990), *A Nation of Homeowners*, Unwin Hyman, London.

Savage, M. (1991), 'Making Sense of middle-class Politics: a Secondary Analysis of the 1987 General Election Survey', *Sociological Review*, Vol. 39, pp. 26-54.

Savage, M. (1995), 'Class Analysis and Social Research', in T. Butler and M. Savage (eds) *Social Change and the Middle Classes*, UCL Press, London, pp. 15-25.

Savage, M. (1998), 'Individualism, Class, and the Transformation of Work Cultures', *Sociological Analysis*, Vol. 2, No. 1, June, pp. 25-42.

Savage, M. (1999), 'Sociology, Class and Manual Work Cultures, 1945-1979', in A. Campbell, J. McIlroy and N. Fishman (eds), *British Trade Unionism, 1945-1979*, Scholar, Aldershot.

Savage, M. (2000), *Social Class and Social Transformation*, Open University Press, Milton Keynes.

Savage, M. and Butler T. (1995), 'Assets and the Middle Classes in Contemporary Britain Research', in T. Butler and M. Savage (eds), *Social Change and the Middle Classes*, UCL Press, London, pp. 345-57.

Savage, M., Barlow, J., Dickens, P. and Fielding, A.J. (1992), *Property, Bureaucracy and Culture: middle-class Formation in contemporary Britain*, Routledge, London.

Savage, M., Dickens, P. and Fielding, T. (1988), 'Some Social and Political Implications of the Contemporary Fragmentation of the 'Service Class' in Britain', *International Journal of Urban and Regional Research*, Vol. 12, pp. 455-76.

Scase, R. (1991), *Class*, Open University Press, Milton Keynes.

Schelsky, H. (1965), 'Die Bedeutung des Schichtungsbegriffes für die Analyse der gegenwärtigen deutschen Gesellschaft', in H. Schelsky, *Auf der Suche nach Wirklichkeit*, Düsseldorf-Köln.

Schumann, M. (1999), 'Das Lohnarbeiterbewußtsein des 'Arbeitskraftunternehmers'', in SOFI-Mitteilungen, No. 27.

Schumann, M. et al. (1971), *Am Beispiel der Septemberstreiks - Anfang der Rekonstruktionsperiode der Arbeiterklasse?*, EVA, Frankfurt am Main.

Scott, M., Roberts, I., Holroyd, G. and Sawbridge, D. (1989), 'Management and Industrial Relations in small Firms', Department of Employment Research Paper, No. 70, HMSO, London.

Segura, J., Durán, F., Toharia, L. and Bentolila, S. (1991), *Análisis de la Contratación Temporal en España*, Ministerio de Trabajo y Seguridad Social, Madrid.

Sennett, R. and Cobb, J. (1971/1993), *The hidden Injuries of Class*, Faber (2nd edition, 1993), London.

Seymour, S. and Short, C. (1994), 'Gender, Church and People in Rural Areas', *Area*, Vol. 1, No. 26, pp. 45-56.

Silver, H. (1994), 'Social Exclusion and Social Solidarity: Three Paradigms', *International Labour Review*, No. 133, pp. 531-78.

Sisson, K., Waddingtong, J. and Whitston, C. (1991), 'Company Size in the European Community', *Human Resource Management Journal*, Vol. 1, No. 2, pp. 94-109.

Skeggs, B. (1997), *Formations of Class and Gender*, Sage, London.

Smith, A. (1776), *An Inquiry into the Nature and Causes of the Wealth of Nations*, Random House, New York.

Smith, C. and Willmott, H. (1991), 'The new Middle Class and the Labour Process', in C. Smith, D. Knights and H. Willmott (ed.), *White-Collar Work. The non-manual Labour Process*, Macmillan, Basingstoke, pp. 13-34.

Smith, C., Knights, D. and Willmott, H. (1991), 'Introduction', in C. Smith, D. Knights and H. Willmott (ed.), *White-Collar Work. The non-manual Labour Process*, Macmillan, Basingstoke, pp. 1-12.

Smith, D. (1980), *A People and a Proletariat. Essays in the History of Wales 1780-1980*, Pluto Press, London.

Smith, N. (1996), *The new Urban Frontier: Gentrification and the Revanchist City*, Routledge, London.

Snow, D.A., Benford, R.D., Rochford, Jr., E.B. and Worden, S.K. (1986), 'Frame Alignment Process, Micromobilization, and Movement Participation', *American Sociological Review*, Vol. 4, No. 51, pp. 464-81.

Somers, M.R. (1992), 'Narrativity, Narrative Identity and Social Action: rethinking English working-class Formation', *Social Science History*, No. 16, pp. 591-630.

Sparks, A. (1991), *The Mind of South Africa*, Ballantine Books, New York.

SPD (1984), *Planungsdaten für die Mehrheitsfähigkeit der SPD. Ein Forschungsprojekt des Vorstandes der SPD*, Parteivorstand der SPD, Bonn.

Spiegel-Verlag, Manager Magazin (ed.) (1996), Spiegeldokumentation Soll und Haben 4, Hamburg.

StataCorp (1999), *Stata Statistical Software: Release 6.0*, College Station, Stata Corporation, TX.

Strangleman, T. and Roberts, I. (1997), 'Social Reproduction, Social Dislocation and the Labour Market', in C.J. Kristensen (ed.), *The Meeting of the Waters: Individuality, Community and Solidarity*, Scandinavian University Press, Copenhagen.

Strath, B. (1987), *The Politics of De-industrialisation: the Contraction of the West European Shipbuilding Industry*, Croom Helm, London, New York.

Strathearn, M. (1991), *Partial Connections*, Savage, Rowman and Littlefield, Maryland.

Streeck, W. (1987), 'Vielfalt und Interdependenz. Überlegungen zur Rolle von intermediären Organisationen in sich ändernden Umwelten', *Kölner Zeitschrift für Soziologie und Sozialpsychologie*, Vol. 38, No. 3, pp. 471-95.

Stryker, S. (1997), 'Identity Competition: Key to Differential Social Movement Participation?', *Paper presented at the Conference on Self-Identity, and Social Movements, Indianapolis, April 1997*.

Taboadela, O. (1993), 'Clases Sociales y Acción Colectiva', *REIS*, No. 63, pp. 71-97.

Tajfel, H. and Turner J.C. (1986), 'The Social Identity Theory of Intergroup Behaviour', in S. Worchel and W.G. Austin (eds), *The Social Psychology of Intergroup Relations*, Brooks Cole, CA, pp. 7-24.

Tarrow, S. (1994), *Power in Movement: Social Movements, Collective Action and Politics*, Cambridge University Press, Cambridge.

Taylor, A.J. (1993), 'Trade Unions and the Politics of Social Democratic Renewal', *West European Politics*, No. 16, pp. 133-55.

Thelen, K. (1994), 'Beyond Corporatism. Toward a New Framework for the Study of Labor in advanced Capitalism', *Comparative Politics*, No. 27, pp. 107-24.

Thompson, A., Adamson, D. and Day, G. (1996), 'Bringing the Local Back, in The Production of Welsh Identities', *Britisg Sociological Association Annual Conference: Worlds of the Future: Ethnicity, Nationalism and Globalization*, Forthcoming in 'Thinking Identities: Ethnicity, Racism and Culture, Reading', Macmillam Press, London.

Thompson, E.P. (1968), *The making of the English Working Class*, Penguin, Harmondsworth.

Thompson, E.P. (1980a), *Das Elend der Theorie. Zur Produktion geschichtlicher Erfahrung*, M. Vester (ed.), Campus, Frankfurt.

Thompson, E.P. (1980b), 'Die englische Gesellschaft im 18. Jahrhundert: Klassenkampf ohne Klasse?', in D. Groh (ed.), *Plebejische Kultur und moralische Ökonomie*, Ullstein, Berlin, pp. 247-89.

Thompson, E.P. (1980c), 'Die moralische Ökonomie der englischen Unterschichten im 18. Jahrhundert', in D. Groh (ed.), *Plebejische Kultur und moralische Ökonomie*, Ullstein, Berlin, pp. 67-130.

Toharia, L. (1994), 'Spain: Modernisation of Unemployment', in D. Gallie, C. Marsh and C. Vogler (eds), *Social Change and the Experience of Unemployment*, Oxford University Press, Oxford.

Toharia, L. and Muro, J. (1988), '¿Es Elevado el Salario de los Jóvenes?', *Revista de Economía y Sociología del Trabajo*, 1/2.

Touraine, A. (1986), 'Unionism as a Social Movement', in S.M. Lipset (ed.), *Unions in Transition. Entering the Second Century*, Institute for Contemporary Studies, San Francisco, pp. 151-73.

Touraine, A. and Ragazzi, O. (1961), *Ouvriers d'origine agricole*, Paris.

Trigilia, C. (1985), 'La regolazione localistica: economia e politica nelle aree di piccola impresa', in *Stato e mercato*, No. 14, pp. 181-228.

Trigilia, C. (1989), 'Il distretto industriale di Prato', in M. Regini and C. Sabel (eds), *Strategie di riaggiustamento industriale*, Il Mulino, Bologna.

Troy, L. (1986), 'The Rise and Fall of American Trade Unions: The Labor Movement from FDR to RR', in S.M. Lipset (ed.), *Unions in Transition. Entering the Second Century*, Institute for Contemporary Studies, San Francisco, pp. 75-109.

Trumka, R.L. (1992), 'On Becoming a Movement. Rethinking Labor's Strategy', *Dissent*, pp. 57-60.

Turner, L. (1991), *Democracy at Work. Changing World Markets and the Future of Labor Unions*, Cornell University Press, Ithaca, London.

Twelvetrees, A. (1996), *Organizing for Neighbourhood Development*, Avebury, Aldershot.

United States Department of Labor (1997), 'Union Members Summary', *Developments in Labor-Management Relations*, Bureau of Labor Statistics, online: http://stats.bls.gov/news.release/union2.nws.html.

Valkenburg, B. and Zoll, R. (1995), 'Modernization, Individualization and Solidarity: Two Perspectives on European Trade Unions Today', *European Journal of Industrial Relations*, No. 1, pp. 119-44.

Van den Putte, B. (1995), 'Uit de bond: Bedanken als vakbondslid', in B. Klandermans and J. Visser (eds), *De vakbeweging na de welvaartsstaat*, Van Gorcum, Assen, pp. 87-111.

Van den Putte, B. and Sips, C. (1992), *Deeltijd en lidmaatschap: Met halve kracht vooruit*, Zeggenschap, pp. 50-4.

Van der Berg, A. (1995), *Trade Union Growth and Decline in The Netherlands*, Thesis Publishers, Amsterdam.

Van der Linden, M. and Rojahn, J. (eds.) (1990), *The Formation of Labour Movements, 1870-1914: an International Perspective*, 2 v. Brill, Leiden.

van der Meer, M. (1997), 'Trade Union Development in Spain. Past Legacies and Current Trends', *Arbeitspapiere/Working Papers, 1997/18, Zentrum für Europäische Sozialforschung, Mannheim.*

Van der Veen, G. and Klandermans, B. (1989), "Exit' Behavior in Social Movement Organizations', in B. Klandermans (ed.), *International Social Movement Research*, Vol. 2, pp. 179-98.

Van Ham, J.C., Paauwe, J. and Williams, A.R.T. (1985), 'De vakbeweging in Nederland: Van leden naar klanten', *Economisch Statistische Berichten*, No. 3 505, pp. 468-73.

Vester, M. (1970), *Die Entstehung des Proletariats als Lernprozeß*, EVA, Frankfurt.

Vester, M. (1998), 'Was wurde aus dem Proletariat?', in J. Friedrichs, M.R. Lepsius and K.U. Mayer (eds), *Die Diagnosefähigkeit der Soziologie* (Sonderheft 38 der Kölner Zeitschrift für Soziologie und Sozialpsychologie), Opladen, pp. 164-206.

Vester, M. et al. (1993), *Soziale Milieus im gesellschaftlichen Strukturwandel: zwischen Integration und Ausgrenzung*, Bund-Verlag, Cologne.

Vester, M., Hofmann, M. and Zierke, I. (1994), *Soziale Milieus in Ostdeutschland*, Bund Verlag, Köln.

Vester, M., von Oertzen, P., Geiling, H., Hermann, T. and Mueller, D. (1993), *Soziale Milieus im gesellschaftlichen Strukturwandel. Zwischen Integration und Ausgrenzung*, Bund Verlag, Köln.

Vinelli, A. (1990), 'Service management', in *Sviluppo e organizzazione*, No. 121, pp. 41-50.

Visser, J. (1990), 'Continuity and Change in Dutch industrial Relations', in G. Baglioni and C. Crouch (eds), *European industrial Relations: The Challenge of Flexibility*, Sage, London, pp. 199-242.

Visser, J. (1992), 'The Strength of Union Movements in advanced Capital Democracies: Social and Organizational Variations', in M. Regini, *The Future of Labour Movements*, Sage, London, pp. 17-52.

Visser, J. (1995), 'Het profiel van de vakbeweging', in B. Klandermans and J. Visser (eds), *De vakbeweging na de welvaartsstaat*, Van Gorcum, Assen, pp. 31-65.

Visser, J., Kersten, A., Van Rij, C. and Saris, W.E. (1990), 'Waarom zijn zo weinig vrouwen lid van de vakbeweging?', in C. Bouw et al. (eds), *Macht en onbehagen: Veranderingen in de verhouding tussen mannen en vrouwen*, SISWO/SUA, Amsterdam.

Vögele, W. and Vester, M. (ed.) (1999), 'Kirche und Milieu der Gesellschaft', *Vorläufiger Abschlußbericht der Studie*, Vol. 1 (Loccumer Protokolle, Bd. 56/1999 I), Loccum.

von Bismarck, K. (1957), 'Kirche und Gemeinde in soziologischer Sicht', *Zeitschrift Für evangelische Ethik*, H. 1, pp. 17-31.

Walsh, K. (1985), *Trade Union Membership. Methods and Measurement in the European Community*, Office for Official Publications of the European Community, Luxembourg.

Warde, A. (1991), 'Gentrification as Consumption: Issues of Class and Gender', *Environment and Planning D: Society and Space*, Vol. 9, pp. 223-32.

Weber, M. (1904/05), 'Die protestantische Ethik und der Geist des Kapitalismus', in *Gesammelte Aufsätze zur Religionssoziologie I*, Mohr, Tübingen, pp. 17-206.

Weber, M. (1964), *Wirtschaft und Gesellschaft. Grundriß der verstehenden Soziologie*, Kiepenheuer & Witsch, Köln/Berlin.

Welsh Office (1990), Welsh Economic Trends.

Western, B. (1995), 'A Comparative Study of working-class Disorganization: Union Decline in eighteen advanced Capitalist Countries', *American Sociological Review*, No. 60, pp. 179-201.

White, H. (1992), *Identity and Control*, University of Chicago Press, Chicago.

Williams, G.A. (1980), 'Locating a Welsh Working Class: The Frontier Years', in D. Smith (eds), *A People and a Proletariat. Essays in the History of Wales, 1788-1980*, Pluto Press, London.

Williams, G.A. (1985), *When was Wales. A History of the Welsh*, Black Raven Press, London.

Williams, L.J. and Boyns, T. (1977), 'Occupations in Wales. 1851-1971', *Bulletin of Economic Research*, No. 29, pp. 71-83.

Williams, R. (1958), *The Long Revolution*, Penguin, Harmondsworth.

Williams, R. (1963), *Culture and Society 1780-1950*, Penguin, Harmondsworth.

Williamson, O.E. (1985), *The Economic Institutions of Capitalism*, Free Press, New York.

Williamson, O.E. (1996), *The Mechanisms of Governance*, Oxford University Press, New York.

Winchester, D. (1989), 'Sectoral Change and Trade-Union Organization', in D. Gallie (ed.), *Employment in Britain*, Basil Blackwell, New York, pp. 493-518.

Windmuller, J.P., de Galan, C. and van Zweden, A.F. (1983), *Arbeidsverhoudingen in Nederland*, Het Spectrum, Utrecht.

Wright, E.O. (1985), *Classes*, Verso, London.

Wright, E.O. (1989), *The Debate on Classes*, Verso, London.

Wright, E.O. (1997), *Class Counts: Comparative Studies in Class Analysis*, Cambridge University Press, Cambridge.

Wynn, C. (1992), *Workers, Strikes, and Pogroms*, Princeton University Press, Princeton.

Wypijewski, J. (1997), 'Union Time', *The Nation*, Vol. 2, No. 265, pp. 3-4.

Young, I. (1997), 'The Complexities of Coalition', *Dissent*, Vol. 1, No. 44, pp. 64-9.

Young, K. (1992), 'Class, Race and Opportunity', in R. Jowell, L. Brook, G. Prior, B. Taylor (eds), *British Social Attitudes: the 9th Report*, SCPR, London.

Young, M. (1958), *The Rise of the Meritocracy 1870-2033*, Penguin, Harmondsworth (Deutsch: *Es lebe die Ungleichheit*, Econ, Düsseldorf, 1961).

Zanfrini, L. (1996), *Una promessa disattesa. Lo sviluppo locale nell'esperienza francese*, Vita e Pensiero, Milano.

Zito, A. (1986), 'Sindacato e produttività. Gli accordi nella grande distribuzione commerciale', in *Lavoro e sindacato*, No. 6.

Zweig, F. (1961), *The Worker in an Affluent Society*, Heinemann, London.

For Product Safety Concerns and Information please contact our EU representative GPSR@taylorandfrancis.com Taylor & Francis Verlag GmbH, Kaufingerstraße 24, 80331 München, Germany

Printed and bound by CPI Group (UK) Ltd, Croydon, CR0 4YY

01/05/2025

01858351-0006